FOR LIFE ABUNDANT

For Life Abundant

PRACTICAL THEOLOGY,
THEOLOGICAL EDUCATION, AND
CHRISTIAN MINISTRY

Edited by

Dorothy C. Bass & Craig Dykstra

William B. Eerdmans Publishing Company
Grand Rapids, Michigan / Cambridge, U.K.

Published 2008 by
Wm. B. Eerdmans Publishing Co.
2140 Oak Industrial Drive N.E., Grand Rapids, Michigan 49505 /
P.O. Box 163, Cambridge CB3 9PU U.K.
www.eerdmans.com

Printed in the United States of America

13 12 11 10 09 08   7 6 5 4 3 2 1

Library of Congress Cataloging-in-Publication Data

For life abundant: practical theology, theological education, and Christian ministry /
    edited by Dorothy C. Bass & Craig Dykstra.
        p.   cm.
    Includes bibliographical references and index.
    ISBN 978-0-8028-3744-8 (pbk.: alk. paper)
    1. Theology, Practical.   2. Theology — Study and teaching.   3. Pastoral theology.
    4. Church work.   I. Bass, Dorothy C.   II. Dykstra, Craig R.

    BV3.F65   2008
    230.071'1 — dc22

                                                          2007052376

Scripture quotations in this publication are from the New Revised Standard Version Bible,
copyright © 1989 by the Division of Christian Education of the National Council of
Churches of Christ in the United States of America. Used by permission.

Contents

Introduction

Dorothy C. Bass and Craig Dykstra

God in Christ promises abundant life for all creation. By the power of the Holy Spirit, the church receives this promise through faith and takes up a way of life that embodies Christ's abundant life in and for the world. The church's ministers are called to embrace this way of life and also to lead particular communities of faith to live it in their own situations. To do this, pastors and other ecclesial ministers must be educated and formed in ways of knowing, perceiving, relating, and acting that enable such leadership.

This set of claims distills the understanding of theological education, Christian ministry, and Christian living in and for the world that will be explored and advocated throughout this book. These claims are general and far-reaching, to be sure, but they are far from abstract. They call to mind countless Christian communities that have emerged over time and across cultures as people respond to God's promise and presence. They assert that faithful and capable ministers contribute in crucial ways to specific communities' capacity to take up life-giving ways of life. They emphasize the importance of educating and forming some Christians to be ministers of this kind. Moreover, they insist that all of these — discipleship, ministry, and education and formation for ministry — are inextricably related to one another and grounded in God's gift of abundant life in Jesus Christ.

Together, this set of claims puts Christian theological education in its proper place — a place of service to ministry, which is itself undertaken to foster discipleship, which in turn exists not for its own sake but for the sake

1

of God and all creation.[1] It also points to the call and capacity of theological educators, as well as other Christian ministers and disciples, to understand the public character of their work and to undertake it in ways that engage with and seek the well-being of a pluralistic world. Many pastors and theological educators are surely in general agreement with this understanding of their basic purpose. At the same time, however, the need to explore the full implications of this purpose is an urgent and challenging matter. Undertaking such an exploration will require sustained and detailed reflection on the character of Christian ministry and the shape of Christian living, as well as on the institutional and intellectual patterns that guide the education and formation of ministers.

Practical theology, the authors of this book contend, offers indispensable resources for this endeavor.[2] This field's attention to Christian life and ministry as crucial foci for theological study and constructive engagement reflects concerns that are widely shared across the theological curriculum. At the same time, practical theology places these concerns in the foreground of attention and takes special responsibility for educating and forming ministers to lead communities in a wide variety of contexts.

Practical theology that is understood in this way necessarily attends to the following questions:

(1) How might a way of life that truly is life-giving in and for the sake of the world be best understood and described, and how might contemporary people come to live it more fully?

1. Theological education, as we use the term, includes not only seminaries and divinity schools but also other institutions that deliberately foster the education and formation of pastors and other ministers, such as teaching parishes, judicatory offices, retreat centers, publications, parachurch organizations, and continuing education programs. The reasons for this expanded understanding will become evident later in the book, especially in the fourth section.

2. This book takes Christian practical theology as its focus and, unless otherwise indicated, assumes a Christian orientation when discussing not only practical theology but also theological education, ministry, and discipleship. The scope and grounding of practical theology can be construed more widely, of course, and the field has been shaped by a wide range of both Christian and non-Christian sources, including, among the latter, Aristotelian ethics and modern social theory. The concerns set forth in this book, however, arise from North American Christianity — a setting in which most practical theology continues to take a Christian approach — and the book's programmatic proposals are meant primarily for this setting as well.

(2) How can the church best foster such a way of life, for the sake of its own faithfulness and for the good of all creation, and how can the church's ministers best lead and encourage this?

(3) What kinds of learning, teaching, and collaboration, both within and beyond theological schools, are necessary and adequate to educate and form ministers who are able to lead and shape communities for discipleship in and for the sake of the world?

(4) How might practical theologians in seminaries and divinity schools best conceive, understand, and undertake their special responsibility to educate and form ministers who are able to embody and foster ways of living that reflect God's promise and gift of abundant life?

These are the questions that will be explored in this book. The last two will receive the most attention — an emphasis that both reflects the vocational location of most of the authors and affirms our shared conviction that excellent education and formation for ministers are indispensable if the church is to know and embody abundant life in the contemporary context.[3]

Authorship and Audience

This book's authors are mostly academic practical theologians, joined by pastors and theological educators from other fields. Our own effort to articulate our deepest calling and specific responsibilities as clearly, compellingly, and effectively as we can has led us to ask the questions listed above of ourselves, and also of one another. Asking and answering these questions is part of doing our work well, we believe. We hope that asking and

---

3. During the conversations that led to this book, it was clear that determining what to call church leaders is a complicated matter. In some Protestant communions, all members are considered "ministers," so applying this term distinctively to ordered, full-time leaders seems mistaken. For many Protestants, "pastor" is a better term for the ordained leader of a congregation, though in common language such leaders are in fact often referred to as "ministers" even so. For Roman Catholics, a "pastor" must be an ordained priest; thus using this term exclusively would leave out the many theologically educated women and lay men who have important leadership roles in local congregations. See p. 41 n. 1 and pp. 71-72 nn. 8-10 below. We use the terms almost interchangeably in this book and intend to include both ordained and non-ordained professional church leaders in our discussion.

3

answering these questions and similar ones can also enhance the work of others who care about theological education, Christian ministry, and faithful living in and for the world. Thus we address this book to a wide range of readers whose work involves them in discerning and building up ways of life abundant. In doing so, we hope not only to ask some challenging questions but also to demonstrate how practical theology can contribute to answering such questions. In the process, we also hope to foster relationships between the academic field of practical theology and other groups within theological education, the church, and society.

The development of this book was spurred and informed by several ongoing conversations.[4] Its authors are grateful for the ways in which these conversations and the work of those involved in them prepared the way for our own conversations and writing. We hope that participants in each of these will receive *For Life Abundant* as an invitation to further engagement with practical theology as we understand it.

One conversation has taken place within the academic discipline of practical theology during the past twenty to thirty years. Thanks to a generation of path-breaking work in practical theology, the present moment is a time of great creativity for the scholars, educators, and church leaders who identify with this theological movement.[5] Indeed, a new profile and agenda have come into view as the intellectual and pedagogical vitality of practical theology has become increasingly evident within and beyond theological education. The academic excellence of practical theology is being nurtured in newly vibrant scholarly organizations and several strong doctoral programs.[6] Meanwhile, a larger academic climate of appreciation for the importance of social practices and for the rich complexity of practical thinking is heightening this field's intellectual significance and engendering respect and collaboration from scholars in other fields.[7] In addi-

---

4. Included in this notion of "conversation" is a wide range of discourse, including books and articles written, courses taught, and constructive proposals offered and enacted.

5. Much of the literature produced during this period of renewal is cited throughout this volume. See especially p. 65 nn. 3-4 and p. 171 n. 3.

6. For example, the American Academy of Religion has recently added a program unit on practical theology, and the Association for Practical Theology (founded in 1984) has grown in size and vitality. For further information see www.practicaltheology.org, a website maintained by the APT. Thomas Long's chapter in this volume considers doctoral programs in practical theology.

7. This climate of appreciation, which has led to important work in virtually every

tion, amid concern about the role of higher education in our society, the commitment of practical theologians to studying human needs and practices not simply for their own sake but for the sake of healing, empowerment, and transformation provides a worthy example of academic public service.[8] Similarly, in a time of concern about the capacity of the church to embody a life-giving way of life and of seminary graduates to shape communities for faithful living, practical theology engages theological education as a whole in fostering the rich ecclesial connections that are crucial if theological schools are to serve church and society well.

The coeditors of this book have come to see practical theology as a movement involving many people in various settings and roles rather than as an exclusively academic enterprise. At the same time, we share with the other authors of this book a deep appreciation for the special role and contributions needed from and made by the academic discipline of practical theology. We hope that the essays presented here will allow readers from a variety of contexts and disciplines to understand with greater clarity the character and significance of contemporary practical theology and to consider their own relation to it. Beyond this, we hope that it will lead such readers to further conversation with this book's authors and other practical theologians, especially within specific institutions where they work together.[9]

As interest in practical theology grows in the academy, sustaining practical theology's vital orientation to faithful ways of living in and for the world is a matter of great importance. Practical theologians (and theological educators of every sort) who neglect the efforts of Christian people over time and today to live in ways that are attuned to God's mercy and justice squander rich opportunities to learn about matters at the heart of

---

field of the humanities and social sciences, has been nurtured by attention to the field-shaping work of philosophers (including Ludwig Wittgenstein, Charles Taylor, and Alasdair MacIntyre) and social theorists (including Pierre Bourdieu and Michel de Certeau), among others.

8. For example, the Association of American Colleges and Universities emphasizes the important role of liberal education in fostering civic knowledge and engagement, locally and globally.

9. In initiating a seminar and book on practical theology, the coeditors sought not only to celebrate the field but also to encourage practical theologians to continue to clarify and strengthen it. The vitality of this field makes this a good time for practical theologians not only to reach out to potential collaborators in church and academy but also to reflect on their own work, which has sometimes failed to attain the excellence that would allow members of this field to provide the leadership and collaboration we believe they can offer.

their work and to make that work as significant and helpful as possible. When the capacity of actual persons and communities to practice a life-giving way of life is their chief concern, however, theological educators can be partners with countless others in nurturing love and service to God and neighbor in and through the ways in which people live in and for the world.

We hope that the academic practical theologians who read this book will ask themselves questions such as these:

- How might practical theologians provide clear, incisive, and comprehensive portraits of the shape of Christian life in our time?
- How might practical theologians in seminaries and divinity schools best conceive, understand, and undertake their special responsibility to educate and form ministers who are able to embody and foster ways of living that reflect God's promise and gift of abundant life?
- What forms of collaboration with faculty colleagues and with ministers and congregations would enhance your own and your school's capacity to prepare ministers of this kind?
- If pastoral education and formation extend into the years beyond graduation, what are the specific contributions your teaching can and must make during the limited time available to you?
- What can practical theologians learn from pastors about the ways of knowing, perceiving, relating, and acting that enable excellent ministry, and how might this learning influence their ongoing teaching and research?

A second conversation framing this book concerns the aims and purposes of theological education. During the 1980s and 1990s, theological schools in North America engaged in a significant and extended reappraisal of the fundamental aims and purposes of theological education as a whole. This so-called "basic issues" conversation has been followed and complemented by more than a decade of work on the character and practice of theological teaching and learning in theological seminaries and divinity schools. These interwoven conversations have resulted in a whole new literature on both sets of issues. Major questions for theological education have been posed and addressed in considerable depth, including: What makes theological education theological? What gives (or should give) theological education its unity or coherence? How shall we understand the relation of theological education to the church and its ministry? What fundamental educational strategies have most power to accomplish theological education's most fundamental aims? In the course of these conversations, issues regarding how practical theology should be conceived and what role it should play in relation to the structure and basic purposes of theological education as a whole have received considerable attention. Indeed, this wider conversation has been an important force in stimulating and shaping the conversations about practical theology described above and in heightening the attention now being paid to practical theology in the theological academy as a whole.[10]

The special responsibility of practical theology for teaching and research on the arts of ministry (including preaching, pastoral care, Christian education, worship, evangelism, and leadership) imbue this field with a crucial role in a theological school's service to church and society. This is a responsibility the authors of this book gladly embrace. At the same time, we do not see teaching and scholarship in practical theology as consignment to the sole "useful" corner of the theological curriculum. Instead, those in this academic discipline propose to help, and often to lead, theological education as a whole in fulfilling its callings to understand and love God truly, to explore the depths and range of Christian faith and life, and to serve church and society. Just as practical theologians need to know the

---

10. Key works in the "basic issues" literature include the following: Edward Farley, *Theologia: The Fragmentation and Unity of Theological Education* (Philadelphia: Fortress, 1983) and *The Fragility of Knowledge: Theological Education in the Church and University* (Philadelphia: Fortress, 1988); David Kelsey, *To Understand God Truly: What's Theological about a Theological School* (Louisville: Westminster/John Knox, 1992); Charles M. Wood, *Vision and Discernment: An Orientation in Theological Study* (Atlanta: Scholars Press, 1985); and Barbara G. Wheeler and Edward Farley, eds., *Shifting Boundaries: Contextual Approaches to the Structure of Theological Education* (Louisville: Westminster/John Knox, 1991). For a full bibliography of this literature and several essays and study guides that provide an excellent introduction to it, visit the website www.resourcingchristianity.org and click on "Theological Education" and then on "Purpose."

The most important literature on theological teaching and learning includes the following: Charles R. Foster et al., *Educating Clergy: Teaching Practices and Pastoral Imagination* (San Francisco: Jossey-Bass, 2006); Malcolm L. Warford, ed., *Practical Wisdom on Theological Teaching and Learning* (New York: Peter Lang, 2004); and Kathleen A. Cahalan, "Strengthening Congregational Ministry: A Report on Programs to Enhance Theological Schools' Capacities to Prepare Candidates for Congregational Ministry, 1999-2003," *Theological Education* 42, no. 1 (2006): 63-114. See also the website of the Wabash Center for Teaching and Learning in Theology and Religion, www.wabashcenter.wabash.edu.

Bible, theology, and history if they are to do their work well, so also do those in other theological disciplines need to honor the practical bearing of their own scholarship and teaching on the life of the church in and for the world (as many surely do). This is a point that both the "basic issues" literature and the literature on theological teaching and learning make eminently plain. The authors of this book hope that our efforts to clarify still further the character and purposes of practical theology will spark conversations with those in other theological disciplines about the hopes and duties shared by all, as well as about the distinctive gifts brought by each.

We hope, then, that theological school faculty members who read this book will ask themselves the following questions:

- What fundamental aims or telos does your school implicitly and explicitly serve? How can this service be identified within the culture and concrete activities of your school?
- How is (and might) your own teaching and research be crafted to contribute to this purpose?
- What do you presently expect of the practical theologians on your faculty? How are they hired and included as colleagues?
- What kinds of learning, teaching, and collaboration, both within and beyond theological schools, are necessary and adequate to educate and form ministers who are able to lead and shape communities for discipleship in and for the sake of the world?
- What arrangements might best enable your school to provide excellent education and formation for ministry?
- What might attention to the pedagogy and perspectives of practical theologians contribute to the enhancement of teaching and research within your own field?
- How can and should your school contribute to the pastoral education and formation that continue after your students' graduation?

We hope that those who serve on the staffs or governing boards of theological schools will also ask themselves and encourage faculty members to ask all of the questions above.

A third conversation shaping this book focuses on efforts to strengthen Christian ministry and discipleship by recruiting, preparing, and sustaining excellent pastors for congregations. During the past ten years, many institutions have been involved in a reinvigorated movement to actively call forth a new generation of pastoral leaders,[11] to develop new strategies for help-ing new pastors get started well in their ministries,[12] and to enhance and expand the opportunities working pastors have for the kinds of personal, professional, and spiritual renewal that will enable them to grow in their capacities to sustain vital ministries over the long haul.[13] A fresh body of research and writing that describes the shape of pastoral ministry in the United States today and helps us understand some of the crucial issues fac-ing it is also being produced.[14] In addition, a theologically rich new litera-ture on vocation and vocational discernment — which has to do not only with the vocation of pastoral ministry, but also with vocation as a crucial dimension of the Christian life — has emerged in recent years.[15]

11. The efforts to call forth a new generation of pastoral leaders include Programs for the Theological Exploration of Vocation on 88 church-related colleges representative of vir-tually the entire theological spectrum; special programs for high school youth that offer op-portunities for theological study and inquiry as well as exposure to the work and ministry of the wider church, sponsored and hosted by 44 theological seminaries and divinity schools; and the fellowship and educational programs of the Fund for Theological Education in At-lanta. For information about programs for high school youth and the work of the Fund for Theological Education (FTE), visit the FTE's website, www.thefund.org. A comprehensive picture of the theological exploration of vocation programs on college and university cam-puses is available at www.ptev.org.

12. The programs that help new ministers get off to a good start in pastoral work are well described in David Wood's chapter in this volume.

13. For information about programs that support working pastors, visit the following websites: www.divinity.duke.edu/programs/spe; www.louisville-institute.org/secondary/pastoralgrants; and www.lillyendowment.org/religion.

14. A good deal of the current research on pastoral ministry has been conducted under the auspices of The Pulpit and Pew Project at Duke Divinity School. The overall project ad-dresses three major sets of questions: (1) What is the state of pastoral leadership at the new century's beginning? What do current trends portend for the next generation? (2) What is good pastoral leadership? Can we describe it? What is the relation of good pastoral leader-ship to the ministry of all of God's people? and (3) How does good pastoral leadership come into being? Visit www.pulpitandpew.duke.edu for comprehensive information about the Project and an extended bibliography. Two key works are Jackson W. Carroll, *God's Potters: Pastoral Leadership and the Shaping of Congregations* (Grand Rapids: Eerdmans, 2006), and L. Gregory Jones and Kevin R. Armstrong, *Resurrecting Excellence: Shaping Faithful Chris-tian Ministry* (Grand Rapids: Eerdmans, 2006).

15. An excellent bibliography of the emerging literature on vocation is available at www.ptev.org. Two key works are William C. Placher, ed., *Callings: Twenty Centuries of Christian Wisdom on Vocation* (Grand Rapids: Eerdmans, 2005), and Mark R. Schwehn and Dorothy C. Bass, eds., *Leading Lives That Matter: What We Should Do and Who We Should Be* (Grand Rapids: Eerdmans, 2006).

The issues and questions that have needed to be addressed with regard to pastoral ministry and vocation demand well-integrated interdisciplinary research that is at once fully theological and rigorously empirical. Addressing these issues and questions well requires both a long historical perspective and careful discernment regarding the contemporary situation, and both clear vision concerning the shape of the future toward which God is calling us and focused attention on concrete action in the present. These topics demand precisely the forms of research and inquiry that, in their chapter in this book, Kathleen Cahalan and James Nieman tell us are characteristic of practical theology.[16] Moreover, crafting on-the-ground projects for specific settings also requires a great deal of practical theological thinking. The strategic decisions people have been making, the education and formation they have been providing, the worship they have been leading, the spiritual direction they have been offering, and the community-shaping leadership they have been exercising have very often been remarkably imbued with practical-theological intelligence. All of these actions, undertaken in the midst of the everyday practice of discipleship and ministry, have created an impetus for many ongoing practical theological conversations, some of which have led to publications that will enable leaders in other settings to join the conversation and to do their own work more thoughtfully.

The people involved in these conversations about ministry and vocation are located in a wide variety of roles and institutions. Some are scholar-teachers in departments of practical theology in theological seminaries and divinity schools or professors in other theological fields. Some are college or university campus ministers, chaplains, or faculty members in a wide variety of fields (from literature and history to engineering and business), student services personnel, provosts, and presidents. A number are denominational judicatory executives. And a great many are pastors of local congregations. This mix has contributed significantly to the conversation as a whole. The degrees of theological sophistication all of these people bring to the literal, face-to-face conversation do vary, of course. Yet it is already evident that the work of academic practical theologians and other theological educators can be significantly deepened by regular conversation with

---

16. See Cahalan and Nieman's chapter in this volume, especially pp. 77-79. Happily, many of the recent publications on these topics do, in fact, provide good examples of practical theology at its best.

those who are actively and thoughtfully engaged in practical theological thinking in the midst of concrete, practical engagements.

Ongoing engagement with working pastors has been an especially important dimension of our work for this volume, and we believe that such engagement needs to be a more regular part of formal theological education. Indeed, this book's argument that preparation for ministry extends far beyond the years of academic theological education could not have been identified, much less elaborated, without the collaboration of pastors, and obviously one implication of this argument is that sustained practical theological collaboration between pastors and professors is urgently needed. Ministers and other leaders, in other words, are partners in theological education not only through their listening to what academic practical theologians have to say, but also in the production of practical-theological thinking and writing from which academic practical theologians have much to gain.

We hope, then, that this book will prompt pastors and those who are responsible for calling, placing, and supporting them through theological education, denominational structures, and congregations to ask questions such as these:

- How can the church best foster a way of life that truly is life-giving in and for the sake of the world? How might such a way of life best be understood and described, and how might contemporary people come to live it more fully?
- How can the church's ministers best lead and encourage this, for the sake of the church's faithfulness and for the good of all creation?
- What ways of knowing, perceiving, relating, and acting enable such leadership, and how can good pastors teach theological educators and others about these?
- In what ways can the church enable its people more fully to discern their vocations as Christians — as members and leaders in their congregations and communities of faith, in the work they do in other settings, in their families, and in public life?
- What forms of support and apprenticeship do pastors and other ecclesial ministers need before, during, and beyond the years they spend in graduate theological education?
- In what ways can leaders of congregations and other institutions contribute to practical theological inquiry and its literature?

Finally, this book continues a conversation that focuses the attention of theologians, pastors, and others on Christian practices and their role within a faithful way of life that takes shape in and for the good of the world. It continues the work of the Valparaiso Project on the Education and Formation of People in Faith, a Lilly Endowment project based at Valparaiso University that has worked for more than a decade to develop ways of thinking about and strengthening Christian practices. We, together with eleven other theological educators and ministers, contributed to this conversation with *Practicing Our Faith: A Way of Life for a Searching People,* which offers an invitation to a broad public to consider and embrace a set of twelve Christian practices.[17] We next joined with a second group, composed mostly of systematic theologians, to write *Practicing Theology: Beliefs and Practices in Christian Life.*[18] This book explores how Christian theology both shapes and is shaped by practices, and it also offers a range of theological interpretations of the role of practices in a way of life that is attuned to God's grace. Some of the essays in *Practicing Theology* also delve into the workings of congregations and seminary classrooms, preparing the way for the attention to teaching and pastoral work undertaken in the present volume.

A practical theological approach like the one set forth in *For Life Abundant* has characterized these books and other Valparaiso Project efforts since the project's inception. *For Life Abundant* makes this approach more deliberate and explicit. It also offers greater attention to theological education and ordered, full-time ministry as crucial components of a life-giving way of life. Here we are not only exploring the contours of a life-giving way of life in and for the world *(Practicing Our Faith)* and situating that way of life within a systematic account of Christian faith *(Practicing Theology).* We are also considering how pastors and the communities they lead can and do come to embrace and embody such a way of life in their own concrete circumstances. As readers will discover again and again in

---

17. See Dorothy C. Bass, ed., *Practicing Our Faith: A Way of Life for a Searching People* (San Francisco: Jossey-Bass, 1997), which explored the practices of honoring the body, hospitality, household economics, keeping sabbath, saying yes and saying no, discernment, testimony, shaping communities, forgiveness, healing, dying well, and singing our lives to God. Craig Dykstra considered more fully the educational implications of the way of thinking set forth in *Practicing Our Faith* in his book *Growing in the Life of Faith* (1999; 2d. ed. Louisville: Westminster John Knox, 2005).

18. Miroslav Volf and Dorothy C. Bass, eds., *Practicing Theology: Beliefs and Practices in Christian Life* (Grand Rapids: Eerdmans, 2002).

the chapters to come, attention to this *how* question is one of the distinctive and immensely helpful features of practical theology.

We hope that those who seek to embrace and build up a life-giving way of life as members of congregations and through their daily work will ask themselves questions such as these:

- What is the shape of a way of life that truly is life-giving in and for the sake of the world, and how can we in this congregation help one another to live it more fully?
- Within the concreteness of this shared way of life, how do we both support one another in faithful living and seek the good of those beyond the congregation, indeed the good of all creation?
- How can and do our pastors and other ministers lead us into a life-giving way of life, and how might we support them and collaborate with them in this purpose?
- Why does theological education for ministry matter so much? How might we support and encourage it?

We hope that reading this book and asking these questions will enrich all four of these ongoing conversations. Even more, we hope that it will encourage conversations across the disciplinary and institutional boundaries that sometimes impede the fullest realization of the shared work of education and formation for Christian life and ministry that matters so deeply to those involved in any of the four conversations.

An Overview of the Book

Through thoughtful engagement with and within situations of personal, ecclesial, and societal existence, practical theology seeks to clarify the contours of a way of life that reflects God's active presence and responds to human beings' fundamental needs. It also seeks to guide and strengthen persons and communities to embody this way of life. Thus practical theology requires stereoscopic attention to both the specific moves of personal and communal living and the all-encompassing horizon of faith. It is undertaken in hope for the well-being of persons, communities of faith, and all creation.

Our emphasis on the telos of practical theology, rather than on its methods or its historic focus on ministerial skills, guides the organization of this book.[19] This book begins, therefore, with the way of life abundant for the sake of which ministry, theological education, and the academic field of practical theology exist. Subsequent chapters focus successively on each of these areas, while insisting always on the relationship among them.

Each of the three essays in the first section, "Envisioning Practical Theology," makes connections across these several areas. However, each places emphasis on one of them, offering an account of its special contributions to the pursuit of the telos that concerns them all. In the first chapter in this section, Dorothy Bass introduces the idea of a way of life that is life-giving in and for the sake of the world and explores how practical theology — including a form of practical theology that is intrinsic to the life of faith itself — contributes to shared efforts to inhabit and extend such a way of life. The next chapter, by Craig Dykstra, emphasizes the importance of good pastors to shaping communities in and for life-giving ways of life. His exploration of "pastoral imagination" explores the nature of the supple and embodied ways of thinking and perceiving that excellent ministers mobilize in the course of engagement in their work. James Nieman and Kathleen Cahalan's essay, which completes this section, focuses more directly on practical theology as such, "mapping the field" in a way that both explains academic practical theology's integral connections to Christian discipleship and ministry and establishes it as an essential component of theological education.

Because practical theology, as we understand it, seeks not only to clarify the contours of a way of life but also to guide and strengthen persons and communities to embody this way of life, attention to the education and formation of people of faith and their leaders is integral to practical theology. The second section of the book thus takes us into the classrooms

---

19. This book's authors ask readers to set aside prior notions of this field, many of which assume divisions between thought and action or theory and practice that are rejected by contemporary practical theologians, as well as by many other thinkers in theology and across the humanities and social sciences. As this book's authors understand it, practical theology is not a matter of "applying" concepts drawn from Scripture or doctrine to real-life situations, or of any other specific methodology. Nor is its guiding purpose to provide techniques by means of which seminary graduates can teach, preach, or otherwise convey what they have learned elsewhere in the curriculum. Further, although many practical theologians make their institutional homes in the curricular area often called "the practical field," contemporary practical theology is not confined within this area but rather welcomes collaborators from across the theological curriculum.

of practical theologians. Kathleen Cahalan, a professor of practical theology in a Catholic graduate school of theology where most students are headed for full-time parish ministry, describes her theological and pedagogical engagement with students' development at two key stages in their education: the introduction to ministry course and the integrative course that comes at the end of the Master of Divinity program. The next two essays explore two different approaches to teaching one of the subdisciplines of practical theology, liturgy.[20] First, John Witvliet, a scholar and teacher of worship and liturgical studies in a Christian Reformed college and seminary, shows how understanding worship as a communal practice performed over time in response to God's grace can transform not only students' relations to the subject matter of this subdiscipline but also their self-understanding as leaders and worshipers. Then James Nieman, a professor of preaching and congregational studies, describes a course he co-taught with a professor of worship. The course's goal was to help students in a Lutheran seminary learn how to shape life-cycle rituals — weddings, healing services, funerals, and baptisms — that both proclaim God's promises and open onto a faithful, sustainable, and culturally-aware way of life. Witvliet's and Nieman's essays display quite different ways of conceptualizing and teaching actual courses, demonstrating that taking practical theology seriously opens onto a wide range of specific performances. At the same time, both essays set forth pedagogies that fully embody the teleological, practical, and theological emphases advocated throughout this book. Finally, Bonnie Miller-McLemore, a professor of pastoral theology and care, articulates some of the characteristic moves of teaching in the practical fields. Her essay sheds light on distinctive pedagogies and argues on behalf of the importance and complexity of "know-how," the knowing-in-the-midst-of-practice that is so central to practical theology.

The three essays in the book's next section, "Practical Theology in the Wider Academy," articulate the distinctive role and contributions of aca-

---

20. Scholarship and teaching in practical theology have often been grouped into specific subdisciplines associated with the several arts of ministry, which typically include pastoral care, preaching, worship (or liturgy), education, evangelism, and leadership. This volume rejects the notion of orienting practical theology as a whole toward these arts, but the authors also honor the importance of the distinctive knowledge required by each and of the focused research and teaching that fosters such knowledge. Considering the full implications of reconceiving each of these as practical theology is an important task for each subdiscipline.

demic practical theology in and to universities and theological schools. Although occupying a specific position within these institutions does not exhaust the meaning of practical theology or limit its publics and purposes, these institutions do surround practical theologians with many of the resources they need if they are to do well the work that both church and society need them to do. Moreover, these essays contend, excellent practical theology contributes in return approaches and insights without which universities and theological schools cannot fully flourish. Serene Jones, a systematic theologian, makes a case for the importance of practical theology to theological education as a whole; it is noteworthy in this regard that she considers practical theology both as a distinct discipline and as a more encompassing movement that can include scholars from across the curriculum. Next, a homiletician and a historian explain how and why each works hard to teach in his respective area in ways that bridge the distance between their two disciplines. Ted Smith, whose approach to teaching preaching incorporates profound appreciation for the development of this form of proclamation across the church's history, collaborates on this essay with historian David Daniels, who incorporates into his courses in a different curricular area a profound appreciation for the practical implications of his subject matter for contemporary communities. Finally, Thomas Long, a professor of homiletics who teaches in one of several new doctoral programs in practical theology, explores the mutual benefits to practical theology and to the university as a whole that can result when this discipline has a secure and well-resourced place in institutions of higher learning.

The book's final section explores "Practical Theology in Ministry." One of most important claims of this book is that pastoral education and formation do not begin with seminary enrollment or end when a student graduates from theological school. Those who will become ministers have learned much from experiences before seminary, and ongoing learning during their early years of immersion in ministry will have tremendous influence on their future work. Christian Scharen's essay sets both seminary education and the early years of ministry within a lifelong process of formation. Scharen is especially interested in how ministers grow, with increasing experience, into a kind of embodied knowing that is especially fitting to pastoral leadership. His essay alerts us to the lifelong character of pastoral formation. David Wood's essay explores the pedagogical possibilities inherent in the early years of ministry in congregations and reports on an experiment in apprenticeship that seeks to make this stage of pastoral formation as helpful as possible. The next essay comes from Peter Marty, who describes the movements of thought and action by which a deeply reflective and imaginative pastor encourages a community of faithful practice to take shape. It is notable that Pastor Marty, giving credit first and last to God, emphasizes all along the community itself rather than the one who leads. Finally, Gordon Mikoski looks closely at the work of one pastor in shaping a life-giving way of life in a very troubled part of the world and shows how Mikoski, a pastor and practical theologian with a strong interest in Christian education, has engaged with this pastor's witness. Mikoski's account provides rich insight into the coherence that undergirds discipleship, ministry, and theological education when all are undertaken for the sake of the life of the world.

In the book's final chapter, we step back to reflect on the overall contours of the approach developed here and to imagine some of the new directions in which it might lead. This conclusion is also a preface that invites readers from a range of disciplines and life settings into the ongoing conversations from which this book emerged and to which we aim to contribute.

The authors of this book hope that those who read it will become our companions in exploring the questions articulated here, as well as other questions that have not yet emerged. Surely many readers are already asking them, and also answering them with great insight, for the theological, pedagogical, and pastoral themes we have sounded here are not ours alone. At a time when interest in practice, particularity, and service is spreading across a range of disciplines and realms, practical theologians are poised to work with others to strengthen theological education, ministry, and the life of faith. And at a historical moment when the importance of faithful living in and for the world could hardly be more apparent, practical theologians are ready to work with others to clarify the contours of a life-giving way of life in and for the sake of the world.

PART 1

ENVISIONING PRACTICAL THEOLOGY

1. Ways of Life Abundant

Dorothy C. Bass

Life Together, Dietrich Bonhoeffer's theological account of life in Christian community, is a book from which we who live during these first decades of the twenty-first century have much to learn. Written in 1938, a year after the Nazis shut down the Confessing Church seminary at Finkenwalde, *Life Together* proclaimed the possibility of Christian community to a world that desperately needed people able to live in hope and to resist injustice. Bonhoeffer was fully aware that Christian community is not necessarily permanent and surely never perfect. Nonetheless, he declared, Christian community embodies God's just and merciful presence to the faithful and, through them, to the world.[1] By sharing with the international church one small community's experience, Bonhoeffer implicitly invited other Christians elsewhere to develop the richer and worthier forms of life together for which they so hungered and which the world so urgently needed.

"Life together" — not a book title here but rather an image of our condition — might instead refer to what we are stuck with, like it or not, on a crowded planet where we are literally surrounded by other people, most of them strangers, some reportedly enemies, a number of them friends. Our

1. Dietrich Bonhoeffer, *Life Together,* in *Dietrich Bonhoeffer Works V,* ed. Gerhard Ludwig Mueller, Albrecht Schoenherr, and Geffrey B. Kelly, trans. Daniel W. Bloesch and James H. Burtness (Minneapolis: Fortress Press, 1996). Peter Marty's chapter, "Shaping Communities: Pastoral Leadership and Congregational Leadership," quotes Bonhoeffer's warning that "Those who love their dream of a Christian community more than the Christian community itself become destroyers of that Christian community even though their personal intentions may be ever so honest, earnest, and sacrificial." *Works V,* p. 36.

lives are interwoven in patterns of commerce and meaning with the lives of people all over the world. Some of these people are near at hand, but most we will never see. In general, though, this surround does not always feel like *life* — certainly not the Christ-centered life, the life spilling over with God's bountiful Life, that Bonhoeffer had in mind. Moreover, in the face of war and countless other forms of conflict, being truly *together* with others can seem elusive, if not impossible.

Some of the most important questions Christian people need to consider in the present historical moment regard the character and purpose of our life together in and for a world whose needs are many and urgent. Have we been given through baptism into Christ's death and resurrection a way to "walk in newness of life" (Rom. 6:4) that will bear good fruit for us and for the world God so loves? If so, what might that walk actually look like, and how can we support one another in it? What might it mean, today, here, to follow one who blessed peacemakers (Matt. 5:19), suffered violence and returned forgiveness (Luke 23:33-34), and said "peace be with you" to those who huddled in fear behind locked doors (John 20:19)? At a time when it is impossible to ignore the harm caused by our own patterns of consumption, how can our life together honor all creation as belonging to God and teach us to dwell rightly and faithfully within this creation? What difference might Jesus' own love for those who are poor make in how we answer these and the many other challenging questions that arise?

Questions such as these touch each of us as individuals, but finding and offering worthy answers require us to explore and to enter a way of life that is shared with others. In its fullest expression, such a way of life makes of Christians a body that shares in, and shares with others, the creative and transforming love of God for all the world. Further, it is God's own merciful and unbreakable participation in the life of the world through Jesus Christ that sustains this body and opens this way of life. This is a way of life abundant — a way that bears the kind of life Jesus said he came to bring (John 10:10).

Those who take up this way of life necessarily do so in a wide range of specific moments in history and in a surprising array of distinct settings all over the world. Yet this way of life is not arbitrary or indiscriminate. Rather it has emerged and continues to emerge — haltingly at times, but sometimes in great bursts of new life — among people drawn together by God's promise and presence. Jesus led those who followed him into such a way of life as he healed and taught, ate and sang, and prayed and died. Later his disciples and those who came after them gathered to celebrate the presence of the Risen Christ, breaking bread together in memory of Jesus, sharing their possessions with those in need, and singing, healing, and testifying — men and women, slaves and citizens, Jews and Greeks, married and celibate, makers of tents and dyers of cloth. Over the centuries, communities that were like these in their deepest source and purpose have taken shape in Syrian deserts, European cities, African townships, American suburbs, and other places all over the world. Like Finkenwalde, these communities are and always have been far from perfect; they are not dream communities but down-to-earth gatherings of sinners who have had frequent occasions to forgive one another (and who have often failed even at that). Even so, it is in and through earthen vessels like these that Christ's gifts of grace, peace, and hope have been received and shared.

Within the unique circumstances of each changing context, actual human beings have sought and still seek today to live in ways that respond to the mercy and freedom of God as they are made manifest and available in Christ. Thus Christians necessarily ask in every time and place: How can, and how do, our lives and our life together participate in a way of life that reflects the Life of God, both when we are gathered as church and when we are dispersed into countless disparate circumstances? What is the shape of a contemporary way of life that truly is life-giving in and for the sake of the world? And how can the church foster such a way of life, for the good of all creation?

I recently posed these questions at a conference on young adults and the church. A woman in her twenties who loves Jesus and longs to find life-giving community in a congregation of her home tradition was excited. "Is that true?" she asked. "We can, even must, ask these questions again in our generation, here and now? I've never heard anyone ask my generation to consider these questions. When can we start?" For all who are concerned about the well-being of the world and the faithfulness of the church at this time in history, these questions are urgent ones indeed. To practice a life-giving way of life is a hope and purpose that is widely shared, even though this way of describing what we are after may be unfamiliar to some. Discerning its contours within a specific context, and receiving and sharing it with others in a host of incomplete though hopeful ways, is the concern of parents and pastors, of educators, health care workers, and public servants,

23

and indeed of anyone called to life in Christ. What does it mean, here and now, to take part in Jesus' reconciling work, such people ask one another even if not in these exact words, and how can we help one another to do so? What need for healing is at our doorstep, or even within our home, and how can we address it? How can we become more generous and more just, especially for the sake of those who are damaged by poverty, disaster, or war, and where should we begin to respond? How might we sing our lives more truthfully, in lament for those who suffer both close at hand and in distant places, and in praise and thanks for God's strong and lasting love for us and for all? Such questions arise over dinner tables, in the meetings of church councils and hospital boards, and in many other settings. These questions are often prompted by crisis or challenge, and they are best considered in conjunction with prayer, Scripture, and reflection on the many factors operative in a particular situation. Addressing such questions requires attention to both the all-encompassing horizon of faith and the specific moves of personal and communal living close at hand. Amidst the shifting conditions of history and circumstance, moreover, such attention needs to be given again and again.[2]

This book as a whole articulates the contributions of a theological movement that foregrounds such questions while looking toward a telos of abundant life in and for the world. Most of the chapters portray practical theology as it shapes the work of academic and pastoral leaders. In this chapter, however, the focus is on the life-giving way of life toward which these professionals teach and write or preach and preside. Without vital connection to this, the contributions of theological educators to ministry and Christian living, and also the work of ministers themselves, lose their point and purpose. Moreover, ministers and church-related academics should care deeply about life-giving ways of life because they too are called to enter these ways as disciples, together with the rest of the baptized.

---

2. In mentioning the need to offer ongoing attention I do not mean that we always start from scratch. Sometimes years of practice prepare us to embody responses to such questions without conscious deliberation or effort. Christian Scharen's chapter offers a very helpful analysis of how deliberation can give way to embodied excellence over years of pastoral practice. A similar development can occur in the life of a lay Christian, for example as families weave hospitality seamlessly into the life of a household, as caregivers recognize need quickly and respond in just the right way, or as friends share in fitting and faithful extemporaneous prayer.

"We Have to Move"

As I ponder how to depict the way of life that is served by practical theology and Christian ministry, my mind keeps returning to one clear memory of yearning, a memory that suggests more questions than answers. I am thinking of an evening several years ago. My twin son and daughter were fourteen years old and in their first month of high school, happy on the whole and very lively but also struggling with issues that anyone who has been that age can remember. They had been confirmed in Christian faith a few months earlier, and now they were cautiously checking out our congregation's youth group. At this crucial juncture, they were wondering with special intensity who to be and how to live.

One Sunday night late that September, my daughter came into the kitchen and sat down at the small oak table where I was reading the newspaper. Her eyes were full of tears, and when she spoke her voice was shaky. "We have to move," she said. "I hate this house. We have so much stuff, and most people in the world hardly have any. I hate this town. I want to live where you don't have to use cars to get places, where people care about pollution and all the other things that are wrong in the world. I hate school. All anyone cares about is clothes and boys and having fun. I really want to live a faithful life, but I just don't think that can be done in this town."

For the previous 48 hours, my twins and I and about thirty other teenagers and adults had been together in Chicago working on a book that invites teens into a way of life shaped by Christian practices. The writing process drew us into an ecumenical and diverse group that my kids found amazing, in part because the adults took the teens seriously and the teens took the adults seriously as well. The three of us had spent most of Saturday in a small group discussing the practice about which we would write, "Taking Time," and three others: "Managing Our Stuff," whose teen author and adult author had covenanted with each other to give away one of their possessions on each day of Lent; "Greeting, Sheltering, and Welcoming," whose adult author had lived in the Sojourners Community in Washington, D.C., for many years and so had lots of experience in offering hospitality to those who are homeless; and "Seeking Justice," whose adult author had been involved in the civil rights movement as an African American teenager in Mississippi.[3]

---

3. The book we were writing was later published as Dorothy C. Bass and Don C. Richter, eds., *Way to Live: Christian Practices for Teens* (Nashville: Upper Room, 2002).

The rich companionship and reflection in this group startled and delighted my son and daughter as they perceived anew the depth and promise of the faith that had been given to them and the way of life it had opened for others. Now my daughter was expressing a yearning to live it as fully as she could. But could this be done in the ordinary town she knew best, Valparaiso, Indiana? Wasn't there somewhere — another town, another country — where a truer, fuller way of life was already in place and easy to live? For instance, wasn't there a different high school where no one would notice if you refused to wear popular brands of clothes — clothes that make money and give free advertising to companies that make other fourteen-year-old girls work in sweatshops? Wasn't there a high school where kids hang out together even if they're from different races or backgrounds? A long conversation followed, one that continues to the present day. I encouraged her questions; I praised her insights; I wept a little too, knowing as she did that the faithful life she envisioned would bear some risks. Dad and I have vocations that keep us here, I said. This is where we live, and the things that bother you are problems in other places too. This is where you are called to be faithful, at least for a few more years. There are people here with whom you can seek ways of living more faithfully. I am one of them, I told her, but there are more. Together, we named them. I realized at once that the promise I was making was one I had already made, together with several of the other people on that list, on the day she and her brother were baptized.

My daughter's soul-searching led me to do some of my own, of course, and this, like the conversation between us, continues. In what ways does our nice house and all the stuff it contains impede my own walk in newness of life? What should we do about our own household's contribution to pollution and global warming? The one complaint on her list of which I was not guilty was caring too much about having fun. Caring too much about work was the charge that would have stuck — another sign of sin, surely, before the generous Creator and Liberator who commanded a weekly Sabbath day for all. I soon realized that my daughter had posed one of the classic questions of the Christian life, one that my friends and I often ask in terms not too different from hers. I want to be faithful, we assert, but my situation thwarts my best intentions. I know I am called to love my neighbor, but do you know how aggravating he is? I would give more money away, but the cost of living around here is pretty high. And so it goes.

A Way to Live

A sense of my inadequacy as a guide to a life-giving way of life, so sharp on that September evening, returns now as I consider how to guide readers of this book to perceive the way of living in and for the world that this book claims is the telos of practical theology and Christian ministry. However, this life-giving way of life is not in its essence a matter of consistently righteous behavior, as the scenario above might seem to imply. Nor can it be gained by intense striving; my family could not have attained it simply by giving away our cars and belongings and becoming strict sabbatarians. Even the most earnest efforts to do good consistently fall short of God's desire and the world's need. And even apparently well-intentioned efforts readily become strategies for establishing our own importance and imposing our own will on the world, bringing to ourselves and others not life but death *Lutheran provés*

Instead, a life-giving way of life is a way of freedom made available only and entirely by the grace of God. Its source is not our own righteousness but that of Jesus Christ, who was given to and for the world out of God's deep and inexplicable love. Faith in Christ dislodges us from our strategies of self-securing and provides a far more trustworthy security as God both holds us fast and gives us a kind of freedom that we could not even imagine apart from God's grace. Faith, as Martin Luther portrayed it at an early and dangerous point in his struggle to reform the church, "is a lively, daring confidence in God's grace, so sure and certain that the believer would stake his life on it a thousand times." In thus daring death, Luther was not being morbid or grandiose; rather he was witnessing to the freedom from fear he had discovered in trusting God's strong hold on him, a freedom-from that was simultaneously a freedom-for. "This knowledge and confidence in God's grace," he continued, "makes [believers] glad and bold and happy in dealing with God and with all creatures. And this is the work which the Holy Spirit performs in faith."[4]

Even though my daughter spoke in moral terms of her yearning to live

---

4. Martin Luther, "Preface to the Epistle of St. Paul to the Romans" (1522), in *Luther's Works*, ed. E. Theodore Bachman, trans. Charles M. Jacobs (Philadelphia: Muhlenberg Press, 1960), vol. 35, pp. 370-71. It is interesting to compare "this kind of knowledge" to Calvin's account of faith (quoted in Craig Dykstra's chapter, pp. 55-56). While denominational and academic habits encourage readers to notice differences between these formulations, Luther and Calvin clearly shared an emphasis on the embodied knowledge of God's grace that is at the heart of the Christian life.

faithfully, I am quite sure that the joy, the high spirits, and the eagerness in relation to God and others that she experienced in that weekend community are a large part of what had awakened her yearning to live somewhere different, somewhere new. These new friends were alert to what she knew were "the things that are wrong in the world." But they were also lots of fun to be with. While seeking ways of living that would diminish the weight of these things in their own lives and the lives of others, they were already enjoying a foretaste of the freedom for which they yearned.

That this life-giving way of life is joyful and free does not mean that it has no shape, however. The grace that frees is also a grace that forms.[5] "Because of it," Luther continued immediately after the last sentence quoted above, "without compulsion, a person is ready and glad to do good to everyone, to save everyone, to suffer everything, out of love and praise to God who has shown him this grace."[6] In the midst of this doing of good, this service, this suffering — in how we use our physical strength and receive whatever suffering may come, in what we say and how we speak to one another, in the concrete forms of life together within and beyond the community that gathers to worship God — a way of life that reflects and responds to God's grace takes shape.

Across the past decade, Craig Dykstra and I have been exploring the form of such a way of life by considering the practices in which those who take up this way of life participate.[7] (The group to which my son and

---

5. Serene Jones, "Graced Practices: Excellence and Freedom in the Christian Life," in *Practicing Theology: Beliefs and Practices in Christian Life*, ed. Miroslav Volf and Dorothy C. Bass (Grand Rapids: Eerdmans, 2002). I will return to the important tension between form and freedom explored in Jones's essay later on in this chapter.

6. Luther, "Preface to the Epistle of St. Paul to the Romans," p. 371.

7. Many other colleagues have been part of this exploration. See Dorothy C. Bass, ed., *Practicing Our Faith: A Way of Life for a Searching People* (San Francisco: Jossey-Bass, 1997), which explored the practices of honoring the body, hospitality, household economics, keeping sabbath, saying yes and saying no, discernment, testimony, shaping communities, forgiveness, healing, dying well, and singing our lives to God; the practice of keeping sabbath is explored more fully in Dorothy C. Bass, *Receiving the Day: Christian Practices for Opening the Gift of Time* (San Francisco: Jossey-Bass, 2000). Craig Dykstra laid the foundation for all this work and also considered more fully the educational implications of the way of thinking set forth in *Practicing Our Faith* in the essays gathered in *Growing in the Life of Faith*, 2d. ed. (Louisville: Westminster/John Knox, 2005). See also Dykstra and Bass, "A Theological Understanding of Christian Practices," in *Practicing Theology: Beliefs and Practices in Christian Life*, ed. Volf and Bass. This literature seeks both to exemplify a way of

daughter and I belonged was part of this same effort, asking what these practices might look like for high school students in the U.S.) Christian practices, we have argued, bear wisdom that has been and continues to be embodied in the actual life together of Christian people across many generations and cultures — wisdom about the nature of the human condition and the needs of the world and about the character of God's life giving response to them in Christ and, through the Holy Spirit, in the people who are now Christ's body. Because communities engage in given practices in a wide range of circumstances, the variety and creativity in precisely how they are performed in specific settings is enormous. Because communities engage in these practices forever imperfectly — faltering, forgetting, even falling into gross distortions — theological discernment, repentance, and renewal are necessary dimensions of each practice and of the Christian life as a whole.[8]

This distinctive understanding of practices has been developed during a period of great theoretical interest in "practice" and "practices" in the humanities and social sciences. In spite of important differences among theories, certain features are common to many ways of understanding what a practice is, including our own.[9] Practices are borne by social groups over time and are constantly negotiated in the midst of changing circumstances. As clusters of activities within which meaning and doing are inextricably interwoven, practices shape behavior while also fostering practice-specific knowledge, capacities, dispositions, and virtues. Those who participate in practices are formed in particular ways of thinking about and living in the world.[10]

---

thinking and to invite readers into more aware and faithful participation in practices and the way of life they comprise.

8. Such discernment, repentance, and renewal can and should take place within specific communities on an ongoing basis. More often in history, however, they have been undertaken in fits and starts across periods of eclipse, decline, or reform. Christine Pohl, *Making Room: Recovering Hospitality as a Christian Tradition* (Grand Rapids: Ecrdmans, 1999), follows change in the practice of hospitality across several historical periods and, further, urges contemporary Christian communities to engage in discernment, repentance, and renewal so that this practice might be embodied more fully and faithfully within our own historical context.

9. Different theories of practice are also reflected in this book, most explicitly in the chapter by Ted Smith and David Daniels; see p. 217 n. 2 for their comparison of the concept of practice used by Pierre Bourdieu with that of Alasdair MacIntyre.

10. Laurie F. Maffley-Kipp, Leigh E. Schmidt, and Mark Valeri, eds., *Practicing Protes-*

In our work together, Dykstra and I have probed theological and normative dimensions that are not necessarily in the foreground for other theorists. One might, of course, identify any complex, coherent, ongoing, character-forming, knowledge-engendering set of activities in which those who call themselves Christian regularly engage as a "Christian practice." The description of a "Christian practice" in this sense would disclose important historical and sociological features of communal behavior that would be of interest and importance to anyone seeking to comprehend the practice. Yet if lacking theological criticism and content — indeed, if lacking God — both this description and the practice itself would ultimately be self-referential and self-perpetuating. It has seemed to us, therefore, that to be called "Christian" a practice must pursue a good beyond itself, responding to and embodying the self-giving dynamics of God's own creating, redeeming, and sustaining grace.[11] This leads us to ask, then: What specific practices give rise to ways of thinking and living that address human existence and the needs of the world in ways that reflect and respond

---

tants: Histories of Christian Life in America, 1630-1965 (Baltimore: Johns Hopkins University Press, 2006), pp. 1-6. This book's introduction includes a summary of theories of practice that identifies two main schools: social scientific thought (with Bourdieu the leading theorist) and the constructive theological understanding developed by Dykstra, Bass, and others. The former, the editors argue, characteristically adopts a critical stance toward the power arrangements embodied in practices, while "Protestant theorists" are more interested in strengthening practices they take to be basically benevolent. In fact, Dykstra and I believe that each "Christian practice" incorporates critical and self-critical perspectives, though it is true that our normative and theological understanding of practices does indeed lead us to see each Christian practice as a whole as good.

11. Dykstra's and my work on practices began with Alasdair MacIntyre's account of social practices (*After Virtue: A Study in Moral Theory*, 2d ed. [Notre Dame, Ind.: University of Notre Dame Press, 1984], pp. 187ff.), but the theological turn we have taken marks a significant break with the concepts developed there. The "goods" that concern us are not "internal" to a practice but are oriented to God and God's intentions for all creation. In addition, our concept of Christian practices is differentiated from that of MacIntyre, on the one hand, and from social scientific concepts of practice, on the other, in that our notion is shaped by a theological anthropology that posits the existence of certain fundamental needs and conditions as belonging to human existence as such. "Christian practices," as we use the term, are clusters of meaningful action (including thinking and representation) that are sizable and significant enough to address these needs (e.g., for relationship with one another, creation, and God; for physical care in illness or injury; for certain material goods) and conditions (e.g., finitude, mortality, and physical and psychological vulnerability). Dykstra and I developed this understanding most fully in "A Theological Understanding of Christian Practices."

to this grace? And conversely, what particular ways of thinking and living are embodied in practices that take seriously God's grace to all the world in Jesus Christ?[12]

Rather than setting Christian practices apart from other human practices and Christians apart from non-Christian communities, Dykstra and I have been most interested in those basic social practices in which people in every time and place necessarily engage in one way or another, by virtue of their humanness, and to ask how the Holy Spirit transforms such practices as communities take up a shared way of life as disciples of Jesus. Examples of such basic social practices (and their Christian forms) would include living in time (embracing daily, weekly, and yearly rhythms of rest and worship); telling stories (testimony); caring for one another in injury and illness (healing, pastoral care); and procuring and using material goods (stewarding the resources of domestic, congregational, societal, and planetary households). In each case, responses to fundamental needs and conditions that exist in every culture emerge through concrete actions that are inextricably interwoven with substantive convictions about how things really are within a world created, redeemed, and sustained by the Triune God. Such practices cut across every realm of life — public policy, family life, a congregation, and more — and each also has distinctive roots in Scripture.[13] This relatively expansive understanding of what Christian practices are, we believe, resists parochialism while also insisting on the irreducibly local, close-at-hand quality of each practice within a given setting. It also honors God's active presence as a gift to the whole world, not

---

12. The question of which comes first in sequence and/or in normative priority — embodied ways of doing things or the ways of thinking associated with them, including doctrine — is one of the most important issues addressed throughout Volf and Bass, eds., *Practicing Theology*, especially in the chapters by Amy Plantinga Pauw, Sarah Coakley, Reinhard Hütter, Kathryn Tanner, and Miroslav Volf. These and most of the other authors of *Practicing Theology* are systematic theologians. Conversations leading up to *For Life Abundant*, as well as some of the chapters in this book, suggest that the more robust notion of and closer engagement with practice belonging to practical theology would make this question of priority a fruitful point of engagement between systematic and practical theologians.

13. See "A Theological Account of Christian Practices," in *Practicing Theology*, pp. 18-19. This understanding of a practice is more expansive than many others and thus covers a lot of social, cultural, and theological territory. Dykstra and I believe that the capacity of this approach to forge conceptual and actual connections across various realms of life is of great value in a social and intellectual context in which such connections are often severed or obscured.

just to, for, or in the church, and it tries to show how the many different things that people actually do might add up to a coherent and meaningful whole that gets embodied in a shared way of life.

Practicing a Life-Giving Way

This summary of a theological and normative understanding of practices interprets practices as the traditioned yet always-emerging patterns through which communities live as Jesus' disciples, responding to God's grace and to the needs of human beings and all creation. It interprets practices, in short, as forms within and through which a Christian way of life takes shape. Thus this interpretation presses us to ask once again about form and freedom, for observation and experience show that practices readily become rigid, as that which is normative crowds out that which is theological. As we become ever more aware of these forms, multiple "shoulds" can weigh heavily upon us, as they did upon me after my daughter's confession and request. Overwhelmed, we forget to notice and lean upon the freeing power of the Holy Spirit. The resulting way of life, though morally earnest, is not likely to radiate faith, hope, and love.

How the forms of a way of life that seeks to respond to God's presence and the needs of the world can be embraced without stifling the freedom that comes with God's saving grace has been a critical question for Christian theologians across the ages. In "Graced Practices: Excellence and Freedom in the Christian Life," Serene Jones brings central themes of Reformed theology to bear on this question. Jones begins by telling of a moment in the life of her congregation when a group of members who were planning new programs to reform the congregation's practices of hospitality and testimony were suddenly overcome by exhaustion and dread. Noticing that the joy and momentum of their initial planning had ebbed, one member asked another how she was feeling about the work that lay ahead.

"I'm sorry," she responded. "I don't mean to be negative, but when I look at this list I feel . . . so tired." Others soon acknowledged that they felt the same. One finally asked, "Is this what it means to be church? Believing that you should do all these things and then feeling worn out and guilty because you can't? Is this the Good News we celebrate?"

Jones interprets this question and the extended theological conversation to which it led as examples of the persistent tension between justification and sanctification in the Christian life, a tension she then goes on to explicate in terms of the Reformed tradition's understanding of the twofold character of grace. Within this congregation, she reports, this understanding proved to be liberating and empowering. If they were justified by God's grace, these lay theologians remembered, they were set free by pure gift rather than by anything they might do or not do (including the visionary projects on their list). Yet if God's grace also "sanctifies" those whom it embraces and provides a basis for understanding the importance of "the excellence of practices," they needed also to take seriously their call to "a pattern of living that reflects the structure of that freeing love." Practices and doing them well do matter, they realized, though not as the basis of salvation for ourselves or for the world. And freedom is real and bountiful, though it does not exist for its own sake but as joyful energy that takes shape in disciplined, beautiful practices. The freedom granted by God's grace, in sum, has a shape.[14]

Jones's reflection on practices in light of these two doctrines and the relationship between them helps to delineate the overall contours of a life-giving way of life by suggesting how freedom and form might cohere therein. As Jones would surely agree, however, theological conversations such as the one considered by this congregation are never finished or fully resolved. Answers glimpsed at one point will vanish at another: someone will make someone else feel the weight of an unfulfilled "should," while another will take freedom as a license for self-satisfaction. To complicate matters further, the play in the tension between form and freedom will surely be different on different days and in different situations. A life-giving way of life cannot thrive without both freedom and form, but discerning how those take shape in a specific time and place and how to guide actual people in embracing them can be exceptionally difficult. This discernment is close to the center of practical theology's concern.[15]

One dimension of practical theology, broadly conceived, is the thinking-in-context of people who are trying to live their lives self-consciously and intentionally as people of Christian faith. This sounds

14. Jones, "Graced Practices," in *Practicing Theology;* quotations from pp. 52-55.
15. I hope in this chapter to note the contributions of both systematic theology (represented here by Jones) and contextual ministry (represented later in the chapter by a gifted youth minister) to fostering faithful living.

pretty grand, but in actuality it is often a down-to-earth matter of figuring out what to do next, and how to do it. In definitional discourses, and even in brief accounts of given practices, it is easy to idealize Christian practices and the way of life they comprise, making them seem more smooth and coherent than they actually are in the midst of everyday conditions. Yet messy everyday practices, embraced humbly yet boldly, are precisely the forms of life that bear help and grace and companionship and challenge for figuring out what to do next within the actual complexities of contemporary society. This becomes clear when a busy mom trying to deal with an overload of demands admits that getting a Palm Pilot and "setting priorities" does not help much, and then discovers that the Christian community over time has developed embodied wisdom and ways of living in time upon which she can draw and in which she can participate. So, in mutual support with others who are also in need of respite and willing to acknowledge their failure to get everything done as a sign of their mortality, she begins to take one step and then another, shaping at least one day each week to receive time as God's gift rather than as a series of demands.[16] Similarly, a Christian practice of "household economics," even when imperfectly understood and undertaken, can reframe the self-understanding and expand the options of a teenager who feels that she is drowning in an ocean of material things. As she discovers that she belongs to a historic and global community that includes many other people who have longed for a different way of dealing with material goods and their consumption and exchange, she enters a context in which she can meet, live with, and learn from others who have experimented in actual forms of life that are guided by human mutuality attuned to the generosity of God. With newfound companions, she too can take one step, then another, as she continues to discover and receive a way of life abundant that is good for herself, for others, and for creation.

Simply to imagine a way of life that prizes an abundance of life rather than an abundance of things to do and things to possess puts a new frame around the world in which many middle-class North Americans live at this point in history.

---

16. In my book *Receiving the Day: Christian Practices for Opening the Gift of Time* (San Francisco: Jossey-Bass, 2000), I try to share the wisdom and ways of living in time that I discovered.

Receiving a Way of Life Abundant

The words that reject the heavily-marketed telos of material abundance and reframe the world are spoken by Jesus in the Gospel of John: "I came that they may have life, and have it abundantly." Parabolically evoking a scene in which sheep seek shelter within an enclosure, going in and out to graze, Jesus says in a rapid burst of metaphors that he is both the gate and the shepherd. The abundance he offers is a pasture — a living pasture, perhaps, a sheep's version of living water (John 4:10) and living bread (John 6:51) — that provides not only nourishment but also the presence and care of a good shepherd. This shepherd knows these sheep, and they know him and recognize his voice. Under his watchful care, moreover, the sheep dwell together in a single flock. For the sake of these sheep, the shepherd is willing to lay down his own life (John 10:1-18).[17]

From the sheep's point of view, this is abundance indeed — abundance of nourishment, safety, community, care. However the text also indirectly discloses that there is trouble in the sheepfold. The community to which this text belonged, the community that saw Jesus as their shepherd and as the source of abundant life, was at risk, even while under his care, from "thieves and bandits" who sneak in over the wall of the sheepfold, as well as from "hired hands" who run away as soon as a wolf appears. What then is the abundant life portrayed and promised here? It is clearly not a life that excludes physical death, which the shepherd himself is about to suffer. Nor is it a condition sheltered from those who would do harm. Rather, it is a life with others that is provided by one whose voice is beloved and whose commitment to his flock is unbreakable. This life is not just a matter of existing. To live "abundantly" is to participate in the true life that comes from God, the Life first and most fully known to this community in the resurrection of Jesus from the dead.

Sheep and shepherds are in many ways remote from the Midwestern town in which I live, and allegorizing this passage in order to identify our local sheep, thieves, bandits, and hired hands would do justice to neither the text nor the town. And yet I believe that many people in this town do know something about a way of life abundant. Many residents gather

17. My reading of this text was influenced by Luke Timothy Johnson, *Living Jesus: Learning the Heart of the Gospel* (San Francisco: Harper, 1999), and Raymond E. Brown, *An Introduction to the Gospel of John*, ed. Francis J. Moloney (New York: Doubleday, 2003).

weekly in communities where we worship God and hear texts like this one, texts that bear witness to a kind of Life that is much more than mere existence and to God who is the source of this Life. There we also receive baptism into the death and resurrection of Christ and gather around a table where we are fed the Bread of Life. There we serve one another in love, even if not as fully as we should, and go out to serve others as well. And sometimes a way of abundant life emerges even here.

Since moving to another town was not an option, my daughter decided to hope for that possibility. She and her brother talked about church, and together they decided to give our congregation's youth group a good try. Barely a month later, a new youth minister arrived in our congregation. Over time, he and his wife and the other kids in that group and the adults who met with them each week became important companions. This minister's yearning to embrace practices that advanced social justice and served the well-being of creation was as strong as my son's and daughter's, and I suspect that he too sometimes wondered if one could live faithfully in Valparaiso, Indiana. Together, however, two or three dozen youth and adults opened themselves to the possibility that they could.

The main thing they did was get together. Each Sunday evening they shared a meal and then gathered in a comfortable part of the church building to sing and pray. Then they broke into consistent, covenanted groups of about six people, with one adult and one of the older teens serving as leaders of each group. They talked about their lives and their faith, sometimes prompted by a talk given after supper or a question prepared by leaders but often just discussing whatever was on their minds. As the evening came to a close, the groups reunited for a time of prayer that often took place in silence around a cross on the floor onto which each person could place a lighted candle. Several times each year they also went on retreats and did service projects together.

I sensed that something special was going on when my kids started refusing to stay home even if Monday's homework was unfinished. When they started wearing the most comfortable old clothing they had — the equivalent of pajamas — I was sure of it. The youth minister's reading of the situation of young people in our town was that their lives were so cluttered and full of demands that they were ignoring God's presence with and for them and offering the Holy Spirit no time and space to work in them. So he taught them to pray and to ponder and to be still, showing them a realm of freedom from the countless rules and expectations imposed on them each day. This freedom was not without form, however. He often re-minded everyone, youth and adults alike, that this freedom comes from God and is constantly nourished by God's Word as it is spoken, seen, felt, and heard through Word and Sacrament. Thus nourished, he continued, this freedom takes shape through the practices through which Christians then go forth to live as disciples in and for the world. The small groups, which had been dreaded at first, became practicing grounds for this shaped freedom, as kids from different cliques and academic tracks devel-oped ties of mutual care and enjoyment and talked honestly about the world in which they lived.[18]

This youth group was not a set program that can be copied and mar-keted to other congregations, even though the resources on which it drew are widely available and its guiding theology was a classic understanding of Christian freedom.[19] What cannot be found online or in a library or class-room is the quality of attention this approach required this minister to give to each youngster and adult and also required them to give to him and one another. Moreover, the contours of the rooms in which it took place mattered, the character of the large public high school just across the street mattered, and the unique gifts brought by every participant mattered. The new life that emerged placed all of these on the expansive horizon of God's judgment and promise, but it grew just one sprout at a time on irreducibly local soil. In a sense, this leader was doing practical theology within his own ministry while also teaching others to do it within their own lives, for the sake of abundant living in and for the world.

---

18. I am drawing on my memory of this ministry and on a paper written by this minis-ter for a theology course he was taking at the time at Lutheran School of Theology in Chi-cago: Jeremy Myers, "Youth Ministry, A Quenching of the Spirit: A Rationale for Imple-menting Christian Disciplines and Practices into Our Work with Youth" (n.p., 2002).

19. This approach incorporated both the contemplative spiritual disciplines developed by San Francisco Theological Seminary's Youth Ministry and Spirituality Project (www .ymsp.org) and the practices of life in and for the world developed by the Valparaiso Project on the Education and Formation of People in Faith (www.waytolive.org and www .practicingourfaith.org). Myers's paper, cited above, drew deeply from theological works that explore Lutheran understandings of justification and the Christian life.

Through Death to Life

My son and daughter, now in college, have moved to another town. Still here, I continue to wonder, with others dear to me, what it really means to embrace a life-giving way of life in a place where so many of the divisions and patterns of consumption that imperil the well-being of the world at this moment in history are manifest. Of course many people eventually leave for one reason or another, and that is as it should be, some following market-driven patterns of mobility while others feel called to life-giving vocations in other parts of the nation or world. Still, even an ordinary Midwestern town full of sinners is part of the world beloved by God, and it is here that those who remain and those who will arrive in coming years will follow Christ.

Often it is a funeral that discloses once again the life-giving way of life that runs right through the very town that my young daughter once suspected was not a promising place for faithful living. Two have done so with special power in recent months. Pondering these moving worship services, I think first of each deceased individual — a crucial aspect indeed, for to see and honor and love the uniqueness of each of these (and indeed of each person anywhere) is an indispensable element of the way of abundant life we are trying to understand. At the same time, I want to convey just as clearly the warmth of hundreds of people gathered together on a cold day, the encouraging sound of voices joined in song and prayer, and the mingling of lament and thanksgiving in the bodies and on the faces of friends and family members. Even more, I want to convey the surprising, grace-filled connection between these two services.

A memorial service for Walt Reiner was held on December 29 in the large Lutheran church to which he had long belonged. Walt, a former football coach at Valparaiso University, died at the age of 83 after a fall in his home and several years of declining health (though only a few weeks before his fall he had been out pounding nails into the roof of a house being built by Project Neighbors, a local organization he founded during the 1980s). During the early 1960s, the civil rights movement jolted him into an infectious activism that never subsided. His approach to change was person-to-person: Love your neighbor by befriending neighbors you would never meet in your own little comfort zone, he would say. He convinced the university that it needed to start an urban studies program in nearby Chicago and moved to a public housing project there with his wife, Lois, a strong and loving colleague in all his work, and their four children.

As they prepared to return to Valparaiso two years later, one of their Chicago friends objected that she and her children did not have the freedom to move to a place with cleaner air and better schools. So the Reiners made it possible for her family — and soon six others — to come too, recruiting hosts and financing from the members of several congregations. At that time, no other African American families lived in Valparaiso, and some hostile residents made threatening calls and burned a cross on the lawn in front of a newcomer's home. Yet five of these mothers eventually graduated from college; most of their children and grandchildren are still in town, and many more African Americans are now here as well. Some of these later formed a congregation that is now part of the United Church of Christ. I remember the tears of joy that streamed down the face of one of the mothers at the first Easter service of Union Community Church in 1989, when the free and expressive worship she had so missed since moving from Chicago broke out in an upstairs chapel at the First United Methodist Church. I also remember my own tears of joy at being embraced by members of Union Community Church that day and across the years, even though I have never left my prior congregation or joined fully in the life of this new one.

Are these signs of a life-giving way of life? In many ways, the story I am telling, which began in the new life of the gospel, led through the valley of death, a valley lit by a Christ-mocking symbol, along a path that still today is strewn with insults and indignities. The town and its established congregations have often failed to practice hospitality as fully as we should have. At the same time, a vibrant community of faith with hope for its children's future has come into being in a formerly forbidding place.

The second funeral took place about two months after Walt Reiner's memorial service, as hundreds of us packed into the largest parlor at Moeller Funeral Home to offer prayer and testimony to God over the body of Bill Thompson, one of the most cheerful and hard-working members of Union Community Church. Bill, a middle-school teacher and husband to Jo, another very capable congregational leader, died suddenly of a massive stroke at the age of 52. His death left a huge hole in the congregation, and I still find it much harder to accept than Walt's. Yet the gratitude that poured forth as dozens of young people, and several older ones, offered testimony about Bill's positive influence in their lives bespoke abundance — the abundance that comes as blessings multiply among people who share their lives with one another in the context of God's care.

Both of these men had flaws, and so did their families and congregations, and so, especially, do I. Yet when I think of Bill Thompson singing with the men's chorus of Union Community Church at Walt Reiner's memorial service, I see life that is astoundingly, surprisingly abundant. If such music could arise only from and among those who always behave righteously and well, that service and every other would be awfully quiet. Music like that is a gift shared by those who have been set free from the power of death in its many forms — free from fear, isolation, and hate, and simultaneously free for participation in abundant life with God and one another. However, this too is crucial: if those making and enjoying that music had not also been formed and engaged in the disciplined beauty of practices that respond to God's grace and embody God's self-giving love, Walt Reiner's funeral would have been awfully quiet for an altogether different reason.[20]

Practical theology in and for a life-giving way of life is often not as visible as that which takes place in classrooms, books, and pastoral conferences. Among the people attending both of these funerals, however, countless deliberations that reflect the kind of knowing pursued by practical theology have taken place, simply because those who found themselves set free to walk in newness of life have had to figure out how to move their feet along an unfamiliar path they could see only by the light of Christ and could navigate only with the help of the Holy Spirit. Disciples in both congregations have considered how generous to be with their money, how trusting to be of new acquaintances, and how to worship God in spirit and in truth. They have preached and listened and prayed and studied, often when facing challenges that were urgent and perhaps even life-threatening. They have learned how to pray with, live with, care for, and mourn the death of a Christian brother or sister from a different cultural background. Not all, not even most, of their thinking has been cognitive; some seem to know what to do almost spontaneously, others seem to lurch along by trial and error, and still others engage in long, earnest conversations. But their thinking has been theological, nourished by Scripture and made possible by a lively, daring confidence in the grace of God. And it has been practical, improvising faith's music within a unique, terrible, and beautiful corner of this world so loved by God.

20. This scene calls to mind David F. Ford's interpretation of the "singing self" in Ephesians (especially 5:18-21). Ford argues that faithful singing communicates God's "abundance" and embodies the transformation that comes with salvation in Christ; see *Self and Salvation: Being Transformed* (Cambridge: Cambridge University Press, 1999), pp. 107-36.

2. Pastoral and Ecclesial Imagination

Craig Dykstra

It is a beautiful thing to see a good pastor at work. Somehow, pastors who really get what the Christian ministry is all about and who do it well are able to enter many diverse situations, whether joyous or full of misery and conflict, and see what is going on there through the eyes of faith. This way of seeing and interpreting shapes what the pastor thinks and does and how he or she responds to people in gestures, words, and actions. It functions as a kind of internal gyroscope, guiding pastors in and through every crevice of pastoral life and work.[1] This way of seeing and interpreting is what I mean by "pastoral imagination."

The pastoral imagination emerges over time and through the influence of many forces.[2] It is always forged, however, in the midst of ministry

---

1. Throughout this essay I will use the terms "pastor" and "minister" to refer to a wide range of pastoral leaders who serve, primarily though not exclusively, in local Christian congregations or parishes. The diverse traditions in Christianity have diverse names and titles for those who do pastoral work in congregations, and behind these names and titles are diverse conceptions of ministry, ordination, and office that all have considerable significance in the shaping of pastoral work and leadership in congregations. In this essay, I will not make any attempt to sort out these many important nuances. Instead, I hope to provide a portrait of the situation of pastoral ministry and its power to shape the people who exercise pastoral leadership, whatever their ecclesiastical office or pastoral role may be. Thus, I would include not only ordained priests and ministers but also lay pastors and lay ecclesial ministers within the meaning of the terms I am using here. What is important for the purposes of this essay is whether those who read it can see themselves as persons who live and work as pastoral leaders in a way that is consistent with what I will attempt to describe. To the extent that this is so, this essay is for and about them.

2. Other essays in this book — especially those in the final section, "Practical Theology

itself, as pastors are shaped by time spent on the anvil of deep and sustained engagement in pastoral work. It is the actual practice of pastoral ministry — the many specific activities of ministry done faithfully and well and with an integrity reflected in the minister's own life — that gives rise to this particular and powerful imagination. There is no other work like pastoral ministry — and, because of that, the pastoral imagination is distinctive, and of immense value.

In spite of its great value, however, no one can go out in pursuit of pastoral imagination as an end in itself. Ironically, even though ministry is hard work that requires considerable preparation and enormous discipline, the pastoral imagination that emerges within it comes not as an achievement but as a gift. It takes shape over time within the daily work of ministry and then somehow surprises one by its presence. As a surprising gift, pastoral imagination is like the other gifts that God showers on those who are caught up in faithful living in a variety of settings — gifts that often are especially suited to the situation and need of those who receive them. As a gift fitting to the pastoral life, the pastoral imagination that comes to ministers is given and received in the midst of a life spent in service to God's people.

Something similar in character may emerge within whole communities of faith as well. Many, many local congregations and other communities of faith are places where people of all ages learn to live lives that truly and abundantly reflect God's grace for themselves and others. There, in community, people learn to experience and to trust the love and mercy of God, and in that context they come alive in ways that accord with the promises of God. I believe that, in and through the church, God in Christ by the power of the Spirit actually makes people's lives better and stronger, more hospitable and gracious, more joyful, generous, and just. This obviously does not always happen, nor in every congregation. But when the people of a community start to learn actually to practice Christian faith, a new and profoundly abundant way of living begins to emerge and eventually flourishes — a way of living that is strong enough to provide a sense of meaning, purpose, direction, value, courage, thanksgiving, and joy even in the midst of conflict, injustice, suffering, evil, and, ultimately, death. Clearly, such communities also

---

in Ministry" — explore how good pastors develop, over time, the kind of imagination I am describing here.

have a way of seeing the world through eyes of faith, a way of seeing I call "ecclesial imagination."

Pastoral imagination and ecclesial imagination live, if they live at all, in a perpetual and dynamic process of mutual interdependence. They are symbiotic. They are caught up with each other in a virtuous cycle. What gives rise to a strong, rich, flexible, attentive pastoral imagination? Pastoral work in congregations made up of faithful people who together share an ecclesial imagination built on the same foundation. And what gives rise to a strong, rich, flexible, attentive ecclesial imagination? In no small part, the presence of pastors who preach and teach the Christian faith and lead congregations imaginatively and intelligently in the light of an ever-deepening knowledge of the grace, mercy, and love of God.

The church's ecclesial imagination is the essential condition for fostering and shaping the pastoral imagination. At the same time, pastoral ministry, undergirded and guided by a truly rich pastoral imagination, is an essential condition for the continual fostering and shaping of the church's ecclesial imagination. Particular congregations and the church as a whole can wither and die — or betray their calling — if they are not consistently fed and led by pastoral leadership possessed of the capacity to perceive, truthfully and deeply, through eyes of faith, what is actually going on in the world of which they are a part; to imagine what new life God is calling God's people to embrace; and to strengthen and enable the people to see it themselves and to live into it creatively.

The point and purpose of practical theology are to nourish, nurture, discipline, and resource both pastoral and ecclesial imagination. That may not be its exclusive purpose or the only good way to describe its purpose and telos, but if practical theology (and indeed theology and theological education as a whole) become in any way disconnected from pastoral imagination and ecclesial imagination, they inevitably forfeit a good deal of their reason for being. They also cut themselves off from essential sources of their own vibrancy.

The South Bronx

The Rev. Heidi Neumark served for nineteen years as the pastor of the aptly named Transfiguration Lutheran Church, a Hispanic and African American congregation situated right next door to the dumps and incinerators where most of New York City burns its trash. The neighborhood is desperately poor, and if anywhere in the United States could be described accurately as God-forsaken, this is the place. But the South Bronx is not God-forsaken, and Heidi Neumark and her congregation know this. They know that the South Bronx is chock-full of God's presence, hard to see as that may often seem.

Neumark's amazing book *Breathing Space* is the best portrait I have seen of a rich and profound pastoral imagination at work — a pastoral imagination forged in the midst of her life with a people whose own ecclesial imagination is deep and strong. Here is just one vignette from Neumark's memoir:

> During one of our Lenten healing services, a little boy named Nelson asked how Jesus knew he was God and how Jesus could be God. Our intern Anita asked him if he was a child of God, and immediately, without missing a beat, Nelson replied, "Of course I'm a child of God!" But in truth, there was no "of course" about it.[3]

When Nelson first arrived on the doorsteps of Transfiguration Lutheran, he was two years old and was joined by a literal parade of twenty other siblings and cousins, all born to Nelson's mother or his aunt. The two women and Nelson's grandmother struggled mightily to care for them all, but against odds that were virtually insurmountable. They were living in various shelters in the neighborhood. Nelson's mother was addicted to drugs and so was her sister. As Neumark describes the situation, "the children lived in chaos. They slept on piles of dirty, smelly clothes. . . . They grazed on what food they found. Discipline consisted of screams and beatings."[4] "Then," Neumark continues, "all twenty-one began coming to church."[5]

> They came in and ran wild. They had never been to church before and had no reference points for any expected behavior. Teaching them was fun — but difficult. There were a number of Sundays when I, who happen to have a high tolerance for disorder (I need it to tolerate myself),

3. Heidi B. Neumark, *Breathing Space: A Spiritual Journey in the South Bronx* (Boston: Beacon, 2003), pp. 108-9.
4. Neumark, *Breathing Space*, p. 109.
5. Neumark, *Breathing Space*, p. 109.

guiltily wished they would not come. . . . Nevertheless, I was really happy to see the children learning stories about Jesus and singing the songs. We made prayer books together. They did everything with gusto — whether singing God's praises or misbehaving.

After about six months, they were baptized. The waters broke and old Sarah gave birth to all twenty-one. *For the creation waits with eager longing for the revealing of the children of God.* I like the J. B. Phillips translation: *The whole creation is on tiptoe to see the wonderful sight of the children of God coming into their own.* The church was on tiptoe to see this prodigious birth drama, as each fine child left the womb of the font dripping wet, foreheads brightly anointed with the seal of their glorious inheritance. "Of course, I'm a child of God!" said Nelson, and St. Paul adds . . . *if children, then heirs, heirs of God and co-heirs with Christ* (Romans 8:17).[6]

But again, of course, there is no "of course" about it. Without Neumark's and the congregation's eyes and ears attuned to regard these children — and their mothers and grandmother — all as "children of God" and as rightful "heirs," the new lives that in fact emerged for many of these children as they grew up in that church would never have been given birth. As Neumark herself says, "Many would consider Nelson and his siblings only as heirs of a family system fraught with abuse and pain, heirs of a cycle that breeds poverty and crime, a future of dry bones."[7] But Neumark and her congregation saw something entirely different. They saw children alive with the promises of God, dripping wet with the waters of God's grace.

Here we see pastoral imagination and ecclesial imagination fully engaged and powerfully at work — in the lives of children, in the lives of parents and grandparents, in the life of a neighborhood filled with people who, in desperate circumstances, are struggling just to find a way to stay alive. What happens? In the context of a small, poor congregation that sustains a palpable sense of the real presence of God and somehow stays continually open to the abundance of God's love and mercy, the people find a way to stay alive. Indeed, much more than this, they find a new way of life, a way of life abundant.

6. Neumark, *Breathing Space*, p. 109.
7. Neumark, *Breathing Space*, p. 111.

The Pastoral Imagination

Almost ten years ago, my colleagues at Lilly Endowment and I decided to try to serve and support pastors in more direct ways than we had in the past. We knew that, in order to do so well, we needed to get to know a lot more pastors personally and learn from them whatever we could about their everyday lives in contemporary ministry. Over the years, we have tried to get to know how ministers think, what they think about, what their concerns are, what their ministries look like, what they do with their time, and how they sustain their ministries over the long haul. As we come to know more pastors, we also involve them in various aspects of our work. We solicit their advice about what we and others might do that would really be helpful in enhancing the quality of life for pastors and their congregations and in building for the future of the ministry.

Several years ago, the Endowment convened, in partnership with the Louisville Institute, two groups of pastors that we came to call Pastors Working Groups.[8] Meeting with those groups provided me the extraordinary opportunity and privilege of meeting over the course of several years with two dozen superb pastors — male and female, black, white, and Hispanic, Catholic and Protestant, serving large churches and small ones. All of us worked together intensively on such questions as these: What makes for a truly vibrant ministry and for long-term pastoral work that has real dynamism to it? Where does such ministry come from, what does it consist of, and what helps most to resource and support it? This venture turned out to be one of the richest sustained theological conversations about ministry I have ever been a part of.

Through conversations with these pastors — plus hundreds more that have taken place over the past decade — my colleagues and I have learned a great deal. We have learned, first, that hundreds and hundreds of congregations all across this country are being served by quite splendid pastors.

8. The Pastors Working Groups were organized by the Louisville Institute, which is a program at Louisville Presbyterian Theological Seminary funded by Lilly Endowment. Dr. James W. Lewis is the Institute's executive director. Over the course of three years, two groups of about a dozen pastors each were convened. Each group met for two-and-a-half days every few months over the course of about a year-and-a-half. David Wood and I convened the first group. William Brosend and Thomas Long convened the second group. Heidi Neumark, who is quoted above, and Peter Marty, one of the authors of this book, were members of the second group.

Even though many of the pastors we are getting to know have a number of specific frustrations and far too many feel at least a bit isolated, they are nonetheless pursuing their callings with a deep sense of satisfaction and even joy. Second, we are learning something very important about how pastoral leaders learn ministry — about what it takes and about how long it takes. We know that pastors are shaped, both as persons and as ministers, by experiences and relationships of many kinds, from childhood through adolescence and young adulthood. We know that what they learn and experience in their seminaries and divinity schools plays a crucial role that has consequences for decades. We also know that their formal training in graduate school never takes place in a vacuum. Graduate theological education shapes and is profoundly shaped by what a person brings to that educational sojourn. As important as all that prepares one for ministry is, however, something at least equally powerful happens after graduation — in the midst of the practice of ministry itself — to those who eventually become especially able and competent pastors.

In a very real sense, of course, each pastor is unique, bearing a distinctive set of personal characteristics and theological convictions and shaped by specific social and cultural influences and locations. At the same time, all pastors necessarily and regularly engage in a set of challenging and substantive activities, including planning and leading worship, teaching, preaching, studying the Bible, being with those who are dying or in grief, and shaping a community's shared life in ways that witness to God's love for the people of this community and for their neighbors. Sustained experience in the actual practice of pastoral ministry somehow takes all that one is and all that one has learned and is learning and refashions it in such a way that the many forces and dynamics working in and through one increasingly gain coherence and are mobilized for the sake of creative and intelligent pastoral leadership. Deep engagement in pastoral ministry itself, in other words, has a powerfully formative effect. Over time, fine pastors develop a distinctive and very special kind of intelligence that enables them to engage in pastoral work of real creativity and integrity, and to sustain it over many years. They develop "pastoral imagination."[9]

The pastoral imagination is just that — an imagination, a way of see-

---

9. While different accents and contextualizations could legitimately be said to give rise to as many forms of pastoral imagination as there are pastors, I believe that the pastoral imagination is, at its heart, a capacity that belongs to all of these.

ing into and interpreting the world which shapes everything one thinks and does. Further, it is an imagination that requires unusual intelligence. It involves specific capacities of mind, spirit, and action that are not only gained during pastoral ministry but also, I believe, essential to doing it well.

Typically, we associate the word "imagination" with "creativity" or even "fantasy." Imagination, in this sense, is all about creating — in our minds or with clay or paint or in work with other people — things that do not exist. It means seeing what is not, and then, perhaps, bringing it into being. Creativity of this kind can contribute in important ways to pastoral work, to be sure, and this kind of imagination does represent one aspect of the pastoral imagination. But there is another meaning of "imagination" that is closer to what I have in mind. It involves what one might call "seeing in depth."[10] It is the capacity to perceive the "more" in what is already before us. It is the capacity to see beneath the surface of things, to get beyond the obvious and the merely conventional, to note the many aspects of any particular situation, to attend to the deep meanings of things.

Imagination is what makes human life meaningful and engagement with the world possible. No human being can really thrive without it. Imagination is the foundation of human perception, of understanding and interpretation, and of whatever deep probings we may make into the significance, meaning, and mystery of human life and reality. It is not just a cognitive phenomenon, although it is the foundation of all cognition. "Its impetus comes," the philosopher Mary Warnock points out, "from the emotions as much as from the reason, from the heart as much as from the head."[11]

Our imaginations develop and grow and change over the course of our lifetimes. As we grow up from infancy to adolescence and as we continue to live as adults, we are constantly affected through our various senses by light and color, touch, smell, sound, and taste, and, likewise, by words and pictures, by events and encounters, and by stories and symbols produced by others. But none of these come to us unfiltered. We receive them actively and engage them responsively, depending on what they elicit

10. See J. Bradley Wigger, *The Power of God at Home: Nurturing Our Children in Love and Grace* (San Francisco: Jossey-Bass, 2003), pp. 2ff. See also Wigger's *The Texture of Mystery: An Interdisciplinary Inquiry into Perception and Learning* (Lewisburg: Bucknell University Press, 1998).

11. Mary Warnock, *Imagination* (Berkeley: University of California Press, 1976), p. 196.

from our memories or evoke in relation to our expectations, fears, and affections, as well as on the reactions and movements of our own bodies. We take all this in by a subtle process of composition that organizes a vast buzz and blur of external stimuli and internal responses into meaningful and apprehensible wholes. This is the work of the imagination. It is really quite a remarkable activity of continuous (though almost unnoticed) creativity.

Every human being lives by the power of imagination. The human imagination is the integrating process that provides linkages between ourselves and our world — and, within ourselves, between our bodies, minds, and emotions, our very souls and spirits. It is by means of the imagination that we are able to come really to "see" and understand anything at all — even, in a sense, to "see" God.[12] Yet each person's imagination is different, in large part because our ordinary life experiences differ. The conditions under which we were raised and in which we now live, the joys and tragedies that have befallen us, our economic and social circumstances: all of these influence the specific imagination belonging to a given person. Our imaginations are also deeply affected by those powerful formative and educational influences that have provided the words we use in our everyday life and work, the stories, images, concepts, and metaphors that frame the ways we interpret our everyday experiences, and the music that sometimes sings itself deep in our hearts. Finally, our imaginations may also be powerfully shaped by our work — especially by demanding, difficult work that requires all that is in us, all that we have of ourselves to give. Work like the work of Christian ministry.

---

12. For further discussion of the nature of the imagination and its relation to the life of faith, see my *Vision and Character: A Christian Educator's Alternative to Kohlberg* (New York: Paulist Press, 1981), ch. 3. There you will find an extended discussion of the sources and uses of the imagination and of the relation between imagination and revelation. The imagination, as Iris Murdoch says, can function in ways that construct "a fantasy world of our own into which we try to draw things from the outside, not grasping their reality and independence, making them into dream objects of our own" ("The Sublime and the Good," *Chicago Review* 13 [1959]: 52). Or our imaginations may be used to reach out to reality. As H. Richard Niebuhr put the matter in *The Meaning of Revelation* (New York: Macmillan, 1960), "The question which is relevant for the life of the self among selves is not whether personal images should be employed but only what personal images are right and adequate and which are evil imaginations of the heart" (p. 72). Some patterns of imagination lead to a realistic seeing of what is going on within us and before us and, hence, to a real meeting with the world. Others lead to delusion and eventually to the destruction of self, others, and community.

In Lilly Endowment's senior leadership there are several very fine lawyers. In working with them closely and personally, I can see that they have been formed — by their legal education and even more by their years of professional work in the law — in a particular way of seeing and thinking that is distinctive to that profession. They have developed what we might call a "legal imagination." It consists of a penetrating way of knowing that enables really good lawyers to notice things, understand things, and do things that others of us simply cannot see or do.

There may also be such a thing as an artistic imagination. Artists in every medium have an imagination and an intelligence that enables them to pull together what they perceive in the world and contemplate in their souls in the process of creating new works of art that in turn help the rest of us apprehend reality in entirely new ways. Like the legal imagination, this imagination relies on individual gifts but is also shaped by the community, education, artistic tradition, and material relations within which the artist works over time.

But what of the kind of imagination I have seen in so many pastors? The pastoral situation itself, I think, shapes pastors in a way of perceiving and understanding and relating to the world that has distinctive characteristics. The unique confluence of forces and influences that impinge on those who engage deeply and well in pastoral work shapes them powerfully, fostering a set of sensibilities, virtues, and skills that characteristically belongs to good pastors.

Every day pastors are immersed in a constant, and sometimes nearly chaotic, interplay of meaning-filled relationships and demands. They attend to Scripture; struggle to discern the gospel's call and demand on them and their congregations in particular contexts; lead worship, preach, and teach; respond to requests for help of all kinds from myriad people in need; live with children, youth, and adults through whole life-cycles marked by both great joy and profound sadness; take responsibility for the unending work of running an organization with buildings, budgets, and public relations and personnel issues. In the midst of the interplay of all this and more, pastors become who they are; indeed, pastors are transformed. The unique confluence of all these forces both requires and gives shape to an imagination marked by characteristics and features unlike those required in any other walk of life. Life lived long enough and fully enough in the pastoral office gives rise to a way of seeing in depth and of creating new realities that is an indispensable gift to the church, to all who are members of it, and, indeed, to public life and to the world.

The pastoral imagination requires a very acute and supple intelligence. Indeed, it requires multiple intelligences. In *Frames of Mind,* the psychologist Howard Gardner has set forth a theory of multiple intelligences that can help us to understand many features of the pastoral imagination. The kinds of intelligence required to comprehend words, numbers, ideas, and concepts and relate them to each other in ways that are tested by IQ and SAT tests are widely acknowledged. According to Gardner, however, several additional, distinct intelligences also exist, each of which helps to shape how various people engage with the world. One of these is what Gardner calls "bodily-kinesthetic intelligence," the intelligence required if one is to have clear awareness of and ability to use one's own body adroitly and effectively (in playing basketball like Michael Jordan for instance, or in dancing, or in presiding in liturgies). Gardner also mentions "musical intelligence," the intelligence that enables one to hear, understand, and create music; and "spatial intelligence," which involves the ability to create physical spaces that make sense (such as sanctuaries and places of communal hospitality) and to inhabit and use them well. "Intrapersonal intelligence" and "interpersonal intelligence" provide the capacities to know, first, what we ourselves, and then, what other people are feeling, and also to know how to respond in appropriate and fitting ways.[13]

Good ministry requires keenness in every one of these multiple intelligences. Further, good ministry also requires that these multiple intelligences be well integrated and that a dynamic coherence among them be constantly engaged, at quite a high level. In fact, pastoral ministry may require a complexity and integrity of intelligence that is as sophisticated as is needed for any kind of work we could think of. To be a good pastor, you have to be very smart in lots of really interesting ways.

Pastors need not only to possess multiple intelligences, however. They must also allow these intelligences to be trained and formed within a lifelong process of learning. Both substantive knowledge — some of it fairly abstract — and practical know-how are required, and because ministry takes place amidst the changing circumstances of life, intelligent adaptation and renewed learning will be necessary as well. Extensive reading and

13. See Howard Gardner, *Frames of Mind: The Theory of Multiple Intelligences* (New York: Basic Books, 1985).

serious observation, along with a great deal of accumulated personal experience, are essential to the emergence of a mature pastoral imagination.

Indispensable to good ministry is a deep, sustained, and thorough-going engagement with the Scriptures and with a sound theological tradition that brings the word of God into an ongoing history of endlessly contemporary thought and practice. Every good minister also has to have a reliable understanding of what makes human beings tick, of who people are and how they operate. This has to be learned from lots of firsthand experience with all kinds of people in all kinds of situations, as well as from novels and poetry, history and psychology, and again, of course, the Bible and theology. Above all, learning humanity requires a disciplined spiritual life through which one enters into the deeper levels of one's own self, encounters one's own deepest hopes and fears, and, placing them in God's hands through sacrifice and prayer, learns to trust the spiritual *terra firma* that enables one to live a faithful and generous life.

To do pastoral work well, a person needs to have a truthful and nuanced understanding of how congregations and other institutions actually work, both on a day-to-day basis and at the strategic level where long-term patterns are identified, shaped, and reformed. Pastoral leaders need to know how to keep the life of a community alive — and how to keep it effectively engaged in a way of abundant life, both for the sake of the specific company of people who comprise that congregation and for the sake of the larger world. All this requires a fairly profound understanding of organizations, and particularly of congregations. Pastors must have a broad awareness and understanding of the world that the church exists to serve, both in its broad scope and contemporary need and in relationship to the specific environment in which one is operating as a pastor and as a congregation. All of this requires continuing study and reflection, but also experienced, practical know-how that has been tested and developed through broad experience, ongoing struggle, and sustained engagement.

Finally, and above all, pastors must have clarity of mind and spirit about what it means to worship God in spirit and in truth.

Pastoral imagination can only in part be brought to the ministry, because deep and sustained experience within the actual exercise of pastoral ministry itself is essential to its ultimate emergence and maturation. But however it comes into being and however differently it manifests itself in very different people serving very different kinds of congregations, I think that we can consistently find that something like the kind of imagination I have been trying to describe lies at the core of virtually every good ministry. Without this gyroscope, it is difficult for pastors to keep their balance in the midst of all that is required of them and all that happens to them, for good and for ill.

The Heart of the Matter

I have talked with several groups of ministers about these ideas of "pastoral imagination" and "pastoral intelligence." From them I have gotten two basic responses. One response finds this way of thinking very helpful. Many pastors say that it gives them a language with which to understand both the complexity and the coherence of the ministry. It helps them understand why pastoral ministry is simultaneously so difficult and so satisfying. It helps them to see that all the many pieces involved in carrying it out are not just shards to be reassembled like broken crystal, but rather essential currents that somehow gather, by the power of the Spirit, into a coherent way of being. And, for many, it validates their own strong sense that pastoral ministry does, in fact, require the very best they have to give — their best thought, their full energy, their deepest engagement. It affirms that pastoral ministry requires real strength of every kind. And these pastors are glad when someone says that, because in our society — and even in the church — the malignant assumption that pastoral ministry does not really demand or require very much surreptitiously undermines both our legitimate expectations of and our sense of gratitude for the Christian ministry.

The second response is really the flip-side of the first, and this is one I typically get from seminary students and new ministers — ironically, especially ones whom I sense to be particularly promising. For them, these ideas can be a bit intimidating. "If that's what it takes to do ministry well," they say, "there is no way I can ever do it! I can't live up to that." A high view of pastoral ministry — of its significance in and for the church and the world, of the importance of doing it well, of understanding all that is involved in and required of a person to do it — can be so daunting as to be overwhelming.

Actually, those who make this second response are right! Ministry is overwhelming. But let us think for a moment about what it means to be overwhelmed. Sometimes we are overwhelmed by the sheer hugeness or complexity of something. We can't get our arms around it. We can't figure

53

it out. We are unable to organize it or to bring it under control. We are overwhelmed in a way that makes us feel small, weak, and inadequate. On the other hand, "overwhelmings" happen in other ways as well. On the shore of a mountain lake at sunset, we are overwhelmed by beauty. At the birth of a grandchild, we are overwhelmed with joy. At a low point in our lives, we are overwhelmed by unexpected generosity.

The British theologian David Ford says that "Jesus Christ is an embodiment of multiple overwhelmings. He was immersed in the River Jordan and then driven by the Spirit into the wilderness to be tempted. He announced the kingdom of God as something worth everything else, a pearl beyond price, a welcome beyond anything we could deserve, a feast beyond our wildest desires. At the climax of his life he agonized in prayer in Gethsemane, he was betrayed, deserted, tortured, and crucified, and he died crying 'My God, my God, why have you forsaken me?' Then came the resurrection, the most disorienting and transformative overwhelming of all."[14] The life of Christian faith, says Ford, is itself the most profound experience there is of being overwhelmed. In baptism we "take on an identity shaped by the overwhelmings of creation, death, resurrection, and the Holy Spirit. We have also entered a community that spans the generations and relates us to . . . perhaps two billion people alive today who are identified as Christians. . . . This is the dynamic of being shaped by being overwhelmed."[15]

The idea that pastoral ministry involves a distinctive imagination and a subtle and complex intelligence can be bad news, indeed — an intimidating and dispiriting "overwhelming" — if we think of them as demands or achievements that each of us on our own can and must individually attain. But the pastoral imagination is not something to be achieved or attained. It comes as a gift. At the very heart of pastoral ministry there lies the good news of a power that is not our own, a labor that ultimately is not our work, a grace that is not of our own doing. The way is not so much one of earnest striving as it is "the 'active passivity' of letting ourselves be embraced, or letting ourselves be fed the food and drink that can energize us for" ministry.[16]

Years ago, when I was a seminary student, I worked for a time at the lo-

14. David F. Ford, *The Shape of Living: Spiritual Directions for Everyday Life* (Grand Rapids: Baker, 1997), p. 46.

15. Ford, *The Shape of Living*, p. 49.

16. Ford, *The Shape of Living*, p. 89.

cal YMCA, teaching swimming lessons. My students were three- and four-year-olds. Each Saturday morning at 9:00, down the steps they would come from the locker rooms into the pool area. As their parents sat along the wall, watching warily, the little ones wandered over towards the shallow end of the pool, where I was waiting.

You know how little kids hold themselves when they are cold and at least a little bit nervous. They clutch up and shiver. They hold themselves tight and grit their teeth. Well, it is a law of nature that you cannot swim while cramping your body and gnashing your teeth. So what I would do is take one child at a time off the edge of the pool and into my arms. Holding them close, I would carry them gently into the water. As we went, we talked quietly. I tried to make them smile and ease them into relaxation. Along the way, I would dip down into the water, allowing them to feel the warmth of it and the flow of it across their skin. After a while — maybe on their third or fourth venture with me into the deep — I would sink them lower and let them feel the water buoying them up. Eventually I could lay them on their backs and, holding my hands beneath them, get them to begin to relax their knees, let loose the muscles in their necks, and slowly draw air into their lungs. At first, of course, when I would remove my hands, they would panic a bit. They would clutch up again and start to sink. But sooner or later, they would finally get the feel of what it is like to float. And at that point, they could roll over and start to swim.

The first priority in teaching children to swim is to enable them to trust the water. Somehow or another they have to come to a specific kind of knowledge. In a deeply somatic, bodily way — and in a way that is in no small part existential, for it is a knowledge that must be strong enough to address their fears — they must come to know the buoyancy of the water. Buoyancy is not something you can teach children — or anyone else, for that matter — through a lesson in physics. Objective as it is, for the sake of swimming one has to come to know it personally.

So it is with the life of faith. At the heart of the Christian life there lies a deep, somatic, profoundly personal, but very real knowledge. It is the knowledge of the buoyancy of God. It is the knowledge that in struggle and in joy, in conflict and in peace — indeed, in every possible circumstance and condition in life and in death — we are upheld by God's own everlasting arms. In his *Institutes of the Christian Religion*, John Calvin said, "we shall possess a right definition of faith if we call it a firm and certain knowledge of God's benevolence toward us, founded upon the truth of the

55

freely given promise in Christ, both revealed to our minds and sealed upon our hearts through the Holy Spirit."[17] Faith, for Calvin, is not a blind leap into the utterly unknowable, much less mere speculation. No, it is *knowledge*. It is a deep, profound, existential knowledge that infuses not only our minds, but also our hearts and even our bodies. It is knowledge that, as we come to know it more and more deeply, over many years, will give form and substance to our entire imagination, to our whole way of being in the world, to our very existence. It is the knowledge of the overflowing abundance of the grace and mercy and love of God.

When pastors try to master ministry on their own, they are overwhelmed by the fearfulness of it. They can become frightened and defensive, clutch up, grit their teeth, and sink. When ministry is received as a gift of God within a larger life of faith shared by pastors and people, an entirely different dynamic begins to take over. Instead of working frenetically and compulsively to harness their own powers and energies, pastors are somehow set free to receive, draw upon, release, and share in the multiple energies and capacities of the people of their congregations and of the whole body of Christ.[18]

It is beautiful to see how humble and grateful the mature and grounded pastoral imagination is. What the pastors from whom I have been learning talk about most is not their own ministry, but the ministries of their congregations. What focuses their attention and anchors their interest is their congregation, their people — who they are, how they are living, what they are doing together. When I listen to these pastors, what I hear them talking about is the way in which their "being with" their people has given them their ministries. These are pastors who have fallen in love with their people because they have seen in them corporately and individually the Christian life embodied. For them, it is the quality and depth of their people's worship that make it possible for them as pastors to lead

---

17. John Calvin, *Institutes of the Christian Religion*, The Library of Christian Classics, vol. XX, ed. John T. McNeill, trans. Ford Lewis Battles (Philadelphia: Westminster Press, 1960), 3.2.7.

18. This point pertains not only to ministers, of course, but to all Christians; and not only to ministry, but to the entire shape of our living — indeed, to the foundations of our very existence. This knowledge and the power it engenders to live joyously and freely, unencumbered by persistent, fundamental anxiety and fearfulness, is the knowledge that lies at the very heart of a Christian life — and *thereby* at the core of both the pastoral and ecclesial imaginations.

worship with integrity. It is the people's care for one another that makes it possible for them to be caregivers as pastors. It is the people's engagement in the church's mission that enables the pastors to lead the congregation in its mission.

It is the congregation's *ecclesial* imagination that over time gives rise to the pastor's pastoral imagination. It is the congregation's *ecclesial* intelligence that is the source for the pastor's pastoral intelligence. What these pastors tell me is that whatever imagination and intelligence they as pastors may have, it has come to them as a gift given to them — quietly, almost unwittingly, over time — by God in and through the people of faith who comprise their congregations.

Pastoral Imagination and Ecclesial Imagination

Ecclesial imagination is the way of seeing and being that emerges when a community of faith, together as a community, comes increasingly to share the knowledge of God and to live a way of abundant life — not only in church but also in the many contexts where they live their daily lives. Ecclesial imagination emerges among the people themselves, fostering a way of seeing and being that is in some ways different in content, quality, and character from that which prevails in the culture surrounding them. The people talk just a little differently than most. The assumptions they make about themselves and others are not quite the same as the conventional wisdom. They do not pretend to know too much — about others, about themselves, or about God. They are more eager than most to listen and to learn. They possess a kind of humility before reality that enables them to be truly attentive to it. When troubles come or things go wrong in one way or another, they don't necessarily panic in the way others do — or even as they might themselves have done at an earlier time. While they are not necessarily all that optimistic, they are nonetheless a deeply hopeful lot. They invest in their youth and they build for the future, whether they expect to live long enough to benefit from it themselves or not. They seem generous, more likely to give of themselves — and not only of their money, but also of their time, their patience, their care.

Read *Breathing Space* and you will see all this taking place; not in large, grandiose ways, but in little ways — ways that might not be obvious to the naked, unformed eye. Even more importantly, it is possible to see such differences in congregations all over this planet. Wherever the church is alive at all, it is alive because it lives, by faith, a kind of life that is not entirely conformed to the principalities and powers of this world.[19]

Ecclesial imagination is most likely to emerge when pastoral leaders possessed of rich pastoral imaginations make it their primary task to guide and resource communities in embracing this kind of life. The fundamental work of pastoral ministry is to foster such a way of life among a particular people. In his essay in this volume, Pastor Peter Marty describes this as "the pastoral task of shaping community."[20] Pastoral work is first and foremost the work of enabling, teaching, helping, guiding, and encouraging a specific community to practice Christian faith themselves.

This may seem obvious, but I fear that many pastors, including me, lose sight of this all the time. It is an easy trap to fall into. In any kind of hard work (especially work that takes place in public and often under considerable pressure), it is our natural human tendency to attend primarily to our own performance, to our own action, to what we ourselves are doing, to how well we are performing — and, perhaps, especially, to how other people think we are doing.

The genius of a pastoral imagination built on the knowledge of the buoyancy of God, however, is its capacity to attend first and fully to others, to the people, their lives, and their life together. The confidence that arises when pastors themselves know, in a deeply personal way, that they too can rest confidently in God's upholding arms enables them to let go of the anxieties that can plague and eventually defeat pastoral work when it is driven

19. For a splendid essay on the kind of difference being Christian makes in the context of a larger culture, see Miroslav Volf, "Soft Difference: Theological Reflections on the Relation between Church and Culture in 1 Peter," *Ex Auditu* 10 (1994): 15-30. In a shorter piece based on this essay, Volf argues that "*the Christian difference* is always a complex and flexible network of small and large refusals, diverges, subversions, rejections, and more or less radical alternative proposals, surrounded by the acceptance, affirmation, and laudation of many cultural givens. There is no single way to relate to a given culture as a whole, or even to its dominant thrust. There are only numerous ways of accepting, transforming, rejecting, or replacing various aspects of a given culture from within. . . . The trick is to know what the Christian difference is and where precisely it needs to surface and where it does not." See "'It Is Like Yeast': How the Gospel Should Relate to Culture," *Theology News and Notes* [a publication of Fuller Theological Seminary] (October 1994): 12-15.

20. See also Larry R. Rasmussen, "Shaping Communities," in *Practicing Our Faith: A Way of Life for a Searching People,* ed. Dorothy C. Bass (San Francisco: Jossey-Bass, 1997), pp. 298-318.

by compulsive striving. Under such conditions we are freed to do pastoral work that is not mainly about us and, say, our preaching. We are freed to attend first and above all to how the people are proclaiming the gospel in words and with their lives. Our own preaching, we can then come to see, is in service to *their* ways of proclaiming the gospel. Similarly, we can also see that what matters is not our own liturgical leadership but rather the people's worship of God.

A spiral of mutual influence, encouragement, and empowerment takes hold when pastors and congregations give and receive these gifts of God to and from one another. Pastoral imagination is a gift that is given by God in and through communities of faith possessed of deep, rich ecclesial imaginations. Ecclesial imagination is a gift that is given by God through the sustained nurture and shaping ministries of wise and faithful pastors with deep, rich pastoral imaginations. Through eyes of faith, pastors come to see the abundance that is before them and that surrounds them already. Through eyes of faith, they can see what gifts they have been given in the people who, however flawed, are the members of their congregations. Likewise, through eyes of faith, the members of congregations come to see the abundance that is before them and surrounding them, too. And, through those eyes, they can recognize what gifts they have been given in the people who, however flawed, have become their pastors.

Ministry like this has about it a kind of beauty and allure that is almost irresistible. And so it replicates itself by drawing more and more people into it, forming and shaping their lives and imaginations, and launching them into new ministry in turn. Such ministry has about it a freshness, an improvisatory character, a liveliness that is itself infectious.[21] And thus an imagination that is at its heart a "seeing in depth" turns out to be an imagination full of creativity — an imagination that sees what is "not yet" and begins to create it.

Practical theology and theological education as a whole, rightly conceived and well practiced, draw upon and serve in profound and powerful ways both pastoral and ecclesial imagination. After all, all of these share as their telos and purpose the strengthening and renewal of the way of abundant life that emerges in response to God's grace in Jesus Christ.

---

21. For a splendid discussion of the improvisatory character essential to Christian life and ministry, see Samuel Wells, *Improvisation: The Drama of Christian Ethics* (Grand Rapids: Brazos Press, 2004).

In the previous chapter of this book, Dorothy Bass describes practical theology as a theological movement that foregrounds three fundamental questions while looking toward a telos of abundant life in and for the world.[22] The three questions are: How can, and how do, our lives and our life together participate in a way of life that reflects the Life of God, both when we are gathered as church and when we are dispersed into countless disparate circumstances? What is the shape of a contemporary way of life that truly is life-giving in and for the sake of the world? And how can the church foster such a way of life, for the good of all creation?

These questions reside at the very heart of pastoral and ecclesial imagination. They are questions that every good pastor, every Christian, and every congregation or other Christian community that is intentional and reflective about the life of faith is asking in one way or another. Further, these questions will find their best answers when people of faith take them up together in congregations as well as in theological schools, the workplace, public life, and countless other settings, and even more so when the conversations taking place in these diverse settings engage, challenge, and inform one another. This suggests that practical theology in its broadest meaning can and should be a shared endeavor involving Christians who live and work in a wide variety of contexts and circumstances. If this is so, practical theology not only nourishes but can and should be nourished in turn by the pastoral and ecclesial imaginations.

Back in the days when I was teaching swimming lessons — now almost four decades ago — I was also taking seminary courses in Bible and theology. From various sources I was learning more about God and something about grace. Over time it became increasingly clear to me that grace does not primarily have to do with things that might or might not happen episodically to affect our particular lives. Grace instead is more like gravity — a constant, enduring presence — indeed, the constant, enduring presence of a loving and merciful Triune God. Even then, as I taught those little children, it seemed to me that the buoyancy of water and the possibility it creates for us to be able to float and to swim with confidence provided an apt and lovely metaphor for the buoyancy of God, whose everlasting and omnipresent grace enables us to live and to have life abundantly. Just a few years ago, I discovered the same metaphor similarly employed in this beautiful poem by Denise Levertov:

22. See p. 23.

As swimmers dare
to lie face to the sky
and water bears them,
as hawks rest upon air
and air sustains them,
so would I learn to attain
freefall, and float
into Creator Spirit's deep embrace,
knowing no effort earns
that all-surrounding grace.[23]

That poem, entitled "The Avowal," is, of course, a kind of prayer. It is a prayer that I keep close at hand. It is a prayer that I pray not only for myself and my loved ones, but for all of us — for the whole people of God, for all the church's ministers, for theological educators — indeed, for everyone who seeks to nurture and nourish pastoral and ecclesial imaginations in the lives of those they serve and touch.

23. The poem is published in *Oblique Prayers* (New York: New Directions, 1984). Copyright 1984 by Denise Levertov; reprinted by permission of New Directions Publishing Corp.

3. Mapping the Field of Practical Theology

Kathleen A. Cahalan and James R. Nieman

Their work was so basic. Every week, he gathered a dozen of his younger clients to learn what many people took for granted: parenting, nutrition, budgets, ordinary life skills. Twenty-three years in social work had taught him that these skills were far from commonplace, however, and their absence produced a cycle of crisis. As that cycle gradually began to slow, he learned something more: the dreams and disappointments of these people, the fabric of their spiritual lives. As a person of active faith, he had never fully considered that these matters might also need his attention.

They called themselves "The Church in the Middle," an uninspiring nickname. Located halfway down the main street of town, this was also their place on the religious spectrum: neither strident nor secretive, neither dogmatic nor docile, but vaguely in between. Unlike other congregations, however, they held an annual community dinner, simply a time to meet others and enjoy good food. The elders viewed it another way, though: as a way to teach the ropes of leadership to their teens. Other members also saw in it something more, a chance to sit with folks and just listen.

A disastrous decade had left its scars. She was now the fifth pastor in that period, following in the wake of her predecessors' scandals, arrogance, and incompetence. Unsurprisingly, the congregation had become wary, ingrown, steeled against further abuse, and dwindling. Yet there were signs of still trying to be the church, quiet ideas tentatively floated in conversations, meetings, or times of fellowship. "Could we . . . ?" they wondered. "We had this idea . . . would you be interested?" It seemed to her that it must have been a long time since they knew a pastor who an-swered, "Yes."

Earnestly the students performed the funeral liturgy: words correct, voices strong, but bodies leaden. Their teacher recognized not just the plodding, but how this artlessness undercut the mystery of the rite. Quickly clearing the room of furniture, he told them just to start walking in silence, back and forth, round in circles, however it happened. First came embarrassed smiles, next quiet concentration, and finally one of them saw how they were moving like an ensemble, every step in rhythm. How did that happen without a word? And then the learning began.

The panelists, respected scholars in pastoral care and Christian educa-tion, addressed a noble-sounding topic: "Global Perspectives on Child-hood." In truth, though, the homiletics professor attended mostly out of duty, for the subject was far from her research. Besides, she knew all the facts. As the stories emerged, though, tales of poverty, illness, slavery, and violence faced by children younger than her own, suddenly she began to hear. Why had she not considered this worthy of her scholarly attention? What if others in her field began to think the same?

When you hear the phrase "practical theology," what comes to mind? Of-fering a sturdy reply to this question is one of the persistent challenges we face, because the question admits of so many answers. The five scenes above suggest rather different visions for what practical theology can be, yet each seems to have little in common with the others. Of course, they are not utterly unalike. Each portrays actual situations faced by Christians in the course of everyday life. Each involves discerning those situations and what to do next in a faithful, intentional way. Each calls forth a wider wis-dom that offers insight and imagination to that discernment. Yet what are we to make of their divergence? These scenes present distinctive life set-tings, vocational roles, kinds of authority, scopes of impact, and even ways of doing theology itself. Adding to the confusion, scholars have argued that instances as diverse as these are genuine forms of practical theology, but they have not clarified what these situations' connection to each other might actually be.

Our aim in this essay is to illumine practical theology as a field with a wide range of participants, each engaged in that field in distinctive ways that are also linked together in a common enterprise.[1] We understand practical theology as a form of theology that occurs within multiple contexts carried out by a variety of people: as a theological discernment by Christians seeking faithful ways of life, as a theological action and reflection by ministers and church leaders, and as a theological discipline focused on teaching and learning as well as research and study in universities or seminaries.

Common features of practical theology resonate in each of the examples above, but more important are the connections among these various expressions. Understanding the links among different forms of practical theology is a crucial dimension of the field; indeed, practical theology as a whole can thrive only when all those connections are recognized. Further, understanding and recognizing these connections strengthens each instance of practical theology. Authors in this book, for example, focus specifically on showing practical theology in ministry and the teaching of ministry. For all their richness, however, those chapters convey only a portion of the larger picture of practical theology. Our effort in this chapter is to provide a conceptual map of the entire field precisely so that the chapters about ministry and teaching are seen in relation to the larger pattern that comprises practical theology.

Unlike many conventional modern maps, the one we offer does not have as its purpose to label and divide a terrain in order to control it. Its purpose instead is to present a narrative that gives a compelling account of the whole — much like ancient and medieval maps were designed to do —

---

1. In this essay we refer to practical theology as both a field and a discipline, drawing on Sandra Schneiders's discussion of spirituality as a discourse, a field, and a discipline. A discourse is "an ongoing conversation about a common interest" that includes such groups as professionals, specialists, teachers, and practitioners of all sorts. Discourse is widespread, and it "risks becoming a catch-all term for whatever anyone wants." In contrast, a field pertains to "an open space in which activities which have something in common take place" so that in spirituality this pertains to researchers, writers on popular subjects, and practitioners, all of whom are interested in a variety of activities that fall under the category of "spiritual." As a discipline, Schneiders argues that "we are talking about teaching and learning, including research and writing, on subjects specified by the material and formal objects of Christian spirituality in the context of the academy." Sandra M. Schneiders, I.H.M., "The Study of Christian Spirituality: Contours and Dynamics of a Discipline" in *Minding the Spirit: The Study of Christian Spirituality,* ed. Elizabeth A. Dreyer and Mark S. Burrows (Baltimore: Johns Hopkins University Press, 2005), pp. 6-7.

while generating conversation among likely neighbors.[2] For all its diversity, we think there is indeed a common purpose that orients the entire field of practical theology.[3] With that purpose in mind, a conversation becomes possible among the neighbors in that field. Certainly we hope to spark dialogue among those who already have a strong vocational identity as practical theologians, especially those who perceive kinship with and differences between one another's work. We also want to engage those who may not view themselves as practical theologians but whose efforts clearly contribute to the field's common purpose. Further still, we hope to clarify the field for newcomers and outsiders, orienting those unfamiliar with our work while answering those skeptical about its value. In addressing these various interests, however, we are not claiming everything as practical theology.[4] Boundaries are essential for the field, since if everything counts as

2. We employ the idea of mapping in a particular way. The typical map that comes to mind is some version of the Mercator projection, a sixteenth-century innovation used as a tool for exploration and control. Even recent efforts to rectify the errors of that map (most famously, the Gall-Peters projection) still leave its fundamental values in place: accuracy for the sake of description and administration. In suggesting the terrain for practical theology, we find another kind of map more helpful. Pre-modern mapping in the West was oriented by the question of what constituted the center and horizon of the world and therefore what story the map told. This kind of map (like the fascinating thirteenth-century Ebstorf *mappa mundi*) argued for a certain kind of worldview, offering a picture entirely oriented to key biblical narratives and theological commitments.

3. The purpose we articulate throughout this essay develops upon two discernable trajectories in recent practical theology scholarship. Some discussions of practical theology in the 1980s involved a small number of scholars interested in articulating a philosophical basis for the field (which also predominated in much of the European conversation) that also justified a distinctive university discipline. The other, somewhat larger conversation focused on practical theology in relation to the nature of theological education, conceiving the field as being a more socially, ethically, and publicly engaged form of theology. Our intent in this essay is to show in a more direct and explicit way the connection between these trajectories, with practical theology understood both as the praxis of faith and as an orienting focus of the ministry curriculum. Don S. Browning, *Practical Theology: The Emerging Field in Theology, Church, and World* (San Francisco: Harper & Row, 1983); Edward Farley, *Theologia: The Fragmentation and Unity of Theological Education* (Philadelphia: Fortress Press, 1983); Lewis S. Mudge and James N. Poling, eds., *Formation and Reflection: The Promise of Practical Theology* (Philadelphia: Fortress Press, 1987); Barbara G. Wheeler and Edward Farley, eds., *Shifting Boundaries: Contextual Approaches to the Structure of Theological Education* (Louisville: Westminster/John Knox Press, 1991).

4. Don Browning's major contribution to reformulating practical theology has been an important influence on our work. We affirm his fundamental conviction that at the heart of

some form of practical theology, then nothing really is and little has been clarified. Therefore, we attempt a more accessible and public vision for practical theology that encompasses diverse participants in diverse situations while holding to a central purpose that defines the field and relates its constituent parts.

Unfolding the conceptual map of practical theology in the remainder of this essay involves elaborating several connected claims in the following sequence.

1. Practical theology engages Christian ways of life and therefore takes as its basic task the promotion of faithful *discipleship*.
2. Practical theology offers leadership for such discipleship by giving sustained attention to various forms of *ministry*.
3. Practical theology brings wisdom to the formation of ministers and the study of ministry in its approach to *teaching*.
4. Practical theology as a discipline involves the relationship between several distinctive domains of *research*.
5. Practical theology focuses in every instance especially upon the *current events* and the *concrete settings* that must be faithfully encountered.
6. Practical theology employs that focus in order to *discern* existing situations of life and *propose* eventual directions for action.

Our map is not a static overview of fixed locations but a narrative guide to a broad field of play in which disciples, ministers, teachers, and scholars might better encounter one another.

---

all theology is practical concern. We refrain, however, from naming all theology practical theology (or fundamental practical theology), with one of its parts "strategic practical theology" as it relates to ministry. Even though there has been significant agreement about Browning's claim regarding the nature of theology, his specific proposal did not take hold in theological education. We prefer instead to retain the term "practical theology" for one aspect of theology in general, and this essay asserts its distinctive character. Don S. Browning, *A Fundamental Practical Theology: Descriptive and Strategic Proposals* (Minneapolis: Fortress Press, 1991).

Discipleship

The basic task that orients practical theology is to promote faithful discipleship. Perhaps this seems a peculiar place to begin. Certainly much of the existing literature seems to center the field elsewhere, such as in an array of specific pastoral functions (such as preaching, liturgy, counseling, teaching, administration, etc.) and/or the teaching of these areas; in social and political movements of broad human and religious significance (such as liberation movements of various kinds); in broad patterns of human development (including moral, religious, or faith development); in particular forms of human transformation (such as nurture, conversion, or healing); or in sustained patterns of human activity (such as rituals or various other particular social practices). While there is great significance in each of these and each often has profound implications for practical theology as a whole, a serious distortion is created by substituting a component part or aspect for the unifying purpose. We speak of the purpose that sets the basic task of practical theology as supporting and sustaining lived discipleship. Rooted in Christian tradition, practical theology focuses on a called people who manifest a particular faith through concrete ways of life.

Christian discipleship can be compactly described as being called by Jesus to follow. Whether long ago or today, ordinary people encounter this call in the course of their daily lives as the people they already are. They are met by a compelling invitation that originates outside themselves. Specifically, Jesus draws them into a new relationship with God. To submit to that relationship is what it means to follow. This kind of following utterly reorients the existence of disciples toward bearing witness to the new life they now have with God through the Spirit. Although a more complete pattern of discipleship could certainly be elaborated, this simple image is enough for our purposes. It allows us to emphasize three implications of discipleship that affect practical theology.

First, because Jesus gathers to himself all those who are called, there is a *communal* reality to discipleship. In their ways of life, disciples embody a commitment to the common patterns and shared witness of all those who know God through the call of Jesus. In putting on Christ, every disciple is summoned to participate in faithful living through an actual Christian community. Such community takes different shape in family, congregation, and other social forms, each nurturing discipleship in its own way. Even in one setting, a community is ever changing as it actively adapts to emerging challenges to and opportunities for faithfulness. The resources for this adaptation do not begin within the community itself but are drawn from the larger and longer streams of communal wisdom in which it stands. In turn, that wisdom is always deployed in relation to other structures, since Christian community is acted upon by such structures (that is, affected by surrounding social and cultural forces) and can in turn act upon them (showing alternatives amidst other institutional realities).

Second, because this communal orientation makes witness to God's ways, there is a *theological* substance to discipleship. Communities of disciples do not exist for their own sake. Wherever they live, disciples instead seek what will enable their richer service of and witness before others. That is, their service and witness are public, offering a particular claim that can be received in some way by others. Since this is not just any public witness but one that has a divine referent, it is a distinctively theological discourse narrated in and native to the Christian community. On the one hand, that discourse is grounded and tested in relation to the wisdom of Christian tradition. On the other hand, this witness cannot simply repeat the wisdom of another time or place, but must use reasoning and expression borrowed from particular surroundings in order to point effectively to God's new life here and now. Disciples are therefore actively involved in a fully theological task, making sense of the new relationship into which they are called so that same invitation can be extended to others.

Third, because disciples make their service and witness in concrete and material ways, there is a *practical* quality to discipleship. Disciples, their communities, and the patterns of common life are not abstractions. Rather, their commitments are embodied in the actual practices of everyday life — a fact that connects this chapter to the growing discussion of what constitutes practices, although this is a matter beyond our present scope.[5] It is important to note, though, that discipleship foregrounds not

---

5. In recent years, the theme of "practices" has become prominent in practical theology. The term is used in a wide variety of ways, however, both in practical theology itself and in literature in other fields (including philosophy, literary studies, anthropology, ritual studies, and so forth) from which practical theologians draw. In previous publications, the editors of this volume have focused their attention on describing Christian faith as a "life-giving way of life" and have developed a conception of "Christian practices" which they believe are helpful in developing a broad but still concrete way of thinking about the shape and substance of a Christian way of life. For them, as for us, a way of life ("discipleship") — rather than any discrete or particular "practice" — is the proper center and orienting purpose of

just any practices but especially those that contribute to the theological substance already mentioned.[6] Having this in mind will help us to clarify the theological work discipleship actually entails. On the one hand, it is not simply concerned about ideas or dispositions for reflective consideration, which might be remote from the material existence of faithful living. On the other hand, it is not simply focused on acting or doing for tangible achievement, which might easily overlook communal resources for critical discernment. Instead, discipleship is practical in uniting thought and behavior, reflection and action in an ongoing relationship. Discipleship is practical not only in concrete forms, communal roots, or contextual links, but also because these are part of a reflective process that can make subsequent witness more faithful and effective.

Since discipleship is communal, theological, and practical, the field of

---

practical theology. See Dorothy C. Bass, ed., *Practicing Our Faith* (San Francisco: Jossey-Bass, 1997); Craig Dykstra and Dorothy C. Bass, "A Theological Understanding of Christian Practices," in *Practicing Theology: Beliefs and Practices in Christian Life,* ed. Miroslav Volf and Dorothy C. Bass (Grand Rapids: Eerdmans, 2002); Craig Dykstra, *Growing in the Life of Faith: Education and Christian Practices* (Louisville: Westminster/John Knox, 1999); and Craig Dykstra, "Reconceiving Practice," in *Shifting Boundaries,* ed. Wheeler and Farley. Other practical theologians who employ the theme of "practice" in developing their practical theologies include Elaine Graham, *Transforming Practice: Pastoral Theology in an Age of Uncertainty* (Eugene, Ore.: Wipf and Stock, 2002); Denise A. Ackermann and Riet Bons-Storm, eds., *Liberating Faith Practices: Feminist Practical Theologies in Context* (Leuven: Peeters, 1998); and Dale P. Andrews, *Practical Theology for Black Churches: Bridging Black Theology and African American Folk Religion* (Louisville: Westminster/John Knox Press, 2002).

6. In its concern for practice, practical theology seeks to understand what is essential to the practice of faith, how Christians in fact do practice their faith, and the ways in which identity, agency, and belief take form in and through an embodied way of life. Practices have five basic features: the what *(actions),* who *(common),* why *(meaningful),* how *(strategic),* and where *(purposive).* James R. Nieman, "The Idea of Practice and Why It Matters in the Teaching of Preaching," in *Teaching Preaching as a Christian Practice: A New Approach to Homiletical Pedagogy,* ed. Lenora T. Tisdale and Thomas G. Long (Louisville: Westminster/John Knox, forthcoming). This is similar to Elaine Graham's definition of practice "as purposeful activity performed by embodied persons in time and space as both the subjects of agency and the objects of history. Practice is also the bearer of implicit values and norms within which certain configurations of privilege and subordination are enshrined. Forms of practice . . . create and police the boundaries of dominance and subordination, power and powerlessness, upon which any given social order may be constructed. Practice is constitutive of a way of life, both individual and collective, personal and structural." Graham, *Transforming Practice,* p. 110.

practical theology is marked by these same features regardless of where we see it at work. The five scenes of practical theology that opened this essay each showed the reality of called people, the substance of a particular discourse, and the quality of concrete ways of life. Seeing practical theology in relation to discipleship also clarifies the essays in the rest of this volume. To imagine ministry apart from particular communities, settings, or traditions is precluded. To promote scholarship more comfortable with academic or professional terms than the language and mission of the church is troubling. To consider teaching for ministry reduced either to implementing correct ideas or to adopting effective techniques is inadequate. Put another way, without the orienting purpose of discipleship, practical theology can be prone to vested interests of curricular turf, aimless clericalism, and complacent piety. By contrast, practical theology best advances scholarship, educates ministers, and supports believers' faithful living when each of these is related to the others because all are aimed at faithful ways of life in Christian community. This is why the field, in its most basic task, is oriented toward lived discipleship in its contemporary and concrete settings.

Ministry

An important test of this orientation toward discipleship arises when we turn to the topic of ministry. Historically, it was typical to align ministry and practical theology in such a way that the former became the field's entire focus. Pastoral tasks retain an important place in the field, of course, though never as ends in themselves nor as the whole work of practical theology.[7] Rather, the reality of discipleship is the horizon on which the practice of ministry must be considered. Communities of disciples are not naturally or invariably able to embrace their calling and enact faithful ways of life without some sort of accountability and direction, and this is what ministry brings. Through many different forms and by many different means,

---

7. Edward Farley's claim that the clerical paradigm is the primary problem in theological education curricula was widely accepted among theological educators in the 1980s. See Farley, *Theologia*, pp. 127-35. Bonnie Miller-McLemore argues the clerical paradigm is a misplaced critique that had negative repercussions for practical theology and the teaching of ministry. Bonnie J. Miller-McLemore, "The 'Clerical Paradigm': A Fallacy of Misplaced Concreteness?" *International Journal of Practical Theology* 11, no. 1 (2007), as well as her essay within this book, "Practical Theology and Pedagogy: Embodying Theological Know-How."

ministry arises within every Christian community to attend on its behalf to a more ample witness through discipleship. Practical theology is deeply concerned about ministry precisely because ministry's aim is to coordinate and impel faithful ways of life. Within such a framework, ministry takes its ultimate horizon to be stewardship of the practices of discipleship.

In everyday usage, however, confusion can quickly arise about what is meant both by discipleship and by ministry. Simply put, we claim that while all ministers are disciples, not all disciples are ministers. This runs counter to the conventional sense that all Christians participate in "ministry of the baptized" or "ministry in daily life."[8] We believe that to use such phrases risks diminishing Christians' concept and understanding of discipleship, which ought to hold central place in the witness of Christian communities without resorting to other labels. Just as important, it risks misleading communities that realistically do need some persons with special responsibility for the practices of all disciples. At times, some disciples may engage in particular ministries in conjunction with those designated as ministers, but their primary and irreplaceable work is actually discipleship. By contrast, ministry is a distinctive calling that arises among and for the community of disciples. Ministers do not create or compose the faithful community but instead receive it and its disciples as already given by God. While sharing with others a call to discipleship, ministers bear a specific vocational calling that is explicitly affirmed by the entire community that involves assessing and fostering the discipleship in that place.[9]

---

8. We recognize that many church communities use the term "ministry" in reference to the service and activity of lay members of the church. In most cases this has been an attempt to heighten and emphasize the people of God as social and ecclesial agents, responsible for carrying forth the church's mission in the world. We certainly support the ecclesiological claim but think it is more helpful to retain the term "ministry" for Christians in leadership positions in the community and "disciples" for the baptized members of the community. If everything is called ministry, it becomes difficult to distinguish the role of leaders from that of members. Of course, we do not intend a form of clericalism that places ministers above or over disciples. We are claiming instead something much different: that discipleship is the fundamental identity and lived reality of all Christians in the body of Christ. Strong scholarly evidence supports this claim. For example, John Collins argues that biblical usage of the term for "ministry" *(diakonia)* pertains to community leaders and not to members of the community. John N. Collins, *Diakonia: Re-Interpreting the Ancient Sources* (New York: Oxford University Press, 1990).

9. Kathleen A. Cahalan, "Toward a Fundamental Theology of Ministry," *Worship* 80, no. 2 (March 2006): 102-20.

On the one hand, this means that ministry occupies a distinctive place in the community of disciples. It stands not above but within that community by carrying out two related roles. First, through the power of the Holy Spirit, ministry *assembles* the community, guarding the whole in its unity with Christ for the sake of witness. It looks for fractures that can divide or distract from that witness and for loss of those prone to wander away through inattention or dissipation. Second, ministry *builds up* the community, deepening each person, groups of persons such as families, and the community as a whole in maturity of witness.[10] It looks for what weakens the call to follow or renders it unable to face changing circumstances. Both these roles are basic to ministry because discipleship itself is never an attained or finished state, but rather a potential to be realized, a following that is always underway. Ministry monitors this process, noting both the forces that corrode the entire community and the unique abilities of each disciple.

On the other hand, this distinction means that ministry provides a crucial link between the community and its setting in the world. It is not strictly internal to that community but attends to a broader horizon of action by carrying out two further roles. First, ministry *recognizes* that setting for what it truly is and the demands this places upon discipleship.[11] It looks for the possibilities and constraints that discipleship faces because of the pressing claims of its situation. Second, ministry *catalyzes* witness in that setting, engaging disciples in that work rather than becoming a proxy for their witness. It looks for, and sometimes even models, avenues of response that disciples can realistically enter. Both these roles are basic to ministry, which itself requires a special imagination or discernment, moving beyond what is to picture what might be. Ministry suggests new op-

10. "The chief responsibility of the ordained ministry is to assemble and build up the body of Christ by proclaiming and teaching the Word of God, by celebrating the sacraments, and by guiding the life of the community in its worship, its mission and its caring ministry." *Baptism, Eucharist, and Ministry,* II.13 (Geneva: World Council of Churches, 1982). See also 1 Cor. 12:4-11 and Eph. 4:11-14.

11. "In this regard, the term 'recognition' (from the Latin re + *cogniscere,* literally 'to know again') has three senses: honor, familiarity, and insight. As a kind of honor, we recognize others by respecting their intrinsic dignity. As a kind of familiarity, we recognize others through the growing appreciation we develop for them over time. As a kind of insight, recognition of others leads to a reappraisal of ourselves and a rethinking of our deepest commitments." James R. Nieman and Thomas G. Rogers, *Preaching to Every Pew: Cross-Cultural Strategies* (Minneapolis: Fortress Press, 2001), p. 7.

portunities, resisting resignation to the context by offering a lively, open sense of what faithfully can be done.

Ministers rely upon several concrete means in fulfilling these roles. Some pertain to ministers' relationships to the community of disciples. Identifying gifts of discipleship, ordering these into a coordinated response, and testing these against the larger wisdom of the church are means that contribute to the roles of *assembling* and *building up.* Other concrete means pertain to the community's setting in the world. For example, naming the times and seasons, judging the adequacy of the community's response to various situations, and being publicly accountable beyond the Christian community are means that contribute to the roles of *recognizing* and *catalyzing.* Still others pertain to the special place of ministry as a distinctive calling. Keeping custody of the strong symbols of the faith, risking to pioneer new forms of witness, and acting in concert with other ministerial colleagues are all means that distinguish this calling.[12]

In the field of practical theology, ministers are key thinkers and actors. They engage practical theology precisely through intentional reflection on and engagement with discipleship and ministry in a local setting. Ministers stand in a unique place between disciples and scholars in the field of practical theology. They are intimately connected to the lives of disciples, serving as the key communicators and interpreters of the lived reality of the faith within their local settings. In this regard, they are an indispensable source for scholars who seek to understand the pressing demands of discipleship as well as the signs of the times. In addition, ministers are largely responsible for interpreting the insights and research of scholars to communities of faith. They draw insights from biblical, historical, ethical, spiritual, and theological resources to help people make sense of their lives.

12. It may seem surprising that in our conceptual map of practical theology we have not portrayed ministry in conventional terms. For example, we avoid traditional images for ministry such as prophet, priest, herald, shepherd, servant, or steward, as well as familiar categories for pastoral practice in theological education, such as homiletics, liturgics, pastoral care, religious education, and administration. These are obviously crucial and important ways of describing ministry, but we are attempting to present, prior to any distinctions, the central feature of ministry that provides a common foundation for these various images and practices. Further, we claim that these images and practices are intimately linked and stand in relationship to each other precisely because of their orientation to discipleship. Our approach is not to be utterly novel but instead to keep ministry centered on a basic test of discipleship, using language that might allow us to imagine new approaches and tools for effective kinds of ministry needed today.

Significantly, they not only interpret these two to each other but are also well-situated to make distinctive contributions to scholarly knowledge and insight about both discipleship and the practice of ministry.

Teaching

The forms of ministry we have just detailed do not arise spontaneously or develop naturally within Christian communities. Like the call into discipleship, the call to ministry must be identified, nurtured, and supported. A sustained and intentional teaching effort is needed, whether within a local congregation or through specialized communities established for that purpose, such as universities or seminaries. Indeed, to affirm a place for such effort makes a bold claim that ways of ministry can actually be taught to others. They are neither the private property of the already talented and lucky, nor the automatic outcome of gifts conferred by the Holy Spirit. Practical theology has developed a special wisdom about teaching in theological education, a wisdom with implications not only for learning ministry in more structured academic settings but also for formation of discipleship wherever it may occur.

Whether it takes place in communities of disciples or schools for ministry, all teaching in the field of practical theology is oriented toward discipleship because it is marked by the essential features of discipleship. Teaching has a communal reality that draws on the broader ecclesial wisdom in an ensemble performance, a theological substance that articulates a more effective witness to God's ways for us, and a practical quality that uses a persistent, grounded movement between action and reflection. In the congregation, discipleship is the ever-present foreground of learning, but in universities or seminaries it constitutes a horizon. Attention to this horizon typically means that practical theologians teaching in universities or seminaries are more focused upon faith communities as such, especially how these are guided and encouraged, since their proximal teaching is with ministers. By contrast, when ministers teach in congregations, both their proximal teaching and their ultimate aim are disciples and their witness.

The special demands of ministry therefore suggest the broad *contours* of how practical theology approaches teaching those who are called to ministry. Our foregoing account of the concrete means of ministry suggests some of what is taught, whether under traditional titles (e.g., worship, pastoral care) or new (e.g., contextual analysis, strategic planning). Although specific substance and standards affect how each is taught, to be taught effectively they must also be consistently related to the four broad roles that pertain to all of ministry. Regardless how conventional or novel the specific area being considered, effective teaching always asks how, through enacting that form of ministry, the community of disciples is guarded in its unity (assembling), maturing in its witness (building up), attuned to its setting (recognizing), and impelled to its witness (catalyzing). From the perspective of practical theology, specialized tasks or particular functions of ministry are integrated into a whole that engages a whole discipleship.[13] Of course, that integration must occur not only in the aim of ministry but also within the life of the minister. Teaching in ministry therefore becomes a matter of formation into a new ministerial calling, one that deepens that person's lifelong call to discipleship alongside others.

Within these broad contours, several implications for actual teaching can be elaborated to show the considerable wisdom practical theology brings to the learning process. We may consider particular *moments* in teaching that are characteristic of the field. A specific ministry practice may itself be closely scrutinized to tease apart the underlying moves, standards, wisdom, and aims that suggest how it can be taught or enacted. Environments for mutual participation and performance may be created to enable a fully embodied knowledge of a form of ministry. Difficult tasks may be stripped down to basic components that are first repeated and internalized, then gradually made more complex. Roles and routines of ministry may be inductively studied to discern rules of thumb or tricks of the trade that contribute over time to intuitive, natural performance. When informed by the wisdom of practical theology, none of these options are mere techniques but instead reflect in their strategies a serious awareness of the complicated layers in learning what it means to be in ministry.[14]

---

13. The problem of academic specialization in theology (as well as in the subdisciplines that make up practical theology) poses the serious threat that students move through seminary education lacking an integrated view of theology, ministry, and the Christian life. Edward Farley, "Why Seminaries Don't Change: A Reflection on Faculty Specialization," *Christian Century* 114, no. 5 (5-12 February 1997): 133-43.

14. Two essays in this volume explore these issues in greater depth in relationship to the seminary classroom: John D. Witvliet, "Teaching Worship as a Christian Practice," and Bonnie J. Miller-McLemore, "Practical Theology and Pedagogy: Embodying Theological

Practical theology can likewise help us discern implications for the *processes* of teaching. We noted earlier that such teaching bears the practical quality of a persistent, grounded movement between action and reflection. This means that the larger plan for teaching in the field often involves a back-and-forth rhythm between performance and critique, a spiraling process essential to embodying what is being taught. Courses are often constructed to loop back to previous insights or experiences but at deeper and richer levels. This in turn reflects that the aim of such teaching (ministry that promotes discipleship) is not to attain a final point but rather to guide learners into an ongoing dynamic. These iterative processes also incorporate a strong recognition of the personal costs of formation in the calling of ministry. Teaching in such circumstances is therefore not a remote affair but requires close mentoring and appropriate modeling, often employing apprenticeship so that growth can emerge over time. Once again, such processes are not pedagogical gimmicks; rather, they convey the very nature of the practices and roles being learned.

In sum, practical theology views teaching for ministry and discipleship as a theological action in itself. Although the field, like others in theological education, surely tries to convey theological warrants, methods, and ideas, it also calls for a theological pedagogy, a way of teaching theologically. For example, if we are serious about theological anthropology, then learners are not passive receptacles but are treated as fully human, created in God's image with agency and responsibility. Moreover, the ministry for which these learners prepare is aimed at discipleship, a necessarily serious and risky commitment that requires nothing less than an astute integration of Christian wisdom with contemporary realities. Finally, one of the chief means by which such learning transpires is through teachers who already exemplify ministry to these learners and thus, in the practice of teaching, must exhibit a faithful witness. In all these ways, practical theology seeks a teaching that truly befits the aims of theological education, calling on those in adjacent fields to share more fully in that vision.

Know-How." Two others address learning ministry beyond the seminary: David J. Wood, "Transition into Ministry," and Christian Scharen, "Learning Ministry over Time: Embodying Practical Wisdom."

Research

Historically, practical theology has been viewed as the area of theology that focuses on certain core practices of ministry. This important role is well worth retaining, but we believe that practical theology as a theological discipline involves vastly more. In the university or seminary curriculum, it fosters teaching and learning about the lived practices of faithful disciples and how ministry relates to these practices.[15] More broadly still, it involves research and writing about every dimension within the ambit of the field. Therefore, practical theology is not simply a collection of interests, but a comprehensive discipline of teaching, learning, research, and writing focused on its own scholarly enterprise. As a discipline, then, what typifies practical theology's research agenda? We believe that the web of varied concerns already mentioned in this essay suggests a pattern of significant domains for practical theological research that benefits both academy and church. These domains are areas of ongoing consideration, persistent spaces of inquiry that scholars regularly enter.

What comprises truly faithful ways of living? This is the research domain of *lived faith*. Practical theology is deeply interested in the formation of believers and the support such formation receives in actual domestic and ecclesial settings. One area of its research therefore seeks to understand what contributes to the disposition and practices of discipleship in actual communities of faith. This naturally includes the communal practices that generate such formation and how ecclesial traditions interface with individual faithfulness. It also involves recognizing the larger social conditions and challenges that bear upon discipleship. Many different partners share in the inquiry of this particular domain, from adept disciples who reflect upon their own growth in faith, to ministers who attend to matters of catechesis or care, to scholars who study congregations and the communities in which they reside. Every aspect of the Christian life as lived faith in concrete settings is open to scholarly examination and exploration.

What guides greater ecclesial faithfulness? This is the research domain of *communal stewardship*. Naturally, this involves those in ministry who have received a special calling to oversee and encourage a vigorous witness.

---

15. Given this understanding, practical theology retains a place in theological education for ministry but can also make important contributions to the teaching of undergraduate students in colleges and universities.

Practical theology has long been concerned with understanding the exercise of historic and publicly recognized forms of ministry like *kerygma*, *leitourgia*, *didaskalia*, and *diakonia*, including their communal, theological, and practical features. Beyond this classical impetus, practical theologians also look to other ways ministers guide and sustain disciples in affecting concrete situations by the study of leadership, transformative pedagogy, strategic planning, and social action. Finally, the discipline also takes an interest in both how the gifts of disciples are discerned and guided by ministers and how persons with particular gifts for ministry are themselves recognized and formed.

What enhances lived faith and its communal stewardship? This is the research domain of *theological pedagogy*. Virtually every context in which practical theology is done involves some educational dimension, so that questions of teaching and learning are commonplace regardless of the explicit focus of the research. Beyond this, by virtue of being an umbrella for several classic subfields in formal theological education, the field has developed something of a common discourse about the teaching of practices in general, whether those practices pertain to ministerial roles or to the daily life of individuals and communities. For similar reasons, the discipline brings a distinctive voice to the table of theological education, often with a special sophistication about how to engender formation that integrates a range of otherwise disparate learnings. In short, scholars in practical theology perennially monitor the educational implications of whatever they study.

What insights best support the discipline? This is the research domain of *disciplinary reasoning*. Practical theology generates a body of scholarship that preserves its wisdom and explicates its theories, both for others within the field and in ways that are accountable to those beyond it. The discipline's discourse emerges first through its own direct research in such areas as particular practices, congregational realities, ministerial roles, or educational approaches. It also develops in conversation with adjacent fields in theological education (biblical studies, theology, history) and those beyond it (sociology, psychology, medicine), as well as forms of study outside of academic institutions (for example, in spirituality, leadership, or development). These conversations aid practical theology in seeing how its various contexts can be better described and shaped. They also bring other fields and areas into contact with practical theological reasoning. This domain will understandably involve a smaller number of scholars. Even so, the growing collaboration between academic scholars and ecclesial practitioners has enriched the field and diversified its insights.

What new situations will the discipline encounter? This is the research domain of *public engagement*.[16] Practical theology, though oriented toward discipleship and ministry in faithful communities, always looks outward to explore its mission in the world. If disciples and ministers are to make a witness, and if practical theology is to contribute to that work, then matters of general practice become a significant horizon. The field therefore seeks to connect with wider publics especially in order to focus on practices where there may be a shared interest. It connects with other religious traditions. Practical theology examines those practices that can account for the complexity of these other traditions and suggest strategies for genuine dialogue and mutual respect. It also connects with other guilds or professions in order to consider the occupational practices that surface in the ordinary lives of the faithful, since these often carry meanings, implicit values, and even critiques that affect discipleship. Given the prospective and experimental nature of such research, it is perhaps unsurprising that this domain remains underdeveloped in comparison to others.

Current Events and Concrete Settings

Our conceptual map of practical theology has thus far been shaped by a strong substantive claim: discipleship is the basic task that orients the field at every level of its work, including the specific areas of ministry,

16. David Tracy's discussion of the social location of the theologian posits three publics in which theology is engaged: the academy, the church, and the society. He further identifies three aspects of theology that correspond *primarily* though not exclusively to each of these publics: fundamental, systematic, and practical theology. He understands practical theology as "concerned primarily with the ethical stance of responsible commitment to and sometimes even involvement in a situation of praxis." Although Tracy emphasizes that fundamental, systematic, and practical theology are related to each other and share in each other's publics, it is unclear how this avoids what amounts to a tripartite division of theology, let alone diminishing practical theology in the academy or rendering it irrelevant to the church and its ministry. We accept Tracy's claim that practical theology has a concern for praxis in social, political, and cultural worlds, but claim that practical theologians are equally and necessarily engaged in research and scholarship related to the academy and church. David Tracy, *The Analogical Imagination: Christian Theology and the Culture of Pluralism* (New York: Crossroad, 1981), pp. 56-57.

teaching, and research. In the remaining sections of this essay, however, we take this mapping a step further by highlighting what methodologically orients our efforts. If we have demonstrated *that* practical theology seeks to promote faithful discipleship, what might hold the field together regarding *how* that task is approached? We think that such unity can be discerned in the distinctive ways practical theology carries out being both contextual and interpretive. The first of these methodological areas is the topic for this section.

At every level of its work, practical theology claims the particularity of contexts as central to its interests. It does not seek universality or uniformity, but wants instead to understand the extant realities and actual demands in which faithful discipleship is lived. This attention to context has temporal and spatial dimensions. On the one hand, the field looks closely at faithful practices as they occur especially in the *present and near future*. Discipleship obviously exists in a sweeping continuum unfolding from the past and stretching into the future, so that attention to both ends is integral to the overall work of practical theology. The field brings such memory and anticipation together in a distinctive way, however, by focusing on the most pressing, current slice of that larger flow: what is and what is soon to be.[17] The field neither overlooks the past, the forces and changes that influence and constrain how we live today, nor ignores the future, the horizon of anticipation in which the meaning of our lives ultimately unfolds. Both these directions of time obviously condition discipleship in the present. Yet practical theology adopts a special perspective within this larger temporal range, foregrounding what is currently within our grasp to do.

On the other hand, the field carefully examines faithful practices that happen especially in *local and nearby situations*. Again, discipleship and the communities in which it is nurtured are not isolated from the world. Believers and leaders are embedded in ever-expanding sociocultural ecologies and spheres of influence that affect and even encroach upon what can be done in any one place. Knowing this, practical theology simply stakes out a place to stand in order to engage these wider connections. Its sustained attention to the local actually makes the web of our larger relation-

---

17. This of course does not exclude the distant future, which is also of concern for Christian faith and witness. Questions about how to forestall long-term consequences and problems, however, are most often taken up with what can be done now and over time.

ships more apparent and thwarts any attempt to remain secluded or insulated. Disciples live and act somewhere, in particular places. Beginning with what is close to hand grants us the perspective essential for a more contextually astute witness, living faithfully in the actual ambit of everyday existence.

The special significance given to current events and concrete settings gives the field a distinctive role in three ways. First, its work remains grounded in the genuine conditions of life that are before us. Because it is trying to promote discipleship, practical theology must always reject whatever tendencies it might have to let its efforts become vague and abstract. It focuses instead on what is: this living assembly of believers, this pressing human need, this dynamic teaching moment, and so forth. Such attentiveness enables practical theology to offer a persistent honesty to the church in its mission rather than escaping into ideas or ideals.

Next, the contextual focus of the field is a starting point for connecting to other temporal and spatial aspects of the faith. That is, practical theology embraces an actual and concrete perspective precisely to forge a bond with the breadth of Christian tradition, understood both historically and globally. Such tradition is rich with norms, rites, symbols, narratives, and practices from other times and places. It therefore holds a storehouse of critical perspectives for contemporary and situated practices of discipleship and ministry. By attending to specific settings, practical theology opens a window onto this larger tradition. At the same time, it enables that tradition itself to be challenged by particular communities, corrected and enriched through emerging local expressions. By standing here and now, the field can launch a mutually critical conversation between any one community and the larger streams in which it stands.

Finally, by maintaining this perspective on contemporary situations, practical theology distinguishes itself from other fields in theological education. To be sure, teaching and research in biblical studies, history, and theology also share a concern for faithful communities and effective witness in our midst. For quite appropriate reasons, however, they do not place these current and concrete aspects in the foreground of their work. For example, the fields of biblical studies or history usually have primary concern for the texts or artifacts of the past, while those of theology or ethics reflect deeply on interrelated claims and meanings, even though all these fields aim to affect ministry and discipleship here and now. Moreover, practical theology depends on these other fields for the more

81

complete sense of the Christian faith each can bring. At the same time, though, these fields need practical theology realistically to assess the present conditions of Christian life and to strategize how the insights of those fields actually contribute to witness. In this sense, practical theology brings a distinctive and irreplaceable voice to the table of theological education.

Discerning and Proposing

The other kind of unity in practical theological work can be seen in the distinctive way in which it is interpretive. Although current events and concrete settings are what focus the field's attention, no context as such can make sense of itself. A further act of interpretation is required in order to clarify what has been encountered and to convey the significant meanings evident in a particular situation. Taken this way, interpreting is not so much a matter of translating something completely unfamiliar as it is making public something that would otherwise remain unnoticed and undeveloped. In practical theology, this interpretive concern can be thought of as having two closely related verbal moods, the indicative and the subjunctive.[18]

In its indicative mood, interpreting *what is,* practical theology works at *discerning.* It seeks to recognize, describe, identify, and understand the context before it. What are the forms and expressions of discipleship, and what are the opportunities and constraints affecting a response? Where does a community of believers find itself, and how does it make sense of its place in the world? Who are the people being trained for ministry, and what are the experiences they bring and the hopes they bear? These are areas for discernment in practical theology, and they occur at every level where the field operates. For this reason, practical theology will make use of the tools and

---

18. The more empirical approach to practical theology can be found in: Johannes A. van der Ven, *Practical Theology: An Empirical Approach* (Leuven: Peeters, 1998); and Gerben Heitink, *Practical Theology: History, Theory, Action Domains* (Grand Rapids: Eerdmans, 1999). The more methodological and hermeneutical approach to practical theology can be found in: Browning, *A Fundamental Practical Theology;* Thomas H. Groome, *Sharing Faith: A Comprehensive Approach to Religious Education and Pastoral Ministry* (San Francisco: HarperSanFrancisco, 1991); and Richard R. Osmer and Friedrich Schweitzer, *Religious Education between Modernization and Globalization: New Perspectives on the United States and Germany* (Grand Rapids: Wm. B. Eerdmans, 2003).

methodologies of the social sciences (psychology, sociology, economics, and anthropology) as well as those of neighboring theological fields (biblical studies, historical studies, systematic theology). Regardless the source, practical theology always employs multiple approaches to discern from participants themselves what is happening in current faith practices.

We hasten to add that within practical theology, discerning is by no means a neutral or objective process. To the contrary, it is already freighted with theological interests. For example, practical theology discerns particular situations with an eye for what is missing, forgotten, or distorted within the practices of disciples and their Christian communities, particularly in their alienation from God. Interpretation in the indicative mood intentionally includes both views about life from within the faith and critiques of harm made by those outside it. Similarly, discernment of human life not only happens from a social scientific perspective but also through the lens of theological anthropology. Christian perspectives on finitude, worth, dignity, agency, and repentance are all needed to give an account of what it means to be truly human in a given time and place.

In its subjunctive mood, interpreting *what might be*, practical theology works toward *proposing*. It seeks to evaluate, assert, guide, and strategize about what faithfully can happen next. Which response could disciples adopt, on the basis of what shared vision and with what means for reaching it? What can a given congregation imagine as the mission into which God is calling it and how does it plan the next steps in undertaking that mission? Where will ministers actually be serving, and how can their education accurately anticipate and prepare for their stewardship there? These are areas for proposals in practical theology, and once again, offering them is essential to every ambit where the field operates. Toward this end, practical theology has often relied on sources outside of academic institutions, such as consulting work in leadership and development. Obviously these are not the only available tools. Within theological education, the fields of ethics or religious education, for example, offer specific ways to listen for alternatives and teach toward transformation, while historical and liturgical studies can remind us of other narratives and symbols by which future challenges can be engaged. In any case, no single method suffices for crafting proposals.

Many find it much easier to see how this portion of the interpretive process is theological. This is especially the case because theology is often thought of as deploying the strong warrants of Scripture or tradition as norms for evaluating current and concrete practices. While there is a place for this, it can also unduly restrict theology to roles of regulation and judgment. It is equally important to recognize that the task of proposing in practical theology is an imaginative enterprise as well, sketching a future that is more attuned to God's promise of abundant life. Moreover, the field uses theological resources with humility, admitting at this point in the process that our best strategies and intentions are still subject to sin and evil. Put another way, practical theology does not offer ideological proposals for optimistic progress, but theological ones aimed at new forms of faithful service that take risks within our own time and place.

Whether in discerning or proposing, then, practical theology interprets Christian ways of life amidst present realities. Its approach is not linear but iterative. Like the systole and diastole of the heart, it involves an ongoing rhythm between indicative and subjunctive moods, a pattern of examination and recommendation that calls forth long-term commitment from disciples and faithful communities. This rhythm may just as easily begin in realizing what might be, which leads back to recognizing what actually is. Regardless the starting point, the entire process will necessarily remain incomplete. Disciples cannot completely comprehend the challenges and demands they face and cannot fully anticipate the outcomes of even their most faithful actions. In its very methodology, practical theology must remain open to God's future.

Such openness, however, is not without commitment or investment. As we have argued above, practical theology is theological throughout its interpretive work, with every moment of that process grounded in Christian perspectives. This has implications for methodology in the field. For example, other views of practical theology have proposed three or four distinct stages of operation, such as "see-judge-act" or "describe-interpret-evaluate-strategize." Besides being needlessly complicated and unidirectional, these models do not fully appreciate what counts as theological work. On the one hand, they treat certain moments in the process as relatively value-free, especially efforts to describe the context. Yet if the very reason for practical theology is to promote discipleship, then we approach any situation interested in what Christian faithfulness entails. That very stance enables us to grasp the human plight and symbolic depth of the here and now more completely than supposedly objective methods. On the other hand, other proposals often relegate theology to matters of assessment and correction. Ironically, this reinforces the stereotype that practical theology concerns only the application of Christian thought to actual situations that have first been understood by other means. Worse still, this view reduces theology entirely to its normative and imperative dimensions, losing the indicative and subjunctive moods so important within practical theology. It is for the sake of an honest view of the present and a richer vision for the future that we see the field as thoroughly theological.

Conclusion

Practical theology is a field in which there are many different players spread across a range of settings and challenges: Christians living and witnessing in everyday circumstances, ministers working alongside disciples to build up the body of Christ, and scholars whose disciplined reflection on teaching and learning leads to research and writing about these matters. These diverse dynamics and their constant interplay make practical theology persistently fascinating and occasionally frustrating. In this essay, we have mapped the field to highlight not only the elements distinctive to each player but also the interrelations and features all of them share. This conceptual mapping is intended not only as a guide through the landscape but also as a prompt for conversation among likely partners. It is crucial now for those in practical theology to take up that conversation, affirm their mutually critical relationships, and make explicit what has long been only implicit. This is a particular service practical theologians can render today to both church and academy, that ministry and discipleship may flourish.

PART 2

Practical Theology
in the Classroom

Part 2
and
Introducing Ministry and Fostering Integration

The authors whose essays appear in this section, "Practical Theology in the Classroom," are known as gifted and thoughtful teachers in the practical field. In the seminar that developed *For Life Abundant,* colleagues asked them to describe the theology and pedagogy that shape what they do in a course or set of courses. What do they hope students will learn to perceive and understand and do, and why? What specific moves in pursuit of these purposes do they make through readings, class sessions, and assignments? Further, what is theological about these choices — that is, how does their sense of God and of their students, materials, and purposes in relation to God inform their pedagogy?

As these chapters make evident, planning and conducting a practical theology course require a teacher not just to describe practical theology but also to engage in it. To borrow language from the previous chapter, these teachers work hard to "discern existing situations of life and propose eventual directions for action" within the "concrete setting" of a specific school with distinctive traditions, students, buildings, schedules, colleagues, and requirements. As John Witvliet points out, the existing situations of life that a teacher of worship must understand include the actual experiences and preferences regarding worship that students already have. Proposing directions for action includes selecting readings to assign, structuring in-class time, and crafting assignments that are more than the "usual end-of-semester sales tax," as James Nieman puts it. In these chapters, therefore, we see practical theology itself in play, as the authors articulate how they exercise the distinctive "know-how" that belongs to good theological educators.

The author of the first chapter in this section, Kathleen A. Cahalan, is associate professor of theology at Saint John's University School of Theology and

Seminary, a Roman Catholic institution in Minnesota. In this chapter, Cahalan analyzes a pair of courses taken by all ministry students in her school. The first introduces students to ministry and the study of ministry, while the second, which comes at the end of their studies, requires them to integrate learning from every field into a pastoral response to a specific problem they are likely to encounter in ministry. In keeping with the methods of practical theology itself, Cahalan shapes the content of each course toward specific ecclesial context of Saint John's. Even so, the issues she explores are familiar to theological educators in a wide range of settings. Treating the introductory and capstone courses as a pair — in this chapter but more importantly in the curriculum itself — and reflecting carefully on what each must contribute, Cahalan engages quite directly with the pedagogical dimensions of questions such as these: What is the educational import of experiences students had (or did not have) before they arrived in graduate school? What are the settings to which students will go after graduation, and what issues will concern them there? What difference can the two or three years they spend in a Master's degree program make within their lifelong process of learning and offering ministry? What do they most need to accomplish while in this degree program, and how does a particular course contribute to that?

Readers will note that some of Cahalan's specific educational strategies draw her students into the moves of practical theological thinking that she and James Nieman set forth in the previous chapter. For example, her account of the process by which she helps students to shape their integration projects provides a window onto such thinking and summarizes an approach that can be brought to bear on any number of issues. The theological and ministerial integrity that is the goal not only of these projects but of ministry studies generally is a goal she invites those who teach in other fields also to prize and pursue in their teaching. This chapter suggests to us that questions about how to begin and end the graduate school portion of a minister's learning would be a generative focus for faculty conversation about this crucial matter.

4. Introducing Ministry and Fostering Integration: Teaching the Bookends of the Masters of Divinity Program

Kathleen A. Cahalan

When I applied for a position in pastoral theology at Saint John's School of Theology and Seminary, I was asked to teach two required courses for ministry students: Introduction to Ministry and the Pastoral Seminar.[1] During the interview I inquired about the goals and content of the two courses. The hiring committee was able to say little about either course though I do remember what they said about the seminar: the course was a chance to cover issues about ministry that had not been covered in the curriculum but were deemed necessary before graduation. "What issues?" I asked. "Topics like finance and budgets," replied a committee member. I told the committee that I could not teach the course, mostly because I knew little about parish budgets and because such a topic should be addressed in a course on administration and finance. What I learned in the interview was that the seminar was functioning as a catch-all for topics that were not finding their way into the curriculum; it was certainly not a culminating exercise in the practice of integration.

When I accepted the position I knew I faced several challenges: designing the two courses from scratch, finding a way to relate them to each other and the other ministry courses, designing a course in parish administration and identifying a qualified teacher, and the long-term goal of relating the ministry curriculum to the entire curriculum. Together, the faculty was facing the larger issue of curricular strategies and goals and what teaching

1. Both courses are required for the Master of Divinity degree and the Master's degree in Pastoral Ministry. I later changed the name "Pastoral Seminar" to the "Integration Seminar."

toward integration means. But I also knew they were eager to have someone come in and "fix" the problem.

Most theological educators recognize the bookend dilemma, what
Charles Foster and his colleagues who authored *Educating Clergy* refer to as
vertical integration: how to move students from introductory to advanced
courses.[2] Such movement involves further questions: What characterizes a
good introductory course that initiates theological education, and what characterizes a good capstone experience that draws it toward a culmination? And
who will teach such courses? Given highly specialized faculties in most seminaries, it is sometimes difficult to identify a faculty member who is interested
or feels qualified to teach either course; oftentimes faculty are uncertain
about what the content and purposes of the courses should be. Yet because
integration remains an important goal for theological educators, defining
what constitutes good introductory and capstone experiences is important.[3]

Teaching the bookend courses has challenged me to define what it is to
introduce students to ministry and to test their capacity for integration before they graduate. At the outset, it means attending to who they are and
what they know when they enter the school, as well as providing a variety
of learning opportunities that coalesce and accumulate in a pattern that is
meaningful and challenging. Because an increasing number of students
enter as novices, while some are advanced beginners, and a few proficient,
it requires intentional teaching to engage students in theological education
that helps them mature no matter their starting point.[4] How can I, and the
school, attend to the knowledge students acquire, the ministerial practice

2. Charles R. Foster, Lisa E. Dahill, Lawrence A. Golemon, and Barbara Wang
Tolentino, *Educating Clergy: Teaching Practices and Pastoral Imagination* (San Francisco:
Jossey-Bass, 2006), p. 330. Foster et al. also refer to theological thinking and horizontal inte-
gration as two other types of integration.

3. See the Degree Program Standards, Association of Theological Schools, A.3.1.0,
which states: "The M.Div. program should provide a breadth of exposure to the theological
disciplines as well as a depth of understanding within those disciplines. It should educate
students for a comprehensive range of pastoral responsibilities and skills by providing opportunities for the appropriation of theological disciplines, for deepening understanding of
the life of the church, for ongoing intellectual and ministerial formation, and for exercising
the arts of ministry." This definition is similar to the one set forth in Foster et al., *Educating
Clergy*, esp. ch. 11, pp. 329-54.

4. See Christian Scharen's discussion of the six stages of learning in this volume. There
is preliminary evidence that the average age of seminary students is declining, with several
schools enrolling more students in their twenties.

they will engage, and the vocational identity being formed, in each of our classes and over the entire curriculum?

The view from the other end, at the conclusion of the M.Div. program, raises another set of questions. What knowledge do I think is indispensable for students to learn over the course of their studies that makes the integration experience particularly informing and worthwhile? What ministry experiences and contexts need to be explored? How best can we assist students to develop and refine the practices of teaching, preaching, and caring for souls? How does the teaching and learning environment invite students to explore their identity and vocation as ministers in the Catholic community at this time? Certainly, theological educators are humble enough to admit that we cannot teach students everything they need to learn about theology or ministry before they graduate. But what should a culminating experience require of students as they take leave of the seminary and move into various ministerial roles in the church? What is indispensable to theological education that can lay a basic foundation for students' ongoing learning and development as they embark on the vocation of ministry? And, as David Wood asks in his chapter later in this book, what types of learning experiences do graduates need as these leave the halls of the academy and move into ministry settings that can deepen and strengthen the knowledge, identity, and skill acquired in seminary?

Introducing Ministry

A primary goal in introducing students to ministry is to help them gain a broadened understanding of what constitutes ministry and a deeper appreciation for its diverse, plural, and complex forms in the tradition. To achieve this goal, the course is organized around six questions: Who is the minister? *(form);* What are the tasks of ministry? *(function);* Where does ministry take place? *(social and ecclesial contexts);* When? *(historical context);* How is it accomplished? *(methods);* and, Why does the church engage in ministry? *(rationale).* The six questions engage descriptively and theologically the person, context, and practice of ministry.[5]

---

5. The pedagogy for the course combines interactive lectures, case studies, historical readings, research papers, short student presentations, and examination. Because the ma-

The question of who is the minister in the Catholic community has received significant theological attention, due to contemporary developments in ecclesiology but also because of the decline of ordained priests and women religious and the increase of ordained deacons and lay ecclesial ministers in local parish ministry. For example, I teach men who will be ordained to the presbyterium (mostly Benedictine monks), the permanent diaconate (for the Saint Cloud diocese), and lay ecclesial ministers, who constitute the majority of our student body and are mostly women.[6] The School of Theology believes that ordained and lay ministers ought to be trained together in order to foster collaborative ministry. But this is new territory for most Catholic seminaries. Just a few years ago an introduction to ministry in a Catholic seminary would have been an introduction to the priesthood.

Because we are facing a large number of people called to do ministry

---

jority of students in the course will be enrolled in their first course or first semester in graduate school, I want them to learn the expectations and demands of graduate-level study of ministry and to maintain high academic standards in a ministry course. The first challenge is not difficult to achieve by being attentive to learning at the right pace, keeping anxiety at a manageable level, giving constructive feedback on written and oral work, and helping students find resources outside the class if they are not mastering research and writing. The second challenge has to do with both the culture of the school and the expectations of the students. Part of our culture retains a sharp distinction between "academic" and "ministry" courses, and I have tried to change that perception by emphasizing that ministry courses must be taught with academic integrity and rigor. Ministry courses are academic insofar as a body of knowledge exists to be engaged critically. Some faculty members hold a view of ministry courses as different from other subject matters: ministry courses entail more personal sharing, they focus on process rather than content in both class time and written assignments, and they are not difficult. I have aimed to make the course academically rigorous while at the same time honoring student agency, development, and insight in class discussions and work. Though much of the academic bias still lingers, I realize that the course cannot be academically rigorous in an effort to show colleagues that practical theology can be like their disciplines; it must strive for academic rigor because the ministry deserves serious intellectual consideration from a wide variety of disciplinary perspectives including history, philosophy, the social sciences, biblical studies, and theology.

6. In this essay I use the term "minister" as a broad category that includes ordained presbyters, deacons, and lay ecclesial ministers. For a comprehensive description of these three categories of ministers in Catholic theological education, see Mary L. Gautier, *Catholic Ministry Formation Enrollment: Statistical Overview for 2005-06* (Washington, D.C.: Center for Applied Research in the Apostolate, 2006).

outside of the traditional avenues of ordination, I devote a great deal of attention to the developing theologies of the minister, including a survey of the history of the minister in our tradition, that considers the episcopacy, presbyter/priest, deacon, and, most recently, the lay ecclesial minister.[7] The historical and theological focus is important for several reasons. First, the School of Theology emphasizes the history and development of doctrine and tradition because we believe that students cannot understand contemporary theological developments and arguments without a strong grounding in the tradition, nor can they advance our tradition without deep knowledge into its ways of thinking and living in the past. Modern theological developments in liturgy, sacraments, and ministry owe a great deal to patristic models, which both correspond to and deviate from medieval developments. The tension between these two streams of our tradition is what is largely at stake today in redefining theologies of ordained and lay ministry.

Second, issues related to who is the minister are the hot-button topics in the church today: those relating to celibacy, married priests, women deacons, women priests, homosexual ministers, and sexual abuse of minors by ordained ministers. Most students know little of the tradition's development in terms of teachings and practices related to ordained ministry; most come into class advocating change but lack the theological knowledge to advance compelling arguments from within the tradition. As ministers in local communities, students will be called upon to represent and explain the tradition. They must teach the tradition in a way that assists church members in understanding what is essential to the minister and what changes over time.

Third, students must develop a sense of ministerial identity and vocation in a changing, ambiguous, and often contentious ecclesial atmosphere. They must forge an identity by wrestling with the tradition, discovering concepts and interpretations that help them define their roles, negotiating the ambiguity of our situation, and, for some, finding the courage to forge ahead not knowing what will change and when. Ministerial identity is a deeply personal and vocational issue, but it is also an

7. See Paul Bernier, *Ministry in the Church* (New London, Conn.: Twenty-Third Publications, 1992); Susan K. Wood, ed., *Ordering the Baptismal Priesthood: Theologies of Lay and Ordained Ministry* (Collegeville, Minn.: Liturgical Press, 2003); and David DeLambo, *Lay Parish Ministers: A Study of Emerging Leadership* (New York: National Pastoral Life Center, 2005).

ecclesial one. Through theological study, ministerial practice, and spiritual formation, all students must find some way of claiming their vocation as ministers within the contemporary ecclesial and cultural setting.

It can be quite easy to give the entire course over to the question of who is the minister. In fact, I have come to realize that when Catholic theologians talk about a theology of ministry they are actually addressing a theology of the minister.[8] But of course, the theology and identity of the minister are just part of a much larger puzzle. Clearly, even if, in the Catholic community, we had all the ordained and lay ecclesial ministers we need, the fundamental issues of *doing* ministry would remain. What, then, constitutes our understanding of the practice of ministry? How do we define ministry? What is it that ministers do, as distinct from other forms of service in the community or professions in our society? How do they do it? And why do they do what they do?

The questions of "what" and "why" are addressed through an examination of six practices of ministry: teaching, preaching, worship, pastoral care, administration/stewardship, and prophecy/social ministry.[9] Interestingly, the term "ministry" is new to Catholic vocabulary, gaining widespread usage since the Second Vatican Council.[10] It has now been re-

8. This is partly due to a traditional bias against functional understandings of ministry in favor of ontological definitions of ordained ministry.

9. I define ministry as "leadership of disciples through teaching, preaching, leading worship, pastoral care, prophecy with social outreach, and administering organizations; for the sake of discipleship lived in relationship to God's reigning presence; as a public act discernable in word, deed, and symbol; on behalf of a Christian community; as a gift received in faith, baptism, commissioning, installation, and ordination; and as an activity that calls forth the fullness of discipleship in each member of the community by attending to ministry as a whole and in each of its specific parts." See Kathleen A. Cahalan, "Toward a Fundamental Theology of Ministry," *Worship* 80, no. 2 (March 2006): 120. While there are many ways to identify the core practices of ministry, in the context of this course, I define these six areas, primarily because of (a) their Christological, biblical, and historical expression in the community, and (b) our curriculum's requirement that students take a course in each of these areas. The six practices also provide a way to discuss ministry in terms that are both broadly ecclesial (how does the parish express these dimensions of ministry?) and vocational (how is calling to ministry a calling to each of these practices?). I concur with Peter Marty's claim in his essay in this volume that ministry is not just a set of discrete tasks, but the whole work of shaping communal life together.

10. Prior to the Council Catholics often dismissed the term "ministry" and "minister" as too Protestant, but through biblical and patristic studies the term was adopted at the Council, being used 76 times in the documents.

claimed in its biblical and patristic meanings, but discussions about what it is and how to define it have been relatively recent.[11]

At least one third of the course addresses the "how" question. My goal is to introduce students to a basic method of ministry that I believe undergirds the six practices of ministry. We employ the shared praxis approach developed by Thomas Groome, which is one practical theology method that has enjoyed widespread influence in Catholic ministry.[12] Because I want students to engage a praxis method in relationship to all practices of ministry, I use case studies that address situations in liturgy, preaching, faith formation, pastoral care, social ministries, and administration. I want students to gain an appreciation for how to think theologically and practically in each of these areas, but also to begin seeing the ways these "ministries" interconnect in real time (e.g., liturgy and pastoral care; preaching and faith formation). I also want to begin challenging notions of specialized ministry, which dominates Catholic ministry roles today.[13] For example, a student may come with a great deal of experience in youth ministry, but not understand or engage aspects of preaching or administration. Or they may come as a chaplain, but lack experience in faith formation.

I have determined that the course cannot be an introduction to practical theology as a theological discipline.[14] Rather its aim must be to introduce students to a "theory of practice" by way of a basic method that enables one to think *about* practice as well as think *in* and *during* practice. Groome's five movements of shared praxis roughly correspond to the general pattern of practical theological thinking: description and analysis (what is going on?); theological interpretation (what does it mean?); and, decision and action (what should we do?). Using the case studies alongside

---

11. See Richard P. McBrien, *Ministry: A Theological, Pastoral Handbook* (San Francisco: Harper & Row, 1987); and Thomas F. O'Meara, *A Theology of Ministry,* rev. ed. (Mahwah, N.J.: Paulist Press, 1999), p. 141.

12. Thomas Groome, *Sharing Faith: A Comprehensive Approach to Religious Education and Pastoral Ministry* (San Francisco: HarperSanFrancisco, 1991), pp. 155-283. The five movements are (1) naming/expressing "present action"; (2) critical reflection on present action; (3) making accessible Christian story and vision; (4) dialectical hermeneutics to appropriate story/vision to participants' stories and visions; (5) decision/response for lived Christian faith. Another important source for a hermeneutical approach to practical theology is Don S. Browning, *A Fundamental Practical Theology* (Minneapolis: Fortress Press, 1991).

13. See Cahalan, "Toward a Fundamental Theology of Ministry," pp. 104-11.

14. John Witvliet makes a similar point in his chapter in this volume: the practice is in the foreground in our classrooms, and the discipline in the background.

the theory of the method allows students to "practice" the theory and test it against their own practice as they simulate the case study situations. It is clearly an artificial environment, for students are not actually doing ministry, but they are practicing one of what John Witvliet has called the "scales" of ministry.[15] The theory becomes a practical method through repetition both in the course and by utilizing it in other ministry courses, in field education, and eventually in ministry. I am betting that such an intellectual disposition will become a *habitus* as they learn to ask reflexively in each ministry situation: What is going on here? What does it mean theologically? What should we do?[16]

I also use the shared praxis method because it provides a *theological* theory of practice. In other words, it is not a theory of practice drawn from the social sciences, but a theory of practice for ministry, and in that sense its beginning and ending point are theological. For example, Groome makes explicit both his theological anthropology and theology of revelation and history from a moderate and liberationist Catholic perspective: Who are we as made in the image of God and what are God's purposes for us and the whole creation? Students are able to begin engaging why it matters what ministers think about the human condition and about what God is doing in relationship to humanity and the world. Further, because the method asks ministers to articulate each movement as they move toward more faithful praxis, students are challenged to explain where they are leading people and why. What do they as ministers want or hope people will be able to know or do, or change or convert, by this particular faith formation experience, or homily, or pastoral care encounter?

The method is also hermeneutical and initiates students into basic practices and norms of Catholic biblical interpretation and theological reflection. It also engages what I would call "ministerial interpretation": the

---

15. The "artificial" nature of practice in the classroom is important because, as Bonnie Miller-McLemore points out in her chapter in this volume, the more deeply one is immersed in practice the less time there is for theorizing.

16. Foster et al. discuss how theological thinking can become "second nature" for students. See *Educating Clergy*, p. 341. Learning a practical theory can be very helpful for beginning students, but there also comes a point when practical engagement itself begins to raise questions about the theory behind it. A student who was quite enthralled by Groome's method mentioned to me one day after class, "I wish we could keep doing this over and over until we figured out what was wrong with it. I'd like to really take this theory apart." The critique of theory comes through putting it into practice, not learning more theory.

minister's capacity to interpret a situation through stories, symbols, and doctrines for the sake of the living, embodied faith in a particular community. In other words, I want students to see that ministry entails learning theology, history, and Scripture, not as ends in themselves, but as sources of wisdom that the minister continually draws upon as she or he interprets, explains, cajoles, comforts, challenges, and calls forth living faith today.

Organizing the course around the questions, *who, what, how, where, when,* and *why,* has helped provide a conceptual map for our class discussions, lectures, and student research.[17] Each question can be addressed historically, theologically, and through an analysis of contemporary practice. In order to understand ministry, no single question can be treated in isolation — only through exploring and studying the questions in relationship to each other can we fully understand the scope and depth of ministry. The challenge of introducing students to ministry is helping them see ministry as a whole with many related parts, a vantage point they can rarely gain from standing in any one position.

At the Other End of the Curriculum: The Integration Seminar

Students enter the seminar in their final year of studies with knowledge about the course requirements. In the introductory course, as students begin to learn the praxis method, I share with them the project they will embark upon in the seminar. In addition, I encourage them to attend the oral presentations given by seminar students at the end of the semester. And, of course, student gossip spreads the word about what to expect. In fact it is common for students to meet with me one or two semesters prior to enrolling in the seminar to "check out" a topic.[18] This is exactly what I hope

17. I explore the *where* question regarding context through a variety of avenues: first-person accounts of ministry including student experiences; studies of ministers and their communities (e.g., Samuel G. Freedman, *Upon This Rock: The Miracle of the Black Church* [New York: Harper, 1993]); and analyses of cultural trends and their impact on the church (e.g., William Bausch, *The Parish of the Next Millennium* [New London, Conn.: Twenty-Third Publications, 1997]).

18. I have tracked student projects over the past seven years and have found that their projects tend to fall under one or two of the following areas: (1) responding to people with particular developmental needs (e.g., children or the elderly), health issues (e.g., AIDS, premature births), emotional difficulties (e.g., grief, depression), issues of membership and

happens: students begin to see the seminar as a culminating experience into which they can bring knowledge and experience from other courses and field education opportunities. I challenge students to think about how they could explore some aspect of their topic in a Scripture or history or ethics assignment, and how they could gain some experience in practicing the ministry they are interested in addressing. They know they will have to demonstrate in public their capacity for practical theological thinking. A brief description of three student projects helps to demonstrate vertical and horizontal integration in the curriculum as well as vocational identity and formation in the seminar.

Regina enrolled in graduate theological education after many years working as a church musician. Her experience gave her a deep working knowledge of the day-to-day practice of liturgical ministry in the local parish, and yet she was eager to explore new possibilities. She came to the first course asking, Is it possible to incorporate music into our care for the dying? As a musician, she was well-versed in the use of liturgical music in healing services and funerals, but she had little experience or knowledge of whether music could play a part in pastoral care in hospitals or hospices. In two written assignments, Regina explored three ways in which music is currently used in care for the dying, and utilized a praxis method to begin defining how she might use music in a home or hospice setting. Two years later, Regina enrolled in the seminar with the project clearly defined: she wanted to design a discernment and training opportunity for parish musicians that would engage them in the question, Can you serve the sick and dying through your music ministry? Not only had she explored the topic in

identity (e.g., oblates, religious), or issues of social justice (e.g., women, persons with AIDS, homosexuals, individuals who are divorced); (2) changing an aspect of ministry practice (e.g., preaching using technology or in the wake of a crisis), pastoral care (e.g., incorporating music into ministry to the dying, using non-sacramental rites, utilizing touch), youth ministry (e.g., using appropriate music, developing spiritual formation in schools), catechesis (e.g., introducing young adult ministries), or liturgy (e.g., SCAP, or Sunday Celebrations in the Absence of a Priest); (3) grappling with Church teachings that pose a challenge in view of current social norms (e.g., ministry to divorced and remarried Catholics, ministry to homosexual persons, SCAP liturgies, low Sunday liturgy attendance among youth); (4) analyzing organizational issues that impact ministry (e.g., effective parish models, parish council structures, closing parishes, clustered parishes); and (5) exploring issues that face the profession of ministry (e.g., paying ministers a just wage, educating youth ministers, sustaining youth ministers, defining a ministerial role such as liturgical ministers or pastoral associates, formation of deacons).

previous coursework and discovered creative uses of music in pastoral care, she had also sought out a CPE program that gave her first-hand experience.

Jeff came to theological education from a different place. A young student, he was out of a college a few years working in a local business when he felt a desire to work in ministry. A faithful churchgoer, Jeff decided to explore graduate theological education to discover whether he had a vocation to ministry and what that might be. He entered school with no previous theological education and limited ministry experience, having served two years on a college RCIA (Rite of Christian Initiation for Adults) team. In the introductory course, he explored basic questions such as, What is faith formation for adult Catholics? And two years later, when he enrolled in the seminar, he was discerning whether to pursue either faith formation or parish business administration after graduation, having gained some knowledge and field experience in both areas. For his seminar project he focused on the role of parish business administrators and how they incorporate Catholic social teachings into financial, personnel, and resource decisions in the parish. Vocational issues were also present: Jeff was discerning whether his call to ministry included ordained ministry or lay ecclesial ministry, and his discernment was not settled as graduation approached.

Annette came to graduate studies with seventeen years of experience teaching in Catholic primary schools. As a member of the Sisters of Charity, her vocational identity was largely shaped by the order's heritage of teaching and service in parish schools. But a transformation happened to Annette during her studies: she discovered something new in ministry and her calling. She began considering a call to serve as a pastoral associate in a parish. She was somewhat alarmed at considering the possibility of leaving teaching, but she decided to explore the work of the pastoral associate in her field experience.[19] A crucial experience defined her seminar project. Annette visited three parishioners on a memory-loss unit in a residential facility. She brought communion to the residents, performed the ritual correctly (as taught in a liturgy class), but felt inadequate in the pastoral care she offered to each person. She had a sense that the experience of communion had been reduced or lost. Though she understood her role as representative of the community and the powerful sharing of the Eucharist brought from the parish communion table, she had a sense of not con-

---

19. For a description of the current role of pastoral associates in Catholic parishes, see DeLambo, *Lay Parish Ministers.*

necting with the patients and was concerned that the community was not present in other ways. She wanted to find out if there was more a minister and parish members could do to address the spiritual needs of this special population.

Interestingly, each time I teach the seminar I face students with a similar range of intellectual capacity, vocational awareness, and ministerial skill. The course is described as "a culminating exercise of practical and theological analysis," the purpose of which is to have students "demonstrate their capacity to integrate Scripture, theology, history, and ministry resources in an analysis of a contemporary situation." Because students come to the course with such varied experience and knowledge, I have written the following course description, referencing the concept of integration in a fairly general way:

> Integration refers to the way in which ministers relate the three aspects of practical theological thinking in a coherent and creative way in order that ministry is thoughtful, effective and constructive. The course is based on the premise that ministers are leaders, theologians, and interpreters of sacred texts, traditions, and human experiences. To be effective leaders ministers need both a breadth and depth of knowledge about the Christian faith as well as insight into living the faith in particular cultural and historical contexts. What are essential, then, are *both* what a minister knows about the good news, its various expressions in Scripture and tradition, and how that knowledge informs and shapes teaching, preaching, worship, social ministries, and the care of souls in particular ecclesial settings.

The course goals aim to assess students' capacities to:

1) describe a ministry situation in regards to its personal, social, historical, cultural, and religious dimensions, drawing upon the social sciences where appropriate;
2) interpret the situation by utilizing insights from Scripture, history, systematic and moral theology, and ministry;
3) construct a response that offers insight and guidance for ministers and communities of faith;
4) integrate description, interpretation, and analysis for the sake of constructive thinking and planning; and,

5) collaborate in an environment of listening, critiquing, and learning with peers in ministry.

The course requires students, as I have already said, to complete an integration project and prepare a public presentation.[20] Students begin their projects by identifying a situation that is important to their ministry — a problem, question, opportunity, or challenge facing particular persons or a community. It is important that they define the situation in concrete and specific terms, and this often means I help them negotiate from a broad topic to a specific issue, partly because of the time limits that will constrain their research, but also because ministry is a concrete and local practice. While there are many situations that have significance for the wider church (e.g., should the age of Confirmation be changed?), for the purposes of the seminar I want students to focus on a concrete, particular situation (e.g., Should St. Mark's parish in New Prague, Minnesota, confirm children when they receive the Eucharist, and if so, what needs to happen

---

20. The paper is a minimum of 25 pages and the presentation is 45 minutes in length. There are generally two required texts for the course. An excellent source for helping students hone a broad topic into a focused question and develop an argument to persuade their audience is Wayne Booth, *The Craft of Research,* 2d ed. (Chicago: University of Chicago Press, 2005). I also select articles or books that exemplify practical theological thinking, among them Richard Gaillardetz, *Transforming Our Days: Spirituality, Community, and Liturgy* (New York: Crossroad, 2000), and Dorothy C. Bass, *Receiving the Day* (San Francisco: Jossey-Bass, 2000). The first half of the course is designed around a series of exercises that move students through each of the three main aspects of the written assignment: how to describe the situation; how to interpret the situation; and how to construct a response. Over a four-week period I lecture, use examples and excerpts from good ministry writing, and require written exercises aimed at constructing the main set of arguments at the heart of each section of the paper. By the midterm, students have completed an outline, a bibliography, a first draft, and any qualitative or quantitative research for the descriptive aspect. My pedagogy then shifts toward coaching the writing process through various drafts and facilitating conversation and critique of students' work by each other. Students read and critique each other's work as the semester progresses. My goal is to have students learn how to affirm, question, and help other ministers think through their projects. I model how to raise questions that help students improve their projects, but this is not always easy for students to do for each other. Working through several drafts of the written project can be a difficult part of the course for some students: they get stuck, overwhelmed, tired, and don't know how to push forward with the research and writing. It is important for me to keep communicating with these students about their progress, with both encouragement and correction. The seminar format is an example of what Foster et al. call integration in community and "learning together." See *Educating Clergy,* pp. 348-52.

to make this change?). A situation, as I define it, is a real-life issue facing real people that has significant consequences if nothing is done to address it.[21] The situation poses a question that necessitates an answer. This does not mean every situation is a crisis or a problem; it can also be an opportunity, but even opportunities raise questions for communities that require an answer, and if unheeded have repercussions.

Part One: Description. In describing the situation students are asked to offer a clear and compelling explanation of the facts, moving beyond their own and the community's commonly held opinions and assumptions. The student's aim is to understand deeply what is going on in the situation and to present it in such a way as to mobilize interest and concern by the audience the student hopes to convince. The student is developing an argument about the situation for which evidence must be presented. Students are guided by the following set of questions for the first part of the project:

- What is the situation that is being addressed?
- Who are the people involved? What group or community faces this concern and why?
- What is the history of the situation? What are its social, cultural, and religious aspects?
- What is being done to address the situation, or not? Is it effective?
- Why is this situation a concern for ministers? Why is it a particular concern for the student?

Research may involve analyses of demographic information; historical studies; qualitative and quantitative studies that help to explain some aspect of people's feelings, knowledge, opinions, and behaviors. Students may utilize opinion polls, surveys, or interviews to help them understand something about a particular group of people involved in the situation.[22] I encourage students first to locate social scientific research related to their

21. Booth, *The Craft of Research*, chs. 3-4. Kathleen A. Cahalan, *Projects That Matter: Planning and Evaluation for Religious Organizations* (Herndon, Va.: Alban Institute, 2003), pp. 6-9. See also Edward Farley, "Interpreting Situations: An Inquiry into the Nature of Practical Theology," in *Formation and Reflection: The Promise of Practical Theology,* ed. Lewis S. Mudge and James N. Poling (Philadelphia: Fortress Press, 1987).

22. A particularly helpful resource for quantitative and qualitative research in ministry is Scott L. Thumma, "Methods for Congregational Study," in *Studying Congregations: A New Handbook,* ed. Nancy Ammerman (Nashville: Abingdon, 1998).

situation, and then to complement that with their own surveys or interviews. A few students have become overwhelmed with constructing and
analyzing surveys, which usually culminates in a project that is a summary
of survey responses. I have learned to guide students more prudently in
this first step: they cannot conduct a full-scale research study that strives
toward validity and generalization, mostly because of time, but also because it is not necessary. My goal is that they learn some basic data gathering skills so that in the practice of ministry, when faced with a challenging
situation, they know how to go about understanding the situation by using
appropriate tools of description and analysis.[23]

But their description and analysis is not meant to be a neutral, dispas-
sionate exercise; rather it includes an evaluative perspective. The first part
of the project offers a rich and compelling portrait of the situation, based
on good factual evidence, as well as an assessment of what is happening, the
strengths and weaknesses of various responses to the situation, and a claim
about what, in particular, needs to be addressed by the minister and community. The description is closely linked with the third part of the essay: the
argument for what strategy to pursue as a response to the situation.

The first part of Annette's project consisted of research into the physical, emotional, and spiritual needs of people with dementia. She also examined ministry resources to discover what pastoral care providers do and
how they relate to persons with dementia. She was able to provide an in-
depth account of the stages of dementia and what care providers should
know as they relate to the person over the course of the disease. From both
social scientific and ministry resources, she was able to evaluate her own
shortcomings as a minister, as well as those of the parish where she served:
she had discovered, and was ready to argue, that there was much more to
offer when bringing communion to patients.

Part Two: Interpretation. The second part of the assignment requires
students to offer a theological interpretation and analysis, both in relation
to the situation (as described above) and as a rationale for the response in
the third part. This requires theological interpretation that opens up and
identifies the theological issues within the situation and then turns toward
the theological meaning and import of the community's response to that
situation. Students are asked to explain the following:

---

23. This is akin to Dykstra's claim in his essay in this volume about learning the capacity to see into situations, and to Witvliet's goal of training for perception and intuition.

- What are the central theological, moral, and spiritual issues in the situation?
- What Church doctrines and teachings apply to the situation?
- What stories and images from Scripture help illuminate the situation?
- What major Christian symbols help us understand the situation?
- Are there historical analogies to this situation? What can be learned from other Christian communities who have faced similar situations, in the past and today?

There seems to be a persistent concern by faculty that ministry students are not able to "do" theology very well. This is partly true but not always the students' fault. One of the problems is that theology is comprised of many aspects, including biblical narratives; dogmas and doctrines; liturgy, sacraments, and symbols; canon law; systematic treatments of the faith; moral arguments; spiritual writings; and, of course, the history of practice that embodies theological norms and content in context. Students have to move from the general realm of theology to the concrete and particular realm of ministry: they are challenged to do some theological "repackaging" of the doctrines, narratives, and symbols of the faith to make them concrete and explicit to the situation they are addressing. To help students learn how to draw theology into their projects, I focus their attention on four forms of theology — doctrines, narratives, symbols, and paradigms — and how each can be used in ministerial practice.[24]

Doctrines are teachings that are presented as formal propositions of the faith. Ministers need to know the basic doctrines of the Christian faith and how they apply to certain situations. For example, a student wrestling with the church's teachings on divorced Catholics needs to know the requirements for the reception of communion. But students do not always understand the development and status of doctrine in the Catholic community: a few students think it is sufficient to quote the *Catechism* or a papal document to "prove" what the church teaches. In these cases, doctrine is not used to illuminate the situation, but to make a final declaration.

There are clearly some important ways in which doctrine relates to

---

24. Students are required to use at least two of the four forms in their project. See David Kelsey, *The Uses of Scripture in Recent Theology* (Philadelphia: Fortress Press), chs. 2-4; Avery Dulles, *Models of Revelation* (Maryknoll, N.Y.: Orbis, 1992); and Groome, *Sharing Faith*, pp. 178-80, 196-98.

practice. In many though not all situations, doctrine provides clarity and clear boundaries for the community. It provides the community a solid foundation for catechesis and is essential for developing identity. Doctrine is the indispensable core of ideas that animates the community's life and witness; it provides substance for a Christian way of life.

Annette began her theological interpretation by surveying church teachings that pertain to the sick and elderly, with special reference to persons with dementia. She was able to locate, summarize, and quote extensively from church teachings about the elderly from the U.S. Catholic bishops and a pastoral letter from John Paul II, which combine elements of Scripture and Catholic social teaching that focus on the dignity and worth of each person, regardless of age or mental capacity. She was able to provide a solid doctrinal foundation for the ministry.

As students learn to draw on doctrine in their interpretation of the situation they must be aware of several elements: the context of the development of doctrine that includes the situation in which the doctrine arose; the *sensus fidelium;* levels of teaching authority related to church documents; various ways the doctrine has been interpreted in particular settings; the relationship of doctrines to each other; contemporary discourse about a doctrine; and the prudent explanation of doctrine when it conflicts with people's understanding and desires.[25] Ministers are challenged to move from the general and somewhat abstract formulations of doctrine to the key insight that can illuminate their particular context. For example, Jeff asked in his project: What do Catholic social teachings on just wages mean in terms of what the St. Cloud diocese recommends to parishes as a pay scale for ministers?

Doctrine can be used in inappropriate ways by ministers: as a trumpcard that diminishes experience, questioning, and dialogue. It can, if presented inappropriately, lack historical perspective and be overly rational. Because doctrine is often presented to the community in propositional language, it can appear dry or passionless, perhaps disconnected from our everyday reality. Because of this "distance" for some members in the community, it is imperative that ministers learn ways to bring doctrine alive and stay present to those who struggle to understand and accept doctrines they don't understand or reject. Ministers learn quickly that doctrine alone

---

25. For an excellent resource on the teaching authority of the church, see Richard R. Gaillardetz, *Teaching with Authority: A Theology of the Magisterium in the Church* (Collegeville, Minn.: Liturgical Press, 1997).

does not make for persuasive, compelling speech and rationales; but combined with other theological language it is an important expression of the community's identity and faith.

The second area of theological interpretation is narrative, which emphasizes the language of story. It emphasizes the Bible and tradition as the stories of the living faithful in response to God's action and presence in history.[26] Students are encouraged to examine Scripture and tradition for stories that help to illuminate the situation of the people they are addressing in their project. They are to search for wisdom figures, prophets and radicals, sages and mystics, theologians and teachers, pastors and ministers, artists, and saints and martyrs. The emphasis in the narrative approach is to demonstrate the ways that God is present in everyday life, both in the past and the present. Faith is an active response to an active God.

Using narratives in practice provides vivid portraits of people drawn into relationship with God through a wide variety of life situations. Such portraits are compelling, inviting, and motivating in ways that doctrines rarely are. Such narratives provide continuity with the past and allow people to see the connection between their lived experience and people from the past: they are connected to the story of salvation history. The minister's challenge is to both *know* the tradition well enough to draw out the stories and *interpret* them in a way that opens up their meaning for today's situation. Regina drew on a story from the eleventh-century monastery at Cluny, which developed elaborate practices of singing and praying as monks accompanied their dying confreres in their final journey of life.

The narrative approach can be used poorly by student ministers. They can overemphasize God's actions in the past, leaving aside what God is doing today; they can romanticize the past or read it too literally; they can argue for reconstructing the past because it is superior to the present situation; they can construct heroes to whom few can relate. At times, students make the mistake that telling stories is enough because the message is so obvious. But stories and narratives bring the community only so far: they do not, in themselves, provide all the insight necessary to inform the community about what they should do in the present situation. Ministers must

26. In many ways, theology as narrative is much stronger among Protestant theologians and ministers than it is for Catholics. Catholics traditionally have not utilized a biblical narrative approach; doctrine and symbol are the dominant modes of theological discourse because of the primary importance of law and liturgy.

take the story another step into their context and use it to build a rationale for where they want to encourage the community to move.

A third way ministers engage theology is through the interpretation of symbols. Symbols are perhaps the most complex form of divine-human communication, yet one of the richest theologically. At the same time that they reveal profound truths about who and what we are and who and what God is, they also conceal, never completely revealing the mystery they express. In language, symbol is metaphor, parable, myth, and analogy, but symbol is also expressed in material form in buildings, objects, bodily movement, and artistic expressions. Symbols move beyond both proposition and narrative toward the aesthetic, but are never divorced from either. Doctrines and stories become embodied and embedded in faith symbols. Theologically, humans are symbol-making creatures and encounters with God are most commonly mediated through some symbolic form.[27]

Symbols, like doctrines, hold essential truths about the faith and, like stories, arise from powerful narratives. Symbols open out common human experiences that can draw people into a larger horizon of religious meaning, and they can do so through aesthetic forms that capture the ineffable (e.g., music, art, poetry, architecture, etc.). Because symbols are multivalent forms of communication, they require catechesis by ministers. They are not always self-evident, and in fact, ministers cannot take for granted that people understand either the basic or the deep meanings of Christian symbols. Symbols must be uncovered, broken open, explored, and critiqued if Christians are to have access to their deep meaning for their lives. But ministers should never only explain symbols in a didactic way; they need to provide multiple encounters with symbols that enlighten and enliven people's imaginations.

Regina chose the crucifixion story from John's Gospel as the narrative and symbol that music ministers can consider as they discern the charisms necessary to accompany the dying with music. The gospel story tells of the community gathered at the foot of Jesus' cross — the dying are not abandoned but accompanied by friends and relatives. In the training program she developed, she drew on artistic renderings of the crucifixion and hymns that drew out the theological meaning of the cross and the demand of Christian service.

---

27. This approach to faith and theology is clearly the dominant one among twentieth-century Catholic theologians such as Karl Rahner, Edward Schillebeeckx, and David Tracy.

How do students use symbols to interpret situations? First, they must discern which Christian symbols illumine the heart of the situation and how to interpret those symbols in ways that draw forth meaning and insight.[28] Annette identified lepers as biblical figures who faced isolation and misunderstanding because of their illness. Despite their social isolation, Jesus reached out to touch them. She argued that dementia creates multiple dimensions of isolation that separate people with dementia from the community and themselves: isolation that is physical (if they have to live outside the home and parish), mental (as they begin losing memory), social and ecclesial (the nature of their relationships change, and they are increasingly absent to the parish community), and personal (they become alienated from themselves). By seeing communion as a form of relationship that connects us physically, mentally, socially, ecclesially, and personally to each other and to God, Annette connected this basic Christian symbol to the community's ministry to persons with dementia.

Symbols must be interpreted wisely, but sometimes ministers miss the mark. They can be experienced in a purely subjective way and lack communal and historical grounding. Interpreting symbols for and with the community requires that the minister not be an authority unto himself or herself, but engaged in the ongoing interpretation of their meaning in the tradition.

The fourth approach to theology identifies paradigms that correlate with the situation. By paradigms, I mean something akin to the wisdom tradition: not absolute rules or laws, but ways of living, guidelines, and models that provide paradigms of how people have figured out how to live faithfully in a particular situation, how they have found a "way of life." Interpreting paradigmatic sayings, stories, or figures means understanding the context with particular attention to the limitations and possibilities available to the community, how the community came to decision, and the consequences of their choices.

Ministers who draw on wisdom paradigms seek moral guidance to address particular situations. Wisdom paradigms emphasize spiritual growth and maturity, not the moral minimum. They keep the complexity and particularity of the situation before the community and discourage a simple

---

28. Granted, every Christian symbol could be used to interpret and illuminate a given situation, but for the project I want students to be intentional about selecting and interpreting a symbol and explaining why this symbol fits the situation in a particularly helpful way.

one-size-fits-all solution. Seminar students who have used wisdom para-digms ask questions such as: Can the ascetical tradition be a resource for women today in light of eating disorders? Should Benedictine monasteries practice daily Eucharist?

Ministers can misuse the paradigm approach to theology. It can be-come subjective and individualistic and lack communal engagement. Per-sons can adopt their own norms and reject guidance from the ecclesial tra-dition. Ministers who use paradigm models must be well-versed in communal models of discernment, prayer, and spiritual guidance.

For theology to become "second nature" for ministers they need to "practice" drawing upon the doctrines, narratives, symbols, and para-digms that constitute the Christian tradition. As they become more adept and confident, they also become more creative and imaginative. But such facility takes time and practice.

Part Three: Response. The project's final part requires students to pro-pose an informed, constructive response that includes a concrete plan that helps their audience (usually ministers and members of a particular com-munity) understand the nature of the situation, what needs to change, why it needs to change, and how the situation might be changed. This requires strategic thinking in the form of practical reasoning. Students are asked to engage the following questions:

- What responses to the situation are currently employed? What are the strengths and weaknesses of these approaches?
- What is a more adequate response? Why?
- What change needs to happen for a more adequate response? What do people involved in the situation need to do? What must ministers do in the situation? What systems must change?
- How might this response be carried out by the community that faces the situation?
- What is a concrete plan with realistic goals for the response?
- What is the theological rationale for the response? Why should people address this situation in this way?

These questions serve as a template for students as they construct a re-sponse to the situation and an argument for why the community and min-isters should consider what the student proposes. While there is no prede-termined way in which the student must spell out the response, there are clearly examples of excellent and poor attempts. For me, this is the crux of the assignment. If students understand and demonstrate creative and constructive thinking about what to do, they have acquired a certain competence; they will acquire more when they engage in the ministry and are able to learn from what they are doing. For now, the seminar is providing an environment for thinking, planning, and defining. Excellent responses combine a fair and thorough understanding of what is currently happening with a formulation of a response that is based on a thoughtful critique and is appropriate to the particular community in its time and place. Further, excellent responses draw the theological material through and demonstrate the theological fiber that connects the practice to the tradition and community.

Annette described ways in which parish ministers can address physical, mental, social, ecclesial, and personal isolation through concrete steps and practices. She drew considerably from ministry and social service resources, but she was also able to give this material theological meaning and interpretation. She designed a training program for parish members who could visit patients with dementia, especially in the early stages. The program draws upon the teachings, narratives, and symbols she articulated in the project, and the skills necessary to accompany those with dementia — the full embodiment of communion.

Toward the end of the semester students deliver public presentations, which distill the main findings of their projects.[29] The oral presentation is meant to be "performative" in what I call "ministerial rhetoric." It is not meant to be the reading of a scholarly paper or the summation of findings. In the presentation, students are challenged to speak from their role and authority as minister in the local community. Because the audience is largely made up of fellow students, area ministers, and faculty, most presentations aim to convince ministers of the importance of gaining insight and skill into a given situation. This initial foray into ministerial rhetoric is essential as they move out into communities to convince church members of the gospel's demands.

In listening to and engaging students in their presentations, we wit-

29. Each student speaks for 45 minutes, which includes 15 minutes for questions and answers. The audience completes an evaluation of the presentation on the style, content, and analysis of the student. Thanks to the helpful analysis of four key pedagogies in Foster et al., *Educating Clergy*, I see the written project as primarily an exercise in interpretation and contextualization, and the oral presentation as an exercise in formation and performance.

ness all three aspects of integration: the knowledge they have gained from study; the wisdom and imagination they bring to bear in the theological interpretation; their rhetorical capacity to speak clearly, persuasively, and informatively; and the degree to which they portray a compelling strategy for how we might consider addressing such a situation in ministry. But the presentation also draws out each student's identity and vocational issues as well as emotional and spiritual maturity. The presentation "exposes" the student in many ways, but perhaps mostly in terms of identity and vocation. It is an important formative moment when students claim their voices, authority, and knowledge of an issue. To do so in the presence of classmates, teachers, family, friends, and strangers is both challenging and exhilarating. I recently spoke with a former student who told me she used what she learned from the seminar presentation in preparing for a presentation to the parish council. She was able to put forth a persuasive theological and practical argument in a way that invited dialogue and learning.

Teaching toward Integration

Integration is an auspicious goal for theological educators. We know the fully integrated student-minister, the person with full knowledge, complete competence in all ministerial skills, and a fully mature vocational identity is beyond our reach; it is only anticipated in seminary but discovered and refined in the practice of ministry. And yet, courses such as this seminar serve as a benchmark, a time in the educational process to attend intentionally to how the intellectual, ministerial, and vocational capacities of a student are merging into a whole.[30] Integration as a benchmark can be frustrating for theological educators, according to Vic Klimoski, if faculty have one set of measures by which all students must be judged. Clearly students by the third year of the M.Div. program are at different places in their capacities to execute an integrative exercise, and some do not do it nearly well enough.

Of course the frustration becomes most apparent when it is public. There have been a few times when a student presents a project to the faculty and student body and I know that the project is weak — the level of

---

30. See Victor J. Klimoski, "Seeing Things Whole: A Reflection on Integration," in *Educating Leaders for Ministry: Issues and Responses* (Collegeville, Minn.: Liturgical Press, 2005), pp. 49-74. Klimoski discusses integration as benchmark, process, and educational strategy.

analysis and insight is slim and the response is at best general and self-evident. It is a moment of public embarrassment and doubt for all. Often the students presenting these projects know they have done an inadequate job, as they can judge their work against that of their classmates; I am embarrassed that I have not been able to guide the student in a more productive way; and there is doubt written on my colleagues' faces about whether the seminar is worthwhile if this is all students can produce. In many ways, students' failure is an indictment of us all: the student, the instructor, other faculty members, and the curriculum. But rarely do faculty members come away from this encounter asking, "What could we be doing to help students be better prepared for the integration project, the benchmark of our curriculum, and for the ministry they are soon to embark upon?"

This question provides a good place to begin faculty discussion about how integration can be an intentional learning process that takes account of different levels of integrative capacity on the part of students in the same course.[31] Faculty could discern the best ways of challenging students to move at a developmentally appropriate pace. Integration then becomes an educational strategy that faculty employ by engaging students intentionally in how what they are learning about Scripture, theology, history, and ministry can be brought to bear in concrete particular instances of practice in Christian life.

I was initially frustrated the first few times I taught the seminar when I realized that integration was "happening for the first time" for many students.[32] The assignment and way of practical theological thinking I was encouraging were mostly foreign to students. I had to assess what I was teaching in the introductory course that could begin the journey toward the integration project at the conclusion of the degree. I began making the method of practical theological thinking more central and explicit. But the additional challenge is creating a culture of integration where all faculty members are intentional about how their teaching encourages a heightened sense of practical theological thinking in ministry, even though they may not address such issues directly. It entails creating movement back

31. Klimoski suggests that theological school faculty utilize a developmental perspective on understanding developed by Grant Wiggins and Jay McTigue. See Klimoski, "Seeing Things Whole," pp. 65-73.

32. Klimoski reports a similar experience by a theological educator. See "Seeing Things Whole," p. 54.

and forth between the general and the particular, the historical and the present, the systematic and ethical to the concrete and local.[33]

When theological educators strive to make integration a goal, a process, and a strategy in theological education, we are essentially seeking to form and educate a person with integrity. In such an integrated student, we are seeking to identify a kind of unity and a proper balance between intellect, practice, and identity because we are convinced that this three-part composite is fundamental to good ministry. And that should be our ultimate criterion: what is the integrity at the heart of good ministry toward which we aim?

My sense is that integration in ministry is the minister's capacity to discern, evaluate, and judge situations in light of the community's beliefs and practices with the aim of nurturing ever deeper and more faithful forms of Christian discipleship. And in order to become wise practitioners in the course of the day-to-day realities of ministry, ministers must develop dispositions for continued learning and reflection on Scripture, history, and theology; for honing their descriptive, interpretative, and rhetorical skills; and for strengthening their faith as lived out through their calling to ministry.

33. See Cahalan and Nieman, "Mapping Practical Theology," in this volume.

Teaching Worship as a Christian Practice

John Witvliet teaches in both a college and a seminary and also directs a program that hosts conferences and workshops for ministers, musicians, lay leaders, and others who lead Christian assemblies in worship. Thus his teaching takes place in a wide range of settings and serves many kinds of students. Witvliet clearly enjoys this diversity — perhaps because virtually all of these learners are Christians who worship God and who are therefore already engaged, and likely to be engaged for the rest of their lives, in the very practice he teaches. He offers them all, he writes in this chapter, "a pedagogy of and for deep participation."

Rather than describing one or two actual courses, Witvliet sets forth in this chapter an approach to teaching worship that could be used in many different courses and settings. The radical moves that shape this approach are his understanding of worship as a Christian practice that participates in a life-giving way of life in and for the world and his commitment to teach this practice in ways that honor its depth, diversity, and ethos. This reframing provides a basis for integrating material from other disciplines while always keeping the practical needs of particular congregations for truthful, vital, and beautiful worship in the foreground of concern. Witvliet shows, for example, how rigorous engagement with historical or sociological research on worship can be arranged and queried not first of all to display and advance the academic field of liturgical studies but rather to expand and illumine students' capacities and comprehension as worshipers and leaders of worship. The chapter includes many creative pedagogical proposals for pursuing this purpose.

John Witvliet is Director of the Calvin Institute of Christian Worship and Associate Professor of Worship, Theology, and Music at Calvin College and Calvin Theological Seminary.

5. Teaching Worship as a Christian Practice

John D. Witvliet

Walk into a worship service in any given congregation on any given Sunday morning, and you will encounter a world that even a lifetime of study cannot fully comprehend. Cultural anthropologists have methods to assess some of this complexity: the interplay of symbols, texts, gestures, rites, power relations, gender, ethnicity, tradition, and culture. Perceptive psychologists and social workers perceive other dimensions of the gathering: the interplay of anxiety, hope, ambition, fear, shame, and gratitude that powerfully shapes how both entire communities and individual participants will experience it. Artists of various kinds sense still other layers of significance: the way in which fabrics, melodies, rhythms, metaphors, and architecture reflect beauty, evoke emotion, and convey convictions. Theologians offer yet another perspective, drawing on biblical narratives and several centuries of theological reflection to hone language for describing the ways in which God's Spirit works through all of this to comfort, challenge, disturb, or nourish the faith of those gathered. The complexity of it all resists complete understanding.

Yet in any given congregation in any given week, some people walk into this assembly not merely with the task of understanding it, but with the holy challenge to give shape to what happens there. These are the people — the preachers, musicians, artists, pastors, deacons, and others — who will form the language, select the texts, choose the music, offer the gestures, and prepare the space, all to make possible this central activity in a congregation's life. Given all of the event's complexity, what could ever prepare them adequately for such a task?

This essay arises out of profound awareness of how difficult this question is, especially for those who teach courses in worship, liturgy, church music, or liturgical arts in a formal academic context.[1] It builds on a hunch that recent discussions about the deep texture of Christian practices offer a promising foundation for effective pedagogy for courses on Christian worship, and thus it attempts to answer the simple question, How would the teaching of Christian worship change if it were more firmly rooted in a theologically robust understanding of Christian practice?[2] That is, if vital Christianity is truly about participating in practices that comprise a life-giving way of life in and for the world,[3] then how should teachers of worship present and probe Christian worship?

I will attempt a provisional answer to these questions by suggesting a series of innovations or adjustments in pedagogy, some of which are already taking place in some settings, others of which are more theoretical possibilities at this point. My aim is to describe an approach that presses beyond teaching mere technique or honing objective analysis of worship to an approach that forms students in the constellation of knowledge, wisdom, skills, and capacities needed for faithful practice. I will do so by addressing the overarching goals, starting points, pedagogical methods, and classroom ethos for teaching.

Overarching Goals

Training for Participation

First, grounding the teaching of worship in a robust understanding of Christian practices would transform courses from being mere introductions to the discipline of liturgical studies into being a kind of training camp for "full, conscious, active participation" in worship as part of faithful Christian communal life. The goal is not simply to think about wor-

---

1. In addition to the many helpful comments of participants in the Seminar on Practical Theology and Christian Ministry, I am grateful to participants in the Calvin College faculty seminar "How to Teach Worship in Congregations and Schools" (Summer 2005) that helped shape many of the thoughts summarized in this paper, as well for the work of my Calvin faculty colleagues David Smith and Claudia Beversluis on pedagogy.

2. This essay builds on prior work on this theme in my book *Worship Seeking Understanding: Insights into Christian Practice* (Grand Rapids: Baker Academic, 2003).

3. This claim is at the heart of the fourth conversation that informs the present volume. See Dorothy Bass and Craig Dykstra's introduction, pp. 12-13.

ship, but to practice it more profoundly. Over the past several years, many worship courses have functioned as a kind of introduction to liturgical studies, much like a liberal arts college might offer Introduction to Sociology. In Introduction to Sociology, the learner is challenged to come to terms with the vocabulary, methods, and key concepts in the discipline, but is not usually trained to "do sociology."

Yet while introducing students to the vocabulary, methods, and key concepts in the practice of worship is a worthy goal, it is not only possible but also critically important to aspire to something more. As Sharon Daloz Parks notes in her study of leadership training, "It is one thing to teach knowledge in the field, and it is quite another to prepare people to exercise judgment and skill needed to bring that knowledge into the intricate system of relationships that constitute the dynamic world of practice."[4] A baseball coach is not interested primarily in producing effective baseball journalists or statisticians, but baseball players. A course in master gardening is designed to prepare students to actually garden. Likewise, a worship professor (at all but the Ph.D. level of instruction) is not primarily interested in producing worship professors or liturgical critics but rather worshipers (and, in the case of seminary education, also presiders or worship leaders) who participate in worship more fully, actively, and consciously as part of a vital, faithful Christian life. Said another way, worship courses can

---

4. Sharon Daloz Parks, *Leadership Can Be Taught: A Bold Approach for a Complex World* (Boston: Harvard Business School Press, 2005), p. 5. In addition to displacing the "introduction to the discipline" approach to teaching, this overarching purpose also contrasts with some other typical pedagogical goals. Teaching worship from a practices point of view would not primarily be designed to offer training in liturgical techniques: we want to do something more than teach how to prepare ashes for an Ash Wednesday service or how to choose songs in the right key. Nor are we training contestants for a game of liturgical *Jeopardy!* We need to do more (though not less) than impart a body of facts. Nor are most of us training academic liturgical historians or social scientists. The point of teaching the fourth-century Eucharistic Liturgy of St. James, for example, is not so that students can date the document. The point is that students can better understand the historical shape of Lord's Supper celebrations, perceive the implicit meaning of their form, and sense what is required to bring contemporary forms to life in their congregations. Similarly, the point of reading ethnographic accounts of congregations or analyzing survey data is not merely to make students experts at ethnography or connoisseurs of social research. The point is to give them both deep insight into the complex dynamics of the practice of worship and tools through which to better understand and value the people with whom they worship, and perhaps also those with whom they are called to serve as worship leaders.

aspire to more than "exploring" Christian discipleship in the area of worship. They can aspire to actually being a part of that discipleship.[5]

This move toward teaching for participation is significant enough that it warrants attention as we describe, outline, and present our courses. The overarching goal of deep participation in worship is not something I want students to simply discover along the way. Given the temptations I face to pull back the teaching of liturgy into the comfortable environs of the discipline that I know better than my students do, I want them to hold me accountable to focus attention on deeper goals, goals that place me alongside them as a fellow-worshiper.[6]

But this change of orientation involves far more than what appears on the course syllabus. It becomes the fundamental orientation for every class lecture and discussion. For example, it is customary for discussions of eucharistic theology to outline various examples of theologies of transubstantiation, consubstantiation, and "non-substantiation." Practice-oriented discussions might move beyond this to discern what implicit understandings of divine presence and absence are at work in congregations and what biblical and liturgical texts, metaphors, and gestures might help those communities live more deeply into the gospel mystery of the Lord's Supper. In the same way, discussions about baptism would continue to rehearse the standard arguments for and against infant baptism, unpack

5. For other moves in this direction, see L. Gregory Jones, "Beliefs, Desires, Practices, and the Ends of Theological Education," in *Practicing Theology: Beliefs and Practices in Christian Life,* ed. Miroslav Volf and Dorothy C. Bass (Grand Rapids: Eerdmans, 2002), pp. 185-205. The obvious danger here, readily apparent to most academics who read this, is that our students will think of such a course as merely a devotional exercise. The easiest ways to remedy that are by developing challenging and compelling assignments, asking probing questions about historical and cross-cultural examples, and requiring significant engagement with local worshiping communities. Overcoming the notion that devotional vitality and rigorous learning live in opposition is best accomplished by vigorously promoting both at the same time. This is a perennial theme in Christian experience and is found even in places where it is least expected. For evidence of a strong emphasis on heart knowledge in the context of scholastic precision, see Richard A. Muller, "The Era of Protestant Orthodoxy," in *Theological Education in the Evangelical Tradition,* ed. D. G. Hart and R. Albert Mohler Jr. (Grand Rapids: Baker Books, 1996), pp. 103-28.

6. For more on mutual accountability for the purposes of learning as spiritual formation, see Karen Marie Yust and E. Byron Anderson, *Taught by God: Teaching and Spiritual Formation* (St. Louis: Chalice Press, 2006), and Michael Battle, "Teaching and Learning as Ceaseless Prayer," in *The Scope of Our Art: The Vocation of the Theological Teacher,* ed. L. Gregory Jones and Stephanie Paulsell (Grand Rapids: Eerdmans, 2002).

complementary biblical metaphors for baptism, and review the basic out-
lines of baptismal liturgies. But they would also include discussions about
how congregations (as well as the students in our courses) could more
deeply claim and celebrate their own baptismal identity. Almost inevitably, this participation-oriented approach means that there will be class
time for exploring fewer themes. But the practice-oriented teacher will
not let a topic go without exploring how it might strengthen present-day
Christian living.

Training Collaborators

Second, a practices point of view calls for worship courses that highlight
the communal dimension of worship. Worship is a first-person-plural activity. Participants are called to be aware not only of God's presence, but of
each other, and of the world. Effective collaborative leadership needs to aspire to be mindful of the entire congregation that is gathered and all of
those that we hope might join the congregation, as well as all of those who
will never join the congregation. Courses on worship should bring this
widening circle of awareness into the classroom. They should foster a vivid
appreciation for all the varieties of people who come to worship: introverts
and extroverts, visual learners and kinetic learners, rich and poor, young
and old, and people with any number of cognitive, emotional, or physical
disabilities. In a liberal arts college course on liturgy, students need to be
challenged to evaluate practices not merely on the basis of whether they
serve their own felt needs or preferences, but rather on how well they enable a community to practice hospitality. In seminaries and divinity
schools, worship classes must form future presiders to imagine ways to encourage the participation of both children and the elderly, persons whose
participation in worship is challenged either by their career success or
their mental illness, persons who cling to the church as their only source of
community and those who resist the church because of the pain the
church has caused them. Some of this formation is possible through the
art of managing the worship classroom. Many classes are comprised of
students who themselves represent remarkable diversity in terms of piety,
temperament, and past experience. Creating a climate of hospitality for
this diverse pool of students is a beginning point for exploring how congregations might do the same. As shapers of community, worship faculty

need to practice the very kinds of skills and moves recommended by Peter Marty in his chapter in this volume.

For worship courses at seminaries and divinity schools, this communal orientation calls for training leaders who will be "catalysts for collaborative worship ministry" rather than "solo pilot leaders." In most congregations, worship is led by multiple leaders. Even the simplest services often involve a presiding pastor and a musician. Yet some books and courses on worship assume that their audience is a solo pilot, lone-ranger leader. They offer advice about what liturgical form to use, where to sit or stand, what to say and how to say it — everything necessary for a command performance as liturgical presider. What we need instead are books with titles like *Planning Worship Together*[7] that encourage the use of complementary gifts of multiple participants in the process of preparing for and evaluating worship.

One of the most sobering consultations I have attended recently has been with church staff members, mostly unordained, who work alongside clergy. Their guess was that most seminary courses teach pastors to do the work of ministry by themselves, with little attention given to how to collaborate with and empower others. They also guessed that most seminary courses teach subject area content to students without probing how those same students might themselves teach that content to others. Both points hit home powerfully. Since then, I've experimented with adding a subtitle to the Introduction to Christian Worship I help to teach: "Preparing for Collaborative Worship Ministry." Our goal is to tackle each class period's content in ways that explore how the material could best play out in the context of collaborative ministry. This is actually quite a freeing approach. I do not need to convert pastors-to-be into experts in liturgical music or architecture in one course. What I do need to do is offer a way of conceptualizing, teaching, planning, and evaluating worship that can be done in collaboration with others who do have those gifts. At the end of a major worship planning assignment in my introductory worship course, I frequently ask students to evaluate their own strengths and weaknesses in planning. Many students admit, for ex-

7. See Howard Vanderwell and Norma de Waal Malefyt, *Designing Worship Together* (Herndon, Va.: Alban Institute, 2004); Paul Westermeyer, *The Church Musician*, rev. ed. (Minneapolis: Augsburg Fortress, 1997), chapter 8; C. Randall Bradley, *From Postlude to Prelude: Music Ministry's Other Six Days* (St. Louis: Morning Star, 2004), chapters 4-5.

ample, that "choosing a balanced diet of congregational songs was much harder than I thought it would be." I have been gratified that some of them add, "I'll need to seek help with that among musicians in the communities I will one day serve."

A second classroom move with potential to increase communal awareness is that of focusing not only on a given subject, but also on how best to teach that subject in congregations. For example, rather than a lecture on "what students need to know about a Trinitarian theology of worship," imagine a class focused on "how students might effectively teach a Trinitarian theology of worship in congregations." The basic themes of each lecture would be similar, but the focus of discussions changes. Asking students "How would you teach this to third graders in your church?" or "How would you raise this idea in the middle of a worship committee meeting?" or "In what way might you draw on this material in a visit with someone in a nursing home or prison?" or even "What are the strengths and weaknesses in the way I am teaching this material right now?" helps them not only to clarify the relevant concepts in their own minds, but also challenges them to think pedagogically. It brings the people they do or will serve into our awareness in the classroom. It both teaches a practice, and teaches the *teaching* of a practice, a kind of meta-discourse that promises to equip students to keep the momentum of learning going long after a particular course is complete. To use our athletic analogy, our courses are not only training baseball players, but also baseball coaches. We are training "player-coaches" in collaborative worship ministry — an especially crucial move in an era of present or impending clergy shortages, an era in which congregations must equip lay leaders more intentionally.

A Well-Balanced Communal Life

Third, from a holistic, practices point of view, worship courses should be taught with a clear sense of how worship fits into a well-balanced Christian communal life. In college courses, it is tempting for us to teach a discipline or topic by abstracting it out of a well-balanced life. In seminaries and divinity schools, it is tempting for those of us who teach practical theology courses in pastoral care, education, preaching, missions, and worship to suggest that faithful pastors must spend at least 35 hours a week on tasks related to *each* of our own individual specialties. Our enthusiasm for our subjects gets the best of us, and we create expectations for exemplary ministry that are impossible to live up to.[8]

The solution to this dilemma is not to scale back enthusiasm for our particular subjects. The solution comes from learning to perceive how each area of ministry and how each Christian practice is intertwined with the others. The scope of inquiry — even in an academic sub-discipline like liturgy or worship — is nothing less than "a Christian way of life." Rather than focusing on worship in isolation, the focus instead is on worship-in-relation-with-other-practices. Whether worship is conceived as one practice alongside of all these, or as the "mother of all practices" in which all of those other practices are grounded, there is more to the Christian life than liturgy. Indeed, as far back as in ancient Israel, one of the greatest virtues of faithful covenantal life before God was having a proper calibration or integrity between worship and the rest of life. The prophetic critique of Israel's worship did not call for liturgy to be abolished, but for integrity between worship and life to be restored.[9]

Classes also need to rehearse the connecting points between liturgy and life. We need to teach worship aware of how it embodies and influences every other Christian practice — especially if, in the words of Amy Plantinga Pauw, "our communal settings of proclamation, sacraments, and confession frame our hopes for closing the gap between beliefs and practices."[10] We need to teach the Lord's Supper as a corollary of what happens in our soup kitchens. We need to teach that communal liturgical acts of praise and confession are rightly complemented by private doxological and penitential moments all week long. When we begin to make these connections, we find ourselves connecting with and drawing from every other discipline in the seminary curriculum. Imagine, for example, a discussion

8. Especially welcome are books that cross over from one sub-discipline into others. For books that cross over between liturgy and other practical theology disciplines, see, for example, Debra Dean Murphy, *Teaching that Transforms: Worship as the Heart of Christian Education* (Grand Rapids: Brazos, 2004); William Willimon, *Worship as Pastoral Care* (Nashville: Abingdon, 1979); William Cavanaugh, *Theopolitical Imagination: Christian Practices of Space and Time* (London: T & T Clark, 2002); David M. Greenhaw and Ronald J. Allen, *Preaching in the Context of Worship* (St. Louis: Chalice Press, 2000).

9. Walter Brueggemann, *Israel's Praise: Doxology Against Idolatry and Ideology* (Philadelphia: Fortress Press, 1988).

10. Amy Plantinga Pauw, "Attending to the Gaps between Beliefs and Practices," in Volf and Bass, *Practicing Theology,* p. 48.

in a liturgy course on how to prepare worship for a remembrance of the terror attacks of September 11, 2001, or a major earthquake or tsunami. That discussion involves challenges for church education, pastoral care, social justice, mission, and witness, as well as evoking key topics in constructive or systematic theology and biblical studies. In this discussion, a worship course doesn't pull students away from the other disciplines, but motivates deeper engagement with each of them.

In sum, the aims and purposes of teaching worship are to promote vital participation within worshiping communities and collaborative models for leading communities — each in the context of a well-balanced communal life.

Starting Points

These are high aims, indeed. Achieving them is made more complex by all the attitudes, convictions, and preferences that walk into the room on the first day of class. The teaching of worship always happens mid-stream, within traditions that embody complex historical trajectories and to students who are already engaging, with varying levels of commitment, in worship practices. Respecting the complexity of these starting points is essential for effective teaching.

Liturgical History

Most of us implicitly sense that we teach in the midst of a long stream of worship practices. For Roman Catholics, the Mass and Daily Office are givens. For Protestants, certain canons of congregational song — whether Watts and Wesley or Maranatha and Vineyard — form the context in which all class references to music will be judged. We never start teaching from scratch. Our teaching functions as commentary on existing and evolving practices, even as we participate in them.

This changes not only the content of our teaching, but also its ethos. Every time we witness the appointment of a new U.S. Supreme Court Justice we hear (through the deafening din of political rhetoric) a rhetoric of deep respect for the role of the courts and for the law itself. Some of that solemnity and humility rightly attaches to the study of worship — how-

125

ever prophetic we might want to be about its reform. We best begin not with the hubris that assumes that we can figure it all out on our own, but rather with a profound sense of privilege for joining a centuries-old, global conversation.

This happens in the classroom by making sure that courses cultivate some historical depth perception. Learning the origins and development of a practice, often by drawing on works in both social and intellectual history, frequently leads to new appreciation for traditional practices, as well as the best platform from which to constructively criticize prior practice.[11] Learning, for example, the profound piety that led to the adoption of the Isaiah 6 Sanctus hymn as a regular element in Christian eucharistic prayers, the pneumatology behind the practice of a prayer for illumination, the complex social history that gave some United States congregations worship spaces that look like theaters, the social dynamics that fueled the outburst of Methodist camp meetings or Pentecostal revivals, or the life stories of a popular contemporary song writer all have the potential to lead to new appreciation for existing practices.[12] Frequent references to history, even when a course is not an historical survey, at least begin to cultivate this kind of historical depth perception.[13]

11. See Susan J. White, *A History of Women in Christian Worship* (Cleveland: Pilgrim Press, 2003); Martin Stringer, *A Sociological History of Christian* Worship (Cambridge: Cambridge University Press, 2005); Frank Senn, *The People's Work: A Social History of the Liturgy* (Minneapolis: Fortress Press, 2006); Tex Sample, *White Soul: Country Music, the Church, and Working Americans* (Nashville: Abingdon, 1996); for a sample history-oriented academic monograph, see Howard Dorgan, *Giving Glory to God in Appalachia: Worship Practices of Six Baptist Subdenominations* (Knoxville: University of Tennessee Press, 1987).

12. For each of the examples in this sentence, see Bryan Spinks, *The Sanctus in the Eucharistic Prayer* (Cambridge: Cambridge University Press, 1991); Geoffrey Wainwright, *Doxology: The Praise of God in Worship, Doctrine, and Life* (Oxford: Oxford University Press, 1980); Jean Kilde, *When Church Became Theatre: The Transformation of Evangelical Architecture and Worship in Nineteenth-Century America* (Oxford: Oxford University Press, 2002); Lester Ruth, *A Little Heaven Below: Worship at Early Methodist Quarterly Meetings* (Nashville: Kingswood Books, 2000); Grant Wacker, *Heaven Below: Early Pentecostals and American Culture* (Cambridge, Mass.: Harvard University Press, 2001); Matt Redman, *The Unquenchable Worshiper* (Ventura, Calif.: Regal Books, 2001), pp. 27-28, *Blessed Be Your Name: Worshipping God on the Road Marked with Suffering* (Ventura, Calif.: Regal Books, 2005), and *Inside Out Worship: Insights for Passionate and Purposeful Worship* (Ventura, Calif.: Regal Books, 2005); and Michael Card, *A Sacred Sorrow: Reaching Out to God with the Lost Language of Lament* (Colorado Springs: NavPress, 2005).

13. In fact, drawing on history in a course not structured as a historical survey may be

Prior Personal Formation

What is true for traditions more broadly is also true of individuals. Most students come from a stream of worship practices that have formed them, even though for some the stream may not be long.[14] Students also come to class with multi-textured experiences outside of worship that have formed them to respond to certain elements of worship — verbal or visual rhetoric, music styles, use or non-use of electronic projection media — in very different ways. This set of personal experiences is likely to be far more influential than any worship class in shaping their attitudes and habits of leadership. Some interesting recent studies have suggested that how people worshiped when they first became a committed believer is most significant for shaping their views of how worship should go.[15] Only rarely do worship courses make students appreciate and value different music, art, or liturgical forms — despite the fact that many of us who teach worship secretly or not-so-secretly hope it will.

This suggests some illuminating comparisons with other educational ventures. Teaching worship is unlike the classroom training of prospective surgeons, where only rarely will students have been present at surgery in a conscious state prior to the class. It is more like training a golfer or singer who has already developed some persistent muscular habits, however good or bad. The effective golf coach or singing instructor must begin by making their students aware of their acquired habits, and then work to reshape those habits by carefully chosen drills. Failing to acknowledge students' prior habits almost always sets up a golf instructor or singing instructor for failure. The same is true for teachers of worship.

It can be tempting for those of us who teach worship to secretly think that most of what students have already experienced in worship is irre-

---

an even better model for how historical awareness functions inside of vital Christian life and ministry. For more on this broad theme, see Rowan Williams, *Why Study the Past? The Quest for the Historical Church* (Grand Rapids: Eerdmans, 2005).

14. See, for example, E. Byron Anderson, *Worship and Christian Identity: Practicing Ourselves* (Collegeville, Minn.: Liturgical Press, 2003), and Don E. Saliers, "Liturgy Teaching Us to Pray: Christian Liturgy and Grateful Lives of Prayer," in *Liturgy and Spirituality in Context: Perspectives on Prayer and Culture,* ed. Eleanor Bernstein, C.S.J. (Collegeville, Minn.: Liturgical Press, 1990).

15. See Todd E. Johnson, "Disconnected Rituals," in *The Conviction of Things Not Seen: Worship and Ministry in the 21st Century* (Grand Rapids: Brazos, 2002), pp. 53-66.

deemably deficient. We then treat their prior experiences as an unfortunate liability in the classroom. However, if the classroom can help students better understand their own prior experiences and train them to ask certain questions about future experiences, then that whole stream of experience, past and future, becomes a key instructional resource to them — an asset rather than a liability.[16] Thus, effective courses might begin by helping students learn to perceive their prior participation at a deeper level. Asking students to name both "their favorite worship song" and "the song that has most nourished their faith" — and then to attend to the difference between these two questions — can help them reframe their working categories of music. Asking students both "What is your favorite style of worship?" and "What moments in worship have truly transformed your outlook on the Christian life?" begins to detach mere stylistic preferences from deeper questions of formation, but in ways that still deeply honor their own prior experiences. These deeper questions can become some of the best long-term outcomes of a course, offering students a pastorally constructive way to approach any future ministry setting.

Another exercise I have found helpful is a first-day exercise in, of all things, drawing. I simply ask students to depict in some form how they "picture" worship, using any visual language they want (stick figures, cartoon characters, abstract symbols, etc.).[17] I begin by asking them to picture themselves at worship. Usually a cartoonish stick figure appears, in some kind of liturgical posture. Then I ask them to add to their drawing anyone or anything else they are aware of in worship, including some representation of the environment in which they worship. Finally, I ask them to find an appropriate way to convey how they imagine God to factor into this (the cautious rhetoric here betrays a Calvinist sensibility about the second commandment). The results are often dramatic and illuminating. Some pictures are indisputably individualistic. Some students build in cross-cultural awareness. Some find a way to suggest awareness of past events

16. Based on the personal narratives of many pastors, we sense that it is highly unlikely that one course in the middle of a theological curriculum will by itself cement their call to ministry and definitively form their pastoral imagination. But a course in combination with weeks or months of self-aware practices as a member of a worshiping community certainly can.

17. This is one way of getting at what Howard Stone and James Duke refer to as "embedded theology." See Howard Stone and James Duke, *How to Think Theologically* (Minneapolis: Fortress Press, 1996), pp. 13-16.

and future hopes in their understanding, while others leave their depictions entirely in the present tense. Many renderings, significantly, are unmistakably deistic, with no possibility of divine-human interaction in worship. (I often feel as if I have dramatic visual confirmation of Christian Smith's claim that the operative theology of our youth culture is that of "moralistic therapeutic deism.")[18] In every case, this exercise begins a discussion about how all of us carry with us into worship certain ways of perceiving the world (and God) in time and space, sometimes in ways that cohere beautifully with the gospel, but sometimes not.

A way to sum up this point is to say that our teaching is, in part, mystagogical. Wise patristic pastors knew that an abstract sacramental theology would mean little to new Christians. One had to experience Eucharist to understand it. After experiencing it, intentional theological reflection offered a source of deeper insight and participation. This ancient post-experience, mystagogical approach to formation provides a helpful model for practice-oriented teaching today.[19]

Pedagogical Approaches or Methods

The Tangible and the Quotidian

In addition to these specific exercises, a practices orientation also affects the basic methods or pedagogical approaches we use throughout our courses. Most basically, a practices approach calls for worship classes that attend to concrete, observable actions in both extraordinary and ordinary places. Practices are things people do (even if some actions, like contemplation, are quiet and seemingly passive). Teaching worship as a practice requires that students learn certain *knowledge* (e.g., basic liturgical liter-

18. Christian Smith and Melinda Lundquist Denton, *Soul Searching: The Religious and Spiritual Lives of American Teenagers* (New York: Oxford University Press, 2005).

19. See Craig Satterlee, *Ambrose of Milan's Method of Mystagogical Preaching* (Collegeville, Minn.: Liturgical Press, 2002). This historical example is also the central inspiration behind the recovery of the ancient catechumenate in a variety of Christian traditions today. See L. Gregory Jones, "Baptism — A Dramatic Journey Into God's Dazzling Light: Baptismal Catechesis and the Shaping of Practical Christian Wisdom," in James J. Buckley and David S. Yeago, *Knowing the Triune God: The Work of the Spirit in the Practices of the Church* (Grand Rapids: Eerdmans, 2001), pp. 147-78.

acy), certain *competencies* (e.g., the skill of choosing musical repertoire for liturgical purposes), and certain *virtues* (e.g., pastoral discernment, humility), but it also demands that students see how that knowledge, competency, and virtue are carried out or enacted, how they are "performed." In this way, courses in worship are like courses in theater and music: they attend to "performances" that unfold through time.

This means, in part, that classes should not be limited merely to what people think about worship, how they think during worship, or whether they like what they are doing. The object of study is not merely ideas about worship or sociological surveys about worship practices. A significant amount of energy should be reserved for encountering actual practices: concrete examples of gestures, symbols, sermons, songs, images, and environments. Worship is a multi-sensory, multivalent subject matter. This is why worship faculty members might aspire to become their school's resident experts in multimedia presentations, offering photographs, video-clips, and sound recordings of actual worship services. Tangible sights, sounds, narratives, and gestures are the natural centerpiece for many class sessions.

One temptation in giving attention to actual "performances" of liturgical action is to give all our attention to the grandest examples we can find, such as liturgy at Westminster Abbey or Willow Creek, to pick outstanding examples from contrasting ends of the liturgical spectrum. Yet this feels a bit like playing a video of Kobe Bryant at a fifth-grade basketball camp: it's inspiring, but not representative or necessarily helpful. Part of the move toward concreteness must also be a move into the ordinary. Practices-oriented teaching revels in the quotidian. It welcomes home-made video recordings of baptism services alongside high-gloss, mass-marketed recordings of festival services in prominent congregations.

This is not to say that young basketball players should never watch Bryant videos or that worship students should never be taught to better understand the grand drama of a papal funeral or a megachurch Christmas celebration. In fact, seeing the human foibles in these idealized settings — for example, accounts of how worshipers in Calvin's Geneva sometimes didn't understand his preaching — can powerfully reinforce the tangible, quotidian, messy nature of ministry.[20] Overall, what we need

---

20. Robert Kingdon, *The Registers of the Consistory of Geneva at the Time of Calvin: Volume 1: 1542-1544* (Grand Rapids: Eerdmans, 2000).

is the constant juxtaposition of the grand and the ordinary, the rich and the poor, the grand-among-the-poor and the ordinary-among-the-rich that helps students see that what is at stake in *any* liturgical performance can be instructive as they think about their own local, contextualized life in community, as well as for how it reshapes our catholic imagination of the breadth of the body of Christ.[21]

Depth Perception

But looking at tangible and quotidian practices does not mean that the worship classroom needs to be pedestrian or prosaic. In contrast, each tangible, ordinary practice presents an opportunity for loving attention to layer upon layer of meaning. Take the Lord's Supper or Eucharist, for example. Practice-oriented teachers eager to discuss a question like, "What capacities does a congregation need to genuinely experience the rich range of biblical eucharistic metaphors?" might draw on recent work in quite a range of disciplines:

- Studies of how young children experience the Lord's Supper, as described in both ethnographic studies and constructive theological proposals;[22]
- Commentaries — both historical and contemporary — on the central biblical texts about the Lord's Supper;[23]
- Analysis of how confessional statements and ecumenical dialogues clarify common understanding within and across traditions, or how

21. Relatedly, practices-oriented teaching also revels in profound social and cultural awareness of the economic dimensions of liturgical practice. Practices-oriented liturgical professors are grateful for books like photojournalist Camilo José Vergara's *How the Other Half Worships* (New Brunswick: Rutgers University Press, 2005), which helps to rebalance our often gentrified Powerpoint presentations. See also Pete Ward, *Selling Worship: How What We Sing Has Changed the Church* (Carlisle: Paternoster, 2005).

22. Susan Ridgely Bales, *Children's Interpretations of First Communion* (Chapel Hill: University of North Carolina Press, 2005), and Joyce Ann Mercer, *Welcoming Children: A Practical Theology of Childhood* (St. Louis: Chalice Press, 2005).

23. Joachim Jeremias, *The Eucharistic Words of Jesus* (New York: Scribner, 1966), and Francis J. Moloney, *A Body Broken for a Broken People: Eucharist in the New Testament* (Peabody, Mass.: Hendriksen Publishers, 1997).

analytic philosophers clarify the metaphors and concepts commonly used to express eucharistic theology;[24]

- Explorations of how particular issues in congregational life (e.g, generational identity in immigrant congregations, or the leadership patterns in congregations with less than 50 members) change eucharistic practice;[25]
- Rhetorical reflections on what language strategies wise Christian writers use when communicating with general audiences of lay people and seekers,[26] as well as on how cinematic portrayals of eucharistic scenes reveal or conceal key themes;[27]
- Analyses of how visual and architectural gestures evoke, reinforce, or contradict central biblical eucharistic metaphors,[28] and of how the ritual patterns and musical gestures of particular congregations reveal patterns of participation;[29] and
- Discussions of how worshipers experience the difference between

24. Jerald L. Bauer, *Worship, Gottesdienst, Cultus Dei: What the Lutheran Confessions Say About Worship* (Saint Louis: Concordia Publishing House, 2006); Jeffrey Gros, Harding Meyer, and William G. Rusch, *Growth in Agreement II: Reports and Agreed Statements of Ecumenical Conversations on a World Level, 1982-1998* (Grand Rapids: Eerdmans, 2000).

25. See, for example, Karen J. Chai, "Competing for the Second Generation: English-Language Ministry at a Korean Protestant Church," in *Gatherings in Diaspora: Religious Communities and the New Immigration,* ed. R. Stephen Warner and Judith G. Wittner (Philadelphia: Temple University Press, 1998); Su Yon Pak, Unzu Lee, Jung Ha Kim, Myung Ji Cho, *Singing the Lord's Song in a New Land: Korean American Practices of Faith* (Louisville: Westminster/John Knox, 2005); Peter Bush and Christine O'Reilly, *Where 20 or 30 Are Gathered: Leading Worship in the Small Church* (Herndon, Va.: Alban Institute, 2006); and Anthony Robinson, *Transforming Congregational Culture* (Grand Rapids: Eerdmans, 2003), esp. chapter 4.

26. See Debra Rienstra, *So Much More: An Invitation to Christian Spirituality* (San Francisco: Jossey-Bass, 2005), or N. T. Wright, *Simply Christian: Why Christianity Makes Sense* (San Francisco: HarperOne, 2006).

27. Jann Cather Weaver, "Engaging Eucharistic Images in Film: Ecclesiological and Liturgical Meanings," in *Arts, Theology, and the Church,* ed. Kimberly Vrudny and Wilson Yates (Cleveland: Pilgrim Press, 2005), pp. 200-216.

28. Mark Torgerson, *Architecture of Immanence* (Grand Rapids: Eerdmans, 2007).

29. Timothy J. Nelson, *Every Time I Feel the Spirit: Religious Experience and Ritual in an African-American Church* (New York: New York University Press, 2005); Mary E. McGann, *A Precious Fountain: Music in the Worship of an African American Catholic Community* (Collegeville, Minn.: Liturgical Press, 2004); and Gerardo Marti, *A Mosaic of Believers: Diversity and Innovation in a Multiethnic Church* (Bloomington, Ind.: Indiana University Press, 2005).

public worship and private devotional practices,[30] how the prayer texts that accompany the Eucharist evolved over 2000 years, and what kind of process is best suited to their reform and adaptation.[31]

Thus, the libraries of practice-oriented liturgical theologians are fusion experiments that draw on research in a large range of disciplines: social, intellectual, and material history, sociology of religion, rhetoric, ritual theory, developmental and cognitive psychology, religious journalism and photojournalism, ethnography, aesthetics theory, art history, architecture, communication theory, and economics. Especially cherished are works by biblical scholars, theologians, and ecclesial historians — our faculty colleagues — that attend to some of this complexity and speak to the complex fusion of social, theological, and cultural factors in specific practices.[32]

The richness of all this material certainly creates the possibility that worship syllabi can be too sprawling and diffuse to be effective, that treatments of any of these sources will be superficial, and that faculty and students alike will feel the kind of despair described by psychologist Robert Kegan in his classic work *In Over Our Heads: The Mental Demands of Modern Life*.[33] The constant challenge for nearly every topic in a worship course is to find centering, guiding questions that match the complexity of the topic, adequately focus the discussion, and create curiosity in students

30. Peter C. Phan, *Directory on Popular Piety and the Liturgy: Principles and Guidelines: A Commentary* (Collegeville, Minn.: Liturgical Press, 2005).

31. Paul Bradshaw, *Eucharistic Origins* (Oxford: Oxford University Press, 2004); Enrico Mazza, *The Celebration of the Eucharist: The Origin of the Rite and the Development of Its Interpretation* (Collegeville, Minn.: Liturgical Press, 1999); and Ronald P. Byars, *Lift Your Hearts on High: Eucharistic Prayer in the Reformed Tradition* (Louisville: Westminster/John Knox Press, 2005).

32. In biblical studies, see the juxtaposition of Walter Brueggemann, *Israel's Praise*, and Brian J. Walsh and Sylvia C. Keesmaat, *Colossians Remixed: Subverting the Empire* (Downers Grove: InterVarsity Press, 2004), for addressing the problem of idolatry, one of the opposites of genuine worship. In theology, David F. Ford and Daniel W. Hardy, *Living in Praise: Worshiping and Knowing God* (Grand Rapids: Baker Academic, 2005), provides a good example, particularly when set in conversation with David F. Ford's *The Shape of Living: Spiritual Directions in Everyday Life* (Grand Rapids: Baker Books, 1997), and *Self and Salvation: Being Transformed* (Cambridge: Cambridge University Press, 1999). In historical studies, see, for example, the multivolume People's History of Christianity series published by Fortress Press.

33. Robert Kegan, *In Over Our Heads: The Mental Demands of Modern Life* (Cambridge, Mass.: Harvard University Press, 1994).

that motivates further learning. It is especially important for practical theology that these questions are theological. The point of this adventuresome multidisciplinary study, again, is not simply to produce arrogant liturgical critics, but rather to deepen appreciation for how both God's creating and redeeming work and the faithful Christian life are expressed in the complexities of ordinary liturgical assemblies. It is to form both worshipers and worship leaders to live each day "in over their heads" in terms of the richness of both human experience and divine grace.

Case Studies

One promising way to focus discussions is through the use of historical, cross-cultural, and local case studies. Case studies expand our awareness of the diversity of ministry practices, ground theoretical discussions in everyday life, help us perceive the complex interrelated dynamics involved in real life, and train new skills for perceiving what is at stake in any given situation. And they are much more manageable for class discussions than larger surveys of the disciplinary landscape. Analyzing a particular type of liturgical assembly in Calvin's Geneva is much more manageable than outlining the history of Reformation liturgical reforms. Studying Thomas Kane's videos of a contemporary Roman Catholic Mass in the Polynesian islands tangibly illustrates the effects of Vatican II reforms, in ways that efficiently but also accurately convey the complex history of recent Catholic liturgical reforms.[34] Asking students to reflect on the worship life of a particular nearby congregation connects classroom discussions with their participation in worship and begins to form habits of reflection.[35]

Case studies are especially useful for helping us see the whole context of a given situation. Take the practice of medicine for comparison. The practice of medicine is a richly textured set of actions that involves physical skill, detailed knowledge of anatomy and chemistry, business savvy for negotiating the market economics of medicine, and skills in human resource management. Every treatment protocol for a given disease involves

34. Thomas Kane, *The Dancing Church* (Paulist Press, 1997).
35. For methods for studying congregations and creating participant-observer exercises, see Nancy T. Ammerman et al., *Studying Congregations* (Nashville: Abingdon, 1998); and Michael Hawn, *One Bread, One Body: Exploring Cultural Diversity in Worship* (Herndon, Va.: Alban Institute, 2003).

a complex interrelation of each of these elements. Effective medical education must help students see the interplay of these variables. The same is true in other areas of education. What Bennett Reimer says of music education applies as well to a lot of theological education: we give far too little attention to how the parts fit into the whole.[36]

The goal of this case study work is much more than mere description. It is to develop a sympathetic, discerning understanding of what is at work beneath the surface. It is to cultivate, to use a phrase of Tom Frank, "an ethnographic disposition."[37] Conversations explore not only actions, but also motives, social and economic influences, and implicit theological convictions. That is, the point of this work is to train *perception,* to equip students with significant and instructive questions with which to habitually interrogate their own contemporary practice. In other words, we need to form in ourselves and our students a kind of pastoral *intuition,* not unlike the kind of intuition needed by effective counselors. Whether for medical doctors, clinical psychologists, or stock brokers, this kind of intuition or tacit knowledge is formed, as Robin Hogarth argues, by deepening our awareness, acquiring specific skills through a regular recurring set of questions we learn to pose, and then engaging in repetitive practice in multiple situations.[38]

Training perception has been explored in a particularly compelling way in Elliot Eisner's *The Educational Imagination.* Though Eisner is writing about promoting deeper perception of what happens in effective classrooms, his insights apply well to any complex, interactive human endeavor that focuses on matters of ultimate meaning and beauty. Eisner builds his perspective around the claim that "the paradigmatic use of qualitative inquiry is found in the arts" — especially the role of art critic. He values the use of quantitative methods but argues that by itself quantitative work is likely "to lead to work that has little significance for educational practice." Following Ernst Cassirer, Eisner calls for a "binocular vision through complementary forms of inquiry" which together offer a kind of "depth per-

---

36. Bennett Reimer, *A Philosophy of Music Education* (Englewood Cliffs, N.J.: Prentice-Hall, 1970), p. 230; see also Frank Burch Brown's work on "The Aesthetic Milieu," in *Religious Aesthetics: A Theological Study of Making and Meaning* (Princeton, N.J.: Princeton University Press, 1989).

37. Thomas Edward Frank, *The Soul of the Congregation: An Invitation to Congregational Reflection* (Nashville: Abingdon, 2000).

38. Robin M. Hogarth, *Educating Intuition* (Chicago: University of Chicago Press, 2001), p. 215.

ception" of a given reality, such as an effective classroom. Effective critics must themselves become connoisseurs of a given event, and then write in a way that invites those who are not yet connoisseurs to see deeply into the central significance of that event.[39]

Of all the kinds of historical and cross-cultural writing that are most helpful to the liturgical/practical theologian, the literature of art or music criticism presents an especially fascinating (and largely unexplored) model. My colleagues in history of art, for example, read widely in intellectual and social history, but in class they weave together the rich tapestry of details from that reading, all while trying to help students see deeply into a painting that is projected before them. And while they may comment on the chemistry of the paints used, the techniques the artist used to render the work, and the social context of the artist, they ultimately are interested in disclosing what is beautiful or prophetic about that artwork. They are interested in discussion of the artwork as an artwork. Likewise effective teaching of liturgy looks to draw on every available type of data in order to understand a given case and then to articulate what is especially pastorally significant and instructive in that case for faithful baptismal living. We teach, that is, in order to illuminate cruciform beauty in others and to foster deeper participation in it ourselves.

Connecting Liturgical Mechanics
and the Deep Meaning of Christian Worship

Fifth, in a practices perspective, worship courses would do much more to connect discussions about the mechanics of liturgy with its deep meaning and purpose — an integrating, synthetic move that is a key feature of pastoral intelligence.[40] In worship, theological convictions and community practices are inextricably intertwined. At their best, worship courses expose the connections between them and probe how to strengthen them. In part, this means that worship courses would become much more explicit about discussing God's being and character.

Part of the educational challenge is simply distinguishing different lev-

---

39. Elliot W. Eisner, *The Educational Imagination: On the Design and Implementation of School Programs* (New York: Macmillan, 1979), pp. 213, 217.

40. This intelligence is explored in Craig Dykstra's chapter in this volume.

els of liturgical participation and analysis. I am grateful for an instructive experience I had near the beginning of my work as a liturgical choral conductor, hearing comments of four worshipers after a service in which my choir had participated. The first, obviously either a veteran chorister or former drill sergeant, remarked: "That choir's procession was as precise and symmetrical as any I have seen." The second participant commented: "I loved the exuberant style of that choir." The third observed, as if making a new discovery: "I couldn't believe how each piece of music went so well with the Scripture readings that preceded it." The fourth, in a noticeably reflective tone, added: "My husband died six months ago, and tonight through your music, I finally have been able to pray." These comments each illustrate a different level of attention and analysis. The first addresses matters of *mechanics,* the second matters of *style,* the third, the *form* of worship; only the fourth evokes worship's deep *meaning and purpose.*[41]

In class, these straightforward categories provide a useful framework for analyzing prescribed practices in assigned readings and students' own liturgical experiences. They call attention to a primary goal in teaching from a practices point of view, which is to hone a kind of stereoscopic vision that is attentive both to concrete liturgical procedures and implicit theological meaning. A technique-driven course would focus mostly on worship's mechanics and style. A theory-heavy course would focus mostly on worship's form and ultimate purpose. An average course taught from a practices point of view would give some time to each. An exemplary course from a practices point of view is interested in the connections among these four modes or levels and regularly rehearses how to move easily and coherently among them. For in practice, these strands of analysis and modes of attention are each intertwined and interrelated.

For this to work, each mode of discourse needs to come into its own. Sustained reflection on both overarching theological themes (e.g., the priesthood of Christ) and discussions of quotidian practices (e.g., how to distribute the elements of communion) should each feel at home. One of the strategies that I have found most helpful for achieving this is that of juxtaposing particular moments in worship with either key theological themes or biblical texts. This method is reflected, for example, in Leanne

41. For a similar vision of linking particularities and large themes and visions in pastoral ministry, see Denham Grierson, *Transforming a People of God* (Melbourne: Joint Board of Education in Australia and New Zealand, 1984).

Van Dyk's *A More Profound Alleluia: Worship and Theology in Harmony*,[42] in which each chapter illustrates how particular liturgical moments (e.g., Eucharist) both reflect and shape attitudes toward key doctrinal loci or themes (e.g., eschatology). Each chapter is followed by two hymn texts that are themselves liturgical documents, but that also speak memorably and evocatively about a given theological theme.

Oddly, the type of connection most in need of exploration (even resuscitation) is the connection of worship to God. It is remarkable that so many books and courses about worship say so little about God. So much attention is given to architecture, musical styles, language, prayer forms, vestments, and patterns of leadership that there is little room to speak about the God who is addressed in worship. This is like speaking of a day on the beach without reference to sunshine. True enough, the practice of worship is a tangible activity that involves material objects and physical actions. But these objects and actions both influence and are influenced by how communities conceive of the deity they address. Effective practice-oriented education must uncover and explore this connection.

Every semester my Asbury Seminary colleague Lester Ruth gives his students one overarching question for his introductory courses, such as:

- "If Jesus Christ is truly and fully the incarnate God, what impact should that have on Christian worship?"
- "If the gospel is a comprehensive story remembering God's activity from beginning to end, what impact should that have on Christian worship?"
- "If Christian worship forms us to be certain kinds of Christians, then what should our priorities in worship be?"
- "If God is triune, does that make any difference in how we worship?"

---

42. Leanne Van Dyk, ed., *A More Profound Alleluia: Worship and Theology in Harmony* (Grand Rapids: Eerdmans, 2004). See also Gordon W. Lathrop and Timothy J. Wengert, *Christian Assembly: Marks of the Church in a Pluralistic Age* (Minneapolis: Fortress Press, 2004); Christopher J. Ellis, *Gathering: A Theology and Spirituality of Worship in Free Church Tradition* (London: SCM Press, 2004); Geoffrey Wainwright, *Doxology: The Praise of God in Worship, Doctrine, and Life* (New York: Oxford University Press, 1980). Note that this move is different from what has come to be called "liturgical theology," which attempts to articulate the implicit theology contained in a given worship practice. This, in contrast, involves analysis of a worship practice in light of doctrine. Each project, I would add, is worthy, provided that students remain very clear about the basis on which normative judgments are made.

Without naming questions like these, we run the risk of teaching that perpetuates the idea that doctrine and practice are unrelated. More profoundly, we risk promoting worship practices that continue without any real awareness or expectation of God's presence. The study of worship — and all practical theology — suffers when it ceases to be theological. It is at this essential point that practices-oriented teaching most resists reduction to mere technique, as well as to any approach that is content with using only social scientific methodologies.

Sometimes grand theological visions come to us through sustained attention to big questions like these. Sometimes grand visions come to us indirectly through discussions on almost anything but theology. The following is a short list of themes that emerged out of classroom discussions of everything from the economics of church construction to what instructions to give a local parish flower committee. They are little theological vignettes, usually in the form of prescriptive statements about how we might best approach liturgy:

- "We don't worship to make God love us, but because God loves us. Nothing in worship should imply otherwise."
- "Remarkably, God welcomes the entire range of human experience in our prayer. Honest prayer and balanced worship involve confession, thanksgiving, praise, and lament."
- "We don't sing in order for God to be present, but because God already is present. Nothing in worship should imply otherwise."
- "Praise affirms and adores God. By implication, it denies false gods and idols. It protests gods our culture erects in place of God. Good liturgy should show both the 'yes' and 'no' implied in our praise."
- "What we remember and what we anticipate define our identity. Good worship forms us in Christian identity by active recall of the past and active anticipation of the future. Good worship doesn't dismiss the past as irrelevant or the future as too vague to anticipate."
- "When we show up for worship, we don't create the song of praise. We join in to a continuous song of praise that includes the music-like praise of animals and oceans, and believers from every time and space. Good liturgy helps us see that expansive vision."

Even for those of us who might feel reticent to structure a course around Professor Ruth's questions, many of us who teach could be more explicit about how our liturgical patterns imply theological convictions and then form us in them. We also need to be more explicit about how our pedagogy also implies theological convictions and then forms us in them.

Practicing Basic Skills for Improvisatory Ministry

Further, from a practices point of view, worship classes in a seminary or divinity school would not only describe or prescribe exemplary leadership practices, but would give students opportunities to engage in them in close collaboration with a mentor. Again, the similarities between ministry and both music and sports are legion. In each field, practitioners engage in activities that involve both skill and artistry. Actions are repeated numerous times, but they are carried out in an improvisatory or extemporaneous way, in response to local situations and conditions. Yet the training of at least some ministers remains quite different from that of pianists or soccer players.

First, students of piano or soccer spend much of their training time actually fingering the keys or dribbling the soccer ball. Training sessions are set up on the field of action. Master teachers spend most of their time responding to student moves. In contrast, much of ministerial education is spent learning the equivalent of the music theory that explains why the scales are important.

Second, when we learn to play piano or soccer, one of the first things we learn is how to practice. Before basketball teams scrimmage, they engage in seemingly endless dribbling and passing drills. Students of violin or voice spend much of a private lesson actually singing or playing, not merely talking about singing or playing. The role of a teacher is often to suggest muscle memory exercises that isolate and develop areas of weakness or potential growth. The key to success is repeated, disciplined rehearsal of key skills. I vividly recall my voice teacher patiently listening each week not only to my halting attempts at singing Italian art songs, but first — at some length — simply listening to me sing scales. As any veteran athlete or musician knows, these drills and scales are a critical part of the work, an activity from which one never graduates. Tiger Woods spends hours on the practice tee before each round of golf, probably more than most rookie professional golfers.

While a repeated theme in this book is that practical theology is about much more than ministerial technique, it would be as problematic to ignore technique as to limit our inquiry to technique. The goals, rather, are to embed technique in a much larger vision and to practice what kinds of skills reinforce and refine a larger vision, contributing ultimately to faithful, vital Christian living. This is, to use a phrase from Charles Foster's recent work, a pedagogy of performance.[43] It is a pedagogy that practices skills, but in ways that shape the identity of liturgical presiders and hosts.[44]

In the teaching of future ministers, I find the teaching of basic skills to be the most difficult part of my work. In the environment in which I teach, as in most seminaries, field education is independent from introductory coursework. I teach students for one nine-week quarter in their first year, and then I may not see them again until graduation day. They have at least two years to unlearn everything I've tried to teach. But the largest barrier here, I find, is myself. I want to use my 27 hours of teaching time to engage in discussions of content, not to practice skills. And I certainly don't want to grade multiple student exercises. What I have been painfully learning over the past ten years is how important it is for me to find very efficient ways of setting up short scale-like worship planning exercises, such as:

- Identify a balanced set of five songs that would be appropriate for a service of remembrance for 9/11.
- Prepare liturgically useful one-sentence introductions to the Scripture readings.
- Practice a gesture to accompany leading a prayer that communicates warmth and hospitality.
- Write out a sample extemporaneous welcome that might be needed on a particular Sunday in a particular congregation.
- Memorize a one-verse call to worship from the Psalms and practice saying it in an inviting, engaging way.[45]

43. Charles R. Foster et al., *Educating Clergy: Teaching Practices and Pastoral Imagination* (San Francisco: Jossey-Bass, 2006), pp. 156-86.

44. William Seth Adams, *Shaped by Images: One Who Presides* (New York: Church Hymnal Corporation, 1995).

45. See Paul Ryan, "Consider Those 'In Between' Words: Spoken Transitions in Worship," *Reformed Worship* 79 (March 2006): 18-19; see also Daniel T. Benedict Jr., "No Cowardly Spirit: Teaching Pastors and Priests to Preside," *Liturgy* 22, no. 2 (2007): 27-34.

Some of the exercises feel pedestrian, but then isn't a C-major scale for beginning pianists also pedestrian? It is also possible to press on to exercises with deeper significance:

- Watch the nightly news each night and then prepare one discerning intention or component for the following Sunday's intercessory prayer.
- Study an assigned Scripture text and choose from the vast storehouse of visual art now readily available over the Internet an especially apt artwork that evokes or unpacks the text in a provocative way.
- Follow up one formal or informal pastoral care encounter by choosing a song that could be sung at the next Lord's Supper service in a way that would best weave together the needs of that particular individual and the grand, communal, eschatological nature of the Lord's Supper.

There is an irreducibly aesthetic dimension to these kinds of exercises, a kind of mental activity that awakens creativity, allusion, and nuance. As Elliot Eisner observes, exercises in creativity tend to create momentum, gradually deepening our capacity to see the world in new ways, expressing the ineffable, and celebrating the non-instrumental parts of human experience.[46] There is also an irreducibly affective dimension to these skills, as in all of worship leadership.[47] Pastoral leaders need both confidence and humility, both authentic empathy to make their leadership of intercessory prayer genuinely pastoral and a sturdy spine to accompany a strong prophetic sermon. Daniel Goleman has probed these elusive qualities in his work on emotional intelligence.[48] While pastoral intelligence involves more than emotional intelligence, it rarely involves less.

All of this prepares students to engage in the inherently improvisatory nature of Christian ministry. Every golf and tennis shot is finally about the art of improvisation, about taking the timeless virtues of a good swing and calibrating them to the wind conditions. So, too, both the Christian life and the practice of ministry involve taking habitual questions and actions and calibrating them to particular cultural conditions. This is especially important because of the number of times we face conditions of uncer-

46. Elliot W. Eisner, *The Arts and the Creation of Mind* (New Haven: Yale University Press, 1994), p. 19.

47. Don E. Saliers, *The Soul in Paraphrase: Prayer and the Religious Affections* (Cleveland: OSL Publications, 1991).

48. Daniel Goleman, *Emotional Intelligence* (New York: Bantam Books, 1995).

tainty in ministry. Books about worship and worship courses can so easily be written and taught in ways that assume fair weather conditions. Yet worship leadership often happens, and is often most pastorally significant, in times of crisis, conflict, or transition.[49]

In seminary training, one of the best places to work on learning the dynamics of improvisational ministry is in field education placements in congregations. But this can also be anticipated in the classroom. With relative ease, the classroom can be turned into a meeting of a local church council, board, or session to work through a particular issue. Imagine turning a classroom into a church council room for discussions of:

- how a pastor or presider could best lead the congregational prayer when ministering in a small town plagued by factory lay-offs, where both union bosses and corporate heads sit next to each other in worship;
- what kind of liturgical response is most needed when a congregational leader resigns because of some kind of tragic personal failure; or
- how a baptism service might unfold in a week in which a member of the congregation has tragically died.

The exercise can be even more immediate when the topic can be something related to the worship life of the college, seminary, or divinity school. These richly textured examples provide instructive ways in which to learn the dynamics of improvisation, to see how the scales of ministry skills come to life in particularly musical ways in everyday ministry.

Ethos

Finally, consider how a practices approach might affect the overall feel of a course on worship. Every class in a seminary — just like every act of Christian ministry — reflects a certain undertone, often an undertone of fear, guilt, pride, or gratitude. It is terribly tempting to teach worship with an undertone of guilt ("if you don't do it this way, be shamed"), fear ("worship practices out there are pretty bad, and getting worse"), or pride ("how fine indeed it is that we don't pray like those [fill in the blank] publicans").

49. Kathy Smith, *Stilling the Storm: Worship and Congregational Leadership in Difficult Times* (Herndon, Va.: Alban Institute, 2006).

But a gospel undertone for both worship and discussion about worship — even in the bleakest days — is most fittingly that of gratitude. Ultimately, gratitude itself is a gift we receive. We can't engineer it. But we can hope for it, pray for it, and celebrate it when it arrives, even in the middle of a college or seminary class. Two moves — from legalism to wisdom, from didacticism to doxology — set the tone for a more fruitful kind of learning environment, better attuned to the topic of worship.

A Rhetoric of Wisdom

Sooner or later in most worship classes, students ask about the "right" way to do liturgy. It is a form of rhetoric that is common across traditions and styles of worship. Tenacious codes of conduct emerge around both monastic matins and seeker services, both feminist liturgies and Promise Keeper rallies. It is tempting for most of us who teach to simply answer these questions and move on. Most of us have a pretty clear sense of what we would like to see happen more in worship, and we sense a golden opportunity to advance our cause in our moment of classroom influence. Yet such power plays can end up stymieing deep learning as well as the very practices we would be inclined to promote. In contrast, as Karen Marie Yust and Byron Anderson argue, the most effective and virtuous teaching "resists powerfulness."[50] Questions about "right liturgy" deserve more than an answer. They beg for a discussion of underlying rationale.

A primary reason for this is that the rhetoric of "right liturgy" places us precariously over a precipice of legalism that can plague students and teachers alike in their ministries. It is fearsome indeed to find a new seminary graduate off to his or her first charge with the message that all the old worship practices there are wrong and need to be fixed, or to find college students whose worship class has bred in them the kind of judgmentalism that will forever keep them from appreciating the strengths of any congregation. The old joke about worship types — "What is the difference between a liturgist and a terrorist? You can negotiate with a terrorist!" — has just enough truth in it to keep it perpetually alive.

What is needed is something to reframe discussions about right and

---

50. Karen Marie Yust and E. Byron Anderson, *Taught by God: Teaching and Spiritual Formation* (St. Louis: Chalice Press, 2006), pp. 158-61.

wrong, better and worse in ways that appreciate the excellencies of some approaches, but with a sense for the contingency of that practice in certain cultural contexts. What we need to recover is a "rhetoric of wisdom." For most of us who teach in Protestant seminaries, at least some students come to class with deep suspicion of practices like the traditional Christian year or the traditional shape of the eucharistic prayer. What we need are not simply assertions that these are the "right ways" to worship, but rather explanations of the inner logic of their strengths: "Wise is the congregation that orients its life to the life of Jesus and to a balanced diet of scriptural themes and Christian affections" or "Wise is the congregation that learns to pray out of both Christ-centered memory and hope." We also need the kind of cultural peripheral vision to understand that this deeper wisdom may, in certain cultural contexts, lead to very different practices than the use of the Christian year or the traditionally shaped eucharistic prayer. Rehearsing the wisdom of particular practices equips students to teach their congregations, answers student skepticism about new or unfamiliar practices, and helps those who may take a given practice for granted to new appreciation. At their best, church polity or canon law documents are a form of wisdom literature. So are the classic liturgies of the Christian faith. Regardless of whether we might want to change them, we gain much by learning how to discern their wisdom and to speak a rhetoric of wisdom ourselves, lest our own liturgical practices end up being propped up by destructive kinds of legalisms.

Of course, the opposite problem — an anything-goes approach — is also a plague. Students who develop little sense that worship *matters* for good or ill will lack the motivation to diagnose and treat the liturgical diseases that keep congregations from genuine spiritual health. Indeed, a worship course only deepens a student's ability to discern what is best if it not only commends certain practices, but also questions others. Fortunately, the rhetoric of wisdom is well-suited to meet this challenge. Every attempt to articulate a statement of liturgical wisdom is, in fact, an attempt to frame a normative statement: "Wise is the congregation that sings songs with a balanced diet of theological themes"; "Wise is the congregation that practices hospitality not only in social programs, but also in worship"; "Wise is the congregation that encourages both contemplative and celebratory piety"; "Wise is the congregation in which Scripture is presented in ways that both comfort and challenge worshipers." In the book of Proverbs, and in contemporary church life, a rhetoric of wisdom helps us navigate a course that avoids legalism on the one hand and libertinism on the other.

Worshipful Teaching and Learning

Finally, teaching worship from a practices perspective invites worship classes that will themselves become more worshipful. Every single class on every single subject inevitably introduces students not only to a set of concepts, terms, and essential questions, but also to an ethos for engaging the material. Courses in military training and water polo, Italian cooking and bowling, differ not only in subject matter, but also in ethos.

Some of the more interesting work in pedagogy of late has focused on the formative power of a course's ethos. Philosopher of music education Bennett Reimer has called for more direct attention in musical education to actual musical experiences. Music education, he argues, should itself be musical, attentive to the aesthetic as well as technical dimensions of music. Likewise, a recent conference on pedagogy at Calvin College explored the theme of "spirituality, justice, and pedagogy," advancing the simple but transforming idea that justice is not only a topic to be discussed in class, but a way of life to be modeled and honed together in the classroom. Sharon Daloz Parks describes the provocative teaching methods of Ronald Heifetz, whose courses not only teach an adaptive approach to leadership, but give students a chance to practice adaptive moves in negotiating the course itself.[51] When congruity between subject matter and pedagogy becomes a key criterion, we begin to sense the incongruity of philosophers waxing eloquent about human imagination and creativity from a twenty-year-old set of lecture notes, or of educators merely lecturing about learner-centered teaching techniques.

The obvious question for those of us who teach liturgy, haunting in its directness, is simply, how can worship courses be taught in a worshipful way? Attention to how classes begin and end provides part of the answer. Just as Karen Marie Yust calls for deepening church committee meetings by giving them a liturgical frame, so too worship class sessions gain much when some kind of liturgical gesture is made as they begin and end.[52] The best class sessions I remember as a student began not with some pro forma prayer or with principled omission of a prayer, but with something that intention-

51. Reimer, *Philosophy of Music Education*, pp. 66-68; Parks, *Leadership Can Be Taught*, chapter 2.
52. Karen Marie Yust, *Attentive to God: Spirituality in the Church Committee* (St. Louis: Chalice Press, 2001).

ally inducted us into a worshipful ethos. The published classroom prayers of Walter Brueggemann are a well-known example of this doxological move.[53] Similarly, the best sessions I remember ended with some word or gesture that was fittingly doxological, prophetic, or benedictory.

The same kind of evocative and worshipful rhetoric is also fitting (and often surprising to students) right in the middle of class. The apostle Paul sets the pace here with his famous mid-course doxological interruptions (e.g., Rom. 11:33-36). Jonathan Edwards, in the middle of his work on the doctrine of the Trinity, once remarked: "God has appeared glorious to me on account of the Trinity."[54] It would be odd for us to rule such professorial interruptions out-of-place in a worship classroom. As in worship itself, one capacity to cultivate in the study of worship is an openness to being inspired.

In terms of ethos, much can be gained by assigning readings that are themselves beautiful and worshipful: Psalm 63, Revelation 5, Egeria's diary of a fourth-century liturgical pilgrimage, Bonhoeffer's *Life Together,* John Wesley's *Instructions on Singing,* or a Pablo Sosa hymn. And much can be gained by asking students to attend to their assignments in worshipful or contemplative ways. Instead of having students skim a 30-page essay on Augustine's view of the sacraments, perhaps they could contemplatively read five pages of a compelling Augustinian sermon.[55] Instead of simply analyzing a baptismal prayer, students can be asked to memorize one. Instead of merely scrutinizing hymns, students can be asked to sing them. To the extent that it forms in students and faculty alike a deeper capacity for wonder, a genuinely doxological ethos may be as important for a course on worship as any particular assignment.

A Triad of Participation, Depth, and Responsiveness

Throughout the history of the Christian church, periods of significant liturgical reform have almost always featured an intense call to deeper, more intentional participation in worship, a deeper pastoral concern for the par-

53. Walter Brueggemann and Edwin Searcy, *Awed to Heaven, Rooted in Earth: Prayers of Walter Brueggemann* (Philadelphia: Fortress, 2003).

54. Cited in Amy Plantinga Pauw, *The Supreme Harmony of All: The Trinitarian Theology of Jonathan Edwards* (Grand Rapids: Eerdmans, 2002), p. 1.

55. Thanks to David Smith for this suggestion.

ticularities of worship in a given congregation, and a profound awareness of how God works in and through all these particularities in worship to nourish, confront, comfort, and inspire participants. This triad of themes also grounds effective practice-oriented teaching.

First, this is a pedagogy of and for deep participation, a pedagogy resolutely set against disengagement, neutrality, and cynicism.

Second, this is a pedagogy of depth and complexity. This is pedagogy set resolutely against shallow, immature, sentimental, or overly simplistic explanations, proposals, or rationales for liturgical practices. It is a pedagogy of interdisciplinary rigor, a joyful embrace of the multivalent, multidimensional complexity of life in community, always in view of the larger horizon of God's redemptive work in particular times and places. It is a pedagogy of both "depth perception" and "peripheral vision," calling students to see deeply into the dynamics of a particular congregation, and to sense the vast landscape of liturgical communities that surround any particular congregation throughout history and across cultures.

Third, this is a pedagogy of responsiveness to the mercy and freedom of God, a pedagogy designed to correspond to the dynamics of divine grace. In an incarnational faith that embraces particularity and material existence, this pedagogy is oriented to tangible actions by real people. In a communal faith, this pedagogy embraces the messiness and joy of community life for both worshipers and those who lead them. In a faith that calls for the humble, grateful reception of divine grace, this is a pedagogy that practices expectant waiting, spiritual discernment, and genuine gratitude for signs of God's redeeming work.

Inevitably, then, this is also a pedagogy of provisionality. In many of these proposed moves, there is a decided open-endedness. The students we teach are already partly formed. The case studies we analyze are messy. The skills we practice always come to fruition in the context of improvisational ministry. No lifetime is long enough to comprehend the complexity and mystery of it all. Participation in worship, like the God we worship in Jesus Christ, is inexhaustible, full of mystery, wonder, and grace.

Liturgy and Life

In any given course, a professor has only a limited amount of time to make the best possible contribution to students' development as ministers. Therefore faculty members in all fields are wise to ask this question: What do students most need from each element in their graduate theological education? This question raises issues that are substantive (what content is most important and germane?), pedagogical (how can assignments and class time best be structured?), and theological (how can all aspects of the course, including the quality of the classroom community, be shaped to serve a life-giving way of life?). This question also prompts teachers to reflect on the place of a given course within the long arc of learning ministry. (This "long arc" is explored most fully in the chapters in this book by Christian Scharen and David Wood.)

In this chapter, James Nieman shares close-grained reflections on the multiple substantive, pedagogical, and theological choices two teachers made as they developed and taught a course that focused on rites of wedding, funeral, healing, and baptism. Nieman, then professor of homiletics at Wartburg Theological Seminary, and his colleague Thomas Schattauer, dean of the chapel and professor of liturgy, designed the course for students who had recently finished year-long internships in congregations and were near the end of their formal studies for Lutheran ministry. Their strategies, and Nieman's reflection on them in this chapter, address several matters of interest throughout this book, including pastoral formation over time and the integration of theological study across disciplines and between the congregation and the academy. The editors hope that this example will encourage other theological educators to reflect periodically on the convictions and strategies that shape their own teaching.

James R. Nieman is Professor of Practical Theology at Hartford Seminary.

6. Liturgy and Life:
An Account of Teaching Ritual Practices

James R. Nieman

Near the end of the Second World War, the acclaimed liturgical scholar Yngve Brilioth completed a slim volume simply called *A Brief History of Preaching*.[1] Gemlike in compression yet sweeping in scope, Brilioth's approach to this history was clever and appealing. From earliest times down to the present, every epoch of Christian preaching was tested against what he considered the definitive proclamatory event: Jesus' inaugural sermon at the Nazareth synagogue as told in the fourth chapter of Luke. Who could question such a standard? At the same time, who could live up to it? I have wondered whether it might be more useful to write a counterpoint to Brilioth's work, except mine would be called *A Brief History of the Death of Preaching*. No shortage of material there. People may not be clear what preaching really is or why it even exists, but they are fairly vocal when it collapses. In fact, you could trace a pretty compelling tale of all the times preaching was thought to be moribund, noticing the issues at stake, the reforms attempted, and the values thereby exposed. The real difference between Brilioth's book and my imaginary one, however, would not be the title or theme. Far more important is whether the author rests solely on an abstract ideal, or instead carefully explores many actual practices, however flawed.

This contrast has been on my mind in preparing this account of teaching a seminary course on ritual practices and what that suggests pedagogically, theologically, and academically. It would be lovely to begin this account with an ideal. If that were the case, I could simply state the sure

1. Yngve Brilioth, *A Brief History of Preaching,* trans. Karl E. Mattson, in The Preacher's Paperback Library, ed. Edmund A. Steimle (Philadelphia: Fortress Press, 1965).

principles of sound ministerial practice and excellent teaching that should guide the design and execution of any course in the area of practical theology, including this one. To be honest, though, this cannot (or perhaps should not) be done. I know of no such consensus in practical theology or among those who teach ministerial practices, not because matters are in disarray but because the complexity of what we study and teach resists any easy reduction. What is more, even if this ideal picture did exist, it would soon look dated. Like those sleek dream cars of the future I once gazed upon as a boy, ideals project more of present fantasies and anxieties than what finally comes to pass, especially in the classroom. Most important, however, I am relieved not to begin with abstract ideals to be implemented later because that is not how practical theology does its work.

Instead, it will be far more useful to explore what I actually do on a regular basis, however flawed. I teach the practices of ministry. Toward that end, I will review the main moves of a course called "Liturgy and Life," which I taught several times with my friend and colleague Thomas Schattauer. This essay can only gesture toward the practice of that teaching, of course, and it rehearses only one pattern for teaching just a few ministerial practices. It would surely be richer to look beyond this solitary case and encounter a wide range of comparable courses and all the commitments they reveal. For now, however, let this one example serve to show how such teaching works, the theological claims embedded therein, and the glimpse this affords of a broader constellation of proposals in the field of practical theology.

Description

"Liturgy and Life" sought to introduce participants to four formal rites deeply located in Christian tradition that variously engage human life passages: baptism, wedding, healing, and funeral. Connections between that topic and the setting in which it was taught were important to how we focused and shaped the course. Students in the course attended a seminary of the Evangelical Lutheran Church in America (ELCA). Most came from that tradition and were in the final year of preparation for ordained ministry in the ELCA, following a year of parish internship and previous courses in Scripture, history, theology, and ministerial practices. At the time, the ELCA was engaged in a five-year process of revising its worship resources, including proposals for the rites studied in this course. In other words, participants came to the course with both a degree of pragmatic urgency about these topics and several common assumptions that went largely unexamined. Naturally, we would have designed the syllabus differently had we been teaching in another setting, for even apparently innocent matters like enrollment, location, and duration of sessions affect the course plan and its possibilities. Any serious look at the practice of teaching must therefore begin by treating the situation as more than just a field of reception. Situation is integral to the teaching practice, becoming part of the lesson learned and influencing how that lesson will one day be used during ministry and taught to others.

Awareness of the situation was but the first step toward entering the classroom. We next turned to the process of course planning, which was foundational for our teaching practice though largely hidden from view. We began this step by discerning the methods and resources that might be used. Unfortunately, such discernment is often imagined only in terms of selecting assigned readings. To be sure, readings were important due to our particular situation and topic. Secondary texts, for example, helped us reach beyond the constraints of our denominationally and demographically limited seminary setting to consider the diverse religious traditions and cultural practices that inform these rites. Primary texts, by contrast, allowed us to attend to the surprisingly difficult task of learning how to read ritual scripts for the theologies they imply and seek to enact. Relying on texts as our only resource, however, would have produced an impoverished view of the ritual practices we were trying to explore, as odd and lifeless as reducing the texture of a human life to the text of a résumé.

Practices involve people, and we knew that the students had a history and future with these rites that would itself be a resource for the course. No one comes to these rites innocently, so students were bidden at several points to account for their prior, formative experiences with them. These accounts would both uncover the diverse values that affect rituals and challenge the idealism with which they are often treated. In addition, because the students had to move toward competence as future practitioners, learning how to plan and enact the rites needed to be part of the course, and cooperative groups were therefore an essential strategy for learning. Students were helped in these groups to develop a planning process, negotiate this process with colleagues, and rehearse the rite as an event embodied in space and time. Of course, this also meant there had to be actual opportunities to enact what the students had prepared. Finally, a reflective paper added a further step toward future competence, not as the usual end-of-semester sales tax but for students to refine the critical abilities needed in ritual situations they would face long after the course ended.

If people were an essential resource for learning ritual practices, this naturally had to include one other kind of person not yet mentioned: the instructors. An ordinary and regrettable tendency is to view teachers primarily as experts, like human textbooks to be consulted for the right answers. Certainly we brought an expertise to this course that included background research and knowledge of literature that students were unlikely to have encountered on their own. By summarizing and organizing this broad array of material in presentations and discussions, we provided a further technical resource to the learning of these rites and practices. This was only part of the teaching method we personally represented, however, and the lesser part at that.

More central to this course was that we functioned as what Donald Schön called "reflective practitioners." Through years of observing highly skilled practitioners, from master architects to musical virtuosi, Schön detected a pattern to how they passed on insights to apprentices. During close, interactive mentoring, these practitioners tested the problems brought to them, framed these problems into more useful categories, and then called on a repertoire of strategies gained through experience to resolve them. Interestingly, Schön also realized that reflective practitioners were often quite inept at directly expressing the reasons behind their own process of testing, framing, and resolving challenges.[2]

As teachers in this course, we had to become reflective practitioners who, *unlike* Schön's, *were* able to account for why we thought and acted as we did. After all, this was exactly what our students would have to do as pastors, not simply presiding at the rites but also opening up their meanings in diverse settings. Beyond our respective scholarly expertise, then, we had to model the sort of reflection on practices they would eventually use. Therefore, as we planned the course we often stopped to ask ourselves how we first came to think and act as we did about these rites. How did *we* learn to notice what was ritually central or theologically significant in worship? How did *we* learn to plan and enact these rites or assess their effectiveness? How did *we* learn critical skills to challenge old practices or creative open-

2. Donald A. Schön, *The Reflective Practitioner: How Professionals Think in Action* (New York: Basic Books, 1983); and Donald A. Schön, *Educating the Reflective Practitioner: Toward a New Design for Teaching and Learning in the Professions* (San Francisco: Jossey-Bass, 1987).

ness to imagine new ones? How might we now share all that in accessible terms, not as archetypical rules to follow but prototypical schema to adapt? These were daunting questions that required considerable self-examination by us as teachers of ministerial practices.

These reflections helped us articulate several layers of teaching objectives. Some were obvious, like introducing students to present scholarship on and emerging resources for rituals. Others were subtle but no less important, like recognizing the enacted theologies and scriptural impulses in these rites or discerning their relation to life cycle and culture. Some aims related indirectly to rites but directly to pastoral competence, like fostering the abilities to plan, enact, and assess that are necessary for ministerial practice. Others were seeds planted for a coming season, like modeling how ministers could teach about and through ritual practices in a way that reinforces witness in daily life rather than an unfortunate kind of liturgical gnosticism. Of course, certain objectives were purely wild dreams, like expanding the liturgical imagination of the church beyond its bondage to past experiences and personal tastes. In any case, none of these objectives stood alone. They became instead an interacting ensemble typical of efforts to teach the practices of ministry.

These various insights about situation, methods, and aims were then used to shape how the course would unfold over time. The schedule involved a roughly three-week pattern for each of the rites tied to marriage, death, sickness, and baptism, and in that order. Our choice of that sequence is itself worth noting, since the order does not correspond to the human life cycle from young to old, the historical emergence of these rites from early to late, or their theological significance from central to peripheral. Instead, we began with a rite that turns out to be a potent entry point for many students but a source of ambiguity for the church: the rite connected to marriage. By starting there, we could explore a tension between what is culturally prized and what the church values for mission, in order to listen to both streams seriously and deeply. As the course progressed through rites tied to death, sickness, and baptism, we moved toward items increasingly well-attested in church sources but often of diminishing familiarity to students, so that this tension between the claims of culture and church could be preserved and repeatedly examined.

A three-week cycle (using a weekly session that lasted three hours) focused on each rite in turn, and was encountered four times over during the semester. This cycle was shaped by a pattern of reflection we wanted students to adopt and ever more thoroughly embody. By repeating this pattern in relation to each of the rites, we hoped to reinforce a reflective practice that would persist beyond the course itself. In the first session of each cycle, subtitled "Rites, Scripture, Proclamation," we began by reviewing the structure of the particular rite with central attention to its key ritual moments. This called for a close reading of the ritual scripts mentioned earlier, as well as historical background provided by the instructors and secondary readings. For example, we looked at how early Christian groups borrowed or rejected certain aspects of Greco-Roman wedding customs, and noted how the vows form a pivotal action within the rite's larger structure.

Next in this first session came what may seem a strange and sudden shift: reviewing the students' own formative experiences with the rite in question. Students wrote brief reports that both *described* a profound life experience with the rite (a grandparent's funeral, for example, or a period of grave illness) and then *interpreted* that incident by suggesting its main narrative themes. When shared in class, these reports often became poignant and emotion-laden occasions as students recounted the ways such rites had been personally significant, for good or for ill. Diverse social commitments and cultural values were thus brought to light, raising the very issues students would likely face as ministers implementing these rites in congregations. As part of these reports, we also asked for specific questions students wanted to see addressed later.

What followed next in this same session required a bit of daring. As instructors, we tried to bring the theologies evident in a rite into contact with the commitments and values in the student reports, which were themselves often brimming with theological meaning. While none of us could know in advance how this would unfold, the aim was to model how the streams of ritual and experience can interact in practical theological reflection. Students began to see that what was formative for them during a rite could now be seen theologically, and how the rites enacted theologies that engaged or sometimes discounted ordinary experiences. After a few times through the cycle, students often saw these connections more readily than the instructors.

The first session concluded with an examination of the scriptural impulses that warrant a given rite and its enacted theologies. In surprising ways, these impulses often intersected with the central experiential issues mentioned in the student reports. Far beyond the often-paltry list of scriptural texts recommended in the propers of most church hymnals and worship books, we discovered through this process a range of biblical trajectories that conveyed a rite's deepest claims. This in turn provided a scriptural basis for preaching that could speak clearly to the many different participants in a rite. With this entire framework in place, students had received sufficient background to begin the cooperative planning process that would lead to enacting one of the rites in class two weeks hence.

The second session on a rite, called "Foundations, Current Issues, Future Development," was a chance to reinforce insights gained so far by bringing these to bear upon contemporary and emerging challenges. Secondary texts frequently helped to cast these challenges in sharp relief by introducing the many ways the human life cycle is ritualized within and beyond Christianity. It was jarring for students to realize, for example, that certain societies or religions place relatively little weight upon rites tied to death, or that some Christians interpret death not only through unfamiliar practices but also with strikingly different theological intent. Such a moment of defamiliarization allowed us to become clearer about what we take for granted in our own practices and whether our rites actually convey what we always thought they did.

Another major task for the second session was to address the questions from the student reports we solicited earlier. Some of these were further inquiries about the history or structure that had been introduced in the first session. (What really distinguishes a betrothal declaration from a marriage vow?) Others sought pragmatic or technical advice on unfamiliar matters. (How are different forms of human remains to be handled during a funeral?) Still others exposed hotly debated topics unlikely to be resolved any time soon. (What supports or precludes Christian rites to mark divorce or same-sex unions?) In all cases, we tried as teachers to resist the seductive role of answer wizard. Certainly, our own views were freely shared and often differed from one another, which was itself rather instructive to behold. The larger aim, however, was to introduce a thoughtful pattern of conversation that starts a process more than it stakes a position.

Building upon these questions, we then used this same session to present emerging scholarly and ecclesial issues regarding the rites. Aware of what already concerned the students, we could instigate a practical theological reflection toward still more complex issues they needed to consider. One fascinating discussion explored the theological meaning of sickness and healing. Twenty-five years ago, no one dreamed that the then-new Lutheran rites of healing would be as widely used as they are today. What was once imagined as a rite reserved for special parish needs or institutional settings is now frequently a regular congregational event in which all are invited to participate. Without our criticizing or celebrating this trend, it raised important questions for us to consider. If all are presumed sick so no one feels excluded, does this diminish or displace those who face serious suffering? If all are declared healed in some metaphorical way, does this betray cynicism about the possibility of physical cure? Are the sick who come to seek healing merely passive recipients in the rite or are they active participants who thereby shape what it means and declares? Are these rites increasingly popular simply as a substitute for confession and absolution? What do we claim theologically about sickness or symbolize through healing that would cause the church to care about these rites in the first place? Once again, entering such a minefield was a daunting task for us as teachers, often requiring us to reflect more deeply together on our own experiences and commitments.

By the third session of the cycle, the "Practicum," students were ready to enact the rites they had been planning for the past two weeks. In general, the students worked together in two separate groups to implement an assigned portion of a rite. Two weeks before the enactment, one student from the opposite group had drafted a liturgy situation drawn from that person's previous year of internship, which served as the imaginary situation for the planning. Another student from within the group was assigned to preach during the rite, and therefore selected preaching texts (in conversation with the planning group), reflected upon these, and prepared the sermon. The rest of the students within that group were responsible to plan, practice, and enact the rite. (Near the beginning of the course, students had been taught a two-meeting process to use for reviewing core worship concerns, assigning leadership tasks, reaching final decisions, and practicing a rite.) Due to time constraints during this session, only those portions of a specified rite that reflected its most distinctive elements could be enacted, and these were detailed on a practicum assignment sheet. Even so, the emergence of newly developed worship resources meant that significantly different versions of the rites could still be effectively tested and compared.

As stimulating and exhausting as these ritual enactments usually were, this third session did not end there. What remained was a crucial but often underplayed aspect of learning ministerial practices: assessment. Let me be clear about what we wanted to avoid. This was not to be a time to endure the withering judgment of instructors who are only satisfied when students have guessed what was really wanted in the first place. Nor was it to be a place for fellow students to reassert private biases in a collective, taste-based diagnosis that elicits only defensiveness and pandering. Instead, assessment was intended to help these practitioners develop what Elliot Eisner called "educational connoisseurship and criticism." Being a connoisseur means learning to appreciate something after lengthy exposure to it, recognizing its subtleties and shades, realizing what matters or does not. Left to itself, however, connoisseurship is an internal matter. Beyond this, then, Eisner saw the need for criticism, which shapes the private insights of the connoisseur into a public disclosure others can grasp and use.[3] The practices of ministry require critical connoisseurship not only to improve competence in what we enact but also to open these practices for others in a way that strengthens their witness in daily life.

For this reason, we outlined specific discussion topics for each practicum. Since rites involve embodied social practices that happen in space and time, complying with formal rubrics or reciting a script accurately provides little or no sense of true competence and effectiveness. Meaningful assessment instead needs to rely on those who have gathered, who are distinctively able to say whether what happened corresponded to what was intended. To guide this kind of assessment, we used categories and insights from previous sessions to undergird the class's growing connoisseurship about the rites. Typically, this meant focusing on the chief ritual moments in the enactment and examining concrete decisions about the roles of people, movements within the space, and the use of speech and song. Since so many things *could* be assessed, the discussion topics focused us on those that mattered *more* and how to speak about them. What emerged slowly was a critical language that allows ritual practice to become publicly accountable. Perhaps the most challenging of these critical skills was assessing moments of integration, noting how various practices related to each other in the overall impact of a rite. This in turn affected how we discussed the preaching, always relating it to the larger liturgy and its imagined context as one practice among many rather than an independent episode of homiletical self-aggrandizement.

With the assessment of the practicum completed, the three-week cycle

3. Elliot W. Eisner, "The Forms and Functions of Educational Connoisseurship and Educational Criticism," in *The Educational Imagination: On the Design and Evaluation of School Programs,* 3rd ed. (Upper Saddle River, N.J.: Prentice Hall, 1994), pp. 212-49.

for exploring a given rite drew to a close. At the next class session, we began anew the same process for another rite, certainly wearier in subsequent rounds, but perhaps also wiser.

Theology

I remarked earlier that we did not approach our teaching with a set of ideals completely worked out in advance and only then applied to the course's design and execution. To be sure, there was a time when courses in ministerial practices were constructed in just that way, so that doctrinal theology was clarified first, with the expectation that it would later be enacted in the life of the church. While wishing to underscore how differently this course was planned (and likely most others today in practical theology), I am not feigning innocence about having any prior theological commitments. Plainly, our teaching as described bears unmistakable Protestant assumptions, let alone other theological concerns to which we, as instructors, were oblivious. In the end, the course was taught by and for Lutherans in a Lutheran institutional setting, with all the limitations that implies. Any broadening of that theological horizon was either self-generated or else did not occur. At the same time, our entrenched position in a particular tradition often bore certain benefits. For example, we paradoxically felt little need to attend to or defend Lutheran confessional claims, but instead could treat these as a baseline for critical conversation about the rites that were our focus. As a result, we could together examine directly and deeply how Lutherans characteristically interpret their own liturgical resources using their strongest theological warrants. In any case, these underlying theological claims unquestionably affected the teaching we were able to envision and the decisions we ultimately made.

Even so, this summary renders a rather flat account of the theological commitments active in our teaching. A more thorough approach requires us to look beyond the overt theological affirmations we already brought into the course in order to reflect on the actual practice of teaching itself. Indeed, by considering the entire span of the course, we can begin to derive inductively the course's orienting themes. In the case of "Liturgy and Life," a cluster of five such themes emerge, each revealing its own implicit theological commitments. These themes show theology less as a fixed set of direct, positive claims about divine being than as several indirect gestures toward divine activity, enacted through the practices of teaching.

The following remarks are not intended as a theological model for the teaching of other courses in practical theology. I am only reflecting here on the themes and theologies of a single course, which some may find fraught with serious biases or deficiencies. If honestly naming these leads to critique and correction by others, however, then such review has already been valuable. Beyond this, it would be intriguing to use this same approach with a wider range of courses in practical theology (to note any shared theological patterns) and with other areas of theological education (to note theological similarities or differences). With this in mind, let us turn to the orienting themes.

Honoring of people. At every turn, we held firmly to the idea that all participants in the course (including but not privileging the instructors) were persons of dignity who had a role and voice in our common work. Therefore, students were viewed not as passive recipients of learning but as active contributors, just as we hoped they would eventually see their role not as acting upon others in worship but interacting with them. Everyone had previous experiences, current perspectives, and emerging questions to be treated with care and seriousness. Our goal was not an innocuous encounter in which different views were simply aired, however. Course participants also took responsibility to critique and challenge one another beyond what was already familiar. True respect required facing difficult ideas, polarized issues, and unfamiliar tasks. It also meant affirming that we were all part of a larger process of growth, with abilities to be enhanced or newly developed, especially in terms of reflection, planning, cooperation, and assessment. These efforts to honor people were motivated by a theological understanding of human worth as a divinely conferred gift. This commitment had the further effect of freeing us as teachers to risk failure or correction, as well as making us more open and available to regard our students with honesty and mercy.

Relating to traditions. The course topic, its participants, and the institution where it occurred did not fall from the sky but emerged within a vibrant stream of theological traditions. The earlier wisdom or alternative perspectives of these traditions show how ritual practices have intersected with daily life in other times and places, offering insights that can still benefit us now. Attending to primary liturgical texts was therefore neither optional nor burdensome, but more like receiving a treasure. Tradition-laden resources were examined with patient care, especially for a sense of how Scripture, which shows God's ways for us, was enacted in the rites and might be encountered anew through their use yet today. Relating to traditions did not mean obsession or compliance with some kind of static object, but instead a lively interaction. This was further framed within a theological view of the church as a unity we have in Christ with the saints of every time and place. We could therefore trust and value the witness of others in the tradition without considering it to be an ultimate, self-contained good. In fact, since this unity is mediated through Christ, the traditions we examined were subject to ongoing critique and transformation so that, through the power of the Spirit, they might better declare in our time and place the abundant life we share.

Engaging with contexts. Because personal experience can exert immense sway over what any of us can see or learn, we wanted participants to rethink their own perspectives in order to gain a wider vision for enacting rites during and after this course. It was quite important, therefore, to expose the contextual enmeshment of all such practices, including those we personally tend to prefer. We partly did this through secondary texts that showed how different cultures ritually mark the human life cycle. We also introduced the methods of disciplines other than theology that can help us appreciate new aspects of contextual realities. Both approaches made it clear that the contexts in which rites occur are more than neutral fields for enactment and reception. They are, first of all, spaces in which God is already active. Beyond this, contexts are dynamic realities that pose distinctive and unavoidable theological questions, some of which challenge the rites themselves. Engagement with contexts meant taking the time to hear and address these challenges so that the rites might retain their impact and meaning. This engagement also reflected our concurrence with the early Christian view that the church is "doing the world" at worship before God: standing amidst the world, pleading for the world, signifying God's reconciliation with the world. Seeing liturgy and church in this way means we must know the world honestly in order to bear it faithfully in prayer.

Focusing on contrasts. Few important practices show what they truly signify by means of simple, direct assertions. Especially with the worship practices we explored, meaning was conveyed through complex, aesthetic performances containing multiple and even conflicting senses. Failure to engage this kind of complexity might lead students to distort rites in either idealized or functionalist ways. Our teaching therefore tended to highlight the contrasting elements within or opposing views about a rite, so that all its messiness and complexity might become apparent. I noted earlier, for example, that the sequence for examining these rites during the semester tried to foreground the tension between their ecclesial value and their sociocultural adaptation. In a similar way, we frequently explored how the official meanings of rites stood at odds with their personal or public significance.[4] Even the overall logic of the course sought to juxtapose how rites relate to traditions yet engage with contexts. This attention to contrasts served the larger point that potent theological meaning is often disclosed only in metaphorical or paradoxical ways. In this respect, the focal rites of this course and how they evoke theological meaning guided us about how we might teach them. As with these rites, so also our course tried to manifest the irresolvable tensions that open onto an inexhaustible mystery.

Enacting as theology. This final theme concerns a theological method evident in our teaching. Theology certainly appears in rituals through verbal scripts and the larger beliefs to which they refer. Far more importantly, however, theology is found in the shared actions that comprise rites and the overall patterns that lend them structure. This recalls Aidan Kavanagh's recovery of the ancient distinction between worship as the church's *primary* theology (its enacted God-claims) and reflection on those core practices as *secondary* theology.[5] Naturally, students needed to be adept at secondary theology to discern the implications of the rites we explored. It was much harder, though, to redirect their attention to how liturgical practices already declare God in what they do. For this to happen, they needed significant opportunities to participate in the rites fully and directly, entering through them as through an icon upon a divine disclosure. By such activity, we sought to rekindle a wonder for how these ritual practices enact theology. Greater still, we hoped to awaken a desire to teach not only about the rites but through them, less asking "What does this mean?" than boldly inviting "Come, taste and see."[6]

A summarizing remark is in order. In trying to discern the themes and

4. John F. Baldovin, "Varieties of Liturgical Experience: Presidential Address," *Studia Liturgica* 32, no. 1 (2002): 1-14.

5. Aidan Kavanagh, *On Liturgical Theology: The Hale Memorial Lectures of Seabury-Western Theological Seminary, 1981* (New York: Pueblo Publishing Co., 1984), pp. 73-95.

6. For the different modes by which rites convey meaning, especially that of participation, see Roy A. Rappaport, "Ritual, Time, and Eternity," *Zygon* 27, no. 1 (March 1992): 27-28.

theologies of the teaching practices of this course, I became increasingly aware that vocational formation was a consistent passion throughout them all. As teachers, we wanted our students to be drawn into the character and vision of a pastoral calling we already shared, one manifested through the church for the sake of the world. The theological commitments of other courses in practical theology might naturally and rightly be driven by other passions, such as human liberation, evangelical testimony, or group therapy. The point remains that these five themes were not haphazard but rooted in a core passion. An adequate theological account of a course should therefore not only review the themes within its teaching practices but also the passion that draws them into a meaningful ensemble, a matter that will certainly differ from one teacher to the next.

Proposals

So far, I have described the planning and teaching of one course focused on certain ministerial practices, as well as the theological commitments orienting that work. In this final section, I will turn to related proposals for the broader field of practical theology that are implied by this course and its theologies. In offering these proposals, however, I want to avoid the misperception that only teachers in practical theology care about effective learning for the sake of the church's ministry or give sustained attention to theological practices. Instead, the shape of "Liturgy and Life" simply allows me a vantage point for suggesting a pair of claims (the former briefer than the latter) that seem natural extensions from our work in that course. These proposals are intended to stimulate a larger conversation for the mutual benefit of all who share a concern for the role of practices in theological education.

Let me begin with a claim that *teaching the practices has as its aim faithful ministry that impels the church's mission in the world.* When it comes to sound teaching, I suspect that most theological educators agree that information-dumping and self-glorification are not legitimate aims. I imagine we also know that more adequate teaching treats students as agents in their own learning, not as objects; as resources in a mutual process, not as hindrances to otherwise smooth sailing. I hope it is also clear by now, though, that this teaching is a demanding and sophisticated task. It calls for instructors with the scholarly competence and confidence to risk what unfolds and to meet it with a kind of generous, patient, inductive readiness. It also calls for knowing and respecting where students are in the rhythms of their own learning, which Alfred North Whitehead viewed as the interacting stages of romance, precision, and generalization [7] This is why our course used a sequence of topics, patterns of action and reflection, and cycles of repetition as part of an overall rhythm to deepen learning. All of this matters because effective teaching ultimately seeks to equip ministers to convey abundant life to others in word and deed.

Well and good, but for one small wrinkle: the decline of effective teaching in the church as a whole. In a quite different part of my research in which I study local theologies in congregations, I have learned that this decline is both pronounced and distressing. In some cases, it betrays a derisive view of laity as unreflective and unchanging. More often, though, well-meaning and hard-working ministers find themselves stymied about how to reach learners who lack the luxury of extensive classroom time and quiet reflection. How we teach the practices of ministry, such as the rituals that focused our course, could begin to offer an alternative. While awareness of and excellence in ministerial practices is important, the real aim is to teach *through* these practices so that all participants, ordained and lay, can sense new ways to declare the mercy of Christ in unforeseen settings. Creative, vibrant teaching is needed not just so students stay intellectually stimulated during and after seminary, but so all the faithful can eventually account for the hope within them. Anything less leaves the church mute at the doorstep of the world.

My other claim is that *the practices of ministry operate in several publics at once,* a matter that calls for rigorous, sustained scholarship in practical theology in the years to come. Let me recall again our work in "Liturgy and Life." When focusing on rites related to the human life cycle, it quickly becomes apparent that liturgical and homiletical insights alone are insufficient to inform the topic. A fuller understanding has to appeal to areas as diverse as ritual studies, church history, aesthetics, biblical scholarship, ethnography, and ecumenics, to name a few. Even then, other helpful persons wanted us next to include recent work in pastoral care and educational theory — and while we're at it, maybe have local pastors and parishioners offer their insights as well. These are all great ideas which very

7. Alfred North Whitehead, "The Rhythm of Education," in *The Aims of Education and Other Essays* (New York: The Macmillan Company, 1959), pp. 24-44.

quickly would transform our humble course into an amoeba-like creature capable of consuming an entire curriculum. We had to stop somewhere, knowing that we could only gesture toward conversations that might break into other courses or extend long after ours was over. What intrigues me, however, about this inclination to expand the study of these rites (or any ministerial practices, for that matter) is the intuition that they operate in many different publics whose several voices need to be heard.

What does this suggest about where research in practical theology should be headed? To begin at home, I think we need to revisit the frequently interrupted discussion of the place of ministerial practices in theological education. I harbor no hegemonic fantasies about these practices orienting everything a theological faculty does, which would be a truly wasteful use of scholarly diversity. At the same time, I am unwilling to consign the teaching of ministerial practices to being the frantically wagging tail on an otherwise proud and steady dog. An alternative would be to gather first around a common purpose for theological education in the church, which I would venture is to equip people to show, soundly and authentically, the gift of lasting love we know chiefly through Christ Jesus. To such a purpose, every discipline brings unique strengths and blind-spots, so that an ensemble effort of distinctive players is required. In such an ensemble, practical theology focuses more (but not solely) on patterns of shared action that declare such faith amidst our contemporary existence. Other disciplines, bringing their own take on this common purpose, not only perform many crucial roles that practical theology cannot, but also hold it accountable to a more rigorous standard in light of the perspectives each one brings. Such rigor today would include special attention to the emerging questions of what marks or grounds a practice as particularly Christian, and how ministerial practices of clergy interrelate with the daily faith practices of laity for the sake of a more ample witness to the love of God in Christ.

Moving outward from our home in theological education, a new set of publics emerge for practical theology to consider. Christians live in a religiously plural world, of course, and really always have. We know the pressing need for interreligious understanding that might check ideologically fostered hostility, although it is unfortunate if fear is our only motivation. In any case, we often address this need through words and ideas, becoming more familiar with the sacred texts and cherished beliefs of other traditions. This is the model of dialogue or engagement, no simple matter since it requires the genuine risk to be changed by those with whom you speak. What surprises me, however, is the relatively small place afforded in this process to religious practices other than just reading or discussion. Attention to other sites of engagement is essential, however, if we are ever to account for the dizzying complexity within a broad religious tradition, let alone seek at least local strategies of mutual respect. In homiletics, for example, I am struck by the importance of what might be called "strong religious utterance," a practice that moves beyond conventional views of Christian preaching and its Jewish or Islamic analogues into the compelling place that story, poetry, and even chant have in shaping people of other faiths. I think we might benefit more than we imagine by exploring such religious practices as a space for interreligious contact and exchange, and in a way that would be more widely accessible than ideationally oriented approaches.

Beyond even the religious sphere, practical theology encounters one last set of publics. In the "Liturgy and Life" course, we frequently reached beyond familiar partners for perspectives on the rites brought by other schools of thought. Interestingly, there is now a growing discussion in areas such as law, medicine, art, and education about the nature of best practices in these professions.[8] The time is ripe for interaction on such matters, but most efforts have again focused more on texts and ideas than situated actions. It is hard enough to establish even bilateral contact between, say, medical staff and pastoral caregivers about the process of healing, let alone to assist persons undergoing treatment in their multilateral dealings with lawyers, accountants, and social workers. Even so, it seems essential that practical theological scholarship interact regularly with those whose professional practices intersect our own, not least of all so we remember what people affected by those practices actually face. The point is not to have more interesting or influential academic conversation partners, but instead to be challenged anew to make a theological perspective count amidst a range of public practices.

8. The current research of the "Preparation for the Professions Program" of The Carnegie Foundation for the Advancement of Teaching has already become important in this regard, including: Charles R. Foster et al., *Educating Clergy: Teaching Practices and Pastoral Imagination* (San Francisco: Jossey-Bass, 2006), and William M. Sullivan, *Work and Integrity: The Crisis and Promise of Professionalism in America,* 2nd ed. (San Francisco: Jossey-Bass, 2005). See also Howard Gardner, Mihaly Csikszentmihalyi, and William Damon, *Good Work: When Excellence and Ethics Meet* (New York: Basic Books, 2001).

In a curious and quite roundabout way, this brings me back to Yngve Brilioth, with whom I began so long ago. At the outset, I stated that Brilioth built his argument upon a single ideal of preaching rather than drawing from actual practices. In fairness, one might object that indeed he *did* begin from a specific instance of a practice, that of Jesus' preaching in Nazareth. Of course, he actually relied upon a secondary report of that practice, and a spare one even then. Brilioth might have included other preaching by Jesus in Luke or even of Peter and Paul in the larger Luke-Acts trajectory. In any case, it could be claimed that Brilioth's ideal test for preaching began where many of our best insights also do, with a potent, compelling practice.

Even so, what fascinates me is what he still overlooked. Brilioth neatly concluded that Jesus' preaching was liturgical (embedded in synagogue worship), exegetical (evoked by a biblical reading), and prophetic (engaged with a particular setting). As with Jesus, so for Christian preaching, which should also be liturgical, exegetical, prophetic. If you pay close attention to Jesus' actual sermon in Nazareth, however, you might notice other aspects besides. For one thing, it was short, all of nine words in both English and Greek. For another, it was performative, using words themselves as an active force (as when someone is declared guilty or granted forgiveness).[9] In short and simple span, Jesus' words enacted gospel. How would the history of Christian preaching look if tested against criteria like brevity and dynamism? It makes you wonder.

There remains one last part of this practice to notice, though. After the synagogue coffee hour when the implications of Jesus' little sermon had sunk in, his listeners had the intense desire to throw him off a cliff. That is, careful attention to the events in Nazareth leads to the conclusion that his preaching had public consequence. Maybe our preaching could as well, not to mention our attention to ritual and indeed every ministerial practice. What if our teaching of ministerial practices and scholarship in practical theology always had as its horizon this question of public consequence? Bravely, we might first rethink any approach that cultivates leaders only for a safe, "greenhouse" ministry. And then, blessedly, we might carefully study and teach those practices of ministry that embolden us to stand amidst the storm and acclaim the one whose gift is peace.

9. J. L. Austin, *How to Do Things with Words* (Cambridge, Mass.: Harvard University Press, 1962).

Practical Theology and Pedagogy

The courses offered by practical theologians often constitute their most direct contributions to the education and formation of ministers able to shape communities in life-giving ways of life. Further, as Bonnie Miller-McLemore argues in the final chapter of this section, these courses make visible some of the core commitments of their discipline as a whole.

Teaching in the practical field teaches not only *about* practices. It does do this, but even more, it seeks to teach practices themselves. Thus John Witvliet understands that a class on worship must be worshipful, and James Nieman knows that a course on rites must allow students to inhabit liturgical postures with their bodies and to speak the words of rites aloud. Moreover, those who teach a specific ministerial practice are generally expected to perform the practice itself at a high level, and they are often responsible for sustaining a theological school's closest relationships with practitioners beyond the academy. At the same time, and as a necessary dimension of all these pursuits, practical theologians and the courses they teach give sustained attention to biblical and historical texts and artifacts, social scientific interpretations of contemporary situations, and a wide range of relevant theoretical material.

Drawing on the accounts offered in the three previous chapters, the pedagogy of other practical theologians, and her own teaching, Miller-McLemore articulates some of the distinctive contributions of their field to those who are preparing for ministry. While describing and advocating teaching that honors and draws on knowledge from many disciplines, she is especially interested in identifying and developing a kind of knowledge that she argues is of special interest for practical theology and of crucial importance for ministry and Christian living, a kind of knowledge she calls "know-how." Miller-McLemore's attention to "know-how" anticipates the embodied learning in the midst of practice that will be emphasized in the fourth section of this book (practical theology in ministry) and suggests an important focus for conversation with academics in other disciplines, a topic considered in the third section of this book.

Bonnie J. Miller-McLemore is E. Rhodes and Leona B. Carpenter Professor of Pastoral Theology and Counseling in the Divinity School of Vanderbilt University.

7. Practical Theology and Pedagogy: Embodying Theological Know-How

Bonnie J. Miller-McLemore

In the otherwise vigorous academic revival of practical theology of the past few decades, little attention has been given to pedagogy.[1] Only rarely have scholars asked how those in the field actually teach — *qua* practical theologians — at least not as a primary question. Other significant conceptual matters of definition and method have naturally taken precedence.[2] Teaching largely remains secondary to scholarship.

Yet the lively national and international conversation about practical theology among scholars of theological education in recent decades has significantly affected how practical theologians teach. Invigorated by efforts to expand the scope and definition of the field and to revitalize theological education, many faculty in practical theology began to teach in new and valuable ways. But we have yet to explore how we are teaching differently and, more importantly, what it means.

On one level, questions about teaching are straightforward. What qualifies as a course in the area of practical theology? What must it include to be

---

1. A recent and important exception to this observation is Charles R. Foster, Lisa E. Dahill, Lawrence A. Goleman, and Barbara Wang Tolentino, *Educating Clergy: Teaching Practices and Pastoral Imagination* (San Francisco: Jossey-Bass, 2006), a comprehensive study of ways in which seminaries educate clergy and cultivate skills, habits, values, and insights. See also Malcolm L. Warford, ed., *Practical Wisdom on Theological Teaching and Learning* (New York: Peter Lang, 2004). Nonetheless, there is still no major text that focuses entirely on practical theology and pedagogy.

2. For my own initial exploration of this problem, see Bonnie J. Miller-McLemore, "The 'Clerical Paradigm': A Fallacy of Misplaced Concreteness?" *International Journal of Practical Theology* 11, no. 1 (June 2007): 19-38.

so named? How do such courses prepare divinity students for ministry? What distinguishes good teaching in the field? On another level, investigating practical theology in the classroom raises profound questions with far-reaching implications for Christian theology and faith. How are practice and theology subtly intertwined and powerfully redefined in the practical theological classroom? How are distinctions between theological fields and between classroom and congregation both appreciated and transgressed? What is the place of self-examination in practical theology and theology generally? What is the place of proclamation and doxology in this (and potentially in other) academic work? Perhaps most importantly, what counts as theological knowledge, and how do teacher and student acquire it?

In response to such questions, this chapter makes a bold claim: Intrinsic to the practice of teaching in this field is a particular way of theological knowing that has important implications not only for the teaching of practical theology but also for the definition of the field and for the larger enterprise of theology itself. This way of knowing is a form of *phronesis* that, in this context, might be called "pastoral wisdom" or "theological know-how." This claim suggests that practical theologians, who among theological educators stand the closest to the juncture between church[3] and academy and thus must continually assert the relevance of their teaching in the theological academy, possess (or in order to be effective need to possess) pedagogical wisdom. This wisdom challenges common assumptions about the textual and interpretative knowledge needed to do ministry and suggests additional attributes, such as self-awareness, practice, ac-

---

3. I use "church" here for brevity and clarity. I actually mean something broader and more complex than the institutional church. I mean "lived experience" as pastoral theologians such as James Poling and Donald Miller describe it; "practice" and "religious practice" as Dorothy Bass and Craig Dykstra have described a faithful way of life; and "public" and "situation" as David Tracy and Edward Farley respectively describe the practical theological audience and subject matter. See James N. Poling and Donald E. Miller, *Foundations for a Practical Theology of Ministry* (Nashville: Abingdon, 1985); Dorothy C. Bass, ed., *Practicing Our Faith: A Way of Life for a Searching People* (San Francisco: Jossey-Bass, 1997), and Craig Dykstra and Dorothy Bass, "A Theological Understanding of Christian Practices," in *Practicing Theology: Beliefs and Practices in Christian Life*, ed. Miroslav Volf and Dorothy Bass (Grand Rapids: Eerdmans, 2002); David Tracy, "The Foundations of Practical Theology," in *Practical Theology: The Emerging Field in Theology, Church, and World*, ed. Don S. Browning (San Francisco: Harper & Row, 1983); and Edward Farley, "Interpreting Situations: An Inquiry into the Nature of Practical Theology," in *Practicing Gospel: Unconventional Thoughts on the Church's Ministry* (Louisville: Westminster/John Knox, 2003).

tion, exercise, accumulated trial-and-error experience, embodiment, and so forth. In short, how we teach says a great deal about the field, what unifies it, and what those who teach believe — not only about the subject matter but also about Christian faith, theology, and life. It says more than any of us has yet dared to claim or fully articulate.

The classroom is only one piece of a much larger picture, to be sure. As other chapters in this book demonstrate (notably those in the fourth section), not all that ministers need in order to learn to do their work well happens here. In fact, despite its value, practical theologians are often especially attuned to the relative inadequacy of the classroom and to the need to reach both backward to where people come from and forward to where they are going in order to connect what is taught and learned in school to much broader contexts of learning and formation. But even this recognition gets us a bit ahead of the story and into issues that this chapter hopes to spell out.

In naming general themes of practical theological pedagogy below, I mix concrete example with theoretical claim, exploring as I go an epistemological framework and theological rationale that explains and justifies what I think many practical theologians are doing in their courses. The themes mingle with one another, of course, and the act of extracting them necessarily reduces the complexity of pedagogy in action. What follows, then, is more circular than linear or hierarchical and more invitational than exhaustive or comprehensive. I hope this exploration will stimulate an expanding and clarifying conversation about pedagogy within practical theology and in theological education as a whole. Moreover, I believe that a close examination of how practical theologians teach will disclose a great deal about the field, its key commitments, and its central contributions to theological education, communities of faith, and the wider world.

Teaching a Practice

Although it seems obvious, it merits saying: Those who teach in the area of practical theology (e.g., care, homiletics, liturgics, education, leadership, evangelism, mission) teach a practice.[4] This explains a great deal about

4. In this essay I use the phrase "a practice" to refer in most cases to a specific practice of ministry — something pastoral leaders do in the performance of their responsibilities. A "practice" in this sense is a part of and intimately related to the larger "practices of the

why teaching in practical theology is complicated and why the field faces a distinctive challenge. Those who come into the classroom must leave better prepared to do something, whether that be to listen, worship, preach, lead, form, teach, oversee, convert, transform, or pursue justice. They need theological know-how. They need more than just the capacity to "*think* theologically" (the focus of plenty of books on reflective practice[5] and the heart of many treatises on practical theology[6]), but also the capacity to "*practice* theology" by putting theology into action through one's body on the ground. Teachers of practical theology therefore must distill components of practice or a *theory* of theological practice *without losing sight of practicing* in our theorizing.

Orientation to teaching a practice to those who must not only *think* but also *do* (and do thoughtfully) fundamentally shapes those who teach in the practical areas. This stands in contrast to those who orient their teaching around the introduction of an academic discipline or area of study. It was not until retirement, for example, that systematic theologian Edward Farley recognized that his teaching had missed the mark. Rather than focusing on his students' "eventual use" of class materials, he taught it as an academic field of study, largely isolated from the various concrete situations with which students had concerns. He is not alone. According to an essay on teaching contained in a report by the Association of Theological Schools (ATS) on the qualities of a "good theological school," the drive to produce traditional scholarship often subverts exploration of alternative teaching practices geared more directly to the needs of students. Although the authors recommend that lecture no longer serve as the "sole pedagogy," most faculty arrive in schools with little background in "non-lecture pedagogical methods" and little incentive to change this.[7] "Even

---

Christian life" that Dorothy Bass and Craig Dykstra describe in their essays and also in *Practicing Our Faith,* but the meanings of the term are different in the two cases.

5. See, for example, James O. Duke and Howard W. Stone, *How to Think Theologically* (Minneapolis: Fortress, 1996), and John B. Cobb, *Becoming a Thinking Christian* (Nashville: Abingdon, 1993).

6. See, for example, Edward Farley, *Theologia: The Fragmentation and Unity of Theological Education* (Philadelphia: Fortress, 1983), and Don S. Browning, *Fundamental Practical Theology: Descriptive and Strategic Proposals* (Minneapolis: Fortress, 1991).

7. Philip S. Keane and Melanie A. May, "What is the Character of Teaching, Learning, and the Scholarly Task in the Good Theological School?" *Theological Education* 30, no. 2 (1994): 37.

when we are aware of [the] gap between the requirements of our subject or field and the students' post-school interests and pursuits," Farley confesses, "most of us teachers concentrate on the first and ignore the second."[8] This is less true for those who teach in practical theological areas.

Practical theologians confront questions of what it takes to shape the theologically wise practitioner the minute they cross the classroom threshold. Teaching worship as a course in practical theology is different from teaching an "introduction to the discipline of liturgical studies," says John Witvliet. It is a training camp for "full, conscious, active participation" in worship as an art of faithful Christian communal life. Its goal is insight into how theology works "with real people in all their social embeddedness" or, as Kathleen Cahalan puts it, with "real-life issues facing real people."[9] Few students will become worship professors or liturgical specialists, but nearly all will be worshipers and some will plan and preside in worship. In teaching worship leadership and other practices of ministry, teachers must stay attuned to the use to which students put their learning.

Those who teach practical theology actually confront questions about wise practice the day they begin to search for a teaching job. How we practice what we teach is unavoidably an evaluative criterion for employment, and it also determines what we are asked to teach. When Cahalan arrived at her institution, she was immediately asked to take over two linchpins of the curriculum, perhaps the hardest classes to teach and sometimes the least appealing to other faculty, namely the first-year and capstone courses. She must first introduce students to the curriculum as a whole and to the wider goal of maturation in the practice of ministry and then, before they leave, test their capacity for academic, ministerial, and vocational integration, ensuring they have learned something transportable and valuable for their ministry. She cannot ignore what students will do after graduation with the texts they study, the papers they write, and the class lectures they hear. Inescapably she must keep an eye on the wider horizon of Christian practice.

8. Edward Farley, "Four Pedagogical Mistakes: A *Mea Culpa*," *Teaching Theology and Religion* 8, no. 4 (2005): 200.

9. See two essays in this volume: John D. Witvliet, "Teaching Worship as a Christian Practice," and Kathleen Cahalan, "Introducing Ministry and Fostering Integration: Teaching the Bookends of the Master of Divinity Program."

Those Who Teach *Can* Do

The fact that practical theologians teach the actual practice of practices implicates the teacher. "Everything we do in the classroom," observes religious education professor Katherine Turpin, "from how we establish the learning environment to how we . . . negotiate conflict," becomes subject to close examination.[10] Students notice if the candidate for the opening in homiletics cannot preach, if the pastoral theology professor does not listen to their questions, if the professor of religious education seldom leads students in creative exercises for learning, or if worship classes are not worshipful. The *teaching* of a teacher of teachers or the *preaching* of a teacher of preachers or the *caring* of a teacher of care is seen as witness and proof of the professor's embodied theology and real knowledge of the subject. In an odd twist of logic, as Turpin notes, "I teach about teaching by teaching." The classroom itself becomes a laboratory in which the mirror is turned back on the teacher.[11]

As a result, the position of the teacher is transformed. Witvliet becomes a "fellow-worshiper" alongside his students; James Nieman becomes a "fellow practitioner." Neither can fall back on the distance and comfort provided by disciplinary expertise. Both must engage what Nieman identifies as "daunting questions that required considerable self-examination."[12] How did *he* first come to distinguish the theological adequacy of the performance of particular rites? How did *he* learn how to reshape them or encourage congregants to reshape them accordingly? How will *he* move beyond historical and systematic theologies that he knows well to the practice-oriented guidance that will help ministers and congregants live their Christian convictions more fully?

In most cases, those in practical theology do not teach their subject matter without significant efforts to learn and do the practice they teach. This shapes their work in surprising ways. "My clinical supervision [as a pastoral counselor] taught me a new epistemology," pastoral care professor Pamela Couture declares, "that changed my life as a learner, a teacher, and

10. Katherine Turpin, "Distinctive Pedagogies in Religious Education," manuscript from the American Association of Practical Theology, April 2006, pp. 1-2, and forthcoming in *International Journal of Practical Theology* 12, no. 1 (2008).

11. Turpin, "Distinctive Pedagogies in Religious Education," p. 1.

12. See in this volume James Nieman, "Liturgy and Life: An Account of Teaching Ritual Practices," p. 154; and Witvliet, "Teaching Worship as a Christian Practice," p. 120.

ultimately, as a scholar."[13] Her counseling training involved an embodied, full-sensory attending, a strategy for using theory without letting it swamp perception, and dexterity in responding to immediate pain and envisioning wider goals. An "avid note-taker," she eventually stopped taking notes; this knowledge was simply not easily translated into notes. Nor has she forgotten it. For her and many other pastoral care teachers, pedagogical schemas for incorporating practice rely heavily on these formative years in supervised counseling. Many pastoral theologians attempt to sustain a counseling practice as a key part of their vocation, just as those who teach preaching fill pulpits and those who teach religious education make their own pedagogical practice a regular part of class examination. Being engaged in actual practice "keeps us honest," my practical theological colleagues say.

A pedagogy that is developed and continually nourished in relation to clinical, congregational, or other non-academic practice engenders shifts in epistemological commitments. The modern academy, shaped by Western views of rationality, often assumes (or at least is dominated by teaching methods that seem to assume) that one thinks one's way into acting. It assumes, as Farley remarks, that "the primary mode of theology is think-ing."[14] The question of how action transforms thinking has been submerged in the history of higher education in recent centuries. In the last three decades of scholarship in practical theology, however, many have argued that theory and practice "dialectically" influence each other.[15] Often drawing upon neglected but persistent strands in Western thought about the importance of practice, they have planted seeds for an alternative epistemology in the practical theological classroom. In how they teach, many practical theologians presume that practice engenders

13. Pamela D. Couture, "Ritualized Play: Using Role Play to Teach Pastoral Care and Counseling," *Teaching Theology and Religion* 2, no. 2 (1999): 96.

14. Farley, "Four Pedagogical Mistakes," p. 202.

15. David Tracy, for example, depicts theology as a correlation between Christian fact and human situation; Farley talks about a "dialectic of interpretation" of truths and norms of the tradition and concrete situations of everyday life; Juan Luis Segundo decries imposition of doctrinal truth that ignores the "signs of the times." See Tracy, *Blessed Rage for Order: The New Pluralism in Theology* (New York: Seabury, 1975), p. 243, and *Analogical Imagination: Christianity and the Culture of Pluralism* (New York: Seabury, 1981); Farley, *Theologia*, pp. 165, 185; Segundo, *Signs of the Times: Theological Reflections*, ed. Alfred T. Hennelly, trans. Robert R. Barr (Maryknoll, N.Y.: Orbis, 1993), p. 147.

thinking as much as thinking enriches practice. For practical theologians, therefore, a (if not *the*) primary mode of theology is practicing the arts of ministry.

It Takes Practice

As a result of new interest in practice and how practice shapes discourse, many now agree that the study of theology is itself a practice. Academic theology is "a form of cultural activity," says Kathryn Tanner. It does not stand over and above the everyday faith of religious communities as a distant intellectual storehouse of ideas, as second-order theoretical reflection reigning over first-order confession. Each discipline — and theological education as a whole — is "a cultural production," "something shaped by concrete social practice," "a material social process."[16]

What might we see then if we turn such claims back on academic culture itself by looking at one practice in particular — namely, the practice of teaching? Christian theology is not shaped only by the "way altar and pews are arranged," as Tanner acknowledges, but also, I would emphasize, by how chalkboards and desks are placed.[17] No good anthropologist walking into the hallowed halls of our institutions of theological education could possibly bypass close inspection of the patterns of our teaching activity — our rituals, daily gestures, expressive styles, and semester requirements — and how they manifest the distinctive, shaping commitments of each discipline.

In many practical theology courses, our anthropologist will discover desks and chairs oddly rearranged. On the first day of my pastoral care class, she would find us watching the film *Billy Elliott*. Billy loves to dance. He closes his bedroom door and bounces on his bed to music; he skips, hops, taps, and prances down the street; he leaps over fences. From the corner of the boxing ring, right before his opponent knocks him out, he eyes with envy the girls across the gym learning ballet. But in his corner of the world — a tough mining village in northeast England — eleven-year-old boys like Billy don't learn to dance. They learn to fight. So Billy must

16. Kathryn Tanner, *Theories of Culture: A New Agenda for Theology* (Minneapolis: Augsburg Fortress, 1997), pp. 63, 67, 72.

17. Tanner, *Theories of Culture*, p. 70.

not only discover his hidden talent. He must also work extremely hard to realize it.

As the class watches Billy learn ballet, they notice that a great deal shapes the learning of a practice besides raw talent — familial and social prejudice and permission, money, friendship, study, apprenticeship with a demanding teacher, endless repetition of basic moves, repeated failure in increasingly difficult moves, occasional success, emotional support, bodily memory, grit, perseverance, risk, passion, grace. I also show clips from another moving film, *Girl Fight*, about a teen from a black working class family in Brooklyn who wants to box. She's good at it, and it relieves pent-up anger, but she too must work hard to prove her place. "I'll train you," says the coach she persuades to take her on, but, "If you don't sweat for me, you're out of my life."

Indirectly at least, I tell my students they'll sweat in my class. My deeper motive, however, is to open up discussion about what they think learning pastoral care involves. Why do I start my class here rather than with a lecture on the basics of pastoral care or the history of the field? Why does a colleague who teaches religious leadership start with a simulation game of a congregational conflict? Because we want our students to know that this course is about learning a practice and they will have to practice this practice as part of the class, something they may not have recognized or experienced in classes where the main task is learning history or theory. Practical theology courses also teach history and theory, to be sure, and other courses reflect on ministerial practice. But ultimately the primary focus in a practical theology classroom is a practice of ministry that aims to enhance the practice of faith.

Thus an unspoken rule or movement or litany guides practical theological pedagogy: Experience the practice, practice it, tell about it, ask questions about it, read about it, write about it, practice it, do it, empower others to do it. Turpin likens this movement to that of medical students learning a procedure: "see one, do one, teach one." Learning practical pastoral wisdom requires close observation of practitioners, doing the work of practitioners, and eventually teaching what one has learned to the faithful in congregations and at large. This litany or movement begins in but obviously extends well beyond the classroom, first in terms of classroom content and then in terms of the long-term vocational development of the practitioner and those she or he shapes.

Consequently, as Witvliet remarks, a "significant amount of energy should be reserved for encountering actual practices: concrete examples of gestures, symbols, sermons, songs, images, and environments."[18] Reliance on texts alone, Nieman says, would produce an impoverished view of the homiletical and liturgical practices he teaches.[19] An indispensable addition to printed texts, as pastoral theology has argued for decades, is the "living human document," the "living human web," the situation in its fullness.[20]

So we send students to the field to interview, observe, and otherwise encounter the "real," as well as to witness, report on, and learn from actual practitioners. They counsel each other, interview someone in crisis, question someone who is an expert in a practice, compose case studies, assess each other's efforts to embody a practice, observe a congregation's practices of care, or work together on a community project. We also ask them to construct and participate in improvisational exercises that imitate the "real." Couture does this through alternating assigned reading with "ritualized playing" or role plays that put the entire class in action. This, she believes, "creates a learning environment that allows students to 'think on their feet' — to habituate themselves into good-enough practice in pastoral care situations."[21] Likewise, Nieman's course is built around a multi-level exploration and enactment of four particular worship rites.

This interest in show and tell has led some people to question the rigor of practical courses, as Cahalan acknowledges in a footnote.[22] If such exercises do no more than spark personal stories, if they do not connect students back to texts, theories, history, and intellectual ideas, such accusations would be correct. Practical theological pedagogy works hard, however, to make practice an avenue into fuller engagement with history and theory and to bring history and theory to bear in practice. Teachers who employ film, ask people to draw pictures, or experiment with singing use these means because they recognize that the knowledge intrinsic to the

18. Witvliet, "Teaching Worship as a Christian Practice," p. 130.

19. Nieman, "Liturgy and Life" p. 152.

20. See, for example, Charles V. Gerkin, *The Living Human Document: Revisioning Pastoral Counseling in a Hermeneutical Mode* (Nashville: Abingdon, 1973, 1984); Anton Boisen, *The Exploration of the Inner World* (New York: Harper Torchbooks, 1952); and Bonnie Miller-McLemore, "The Living Human Web: Pastoral Theology at the Turn of the Century," in *Through the Eyes of Women: Insights for Pastoral Care*, ed. Jeanne Stevenson Moessner (Minneapolis: Fortress, 1996), pp. 9-26.

21. Couture, "Ritualized Play," p. 96.

22. Cahalan, "Introducing Ministry and Fostering Integration," pp. 93-94 n. 5.

life of faith requires many avenues which cannot be accessed through conventional academic means alone.

Hints, Tips, and Rules of Thumb

Practical theologians teach a practice with the expectation that participation in that practice will cultivate the kind of knowledge, *phronesis*, that deepens students' capacities for further participation in the practice. But the path to theological wisdom is never quick or easy. At certain stages of learning, all sorts of hints, tips, and rules of thumb can be extremely helpful. In spite of criticism from those who worry about a presumed preoccupation in theological education with ministerial skills, many practical theologians, including myself, provide a constant stream of helps and hints to our students as valuable intervening steps toward pastoral competence. When rules of thumb are deeply connected to the beauty of richly embodied, theologically responsible practice, they play a needed (even if always limited) role in helping students move toward practical theological wisdom.

There are, after all, better and worse ways to stand when speaking from the front of a church or raising the bread and wine for praise and blessing. There are better and worse ways to enter a hospital room or to express care when a parishioner looks like she or he needs a hug. There are gestures in preaching that invite listening, and phrases in counseling that open up space. One may feel artificial and forced in making these moves at first, but over time, as one experiments with particular gestures and phrases, practices them over and over, and considers their theological implications, they can become a reliable and authentic part of one's own pastoral repertoire.[23] The development of such a repertoire, of course, only begins in the context of the theological school. It actually develops over a lifetime of the practice of ministry. So neither students nor faculty nor receiving churches should presume that seminary fully prepares students for ministry. Students should expect to be "caught by surprise" again and again, as Couture writes in her syllabus, until "after years of being sur-

---

23. I join Turpin in using the word "repertoire" intentionally here to refer to a range of skills and aptitudes, acquired over time, that one can perform. See Turpin, "Distinctive Pedagogies."

prised" they become "seasoned" pastors.[24] Such maturity rests on regular practice of disciplines of self-monitoring, dialogue with theory, and, of particular note here, facility with "rules of thumb."

Hints, tips, ground rules, and rules of thumb are not the whole game or even a major part. They are small moves that are used strategically to improve enactment of a practice. They still have a place, however, and theological bearing. They shape and maintain "muscle memory," in Witvliet's words, and such memory comprises a needed, if overlooked, part of good pastoral ministry and faithful living. Like technique in the development of musicianship, skills are integral to theological maturation from the very beginning. Both Turpin and Witvliet liken rules of thumb to learning the scales so "one can begin to improvise in a particular key."[25] Just as you "can't be a musician without working on the scales" or "a good basketball player without practicing thousands of free-throws," so also, argues Witvliet, "effective improvisational ministry is impossible without excellent grounding (and constant rehearsal) in basic skills." The best practice embraces both "scales" *and* "artistry," "hard work *and* soaring vision."[26]

What we really need to know then, as Witvliet asks, is what "are the scales we need to practice in theological education?" As Christian Scharen points out in his chapter, those in other fields, such as Patricia Benner in nursing education, have taken this question seriously. Drawing on applied mathematician Stuart E. Dreyfus's and philosopher Hubert Dreyfus's study of chess players, air force pilots, and army tank drivers and commanders, Benner breaks down the component parts and steps of "skill acquisition" in nursing care. Such skills "literally get sedimented" in the "embodied know-how" of the mature practitioner. The expert nurse knows more "than he or she can tell or think to describe."[27] The chal-

---

24. Pamela Couture, unpublished introduction to pastoral care syllabus, 1989.

25. Turpin, "Distinctive Pedagogies."

26. John Witvliet, "Music/Practical Theology Comparison," unpublished manuscript, Seminar on Practical Theology and Christian Ministry, October 8-9, 2004, pp. 7-8, 13.

27. Patricia Benner, unpublished paper presented at the American Academy of Religion, November 19, 2006. See also Benner, "Using the Dreyfus Model of Skill Acquisition to Describe and Interpret Skill Acquisition and Clinical Judgment in Nursing Practice and Education," *Bulletin of Science, Technology, and Society* 24, no. 3 (June 2004): 188-99, and *From Novice to Expert: Excellence and Power in Clinical Nursing Practice* (Menlo Park, N.J.: Addison-Wesley, 1984). See Christian Scharen's chapter in this volume for further commentary on this research.

lenge, as Nieman emphasizes, is that by contrast with the automatic expertise of masters, teachers of practitioners have to account "for how we first came to think and act as we did" and make this knowledge of "scales" available to students.[28]

Hints and helps need not be unsophisticated. The book of Proverbs and the long trial-and-error history that lies behind its pithy sayings of simple truth for living the life of faith — what one biblical dictionary describes as a "philosophy rooted in the soil of life" — models a similar kind of well-worn and reflected-on pragmatic guidance.[29] Our hints and helps sometimes reflect an analogous effort to distill the hard-earned history of therapeutic, relational, spiritual, and theological knowing that has given rise to the theological know-how embedded in the routines of the deeply knowledgeable faithful practitioner. So it is no surprise that Witvliet turns to the rich rhetoric of wisdom literature ("wise is the congregation that . . .") over the ultimatums and imperatives of legal language ("thou shalt not . . .") when he wants to model a way of theological knowing faithful to Christian worship and praise.[30]

Completing the Hermeneutical Circle

At the heart of the practical theological enterprise, then, stands a preferential option for practice. In the context of an intense focus on actual situations, the refrain "what then shall we do?" echoes through all areas of practical theology. To say this more theologically: an incarnational, prophetic, and eschatological theology marks our teaching. That is, convictions about the graced nature of embodied creation, the imperative to act on the gift of grace for goodness and justice, and the provisional incompleteness of all such activity stand behind teaching in the field. Theology is, in Nieman's words, less "a fixed set of direct, positive claims about divine being" and more "indirect gestures . . . to a sense of divine activity." Consequently, practical theologians often talk about theological messiness. "Our teaching," Nieman observes, "tended to highlight the contrasting elements

28. Nieman, "Liturgy and Life," p. 153.

29. S. H. Blank, "Wisdom," in *The Interpreter's Dictionary of the Bible: An Illustrated Encyclopedia* (Nashville: Abingdon, 1962), p. 857.

30. Witvliet, "Teaching Worship as a Christian Practice," p. 145.

within or opposing views about a rite so that all its messiness and complexity might become apparent."[31] In all three preceding chapters in this section of this book, God's presence is described as iconic, metaphorical, paradoxical, mysterious, and "mystagogical"; it comes through shared action, through what practices already declare about what God is doing. As one colleague in our seminar observed, Christian practical theology searches for a "way of living up to the gospel we profess." Our courses are "trajectories," as Witvliet remarks, toward the life-long exercise of faith.

Practical theological pedagogy strives for fluidity between theory and practice in various ways, but in any course in practical theology one should be able to find loops, circles, or spirals in the syllabus itself and in individual class sessions. That is, when those who teach in practical theology come up against the elusiveness of practice and the insufficiency of theology, we move. We jump onto the hermeneutical loop that Cahalan describes in her chapter, moving among description, analysis, interpretation, decision, and action.[32] When students enter the program at the front end, she looks for the questions they bring, anticipates the resources they will need, and aims toward the capacities they will take with them when they leave. The structure of her penultimate assignment leads students through a similar circle of questions: "What is going on here? What does it mean theologically? What should we do?" Similarly, Nieman describes a "cycle" in his class, repeated four times for each rite, around historical and structural description, formative experiences, theological encounter, scriptural examination, and actual enactment of the rite.

Much has been made and should be made of the first move — thick description and interpretation of the situation. Turpin talks about "read-

31. Nieman, "An Account of Teaching Practices," pp. 159-60, 161-62.

32. Cahalan, "Introducing Ministry and Fostering Integration," p. 97. This method has received a variety of interpretations. See, for example, Juan Luis Segundo, *Liberation of Theology,* trans. John Drury (Maryknoll, N.Y.: Orbis, 1976); James N. Poling and Donald E. Miller, *Foundations for a Practical Theology* (Nashville: Abingdon, 1985); Browning, *Fundamental Practical Theology;* Evelyn and James Whitehead, *Method in Ministry: Theological Reflection and Christian Ministry* (Kansas City: Sheed & Ward, 1995); Thomas Groome, *Christian Religious Education: Sharing Our Story and Vision* (San Francisco: Jossey-Bass, 1999); Roslyn Karaban, "Always an Outsider? Feminist, Female, Lay, and Roman Catholic," in *Feminist and Womanist Pastoral Theology,* ed. Bonnie Miller-McLemore and Brita Gill-Austern (Nashville: Abingdon, 1999), pp. 65-76.

ing" the specific and wider cultural context. Witvliet talks about training both "depth perception" and "peripheral vision" to enable people to see any given situation from a wide variety of angles.[33] Pastoral theologians talk about the living human person or web as "document" and "text." Some, such as Mary McClintock Fulkerson, define a "sort of 'phenomenology of situationality'" as the "larger frame" and the chief contribution of practical theology.[34] I would agree with all of these claims but would add that the "larger frame" of practical theology is not satisfied until the loop is completed or until one moves from "interpreting situations" toward response. Students must engage in *phronetic* theological movement from "practice to theory and back again," as practical theologian Don Browning says, or, more specifically, from "theory-laden practice to a retrieval of normative theory-laden practice to the creation of more critically held theory-laden practices."[35] Many courses in practical theology adopt this movement as the implicit structure of the syllabus and the rationale behind specific assignments.

I would not expect those in other fields consistently to run this entire circle. There is place and need for disciplines that delve deeply in each of its specific moves. But practical theological pedagogy suggests that theological education needs more foraging forth by those in other fields than currently is the case. If those in practical theology find themselves drawing from every other discipline in the seminary curriculum, as Witvliet remarks; or appealing to areas as diverse as ritual studies, biblical scholarship, and ethnography, as Nieman observes; or requiring students to analyze demography, locate historical roots of a problem, and consider religious symbols, as Cahalan does, might those in other fields reach to practical theology?

---

33. Turpin, "Distinctive Pedagogies"; Witvliet, "Teaching Worship as a Christian Practice," p. 148.

34. Mary McClintock Fulkerson, "Ministry to Eunuchs and Other Ecclesial Practices: Toward a Theological Reading," unpublished manuscript, p. 13. These ideas now appear in her book, *Places of Redemption: Theology for a Worldly Church* (Oxford: Oxford University Press, 2007). Fulkerson relies on Farley's article, "Interpreting Situations," in which adequate framing of the contemporary situation is seen as the primary subject matter of practical theology and "situation" is defined as the "way various items, powers, and events in the environment gather to evoke response from participants" (p. 36).

35. Browning, *Fundamental Practical Theology,* p. 7.

Instruments of Peace

To "read" a community as a "theological text" one must, according to Fulkerson, take bodies seriously and all the "visceral, affective responses to different bodies," such as her own reaction to the "thin white man sitting twisted in a wheelchair" or "all the dark skin in the room" of the multiracial church community in a working class area of a small Southern city on which she turned her anthropological-theological gaze.[36] A closer theological reading of the community requires attention to desire, fear, and aversion — affective responses — to counterbalance or correct the prevalent intellectualist leaning or cognitive focus of most systematic theological work.

Although Fulkerson does not say so, I would argue that to do accurate affective analysis — that is, to "read" and respond to a situation as a "theological text" with attention to affect — one needs not only ethnographical or other social science tools and theological insight. One must have a certain level of emotional and spiritual health — the much-maligned "therapeutic" vitality that contemporary psychology has often understood better than theology. If this were not true, then seminaries and judicatories would not bother to interview applicants, give them personality tests, or remark that this or that person is really not "cut out for" ministry or seminary teaching. Of course, a call from God or a religious community is not something any of us can be quick to judge, for premature and one-dimensional judgments are often in error. Nonetheless, those teaching care, education, preaching, leadership, and so forth know that personhood matters and find ways to work this into class discussion and assignments, as Cahalan's work with specific students makes most evident. The questions students bring are intimately tied to questions of vocational discernment and identity confronted in "changing, ambiguous, and often contentious ecclesial" times.[37] If faith is not just a matter of beliefs, language, institutional structures, and practices, but also, as in Augustine, a matter of desire and its disorders, then healing ("therapy" in its broadest historical and classic meaning) of personal, relational, and social brokenness matters.

The know-how of practice is actually distinctly person-located. Practical reason or reason that orients action is "different from intellectual rea-

---

36. Fulkerson, "Ministry to Eunuchs," pp. 2-3.
37. Cahalan, "Introducing Ministry and Fostering Integration," p. 95.

son, reason that orients the mind," according to Couture. Drawing on Aristotle, she argues that practical reason is "necessarily imprecise and cannot cover all of the situations it governs." Only wise *persons* then "can make wise judgments in situations with variables for which theoretical reason cannot account." So, practical theological pedagogy has a particular aim: the formation of "wise persons" rather than "only intelligible theories."[38] Perhaps one of the most important aspects of the final assignment that Cahalan requires in her culminating course has to do with what happens to the person him- or herself. Many are transformed, sometimes even in the moment of giving their public presentation. In the course of their degree programs, they change from naïve or terrified beginners to people with voice, presence, and emotional and spiritual integrity that will carry them over the threshold from classroom into ministry.[39]

This final element of engaging the learner holistically raises deep suspicions among some that practical theological courses are not intellectually rigorous or that they have simply succumbed to vagaries of modern psychology. Yet the focus on the person in practical theological pedagogy is not automatically a symptom of sloppy pietism or individualistic culture gone awry. Rather, it is a recognition that each person can become, as in the prayer of St. Francis, "an instrument of peace." Some would qualify Henri Nouwen's famous description of the minister as "wounded healer" by advocating for pastoral leaders that are "healed" or "recovering" wounded healers before they try to facilitate the healing and formation of others, whether through preaching, leading, educating, or other practices. Spiritual self-awareness is just as crucial today as it was for the likes of Augustine, Søren Kierkegaard, and other classic models of the Christian life. Education centered on students' formation can happen with "integrity and rigor," Cahalan insists. She uses means similar to those listed by Witvliet: "assigning challenging and compelling reading, asking probing questions about historical and cross-cultural examples, and requiring significant engagement within the classroom and with local worshipping communities."[40]

Other practical theologians ask students to do "genograms," plotting

38. Couture, "Ritualized Play," p. 97. Couture draws here on Aristotle's *Nicomachean Ethics* in *Introduction to Aristotle*, 2d ed., ed. Richard McKeon (Chicago: University of Chicago Press, 1973).

39. See Cahalan, "Introducing Ministry and Fostering Integration," pp. 92-93, 112-13.

40. Cahalan, "Introducing Ministry and Fostering Integration," pp. 93-94 n. 5; and Witvliet, "Teaching Worship as a Christian Practice," p. 120 n. 5.

relational connections and disconnections as well as patterns of health and pathology over several generations, or to write in first-person singular about themselves with "experience-near analytical" rigor, as pastoral theologian Kathleen Greider remarks.[41] Such assignments point to the need to reach both backwards to where people come from and forward to where they are going. Students have a "history and future" with practices, Nieman acknowledges, that is "itself a resource for the course." When he asks students to describe in detail, "for good or for ill," the contextual history shaping their pre-understandings of particular liturgical rituals, he knows the class period might turn out to be "quite poignant and even emotion-laden." As Witvliet observes, just as a golf coach or singing instructor can make little progress without analyzing "persistent habits" that define a good swing or pitch, so also must seminary teachers begin by raising awareness of the "acquired habits" students bring to the classroom and to the practice of ministry.[42] Those who hope to lead religious communities and organizations need the kind of emotional intelligence obtained by therapists after years of intense training.

There is one additional dimension to this final element: Where theological education often aims at analyzing or deconstructing sacred texts and beliefs and rightfully encourages students to understand their complicated historical and cultural contexts and meanings, practical theological pedagogy takes up the task of post-deconstruction reconstruction. This, of course, is not a task that belongs exclusively to those who teach practical theological courses but raises common questions for all classes. Does this course only take apart or does it also offer ways to put back together? Does it only promote disengagement from religion or does it allow for fuller reengagement? So, as Witvliet asserts, the "ethos" or the "undertone of fear, guilt, pride, or gratitude" of the classroom is important.[43] So also are sightings of grace. Practical theology pedagogy involves what Fulkerson identifies as a discernment of the "'theonomy' of a situation, its openings for God-dependence" or what she also calls "places of appearing," "signs" or "traces" of redemption. These can be theological even when we do not

41. Kathleen J. Greider, "Practical Theology, Pedagogy, and the Case of Pastoral Care," manuscript from the American Association of Practical Theology, April 2006, p. 9 and forthcoming in *International Journal of Practical Theology*.

42. Nieman, "Liturgy and Life," p. 152; Witvliet, "Teaching Worship as a Christian Practice," p. 127.

43. Witvliet, "Teaching Worship as a Christian Practice," p. 143.

"use what are, strictly speaking, 'theological terms.'" The very act of analyzing the site of the "wound" where faith no longer works is "an indirect testimony to God" or to "that alone which can account for such a diminishing of social sin, the reality of God."[44]

Contributions to Curriculum and Theological Education

A closer look at how we teach discloses a great deal about the field of practical theology, its key commitments, and its central contributions to theological education, communities of faith, and the wider world. While practical theologians have searched in many directions for definition of the field, central conceptual and practical agreements have sprung up in our own backyards. We have not thought to look so close to home in part because we have been entranced with a particularly powerful diagnosis of the problems of theological education that discouraged attention to practical theological pedagogy.[45] But now we can see that courses in practical theology uphold a rich definition of theological know-how that recognizes the intelligence involved in practice and the teaching of practice. A closer look at practical theological pedagogy and the social enterprise of teaching provides an intriguing lens to understand theology anew, as it refracts the light of the practice of faith from which it comes and toward which it points.

Practical theologians emphasize not just learning *about* a discipline but also, as Witvliet says, "full, conscious, active participation" *in* it. Even courses introducing practical theological methods, as Cahalan observes, rarely discuss practical theology as a discipline. To learn about worship, one must engage in it; to understand care, one must try it out; one cannot learn to teach without teaching; one must engage concrete particular instances of ministry to do ministry. Ultimately, the teaching practices of practical theologians suggest one knows theology as one embodies it.

This has many pragmatic implications for the curriculum of theological education as a whole and for Christian faith more broadly. I will mention only a few of the more obvious. As I listened to colleagues share syllabi and delve into the strategies behind the readings, exercises, discussions, and re-

44. Fulkerson, "Ministry to Eunuchs," pp. 14, 16.
45. Miller-McLemore, "The 'Clerical Paradigm.'"

quirements of their courses, I was surprised by the common elements that emerged. Clearer theoretical articulation of the features of practical theological teaching — the focus on practice, the interplay between scales and expert performance, the hermeneutic circle of description-interpretation-action, and the role of self-reflection and formation — provides resources to evaluate courses in practical theology. There are criteria that define a course in practical theology and make claims for or against one course or another.

In turn, this list of features provides a way for faculty in other areas to appreciate and incorporate into their own teaching the wisdom of learning a practice so central to the area of practical theology. Reaching across the curriculum should be less unilateral. If practical theology's expertise has been interpretation of and response to situations, should not faculty in other areas turn on occasion to resources in practical theology to understand more deeply particular issues and practices, such as ritual, marriage, suffering, anger, and so forth? Would it not be helpful if faculty in historical and systematic theology were to include good practical theology texts in their syllabi or require participant-observation of practitioners among their assignments? Those in practical theology might serve as guides.

Articulating the key features of practical theological pedagogy invites greater conversation across the disciplinary areas about the marks of excellence in theological education and the nature of doing theology for the sake of the Christian life. Those in practical theology often have insight into what is needed in introductory and capstone courses. But the auspicious aspiration harbored by many in practical theology is precisely what Cahalan names at the conclusion of her chapter: that integration is not something that students encounter only in courses in practical theology or only at the end of their course work. This is a task that must be shared by the whole faculty. Cahalan calls for a "culture of integration where all faculty members are intentional about how their teaching encourages a heightened sense of practical theological thinking in ministry."[46] In such a culture, few courses, if any, would be oriented around introduction to a discipline.

This inevitably requires greater proximity to practice on the part of all faculty. Practical theology confirms an epistemological truth elaborated by performance and ritual theory: performance "creates meaning that cannot

46. Cahalan, "Introducing Ministry and Fostering Integration," p. 114.

be found elsewhere."[47] It is odd that facility in practice among faculty across the curriculum — so important in medical education, for instance — has received so little attention. Without practice of a wide variety of kinds, not only by those who teach in practical theology but by those in all fields of seminary education, can we understand the knowing needed by those we teach?

In short, some of the means and goals of practical theological pedagogy are worth wider emulation. Examination of the epistemological and theological commitments behind the goals and the ways various practical theologians strive to reach them validates teaching in practical theology as more complex, more theologically sound, and more fitting for ministry than has previously been recognized. Theoretically, theologically, and pragmatically, such teaching is a resource both for enriching seminary education as a whole and, perhaps more importantly, for understanding the ways of knowing intrinsic to ministry and faithful living.

47. Charles J. Scalise, *Bridging the Gap: Connecting What You Learned in Seminary with What You Find in the Congregation* (Nashville: Abingdon Press, 2003), p. 120. He cites Jeremy S. Begbie, *Voicing Creation's Praise: Towards a Theology of the Arts* (Edinburgh: T & T Clark, 1991), and Frances Young, *Virtuoso Theology: The Bible and Interpretation* (Cleveland: Pilgrim, 1993).

PRACTICAL THEOLOGY
IN THE WIDER ACADEMY

Part 3
and
Practical Theology in Two Modes

Practical theological teaching such as that considered in the previous four chapters takes place within academic programs that support and require study in a variety of fields. For practical theologians, this multidisciplinary location is indispensable, and it is noteworthy that all of the authors in the previous section describe strategies for incorporating knowledge from other fields into their courses. They also express hope for greater collaboration with colleagues in these other fields. The importance of knowledge from multiple disciplines — including other theological disciplines and the social sciences — to excellent work in practical theology is also a theme in Kathleen Cahalan and James Nieman's essay in the first section of the book, "Mapping the Field of Practical Theology."

This section addresses these concerns by providing detailed examples of work along the boundaries between practical theology and two other disciplines that are also present in almost every theological school — systematic theology and history. It also contains an essay that makes the case for including practical theology among the disciplines included in a pluralistic research university. In every case, the authors identify benefits that flow both to practical theology and from it, enriching the work of all concerned.

In the first essay, systematic theologian Serene Jones argues that there are two kinds of practical theology — the specialized teaching and research that take place within the practical field, and the work of theological educators whose specialization is in another discipline. Both, Jones insists, have practical bearing on ministry and Christian life. Even after describing her own collaboration with a colleague who teaches pastoral care and counseling as a very generative one, however, she likens the relationship between these two sorts of practical theologians to a "construction zone." The work of understanding and fully benefiting from the mutually helpful contributions of each is far from complete, and often the workplace gets messy as disciplinary lines are crossed. Yet within this zone, Jones suggests, the future of theological education as a whole may be coming into view.

Serene Jones is Titus Street Professor of Theology and Chair of Women's, Gender, and Sexuality Studies at Yale University.

8. Practical Theology in Two Modes

Serene Jones

"What are you writing?" asked Al, the contractor who had been a steady presence in my life since my bathroom floor had rotted through my front hall ceiling two months earlier. I'd learned to trust his instincts on just about everything from Moroccan tiles to toilets. I'd also discovered, over time, that he was a pretty good theologian.

I looked up from my desk, which was strewn with folders. By comparison, I saw, his construction zone was a model of organization. "A piece on practical theology," I replied.

"Do you also write about impractical theology?" He grinned. I have to admit that his response made me wince a little. Does calling one discipline "practical" imply in some way that what those of us in other disciplines do is not?

"No, I don't write *or* teach impractical theology," I told Al as calmly as possible. "Everything we do in the divinity school is practical; it's about faith and people's lives." We talked for a while and then turned back to our projects. But as we did so, I realized that each of us was working in a zone where structures were changing. Like my front hallway, the place of practical theology within theology as a whole is presently under construction. My answer to Al will also be part of my argument here: all theological educators are in some sense "practical" theologians. At the same time, I will argue for the importance of practical theology as a distinctive field and will suggest that it has the potential to be a significant factor as theological education builds for the future. Constructing this part of the curriculum in a manner that is both durable and welcoming is, like the rebuilding of my hallway, crucial to the functioning of our theological house as a whole.

Surely almost everyone teaching in a seminary today would agree that teaching and research that specifically explore the practices of ministry and Christian living and help students to engage in these practices more fully are of great importance. What curriculum committee doesn't wonder each year when pulling together course offerings whether they've included the full range of "practical" classes necessary for modern day parish work? Answering this question is critically important to the life and mission of any school, even though answering sometimes proves surprisingly difficult to do. Similarly, what ministerial studies search committee hasn't been perplexed by the challenge of writing job descriptions for teachers who can pass on to students those integrative, down-to-earth skills required to effectively lead faith communities? Designing such positions is essential, and yet, time and again, it is hard to find just the right language to describe teaching of this kind and even harder to find the right person to undertake it. What kind of graduate training prepares someone for this kind of teaching? How are we to define forms of excellence that are more than sheerly academic?

Moreover, as noted above, a lack of clarity about practical theology also exists at a personal level. What faculty member hasn't had a version of my conversation with Al, in which folks want to know, in real-life terms, why our theological teaching matters, and who among us hasn't faltered just a little when trying to answer? It's as if orange warning-cones and yellow tape presently encircle our collective thoughts about practical theology and its relation to other fields, under a sign that reads: "Caution: Construction Work Zone — Enter at Your Own Risk."

As this volume demonstrates, much constructive work has been going on in this zone in recent decades. Over the past three years, I have had the opportunity to engage with this work as a "visitor" from a neighboring discipline, and in this essay I explore the insights that have flowed from those conversations. I am a systematic theologian by training and in spirit; I love the intellectual work of helping students understand the complex terrain of their belief systems and faith commitments, and as such, I have enjoyed working with the conceptual challenges of answering Al's question from my disciplinary perspective, informed by the wisdom of others who are far more practically agile than I. What I offer here, however, is not a summary of "practical theology" according to canons of systematics (as if such a perspective even existed). Rather I offer some reflections on what is unique about practical theology as a distinctive subject matter or field, while also insisting that all good theology is practical in a related but somewhat different way.

Figuring out the relation between practical theology as an endeavor shared by the *whole* theological faculty and practical theology as it is undertaken by *designated experts* working within a distinct curricular area has weighty consequences for the sturdiness of the educational communities we are building for future generations of students. On the surface, this may seem a small question, but since the beginning of this project, it has quietly but persistently commanded my attention in a manner not unlike those hidden but crucial load-bearing walls that builders look for. If you ignore them, you do so at the building's peril. So, too, it is with this theologically load-bearing question.

In my own work, the stakes involved in this question are significant, and I feel them daily. From the start of my teaching career, I have defined myself as a very practical systematic theologian and, as such, as an intellectual companion of those who do practical theology in the more focused sense. It has always seemed to me that any responsible Christian theologian should be, in fact, a practical theologian because — isn't it obvious? — the faith we teach is through and through a practical faith. It lives only insofar as it lives in the tissue of our everyday comings and goings, in our practices, and in our material, communal lives in all their complex, messy, graced fullness. I am well aware, however, that in seminary offices around me sit professors who officially call themselves "practical" theologians and who teach subjects very different than mine. When I listen to them describe what I do as being abstract and highly theoretical in contrast to their own more down-to-earth activities, my disciplinary abode does appear, as Al imagined it, an exercise in impractical theology. My reaction to this depiction is never as straightforward as I would like, for both views of practical theology seem right. I do practical theology in a very broad manner; they do practical theology in a more discretely defined mode. So what is the difference between them? And what might they share?

In the sections that follow, I lay out what I see as the similarities and differences between the two enterprises. I try not to draw hard lines between them, however, or to resolve the vital tensions that their differences inevitably generate. Instead, I argue that our schools are best served by keeping the question of their relationship creatively open-ended. To do this, we need continually to insist, first, that practical theology is an endeavor of the *whole;* as seminary faculty, all are practical theologians, including those who are also systematic theologians and biblical scholars, historians and ethicists. Affirming this insures that theological education stays concretely engaged and theologically faithful in its mission to serve abundant living in and for the world. Secondly, I argue that questions regarding *how* to be concretely engaged are complex and difficult and that we need a segment of our faculty to be devoted to helping us and our students better grasp this "how." By carving out a place for practical theology in this sense, we seek to insure that our collective work is guided by the best and most creative "practical" insights and know-how of the day. Specialized scholarship and teaching of this kind help to keep both students and the rest of the faculty intellectually honest about and theologically engaged in crucial aspects of Christian ministry and life.

In framing my understanding of practical theology in this way — as a dialectical interplay between its broadest holistic aspirations and its varied forms of specialized expertise — I avoid nailing down a rigid definition of the enterprise, instead leaving it intentionally open-ended. My hope is that theological faculties can learn to be comfortable with this tensive indeterminacy, this back and forth between broad aspirations and specialized talents. Doing so will require us to come to grips with the discomfort of living in the middle of a never-to-be-finally-completed construction zone. Learning to tolerate this tense incompleteness, however, will make us better theologians and teachers. After all, so much of life, in both its practices and its confessions, is conflicted and unfinished, and it is important to know that our faith's load-bearing walls will hold up well as we move into our ever-unfolding and still gracefully unfinished future.

What's "Practical" about Systematic Theology?

When I tried to explain to Al that all theology is practical theology and that everyone in a seminary should try to be a practical theologian, the images that immediately came to mind were scenes from my own classroom at Yale Divinity School. Here, day in and day out, I participate in a project of intellectual faith-formation that feels practical through and through. While I experience the practicality of my work in classes ranging from Reformed theology to the doctrine of God, it is most alive for me in my introductory lecture course in systematic theology. After fifteen years of leading it, I still can hardly wait to walk in the door that first day and begin teaching students why and how Christian faith-claims matter. It is vital and energizing. I love talking with them about subjects like God, the church, Jesus, salvation, revelation, providence, and all the other complex concepts that make up the landscape of Christianity's belief system. And in those moments when I am most thoroughly immersed in teaching such things, it feels more like I'm dancing or story-telling or even playing a vigorous game of soccer or poker than engaging in something disembodied and abstract. What is very clear to me, in the midst of it all, is that doing systematic theology is itself a practice — a form of engaged knowing, a disciplined habit of body and mind, a patterned action, a way of embracing the world that is as embodied and ritualized and traditioned and improvisational as any of the other forms of "practical know-how" more typically associated with practical theology.

What are these plays of mind and body — these *practices* of systematic theology — that make my classroom engagement feel this way?[1] At one level, the course unfolds in a very traditional, straightforward manner. I walk students through the major doctrinal loci that structure the Christian tradition's creeds and confessions, discussing as we go their content, their history, and their ongoing role in the life of faith. We explore each doctrine from several perspectives, emphasizing that Christianity is not comprised of a single tradition but several. I insist, however, that even in the midst of these differences, there are core claims that Christians share and that grasping their fullness is enormously important to the life of faith. Why? Because together they create an imaginative worldview in which God is present and calling us to step into the reality of divine grace and to live there fully.

When I open this world of doctrine to students, I try to show them what that imaginative world consists of by teaching them habituated thought-patterns that Christians have devised over the centuries to structure the deep faith plays of mind that comprise the terms of their engagement with the world — the rules of doctrine. Stating it this way makes these rules sound abstract, but they are not. I don't want students to grasp an understanding of grace, for example, as if it were just a mathematical concept or an easily managed set of propositions. I want them to experi-

---

1. These were lessons I tried to learn from my teachers, among whom I include five of the best in the business: John Calvin, Hans Frei, David Kelsey, Letty Russell, and Cornel West.

ence the lived reality of theological claims about grace as they seep into the far reaches of their imaginations and run through their bodies. I want them to know these faith claims not only cognitively, though I do consider that one important dimension. I want them also to imbibe these claims, to taste them, and to believe them.[2] For some students, I pursue this goal by giving them the tools they need to make sense of the faith they have — I do not create it, I simply give them the glasses they need to see what is there already and a well-honed calculus for calibrating the weight of what they already know to be true. For others, the class serves a more constructive catechetical function, and I find that I am opening doors to a faith they may have come to divinity school to discover.

How do I help this happen? As a teacher, I start by entering a particular mindset when I write my lectures. A good number of my students are involved in ministry or community work, so when I sit down to work, I envision them doing theology in various field education sites and write towards those places. I imagine Maggie preaching on Sunday in a downtown New Haven church; I see Juan sitting with the parents of a son killed in Iraq; I picture Lauren coming home exhausted after a contentious finance meeting; I think of Elijah presiding over his first funeral and his first wedding in the same week. With these pictures in mind, I then begin to describe how I understand the rules of doctrines such as the Holy Spirit, Providence, Justification and Sanctification, and Creation coming to life in their midst. The process is deeply integrative. Older models, such as "applied theology" and "reflection on praxis in the light of theory" are not helpful at this point: I do not first have an idea of what a doctrine is and then, with that concept in hand, try to figure out how to apply it to their lives. No, for me, doctrinal rules only become meaningful when they are enacted in the midst of life-stories. In other words, there are no doctrines lying around waiting for me to teach them in principle, as if they could be separated from the narrative, life-filled sites of their enactment. They are what they are, incarnate. This does not mean I cannot explicate their logic

2. The kind of knowledge I long for my students to develop is related to the way of knowing that Craig Dykstra describes as "a deep, somatic, profoundly personal, but very real knowledge" in his chapter, p. 55, and to the "embodied knowing" that is the focus of Christian Scharen's chapter. See also the concluding chapter of this book, p. 357. In the context of learning systematic theology, I sometimes see students bringing this kind of knowing to articulacy and coherence, and I hope that future experiences will connect with the conceptual landscape encountered in my classes in ways that cannot yet be anticipated.

in a certain form of abstracted prose. What it means is that doctrines only take on life when they settle into the stuff of faith's ongoing, practical unfolding.

What this looks like concretely, as a form of practical systematic theology, changes constantly. For example, when we are studying pneumatology, I think of Maggie and try to explain to her that sermons are acts of proclamation, not just good story-telling or public counseling sessions, and then to teach her a play of mind that, when she preaches, allows her to be open to the Holy Spirit. In my judgment, this is how she will best learn the doctrine of revelation and master the logic of pneumatology. Juan's urgent, lived need for a resilient and profoundly honest view of the doctrine of providence shapes how I teach that doctrine. I ask myself, "How might I describe God's providential, caring relationship to the world with enough nuance and substance that he will not make trivial or untrue claims about God's will in the midst of the devastating violence of war?" With Lauren in mind, I focus on the ways in which the doctrines of justification and sanctification might help her see that, on the one hand, her church finance committee is not in charge of saving the world — that is God's work in justification — but that, on the other hand, finance meetings still matter enormously to the faithful functioning of churches (sanctification).[3] What I try to give Lauren is an on-the-ground version of soteriology and a lived doctrine of grace. For Elijah, my hope is that the doctrine of creation might help him understand that, when it comes to funerals, Christians have more to say about finitude and death than just a string of platitudes about heaven, and when it comes to marriage, Christians can find freedom and strength in the realization that human covenants and God's covenant are not identical — and that God's alone is everlasting.

Many of my colleagues in practical theology would find this model of teaching familiar, in that it draws constantly on the lived experiences of persons, sometimes referring to events I know really happened and sometimes conjuring up fictive scenarios based on what I know generally about churches and my students. Teaching to and from embodied, situated particularity is something I think I share with them. The difference between us is not that my teaching is impractical; it is rather that placing embodied, situated particularity within the imaginative landscape of Christian doc-

---

3. Dorothy Bass's chapter in this volume explores the tensive relationship between justification and sanctification in the Christian life in a similar way. See pp. 32ff.

trine is one of my goals. When I do this, I am not using these stories as events to be analyzed using doctrines, as if systematic theology somehow worked like a surgeon's scalpel, dissecting life in a particular way, or as if lived experience were an object to which theology needed to be applied. No, these stories hold the substance of doctrine; the theology I teach has no meaning apart from them. The plays of mind and imagination that comprise the landscape of doctrinal meanings are the same plays of mind and imagination that construct and engage everyday life in all its complex fullness.

In other words, experience happens in the space of these doctrinal plays of mind and not outside of them. Life and doctrine are inseparable. My hope is that when students begin to grasp the logic of faith in this manner, they will know it in their bodies as much as in their cognitive minds because, like learning to walk or speak, they are mastering a patterned set of moves that engage an embodied, thinking agent. In this regard, systematic theology is practical from beginning to end insofar as it unfolds in space the daily practices that comprise life as we actually live it. From where I stand, it is hard to imagine an enterprise more down-to-earth than this.

What's "Practical" about Practical Theology?

Even though my understanding of systematic theology is very practical, what I teach is not the same as the practical theology taught in disciplines that officially bear the name "practical." Making sense of this distinction while also insisting that my own endeavor is pragmatically engaged is a complex matter. I realize, as should anyone who is part of a multiple-disciplinary faculty, that there are things I do not need to teach in my classroom because they are being taught by others who understand them better than I do. This simple insight is one that all of us need to be reminded of regularly. I do not teach my students how to do exegesis because I can just barely read Hebrew and Greek, and I have not mastered the plays of intellect or the structure and the work of biblical scholarship today. The same goes for church history. In my lectures, I make references to the medieval church knowing that students are wrestling with these topics in other classes. This is true for the field of practical theology as well. There are imaginative plays of mind and patterned habits of thought and analysis that are learned in practical field classes that I simply do not have the background or the wisdom to teach thoroughly and well.

Like the intellectual habits and plays of mind belonging to systematic theology, the patterns of practical theology do not fit into nice, clean categories, as the other chapters in this book demonstrate. However, I know them when I see them, and especially when I see them in practice, as I did during a recent experience of co-leading a classroom discussion on "trauma and grace" with a colleague from the field of pastoral care and counseling. Our topic was the Columbine High School shootings and the challenges of being pastoral leaders in situations of catastrophic violence. We began the class by showing a video re-enactment of the events followed by interviews with survivors and on-the-scene footage of student reactions in the immediate aftermath. After these visually powerful presentations, the class turned to the theological and pastoral issues involved in ministering to others in such traumatic environments.

My colleague and I agreed that I would start the discussion, and I began by asking students how they might have responded as pastors and what role their understanding of Jesus would have played in that response. Given the enormity of the violence, I asked them to think particularly about the relation between this event and the Cross, that moment in Scripture where we find a story of devastating violence disrupting history and destroying hope. How do you imagine God-in-Christ being present to humanity in the midst of the violence of the Cross? I asked them. Where was God when Jesus was crucified? And where was God at Columbine? How do your answers to these questions, I further asked, affect your baseline perceptions of the events themselves? Would you have seen the victims as crucified? Would you have viewed the perpetrators as similar to Christ's own betrayers and crucifiers? How would you have interpreted your own role as a pastoral presence? As being Christ-like? As bearing the Cross? Standing with the violated? Taking on the sins of the world?

Given the topic's weight, conversation was slow in beginning, but as the class relaxed, responses began. For the most part, their answers were predictable but wise. They wanted to be pastors who were "with" and "suffering alongside" the high-school students and who, from this position, would be strong witnesses to the reality that God is "with us" and "suffers alongside" humanity in the midst of the world's violence. When asked about the Christology that lay behind this view of ministry, they gave a doctrinal answer we had explored in a previous class, the "solidarity" view of the Trinity. Because God, in the Incarnation, takes on our full humanity, we can be certain that on the Cross God took in Christ's suffering and death, profoundly and completely. This means that in the midst of our suffering, God similarly (by adoption) takes on the full weight of our human plight and bears our traumas fully, in solidarity with us. This Trinitarian model, the students suggested, provides a powerful model for doing ministry in the midst of cross-like traumatic events like Columbine. Here, they argued, one is called to practice a ministry of "solidarity" where clergy similarly "stand with" those who suffer, holding them, bearing their pain and affirming their humanity, albeit in ways appropriately not divine but human.

Following this doctrinal conversation, which I thought went very well, my pastoral care colleague took her turn leading the class. As I had come to expect, she moved the conversation in a different direction, both in style and in the content of her comments. She started by asking the class how they felt watching the clip: Did they go numb? Was it hard to concentrate? Did it make them nervous? Fascinated? Did it provoke other images? Feelings? She leaned towards them as she offered these questions, her voice low and undemanding but fully present. She patiently allowed long periods of silence into which students were gently invited to offer comments if they chose. She also nodded often, and gave affirming "hmmms" after students spoke — and also when they didn't. Watching this artful dance of teaching, it struck me that through her bodily actions and the use of voice she was teaching them important things about how one is pastorally present to persons in the midst of such a crisis — a concrete form of know-how that she was showing them as much as explicitly teaching them.

After what seemed an appropriate period of time, she then began to introduce the literature of her field. She described clinical studies of a phenomenon called "clergy compassion fatigue." This material suggests that frontline caregivers often suffer symptoms similar to the post-traumatic stress responses experienced by those for whom they care, albeit in a secondary, mediated form. She explained that when pastors become too identified with those who are traumatized, they risk carrying the traumatic experiences of others into their own lives. Like the traumatized, they can lose their cognitive capacity to make sense of the world; their own mental boundaries begin to crack open, and in many cases, their agentic confidence fractures, making it difficult for them to undertake daily life tasks with vigor or hope. After describing this phenomenon, my colleague asked the class a number of open-ended but directive questions that elicited from them stories about previous times when they had felt overwhelmed by their proximity to the traumatic suffering of others, and the conversation turned to congregations. A student from Denver talked about the slow disintegration of a church located near Columbine in the years since the shootings; another described a parish in Fairfield County, Connecticut, that still carries, in the church's body, the aftershocks of 9/11. In such cases, my colleague pointed out, not only pastors but communities themselves can take on, at a secondary level, the symptoms of traumatic anxiety and disorientation that the survivors in their midst are experiencing. When this happens, pastors cease to pastor well and congregations begin to fracture and split. She pointed out, as well, that the class's own inability to concentrate as they watched the clips could be, itself, an enactment of this dynamic, albeit in miniature.

As the conversation continued, it became apparent to everyone in the classroom that we were discussing not just a psychological issue but a deeply theological one. The most obvious insight to emerge was that "solidarity" models of ministry might have significant limitations when deployed in situations of traumatic violence. At a pastoral level, ministers may need to practice detachment rather than identification with victims in events like Columbine if they are to be effective caregivers. A second insight followed, namely, that imagining one's role to be "Christ-like" with respect to Jesus' own identificatory suffering might be a hindrance not a help in instances such as these. Out of this grew a discussion of ministry models that do not assume an *imitatio Christi* theology, a conversation with a long and complex history in the annals of Christian doctrine. She further grounded these comments in her own reflections on the pragmatics of teaching traumatic material — how she herself had to detach from it in order to be present to the students as they experienced its often overwhelming force. She once again showed them, in her embodied practice, a practical enactment of the very subject matter she was explicating.

The insights and concrete learning of the class did not end here, however. My colleague's questions forced the class to reach back even further into the theological substance of our discussion in order to explore possible shortcomings of the Trinitarian solidarity model itself. Could it be, the students asked, that the First Person of the Trinity may well have to be imagined as *detached from* — and not just *identified with* — the suffering of the Second Person in order for God to be the one who speaks, loves, acts, and

205

saves in the midst of the traumatic undoing of a crucifixion that silences voice, disables action, and fractures possibility. Could it be that God did, in fact, "abandon" Jesus on the Cross not as a punishment but in an act of salvation and love? As students began to make these connections, the class felt electric, and our conversation felt, well, *true*. The whole picture of what it means to be a pastor and a person of faith wrestling with the meaning of life in the midst of a profoundly broken world — a world that God loves — was coming alive for them. For me as a systematic theologian, it was as if a key had been turned in the lock of my view of the ministry and then, correlatively, of the doctrine of the Trinity — a moment of conversion, almost. Practical theology, I thought, at its best.

Here too, however, my expectations of what constitutes a successful class and good "theology" were challenged by the practice of my practical theological co-teacher. While she was as moved as I was by the theological insight that flowed from our discussion of Divine distance, she pressed beyond it, asking the class to consider whether or not this view of the Trinity would have made significant difference to a high-schooler in Denver on the day of the shooting. While it was clear she did not think that these insights had no pastoral significance, she wanted us also to think in very practical, down-to-earth ways about how these insights might be enacted in concrete forms that are deeper than cognitive knowledge might suggest, in forms perhaps more physical than intellectual, in interactions more invested in touch and sound and feeling than in theological, doctrinal insight. As to how she "taught" these important realties of pastoral life, it was again as much in her doing as in her saying that she engaged and showed what such a presence — at one and the same time distanced and yet compassionately present — might look like in the midst of lived experience.[4]

---

4. The example of my colleague's teaching reinforces several points about teaching in the practical field, including Bonnie Miller-McLemore's argument that teachers in the practical area must perform what they teach as well as describe and analyze it (p. 175); James Nieman's description of practical theological teachers as modeling for their students what it means to be a reflective practitioner (p. 153); and John Witvliet's argument that a class in worship must, at least at times, be worshipful in tone (p. 146), as my colleague's class was caring in tone.

What Is Distinctive about "Practical Theology," and Why Does Systematic Theology Need It?

What did my colleague do well that was different from my own best offerings? Our shared teaching experience suggests several points regarding the relation between systematic theology and practical theology and how work in these two fields can inform and complement one another, especially in the context of sustained collaboration.

First, and perhaps most obviously, our team-teaching reminded me again and again of the value of the distinctive disciplinary knowledges that scholars and practitioners of practical theology bring to the theological curriculum as a whole. In this case, my colleague had access to and mastery over a body of knowledge that was simply outside the purview of my expertise. (Likewise, it seems unlikely that theologians like Jürgen Moltmann, who support the "solidarity" model, ever read a clinical journal article on compassion fatigue.) My colleague had spent years studying literature in the fields of psychology and sociology as well as the growing body of material emerging from the field of pastoral care and counseling. What was powerful about her teaching, however, was not just her disciplinary knowledge but her skill at integrating it with my systematics knowledge as well as the work of other disciplines in order to give the class a more comprehensive sense of how one practically engages the life of faith in the midst of a crisis such as Columbine. In this regard, her lively sense for the cross-disciplinary character of theology was one of her distinctive strengths. Her practical play of mind was richly interdisciplinary — a skill that no doubt the entire faculty could benefit from learning.[5]

Second, as I watched my colleague work with the class, it was clear to me that her training had developed certain habits of mind that were quite different from those formed by the guilds where my own intellectual habits were formed. When she looked at the world of the events we were discussing, her eyes saw things mine did not. When approaching the topic of God's relation to violence, for instance, she was able to notice and analyze

---

5. The final chapter of this book argues that interdisciplinary collaboration is necessary if practical theologians are to gather insights, methods, and resources that are adequate to portray the complex realities on which this field focuses. The complex realities of faith and life mean that this same claim should be made for those working in other theological fields as well.

the patterns of behaviors, attitudes, and actions surrounding the event, particularly as they related to models of pastoral action and to church-communal gestures of heart, hand, and head. Her strength was her ability to read the motions of bodies, the play of unconscious reactions and responses, and the practices — some clear and some cloudy — that were part of the thick texture of our subject matter. She did this not only with regard to the situation at Columbine; she did it with the class as well. She was able to read our students — their own reactions to the films we saw and to past traumas in their lives — in ways that simply escaped me.[6]

Third, my colleague had not only mastered a body of knowledge and a way of seeing/reading practices that were different from my own. She had also mastered a distinctive way of passing on this knowledge — a unique set of pedagogical strategies. When she worked with the class, it was thrilling to see her ability to elicit from students stories that, in their telling of them, awakened them to new insights that my own approach failed to elicit. Using a form of *invitational, directive listening,* she encouraged them to grapple with and open up the world of practices in creative ways that kept their stories at the center of the discussion. She was teaching practical theology using pedagogical practices that made the students' own practices and experience the center of their critical reflection. I try to do this when I write theology lectures aimed at Maggie and Juan's experiences in their field placements, but my colleague was able to do it much more directly than I because her discipline places their experiences and their pastoral work in the foreground of concern. The fact that her own doctoral training included clinical training in counseling likely deepened this capacity in her.

Fourth, she was particularly skilled at the integrative goal of helping students see how the different pieces of our school's multi-sectioned curriculum came together in the context of pastoral ministry. She did this by using their stories and experiences as the landing place of our reflection rather than as just a teaching example or case study. In doing so, she helped the class to bring all our specialized knowledges together in a space of lived faith. In the course of her analysis of the event, she encouraged students to make connections between the insights of the clinical literature on compas-

6. In her chapter in this book, Bonnie Miller-McLemore discusses how clinical training in counseling, which is undertaken by most teachers of pastoral care, influences the pedagogy of teachers in this field; p. 175.

sion fatigue, the practical workings of congregations, the doctrine of the Trinity, their own lived experiences of traumatic violence, and the Gospel of Mark's account of Jesus' cry of dereliction. While it would be ideal if every professor in every field were able to take his or her designated subject matter and show how it fits together with other disciplines in the curriculum and with the on-the-ground challenges of parish work, it was clear to me that my colleague had been trained to put this integrative agenda at the forefront of her teaching agenda. She was skilled at not just explaining and modeling integration but also at guiding students in integrative thinking of their own. In this regard, she demonstrated well one of the principal strengths of practical theology — its thoroughgoing interdisciplinary character. At its heart, it is a multi-disciplinary, intra-disciplined discipline.

Fifth, her process of teaching was not just to take clinical literature and apply it to a ministerial context. The material on compassion fatigue was transformed, in her hands, into a body of literature that could be interpreted theologically, shifting its context and opening up its possibilities. In this regard, she moved the material beyond the social science framework out of which it emerged and situated it within a Christian communal context, thereby theologically recrafting some of the core assumptions of compassion fatigue theorists. It was not a situation, therefore, in which I was doing theology and she, practice. No, her work had its own distinctive, theological substance — a substance that directly impacted the doctrinal conversations about the Trinity I subsequently led. What this suggests is that not only I as a theologian have much to learn, even about doctrines, from the wisdom of the practical fields, but that a good practical theologian like my colleague is guided by some of the supposedly "impractical insights" that mark the work of systematicians like me.

Living in the Construction Zone Where
Practical Theology and Other Disciplines Meet

Using two of my courses as examples, I have described two different ways in which the term "practical theology" can be applied to the endeavors of our theological faculties. On the one hand, it names an *aspiration* that ideally should be shared by the entire theological faculty: when we do our work best, we should all aspire to be practical theologians. This is the highest goal of our teaching. On the other hand, I have also shown how the term appropriately functions as the name for a specific teaching *area* within the curriculum of most theological schools. It is the place marked by distinctive disciplinary habits and teaching competencies that are not shared by the whole faculty because, like all the disciplinary endeavors, it demands specialized know-how and training. The crucial strengths of this disciplinary area, I have suggested, are not only its specialized content (i.e., psychology), but also its ability to read persons and situations, its capacity to foster integration within a multi-disciplinary vision, its effort to teach a practice rather than simply about a practice, its commitment to developing pedagogical strategies appropriate to its subject matter, and its ongoing contribution to substantive theological reflection.

I have also suggested that the tensions between these understandings of practical theology as shared aspiration and distinct area are sources of vitality for practical theology and for theological education as a whole. In my view, the tensions created by the back and forth between the two understandings is productive, and the urge to resolve them should be resisted. One such tension is the push-pull dialectic between practical theology's disaggregating commitment to attending to the particularity of situations and its aggregating drive to develop integrative competencies. A similar tension arises when the desire to define distinctive methods and modes of knowing (a disciplinary episteme) conflicts with the recognition that the patterns practical theology seeks to identify are as intuitive and unconscious as they are cognitive and measurable. Moreover, all of these tensions are influenced by an ongoing tension between doctrine and practice in the life of Christian communities, within which theological affirmations measure practice, which itself shapes theology, which is itself a practice that is, in its incarnate form, irreducibly theological.[7] Keeping such tensions alive is not easy, for the desire to dissolve tensions such as these is strong, and resisting this desire means taking up residence in a construction zone. The conversations, practices, and forms of life likely to emerge in this zone, however, are vital and necessary ones that would be poorer if any of these tensions were to collapse.

In the course of writing this essay, I have learned that many practical

---

7. A predecessor seminar and book to this one, in which I also participated with Dykstra and Bass, explored this tension more fully; see Miroslav Volf and Dorothy C. Bass, eds., *Practicing Theology: Beliefs and Practices in Christian Life* (Grand Rapids: Eerdmans, 2002).

theologians — in both senses of the term — are able to manage these tensions and that as a result the construction zone they occupy is bursting at the seams with energy and insights that are crucial to the future of theological education as a whole. I have come to believe that playing with this set of tensions, keeping them alive and irksomely unresolved, may well be the key to revitalizing seminary education in the years ahead. If this is so, practical theology may well be poised to take a strong lead — over other disciplines — in charting a new, enlivened course for a form of theological education that is both globally responsive and intellectually rich.

As a systematic theologian who is committed to living in this construction zone, I want to call attention to one more tension that is crucial to the ongoing development of practical theology in both senses and to the capacity of theological education as a whole to serve the church and the world. This final tension proposes forms of mutual reliance and accountability that could eventually shape the architecture of a sturdy space within which the sometimes untidy work of education for the sake of Christian ministry and life can thrive.

The specialized practical insights of those who teach in the practical field must themselves be measured by the strong *theological* standards and norms that inspire our schools as a whole. In this regard, specialized work in practical theology must be submitted, as a form of theological knowledge, to the broader measure of Christian faith and practice, a measure enriched by the work of a seemingly impractical field like systematic theology, among others. In other words, those who teach and write in such practical areas as pastoral care and counseling, preaching, and Christian education do not have unilateral ownership of the theological criteria by which their teaching and research are assessed.

At the same time, theological educators in other fields need to acknowledge that the theological criteria guiding their schools are themselves subject to practical wisdom gleaned from faith-on-the-ground, faith as it unfolds in the lived experience of pastors, congregations, and Christians everywhere. While this is not a wisdom for which specialized practical theologians can claim exclusive ownership, they nonetheless have a certain well-earned affinity for it, and because of this, it is to the theological benefit of all theological educators to listen carefully to them.

The relationship between practical theology as a distinctive field and the other fields represented in theological education is an active, unfinished work-site where new possibilities are embraced and enacted with each passing day. It is in a construction zone such as this that the future of theological education can best be imagined and engaged. While it is clear that neither Al nor I could have held up under the pressure of a never-finished hallway, it may well be that a good practical theologian (in both senses of the term) will always feel more at home in the middle of such tensive indeterminacy than she ever would in other more staid corners of theological education — where, alas, far too many systematicians are still to be found.

History, Practice, and Theological Education

This essay, like the next one, explores the rich territory that exists on the frontier between practical theology and another field that consistently receives attention in theological education. Though typically different in their organization, courses in history and practical theology almost inevitably overlap, as teachers in the practical field strive to help students understand the history that has shaped practices of ministry and Christian living, and as teachers in history select from an overwhelming amount of historical material that which has important bearing on Christian life and ministry. As educators in both fields embrace their vocation as "practical theologians" in the more expansive sense that Serene Jones claims belongs to all theological educators, opportunities emerge for fruitful conversation and collaboration between these fields.

Here David Daniels, who teaches the history of Christianity at McCormick Theological Seminary, and Ted Smith, who teaches practical theology at Vanderbilt Divinity School, engage in just such a conversation. As they describe their courses, the characteristic approaches of their home disciplines remain visible. At the same time, however, we learn that their teaching shares an emphasis that both individuals believe provides a generative focus for students preparing for ministry: attention to the historical development of specific practices. This emphasis, Smith and Daniels argue, opens students' imaginations and draws them onto horizons of hope. Moreover, attention to the history of practices enables each discipline to do its own work better and forges salutary connections across the curriculum. It is intriguing to wonder how a similar emphasis on practices might also provide biblical scholars, systematic and philosophical theologians, and ethicists with ideas for renewed engagement with work being done by their practical field colleagues.

9. History, Practice, and Theological Education

David D. Daniels III and Ted A. Smith

"Practice" can be defined in many ways, but all the best definitions remember that a practice is formed over time. So, too, history has many tasks. But every full understanding of the field includes some place for practice. Talk about practice leads to historical work, and work in history invites consideration of practice. History and practical theology call out to one another across the gulf of their separation by the syllabi, departments, and curricula of theological education. Recent years have seen a thicket of bridges across this gap. Historians, for instance, have compiled works like *Lived Religion in America* and *Practicing Protestants*. And homileticians — to take only one "practical" field — have written broad, sweeping surveys like O. C. Edwards's *A History of Preaching* as well as fine-grained studies like Beverly Zink-Sawyer's *From Preachers to Suffragists*.[1] In this essay we try to add one more bridge across the gap between history and practice by considering what it means to tell histories of practice in courses lodged in different parts of the theological curriculum. We are especially interested in ways to use histories of practice in the process of educating people for ministries that lead communities into ways of life that are caught up in God's great work of reconciliation.

1. See David D. Hall, ed., *Lived Religion in America* (Princeton: Princeton University Press, 1997); Laurie F. Maffly-Kipp, Leigh E. Schmidt, and Mark Valeri, eds., *Practicing Protestants: Histories of Christian Life in America, 1630-1965* (Baltimore: Johns Hopkins University Press, 2006); O. C. Edwards, *A History of Preaching* (Nashville: Abingdon Press, 2004); Beverly A. Zink-Sawyer, *From Preachers to Suffragists: Woman's Rights and Religious Convictions in the Lives of Three Nineteenth-Century American Clergywomen* (Louisville: Westminster/John Knox Press, 2003).

As coauthors, we approach the divide between history and practice from opposite sides. One of us, David Daniels, has been trained as an historian. He has taught church history at McCormick Theological Seminary since 1987. Ted Smith, on the other hand, teaches ethics and preaching at Vanderbilt Divinity School. Both of us try to teach histories of practice in our classes. But one of us reaches from history toward practice, and the other from practice toward history. The view is different from each side, and we believe the differences are worth preserving in the structure of this essay.

While we start from different places and work from different definitions of "practice," we both teach history with critical and constructive hopes. Histories of church practices are of more than antiquarian interest. They have the power to demystify practices that have become second nature, and so beyond conscious reflection. By retrieving the historical and social process by which a practice came to be established, we hope to open up critical and faithful conversation. By recalling the reasons given for establishing a practice, we hope to give students vocabulary for sharing in that conversation. And by remembering suppressed alternatives — the losers of historical struggles — we hope to stock the imaginations of pastors with lost treasures. Rummaging through the past can yield historical resources for charting new directions in ministry. But the resources of the past are not endlessly fungible goods that we can use in whatever ways we wish. We believe that the goods of the past also make claims on us. And good histories listen for ways the past addresses the church today.

We also share a sense of the glorious untidiness of the world as it actually exists. Though we use different metaphors, we both try to describe ways in which history can attend to and tell the story of irreducibly complex realities. In particular, we share a confidence that histories will spill over and eventually break up hardened containers for sorting people and practices by race, class, and culture. The actual practices of actual people resist clumping under categories like "Puritan preaching" or "Black Pentecostal piety." Careful historical studies reveal a mixing that extends back as far as we can see — and suggest the possibility of a church that might embrace such combinations in its present and future practice.

Underneath other agreements lies a shared sense of the *disjunctive* nature of historical time. Neither of us tells smooth narratives that connect past, present, and future in an unbroken line. Daniels emphasizes the importance of the rupture with the past: the seventeenth century is a "lost world" to us, and there is no going back. And Smith stresses the break between past, present, and the eschatological horizon. The practices of everyday church life are not technologies that produce the Great Day; they are broken signs that — in and in spite of themselves — bear witness to and even get caught up in redemption.

What really matters, though, are not these larger and smaller points of agreement. The differences might be more interesting than the things we share. What matters most is our sense of a common task: to connect history and practice in teaching for ministry. In this essay we want to deepen the conversation about how to make that connection, and we hope to expand the ways that both practical theologians and historians try to make it. And so we offer not a single unified theory for the connection of history and practice, but examples of two attempts from two different starting points.

Teaching History in a Practical Class

— Ted A. Smith

My reflections on teaching history for ministry are shaped more by hope than experience. I write as an advanced beginner in classroom teaching. I have spent more years preaching on Sunday than teaching Monday through Friday. My coauthor has the wisdom born of long experience in one setting, but my own teaching has been brief and peripatetic. My observations grow out of teaching introductory classes in preaching for Master's students at Candler School of Theology and advanced seminars for Ph.D. and Master's students at Vanderbilt Divinity School. Such experiences — composite in many ways, and from a relatively short period of time — can illustrate this argument for teaching history in practice-oriented courses. But they cannot even begin to justify it. The real justification is in this hope: that theological histories of practice can help form preachers and congregations who understand themselves as caught up in God's presence for the life of the world, and who find ways to extend, revise, and improvise practices in response to that great love.

With these hopes in mind, I try to teach *theological histories of practice.* Each of the key words in this phrase gets used in a vast variety of ways. Clarifying what I mean by those words offers one path into the ways I am learning to teach. In the paragraphs that follow I take up each of the words in turn. In keeping with the hope that animates this essay, I will begin at the end.

By *practice* I do not mean whole forms of life like agriculture, medicine, hospitality, or testimony. In the context of these classes I find it more helpful to use "practice" to refer to smaller-scale habits, to patterned activities like exegeting Scripture, developing an introduction that attracts attention, finding a style that conveys sincerity, and telling stories to illustrate points.[2] Practices like these provide the structure of most introductory courses and texts in preaching. I follow that structure, more or less, but then try to add a historical dimension to the consideration of each practice. For instance, I try to teach students not only how to structure a sermon, but also a history of ways preachers have structured their sermons and why some of those ways got lost while others attained widespread use and common-sense status. The tighter focus of these histories temporarily divides the complex art of preaching into practices that students can learn one by one, even as they learn to bring them together into a whole sermon.

A history of practice in this sense must attend to the quotidian stuff of preaching over time. It is tempting to look elsewhere. Ironically, the every-

---

2. I therefore use "practice" much like Pierre Bourdieu used *habitus:* to describe "regulated improvisation" (p. 79), "subjective but not individual systems of internalized structures, schemes of perception, conception and action" (p. 86), or "systems of durable transposable *dispositions,* structured structures predisposed to function as structuring structures" (p. 72). See Pierre Bourdieu, *Outline of a Theory of Practice,* trans. Richard Nice (Cambridge: Cambridge University Press, 1972). This sense of practice calls for work at a smaller scale than the one suggested by Alasdair MacIntyre's definition of practice as a "coherent and complex form of socially established cooperative human activity" formed around pursuit of "goods internal to that activity." Alasdair MacIntyre, *After Virtue: A Study in Moral Theory* (London: Duckworth, 1985), p. 187.

I don't mean to reject MacIntyre's definition. Bourdieu and MacIntyre do not present mutually exclusive definitions, for they speak in different registers. MacIntyre's register is most useful for framing questions about the telos of preaching as a whole. But Bourdieu's smaller scale helps students see the ways most actual sermons are congeries of practices, each with a telos of its own (for better and for worse). Bourdieu's recognition of practices as "durable" and "transposable" also helps students see the ways in which they may already have undertaken versions of core practices of preaching in other spheres of their lives. And, as I argue above, Bourdieu's tighter focus helps students to learn preaching by letting them pick up one practice at a time. This smaller scale of analysis risks giving up questions of the purpose of the whole. But that work can perhaps be done better by other terms, like "way of life" (as used in the framing essays in the first part of this volume).

day has become less accessible than other forms of preaching and talk about preaching. Narratives about the development of homiletical method, for instance, are ready to hand. They often feature prominently in the education of faculty in homiletics, and they sometimes leak into introductory classrooms. But while stories of the guild's talk about preaching can help illumine the reasons changes got made, a history of practice will also require study of how people actually preached. And because practices are taken-for-granted habits widely shared across social groups, histories of practice cannot be told only through stories about a few exceptional preachers. Virtuoso preachers are important because they offered models that people in their times tried to emulate. And famous preachers may have been especially articulate in explaining why they performed a practice as they did. But what makes a practice a "practice" in the sense I'm using the term here is the sheer commonness of it. And so I try to lead students to accounts of more ordinary preachers preaching more ordinary sermons. The nature of practice demands histories of the everyday.

The *history* I do in preaching classes retrieves the social and historical processes by which practices come to be established as practices. Practices emerge in the lives of communities over time, but they become practices only as they come to be taken for granted. And that taken-for-grantedness requires forgetting the history of their production. Practices come to seem natural and eternal, more like gravity than something made by humans acting in time. I try to retrieve the history of a practice by offering students something like what Charles Taylor called a "genetic" account — a narrative that shows how a pattern of thought and action developed, how it moved from radical innovation to established norm, how it was transformed from something so odd that it could not be recognized to something so obvious that people can scarcely imagine alternatives.[3] It can be

---

3. As with my use of "practice," my sense of what history needs to be comes into sharper relief when contrasted with the work of Alasdair MacIntyre. I think that "genetic" histories avoid the progressivism implicit in MacIntyre's notion of "tradition" and the nihilism he ascribes to "genealogy." A genetic history leaves open, for a time, the question of whether a practice has made progress, turned into ideology, or taken another course entirely. It simply asks how things came to be the way they are. See Charles Taylor, "Philosophy and Its History," in *Philosophy and History: Essays on the Historiography of Philosophy,* ed. Richard Rorty et al. (Cambridge: Cambridge University Press, 1984), p. 20. Cf. Alasdair MacIntyre, *Three Rival Versions of Moral Enquiry: Encyclopaedia, Genealogy, and Tradition* (Notre Dame, Ind.: University of Notre Dame Press, 1990).

hard, for instance, for mainline Protestant students to imagine a sermon without stories of some sort to illustrate its points. It can be harder still to imagine what a story might be doing in a sermon if not "illustrating points." A genetic history of sermon stories would trace the ways this practice came to be so deeply established in our minds, bodies, and communities. It might remember the many forms and purposes of medieval *exempla,* the Puritans' wariness of *exempla* they considered tropological, the redevelopment of stories as illustrations by nineteenth-century evangelicals, the neo-orthodox movement's resistance to extrabiblical stories in the twentieth century, and the great proliferation of uses of "narrative" in the last three decades. Such a history would remember changes in storytelling alongside the rise of phenomena like the novel, the penny press, and the celebrity tell-all — and the kinds of subjectivity that could appreciate such narrative forms. Genetic histories tell the story of how some "we" came to do things "the way we do them."[4]

Genetic histories therefore differ from and complement the case studies described by John Witvliet elsewhere in this volume. Case studies need not be connected temporally to the present moment. Students can study case examples of worship in Calvin's Geneva, for instance, to learn what good practical theology looks like. They can then try to work by analogy in their own contexts. In the logic of the historical case example, there is no need to connect the past moment with the present — distance actually helps to construct the case *as* case, and analogy provides the bridge to present practice. But genetic histories try to connect the dots through time. History itself is the bridge. The genetic histories I use in an introductory preaching class might consider a practice from the sixteenth century, but only as one moment in a longer narrative that ends in the practices some group of people takes for granted today.

Genetic narratives have enormous critical power. They take a practice so obvious that it is invisible and bring it into view. They take a practice so natural that it seems eternal and show how it came to be in time. And the best genetic narratives take a practice that seems inevitable and show all the alternatives suppressed and forgotten in the course of its production. Thus, in Michel de Certeau's words, "History (in the modern sense of the

---

4. For a clear example of what I mean by a genetic history of a practice of preaching, see David S. Reynolds, "From Doctrine to Narrative: The Rise of Pulpit Storytelling in America," *American Quarterly* 32, no. 5 (Winter 1980): 479-98.

word) and revolution are born together."[5] But telling the story of how a practice came into being need not be *merely* critical. Genetic narratives end in nihilism if we assume that any church practice that came to being in time is nothing more than a human invention, driven by interests, and so a fall away from the will of God. There are deep currents in Western thought that push toward that assumption. Students often assume, for instance, that if a practice has not prevailed always and everywhere that it is just "made-up." But Christians have good reasons to reject the idea that historicity, the mere fact of having come into being, automatically degrades a practice. If Jesus Christ was born, crucified, and raised to new life, then the work of redemption has some historical dimension. If the Holy Spirit moves in the life of the church as it actually exists, then historical things are caught up in holiness. And if God is always already active in and for the life of the world, then things of God might come into being in the course of time. A *theological* history of practice begins with affirmations like these. It tells historical narratives in the trust that God moves in history for the sake of redeeming history.

To say that God moves in history is not to say that whatever is, is right. And to attempt to tell theological histories of church practices is not to say that those practices have become simply and perfectly identical to the work of God in the world. A theological history might take something closer to the shape suggested by the poet George Herbert:

> God calleth preaching folly. Do not grudge
> To pick out treasures from an earthen pot.
>   The worst speak something good: if all want sense,
>   God takes a text, and preacheth patience.[6]

The practice itself may fail to accomplish what it promises; the promise of a practice may be kept in spite of the practice. A theological history will remember this. It will remember that church practices hope for ends beyond what they actually accomplish. They point towards a horizon of redemption that they do not achieve in themselves. That horizon judges them,

---

5. Michel de Certeau, *L'étranger, ou l'union dans la différence* (Paris: Desclée de Brouwer, 1991), p. 105. Quoted in Rowan Williams, *Why Study the Past? The Quest for the Historical Church* (Grand Rapids: Eerdmans, 2005), pp. 5-6.

6. George Herbert, "The Church Porch," in *The Complete English Works*, ed. Ann Pasternak Slater, Everyman's Library no. 204 (New York: Alfred A. Knopf, 1974), ll.429-32.

even as it is their glory. A theological history will remember both the judgment and the glory. It will remember how church practices came into being even as it remembers their hope for their redemption. It will be not only genetic, but also eschatological.

In the classroom this means that sources from religious studies or even church history usually provide only a first step. At present the academic disciplines are divided in such a way that historical studies often give excellent genetic histories of practice, but only rarely go on to consider how a practice might be caught up in the love of God for the world. A fully theological history of practice asks students to take that extra step, to hazard a hope for the practice they are considering — and not only considering, but also taking up and transforming in their own ministries. Such hopes cannot be known in the same way that empirical facts can be known. But they are not simply shots in the dark or projections of fantasy. Scripture, reason, and the testimony of the people of God over time provide some guidance. And in the end it may be less important to establish a single theological interpretation than to form students for a way of participating in practices that regards those practices as both fallible historical realities and sanctified responses to God's great love. As a teacher I seek to open both historical and theological questions, and to help students hold them together without reduction.

I teach theological histories of practice in a course like Introduction to Preaching with a set of specific hopes in mind. These hopes have not been realized in every student in every semester. There is no magic here. But it is the students who have taught me to have these hopes. I scarcely could have formed them when I first began to teach.

First, I hope to induct students into informed, humble, critical, contextual conversations about the practices of preaching. Students sometimes find themselves at a loss when trying to think about better and worse forms of preaching. When they take differences in practice as natural facts and attribute those differences to cultural or to individual styles, they often say that they have no tools for evaluating difference. A healthy respect for individual and cultural pluralism leads them to a relativism that cannot make judgments of any kind. When they do make judgments, their evaluations tend to be abstractly pragmatic. They ask what will "work," but without much reflection on what work a practice is supposed to do, or why that work matters. Genetic histories help break such deadlocks of unreflective relativism and abstract pragmatism. Because they trace the reasons why different practices developed as they did, they lead students into communities of reason-giving. Students learn a kind of immanent critique that enables them to evaluate a practice on its own terms. And they learn a new self-consciousness. Practices once so inevitable as to be invisible now come into focus for critical conversation.

For instance, practices for arranging worship spaces often devolve into battles between students who want "traditional" spaces and students who want spaces arranged for maximum "effectiveness." But reading and discussing a thick history of worship spaces in the United States helped one class find new patterns for critical and constructive conversation.[7] The history of practice eroded the distinction between the two camps: traditionalists learned just how much worship spaces have changed over time, and pragmatists came to see the desire for effectiveness as itself part of traditions that have hoped for many different sorts of effects. Individual students came to see the worship spaces that had formed them not as eternal givens, but as incarnations of particular visions of church, worship, and salvation. They came to see even the spaces they despised as making some kind of sense in their own historical contexts. That doesn't mean that the conversation ended in a feast of mutual affirmation. If anything, what was at stake in the disagreements became clearer as the conversation became more precise. Most participants changed their minds in some way. But what really changed was the quality of the conversation. It moved from a surface-level conversation about "likes" and "dislikes" to a much deeper conversation about the meaning of community, the purpose of worship, and the ways those meanings and purposes could be sought in the arrangements of space.

Second, I hope that learning the history of practice will break open naturalized human constructions like race and ethnicity, and so enable more hybrid styles to flourish. Categories like "Black preaching," "Hispanic preaching," "Catholic preaching," and the late-to-self-consciousness "mainline preaching" (which used to think of itself as "just plain preaching," and still can't quite bear to call itself "white men's preaching") have all ossified over time. Like classical, soul, gospel, blues, rock, hip-hop, and country music, the preaching styles appear now as established entities. Each has its own

---

7. We relied especially on Anne C. Loveland and Otis B. Wheeler, *From Meetinghouse to Megachurch: A Material and Cultural History* (Columbia, Mo.: University of Missouri Press, 2003).

genealogy, distribution network, stars, and list of distinctive traits. But just as the history of musical styles is much messier than these neat categories suggest — to what category should we assign Marian Anderson? Dusty Springfield? Ray Charles? Jerry Lee Lewis? — the history of preaching is messier and more interesting than the categories that now organize it. Consider a preacher like Rebecca Protten, a woman of African heritage who joined the Moravian Church and then lit up the island of St. Thomas and the wider Atlantic world with her gospel preaching. Born in 1718, Protten traveled widely between Europe, Africa, and the Americas, soaking up and passing on influences at every stop. Or consider how many of the first white Methodist preachers in the United States experienced conversion in response to the preaching of Harry Hosier, the legendary African American preacher who traveled with Francis Asbury. Essentialized categories of race and culture have a hard time containing tangled stories of hybrid preachers like these.[8]

This is not to say that categories like race and ethnicity should drop out of our historical narratives. On the contrary, these categories have such enormous historical significance that it is impossible to tell the truth about any part of our history, including how we have come to preach in the ways we do, without making use of them. Telling stories of glorious hybridity and rhizomatic vitality without reference to race papers over the violence and injustice of a society still structured along lines of race. An appeal to

---

8. Here I have learned especially from Victor Anderson, *Beyond Ontological Blackness: An Essay in African American Religious and Cultural Criticism* (New York: Continuum, 1999); Uma Narayan, *Dislocating Cultures: Identities, Traditions, and Third World Feminism* (London: Routledge, 1997); and Sherry B. Ortner, "The Problem of 'Women' as an Analytic Category," in *Making Gender: The Politics and Erotics of Culture* (Boston: Beacon Press, 1996), pp. 116-38. On Rebecca Protten, see Jon F. Sensbach, *Rebecca's Revival: Creating Black Christianity in the Atlantic World* (Cambridge, Mass.: Harvard University Press, 2005). On Harry Hosier, see Nathan O. Hatch, *The Democratization of American Christianity* (New Haven: Yale University Press, 1989), p. 106.

In this essay I focus on categories of race, culture, and ethnicity. Gender has also been of enormous significance in the history of preaching, and any complete history must attend to it. I think an argument analogous to the one I make here can be developed in relation to gender. But the differences between race and gender are significant enough to warrant a separate and more focused discussion, a discussion that would outrun the limits of this essay. For examples of what that discussion might look like, see two classic articles: Joan W. Scott, "Gender: A Useful Category of Historical Analysis," *The American Historical Review* 91, no. 5 (December 1986): 1053-75, and Elizabeth A. Clark, "Women, Gender, and the Study of Christian History," *Church History*, vol. 70, no. 3 (September 2001) 395-426.

the messiness of history, as Brad R. Braxton wrote, can become "an ideological construct to obscure the times when history has been more blunt and univocal."[9] Ignoring categories like race and ethnicity also makes it more likely that a history will forget the practices of people who have had less power to shape the writing of history. Dominant narratives exert powerful gravitational pulls, and attempts to tell hybrid histories can quickly become nothing more than the same old stories with a few new characters. Analytic categories like race and ethnicity must appear in any truthful historical narrative. The key, though, is that they appear *within* history rather than *prior to* history. They should not be given unquestioned and invisible power to structure the ways we tell history. Such power treats these categories as if they were natural, given, even ontological. They should rather be remembered as brutally significant human constructions that emerged in time to shape the development of practices over time.

In the classroom, remembering race and ethnicity within history means making their emergence a persistent question on the syllabus, not just an assumed and invisible ordering principle that governs construction of the syllabus. For instance, if a preaching class presents black and white preaching as two completely different styles, and traces a history for each that does not overlap at any point with the history of the other, it not only fails to do justice to complex historical realities but can even slip into naturalizing racial categories as "givens" in structuring the world. A better class might ask, for example, how the great hurly-burly of the Cane Ridge Revival got sorted, over the course of the nineteenth century, into (at least) black Protestant, white mainline, white evangelical, and more multiracial Pentecostal traditions. How did the boundaries get drawn, who drew them, and with what effects? How do present practices repeat and resist those boundaries? Remembering an event like Cane Ridge or a preacher like Rebecca Protten need not make the significance of race disappear. It can rather clarify the ways human actors made race significant in the course of history. It can reveal racial structures as historical constructions rather than ontological givens. And so it can suggest strategies for resistance to those structures and kindle hopes that they might be transcended.

Remembering race as a powerful human construction that never fully captures reality can enable preaching students to break out of racialized categories and develop styles that display real hybrid vigor. When categories

9. Brad R. Braxton, personal correspondence with Ted A. Smith, October 31, 2006.

like "Black preaching" appear as hermetically sealed and eternally given traditions, African American students can feel bound by them and other students can feel as if they have nothing to learn from them. Brad R. Braxton, a colleague who takes up practices honed in both black church pulpits and European universities, described the resistance of a white student to his teaching. He taught black preaching, she said. And black preaching was great for black people. But what could she learn from it? And, more pointedly, how could it be fair to grade her on her ability to do it?[10]

The best answers to such questions will recall the long history of black preachers learning in white-dominated institutions — and the just-as-long history of whites hearing, copying, and adapting black rhetorical practices. Borrowing has gone in every direction, often accompanied by coercion, and for so long that there is always an example prior to whatever example we cite. And the lines that determine what counts as "borrowing" from another culture have been erected and redefined over time. The asymmetries of power across those lines are significant, and no account of borrowing would be complete without outrage at injustice past and present. The past makes claims on us. One way to respond to those claims, I think — one way to work towards a more just church and society — is to reveal the deep mixedness of our traditions, to tell histories that name the power of race to structure practice even as we point to some of the ways that real people have gotten over, under, and around those structures. Such histories of hybridity can inspire and legitimate all sorts of borrowing back and forth. They can support a pedagogy like Braxton's, in which students are encouraged to try on practices associated with races and cultures other than their own. Such borrowings are dangerous — they can descend into new forms of colonial appropriation, self-loathing, or even minstrelsy. But knowing the history of race in relation to a practice brings a critical self-consciousness that makes it more likely that even these awkward borrowings will become steps towards preaching that anticipates a church from every people and nation.

Third, I teach with the hope that history can help clarify the social relationships condensed, developed, and embodied in particular practices. A genetic history shows the ways a practice came into being. It reveals both the interests and the ideals with which the practice allied itself — interests and

---

10. I am grateful to Brad R. Braxton for allowing me to share this story, and for his incisive comments on the essay as a whole and on this section in particular.

ideals which live on in the practice, regardless of whether we are conscious of them. For instance, an informal, conversational, "natural" style has become so common among contemporary preachers as to pass beneath notice. It arose in the wake of the American Revolution, when a preacher no longer had authority simply because he was the pastor of a town's established church. Institutional ties mattered less in a time of legal and cultural disestablishment. The sincerity of a preacher came to matter much more. And preachers could not just *be* sincere; in order to have authority, they had to *show* that they were sincere. Such displays required finding ways to allow congregations to compare a preacher's pulpit persona with his or her true self. That meant acting in public in ways that gave people glimpses into the preacher's private life. Because private life was taken as the home of the real, true self, preachers who used vocal patterns, gestures, and dress associated with private life looked more sincere. Preachers who preached like they were in an old Massachusetts pulpit sounded fake, even when they were telling the truth. And preachers who spoke as if they were in the parlor of a private home sounded sincere, even when they were lying. The question of conversational style, then, links to topics like the disestablishment of religion, the democratization of authority, the differentiation of spheres in society, and the privatization of selves.[11] A whole world of social and political philosophy is condensed into a relatively subtle change in gesture and tone. A good genetic history brings all those issues to light. It helps practical theology to become public theology.[12]

A good genetic history also helps practical theology to become ecclesial theology. The practices of preaching are not just formed by preachers. They arise out of congregations, denominations, and movements. They come to life in and for these wider communities.

Because preaching grows out of and relates to a whole way of life, the best histories of preaching will keep this wider way of life always in view. They will trace connections between practices of preaching and the practices of the whole community. They will ask not only how a practice

11. I try to offer a more complete version of this argument in Ted A. Smith, *The New Measures: A Theological History of Democratic Practice* (Cambridge: Cambridge University Press, 2007), Chapter Five.

12. One of the best examples of this way of seeing social and political currents condensed into church practices comes from an unlikely source: Theodor W. Adorno, *The Psychological Technique of Martin Luther Thomas' Radio Addresses* (Stanford, Calif.: Stanford University Press, 2000).

changed, but also about the agency of ministers and other community members in its transformation. They will consider how listeners heard, ignored, performed, subverted, followed, initiated, and transcended the sermons that preachers offered. They will ask which practices of preaching grew out of and guided communities to ways of life abundant. The massive "listening to listeners" project of contemporary homileticians begins to explore some of these questions for today's preaching. And the turn to social history has produced several decades' worth of excellent studies of the relationships between the practices of preachers, congregations, and wider communities. A good history of a practice of preaching will understand itself as part of a history of a way of life.[13]

Fourth, I teach theological histories of practice because I believe they help form the right kinds of pastoral imagination. The best pastors have some sense of the significance of what they are doing, and I am convinced that knowing the history of a practice helps that significance come to light. Congregational ministry is full of debates about things like whether to use carpeting in the sanctuary — issues that seem completely beside the point. But when a pastor can see the history stored up in such a debate, when she remembers that sanctuaries have aspired to be amphitheatres, natural groves, living rooms, and more; when she remembers the ways these spaces help to order and construct race, gender, and class; and when she remembers the very different visions of the good news proclaimed in each of these models . . . when a pastor remembers all this, then she begins to see the significance of a fight about carpeting. And so the everyday stuff of congregational ministry breaks open and stands revealed as teeming with social issues and gospel hopes.

The richest pastoral imaginations are not individual achievements of vision. Nor are they so collective that they never quite touch the ground in any living person. They arise, rather, when individual pastors come to some reflexive appreciation of the broader, deeper memory of the church. When pastors engage in practices like concluding a sermon with a call to decision, they are already imagining more than they know, for practices themselves are formed through generations of dreams, decisions, actions,

---

13. See Ronald J. Allen et al., *Listening to Listeners: Homiletical Case Studies* (St. Louis: Chalice Press, 2004). One historical account of the work of listeners in appropriating sermons is Charles E. Hambrick-Stowe, *The Practice of Piety: Puritan Devotional Disciplines in Seventeenth-Century New England* (Chapel Hill: University of North Carolina Press, 1986).

and sins. Christian practices embody ecclesial memory. That deep memory usually lives beyond conscious retrieval, even as it is performed in both the daily and the extraordinary stuff of church life. Genetic histories of practice can bring deep ecclesial memory to light. Such histories form pastors who begin to understand the ways they are connected to past and future generations. They form pastors who understand that they are already hoping for more than their immediate situations demand, for they know that they are performing practices that bear within them traces of the hopes of Christian people long ago and far away. Telling history theologically does not mean simply baptizing those hopes and declaring that they will be fulfilled. It means seeing them as prayers addressed to a living God already at work for the redemption of the world. And it means seeing everyday church practices as already caught up in that work of redemption, perhaps in spite of themselves.

Teaching Practice in a History Class

— *David D. Daniels III*

Seminarians enter the history classroom bearing various attitudes and feelings toward the study of history. Amazement at the dizzying array of the variety of Christianity is quite usual. Being appalled at the bloody past of the Crusades and other movements in the history of Christianity occurs frequently. Phobias of drowning in a sea of dates, names, places, events, and ideas afflict some. An antiquarian love of the past, or of a supposedly forgotten golden age in the past, attracts a rare crew, and an ahistorical myopia claims many victims. Always present, yet never the majority, are those possessed by a historical acumen that makes them sensitive to the texture of history.

Peter N. Stearns's essay "Why Study History?" offers some insights that could be recast in order to appropriate them in the education and formation of ministers to lead and shape communities for discipleship in and for the sake of the world. History helps seminarians understand how the church has been a community of faith and how Christians have practiced the faith over time, providing an angle of vision to view the world. History helps seminarians to understand change and how the current church and society were constructed, equipping seminarians to situate themselves and the church within an historical perspective. History also provides for seminarians an arena to engage in moral exploration; by entering the past through history, seminarians can test their own moral sense against the moral decisions of historical figures and denominations or movements. History also supplies untapped resources and a complex heritage from which seminarians can draw in constructing a Christian identity that fosters a way of living that annunciates abundant life.[14]

An intriguing approach for theological schools to introduce or reacquaint seminarians with the history of Christianity is to order the survey around the history of the practice of ministry. When we tell the story of Christianity, we should ponder telling the story from this vantage point, for making ministry central to the study of history aids in convincing seminarians of the critical role of history in the practice of ministry, as well as the critical role of ministry in shaping the church over time. When we teach history, we often tell stories: stories of the forming of an era; stories of events that mark an historical period; stories of practices transmigrating from one tradition to another. While there are historians who resist the idea, there are also many who employ a narrative structure to organize and teach survey courses on the history of Christianity. Narratives of previous eras guide the student back into a different world, a lost world, from the present.

By probing the historicity of a set of practices, such a course provides seminarians with a particular historical angle on ministry. As Craig Dykstra contends, "[a] practice cannot be abstracted from its past, because the past is embedded in the practice itself." He further states that "[a]s people participate in practices, they are involved in their ongoing history and may in the process significantly reshape them." Dykstra also inquires about how practices have "taken on different shape and meaning in various historical and cultural contexts."[15]

The goal of the course would then be to challenge the "presentism" that blinds students from seeing the historicity of Christian ministry and inflicts them with historical amnesia, denying them the heritage lodged within the Christian memory. As presentism is countered and the past is engaged, how might the student and teacher relate to the past?

14. Peter N. Stearns, "Why Study History?" (American Historical Association, 1998); available online at http://www.historians.org/pubs/Free/WhyStudyHistory.htm.

15. Craig Dykstra, "Reconceiving Practice," in *Shifting Boundaries: Contextual Approaches to the Structure of Theological Education,* ed. Barbara G. Wheeler and Edward Farley (Louisville: Westminster/John Knox, 1991), pp. 44, 47.

> What is missing . . . is the possibility of a conversational relationship
> with the past, one that seeks neither to deny the past nor to achieve an
> imaginative restoration of the past but to enter into a dialogue with the
> traditions that still shape our view of the world, often in ways in which
> we are not even aware. Instead of merely addressing the historical rec-
> ord, we need to grasp the ways in which it addresses us.[16]

As we explore the history of a set of practices over time, are we in search of
the ways that the past might address the present? of the historical origins
of contemporary expressions? of continuities and discontinuities between
past and present regarding the practices? or of the ways in which the practices both adapt to and challenge the various historical contexts in which
they are shaped and which they shape?

Since I teach in the history field, the surveys that I teach provide not a
history of practices of ministry but rather a church history survey organized around the practices of ministry. My courses on the history of the
church in North America are currently informed by texts like Rhys Isaac's
Transformation of Virginia, Sylvia R. Frey and Betty Wood's *Come
Shouting to Zion: African American Protestantism in the American South
and British Caribbean to 1830,* E. Brooks Holifield's *Pastoral Care in America,* Douglas G. Adams's *Meeting House to Camp Meeting,* Harry Stout's
New England Soul, Albert Raboteau's *Slave Religion,* and Mechal Sobel's
*The World They Made Together: Black and White Values in Eighteenth-
Century Virginia.* The courses use prayers, hymns, and sermons as primary documents that can be read through interpretive schemas critically
borrowed from these authors. Such an approach gives students strategies
to interpret the different practices of ministry within their historical contexts. Periodization is informed by major shifts in worldview, with attention to the related sensibilities, auralities, temporalities, and spatialities in
which the practice of ministry was embedded historically.

Linear linkings of the past to the present insufficiently capture the
flow of history. Moving beyond this approach presents many challenges
and requires new images of the development of Christianity in North
America as well as new methodologies. Somehow the interplay of religious
traditions and cultures of Europeans, Africans, and Amerindians must be

---

16. Christopher Lasch, "The Communitarian Critique," in *Community in America: The
Challenge of Habits of the Heart,* ed. Charles E. Reynolds and Ralph V. Norman (Berkeley:
University of California Press, 1988), p. 180.

recognized in order to grasp the particularity as well as the historicity of Christianity in North America that shaped the practices inherited from different religions and cultures.

Borrowing from the French philosophers Gilles Deleuze and Felix Guattari to grasp the multiplicity of voices and the plurality of origins that construct the Christian tradition itself, Dale Irvin suggests *rhizomes* as a new image. Rhizomes are "plants with subterranean, horizontal root systems, growing below and above ground in multiple directions at once." Irvin contrasts rhizomes with trees to describe the interlocking character of Christian tradition:

> A tradition . . . is not like a tree, organized with a major trunk and smaller (or minor) branches, and drawing primarily from a single, dominant taproot that likewise grows in one direction. A tradition is more like a rhizome, agglomerating and stabilizing at times around common experiences or locations, but then branching off and spreading rapidly at other times, in several directions at once. It is a decentered, or multicentered, system flowing across multiple material and subjective fields.[17]

This image provides a new way to visualize the relationship between Christianity in North America as the production of various peoples, cultures, and religions, capturing the multiple ways in which Christianity in North America was generated. Consequently we resist teaching the history of Christianity in North America as a mere transplantation of European Protestantism or Catholicism. Instead North American Christianity would be studied as the product of the encounters among Amerindian, African, and European cultures, which created a cluster of religious expressions and sensibilities.

Scholars such as James Clifford may provide help. Clifford proposes developing a conception of culture that takes seriously both (1) the apparent disintegration of various cultures around the world and (2) the integrity of the culture exhibited in its inventiveness. Continuity is not the only trait that indicates cultural vitality, but inventiveness is a sure sign of cultural vigor. "Many traditions, practices, cosmologies, and values," according to Clifford, have been lost, and "some literally murdered; but much has

---

17. Dale T. Irvin, *Christian Histories, Christian Traditioning: Rendering Accounts* (Maryknoll, N.Y.: Orbis Press, 1998).

simultaneously been invented and revived in complex, oppositional contexts."[18] The challenge is to teach students to recognize the inventive nature of North American Christianity within its Puritan, Anglican, Catholic, Presbyterian, Baptist, Methodist, and Pentecostal expressions.

Stearns's essay, mentioned above, also accents some "usable habits of mind" that are fostered by the study of history, including the capacities to assess various types of evidence, scrutinize conflicting historical interpretations, and interrogate continuity and change. Humility towards history could also be included as a usable habit of mind. Seminarians must learn that the sources historians employ are always limited; rarely were they crafted for the use to which historians recruit them. While the social locations of the authors of the sources must be acknowledged, these partial sources can still offer valuable gestures towards the present and glimpses into the past, even into the past of lost worlds.

First, there is merit for students to confront the discontinuity of the past from the present and the ruptures within the past, thereby to explore lost worlds buried in the past that expose starkly the contours of the present. As students explore the history of a set of practices over time, they are encouraged to appreciate the discontinuities between the present world and worlds of the past and to resist the tendency to incorporate the past seamlessly into the present. In a sense, some of the past worlds are lost.

The world of seventeenth-century North American religion, according to E. Brooks Holifield, Albert Raboteau, Mechal Sobel, and Jon Butler, is one such lost world. Even so, students must somehow learn to enter this alien terrain in order to confront the real discontinuity between that era and the twenty-first century. A cultural chasm brackets that world from the present. While real continuities in congregational life and practices persist, my pedagogical task is to guide students in their encounter of this lost world and examination of the practices of ministry within that lost world. Holifield notes that during this era

> They envisioned reality as a vast chain of being that stretched from the heavenly throne of God to the lowest material object. At the summit of the Real was God — uncreated, unchanging, eternal. At the summit of the created order were the angelic hierarchies, numbering in the thou-

18. James Clifford, *The Predicament of Culture: Twentieth-Century Ethnography, Literature, and Art* (Cambridge, Mass.: Harvard University Press, 1988), p. 16.

sands of thousands, dwelling in celestial spheres, yet able also to appear on the earth, which did indeed seem bedeviled by fallen angels — demons and wicked spirits under the command of Satan, the highest of the fallen. A little lower than the angels stood men and women, sharing with the angels a rational nature, and with the world of lower animals the faculties of sensation, memory, and passion.[19]

The work of pastors, within that worldview, included being "specialists in the supernatural," according to Holifield. They prayed to God, reasoned with people, and battled with Satan. Holifield further notes that "wizards and soothsayers" with their "charms, love magic, fortune-telling, divinization, and astrology" competed with clergy in engaging the populace.[20]

Mechal Sobel describes eighteenth-century Virginia as a lost world akin to the world limned by Holifield. Yet in her account blacks and whites together carried this world. They were able to construct a world together because Virginians of African and European descent both held a "rural, prebourgeois and especially preindustrial" worldview. She contends that from around the 1670s to the early 1800s, "the interpenetration of Western and African values took place," producing new culture that blended African and European practices and values. According to Sobel, "the social-cultural interplay was such that both blacks and whites were crucially influenced by the traditions of the 'other.'"[21] During this long eighteenth century, blacks and whites constructed coherent or overlapping worldviews. Virginians of African descent inherited a Christian past which they used to re-envision their present and future, incorporating their African values and perceptions, while Virginians of European descent found their Christian present and future shaped by African sensibilities, sensibilities that resonated with European worldviews.[22]

A crucial and exemplary development in ministry took place through the interpenetration of Western and African values that shaped Christian practice related to death and dying. Sobel argues that Christian death and

---

19. E. Brooks Holifield, *A History of Pastoral Care in America: From Salvation to Self-Realization* (Nashville: Abingdon Press, 1983), p. 38. Also see Jon Butler, *Awash in the Sea of Faith: Christianizing the American People* (Cambridge, Mass.: Harvard University Press, 1990).

20. Holifield, *A History of Pastoral Care in America*, pp. 38-39.

21. Mechal Sobel, *The World They Made Together: Black and White Values in Eighteenth-Century Virginia* (Princeton: Princeton University Press, 1987), pp. 3, 5, 64.

22. Sobel, *The World They Made Together*, p. 67.

dying were transformed from being a forlorn, fearful, and grief-ridden experience that cast heaven as "an unknown land" into being a joyous, welcoming transition from life to afterlife with heaven as a domicile in which kin were reunited. Sobel credits the change to Africans becoming Christian and introducing their views on the afterlife as a reunion with the ancestors and their characterization of death as a "joyful homecoming" into the church.[23] Pastoral caregiving to the dying became rituals of "happy death" for those who bade the world farewell in their quest of "making heaven" home. Instead of whites shunning sorrow and expressions of grief as was the norm earlier in the long eighteenth century, they now grieved as those with a particular hope. The living and dying could exclaim to each that "we shall ere long be reunited never again to be separated from those we love" and "we'll meet in heaven." With death conceived as the gateway to the next life, according to Sobel, "deathbed scenes became ecstatic experiences."[24]

The world of eighteenth-century Virginia, constructed by blacks and whites, would later collapse under the pressures of industrialization, urbanization, and the advent of middle-class culture in the United States. While remnants of this world persist, the coherence of that world, and the world itself, are lost. Nostalgia might promise to take students back to such a world. But history remembers its strangeness to the present. This strangeness brings gifts of its own. Working hard to glimpse a now-foreign worldview can expand the imagination of seminarians and open them to differences of other kinds.

Second, there is merit in students searching for the origins of practice by examining how a practice emerged into a particular form. By drawing upon scholarship akin to Harry S. Stout's study of five generations of Puritan preaching (1620-1776), students can be introduced to how a preaching form persisted. According to Stout, a "plain style," unadorned with extrabiblical authorities, marked the tradition of regular preaching. For five generations Puritan preaching persisted with its sequence of sin-salvation-service. Stout surmised that for three generations there were "few changes in biblical foundation, theological focus, social orientation, or thematic organization from Scripture text to doctrine to application."[25]

---

23. Sobel, *The World They Made Together*, pp. 221-23.
24. Sobel, *The World They Made Together*, pp. 223-24.
25. Harry S. Stout, *The New England Soul: Preaching and Religious Culture in Colonial New England* (New York: Oxford University Press, 1986), p. 154.

Other changes did occur over time. The insular social world of the first two generations of New Englanders was distinct from the imperial social world of the third generation, and changes in preaching were intertwined with changes in the religious culture. Whereas the first two generations could rely on the law requiring church attendance, third-generation ministers "had to persuade their listeners to attend public worship by pricking their consciences." For the first two generations God's goodness was a major theme, whereas third-generation ministers emphasized "God's love for humanity." In the anglicized provincial capitals, third-generation regular sermons possessed an anglicized flair whereas the villages and towns escaped this acculturation.[26]

According to Stout, the fourth generation of Puritan preaching was characterized by the loss of the middle ground occupied by the first three generations of preaching, due in part to the impact of the First Great Awakening. The weight being given to one human faculty over another, together with other factors, produced two varying styles of preaching, both of which displayed a heightened interest in delivery or elocution. The rationalist sermon sought to enlighten the understanding of the congregants. The evangelical sermon sought to inspire their affections. The delivery of rationalist preaching focused on style, "'gravity,' restrained 'reading,' and a literary 'cadency,'" whereas the delivery of evangelical preaching stressed "'affected tones,' 'theatrical' gestures, or 'inspired' spontaneity." The fifth-generation regular preaching perpetuated these accents.[27] In some regards, traces of all these styles can still be seen in various North American congregations today. Understanding these styles requires understanding their history.

Worship also provides examples of continuity. In seventeenth-century New England, according to Douglas Adams, there were two Sunday services: morning and afternoon. Here Adams describes the worship event:

> The original pattern emerged as follows: at the communion table, close to the worshiping congregation, the clergy often presided with lay leaders. Standing there with the people, clergy began the service with prayers of thanksgiving and later led prayers of intercession incorporating concerns spoken out or written by laity. All continued to stand for

26. Stout, *The New England Soul,* pp. 127, 149, 155, 158.
27. Stout, *The New England Soul,* pp. 187, 222.

singing led by laity. Often from the table, clergy read the scriptures interspersed with exegesis so that the word would be heard and not be a dumb reading. Then they went into the pulpit to give the sermon setting forth the bearing of the Bible on any of a wide range of issues related to God's kingdom on earth. Immediately after the sermon as the worship continued, they came down from the pulpit and sat at the table to answer the congregation's questions and hear witnessing by laity, who were free to agree or disagree with what clergy had said. And from the table, clergy gave thanks and gave the bread and wine, as often as each Sunday or least once a month, to lay leaders who distributed communion to the people. After more singing, the people often gave their offerings at the table.[28]

In searching for the origins of this pattern of worship structured around prayer, singing, Scripture reading, and preaching, Adams provides students with clues. He contends that this worship pattern was introduced by the Separatists at Plymouth and became the model for "free church worship," the worship tradition of the "Puritans, Separatists, Baptists, and Quakers in the seventeenth and eighteenth centuries, some Methodists in the late eighteenth century, and Disciples of Christ in the early nineteenth century." We could add that it would also be familiar to various Protestant congregations in the twentieth and twenty-first centuries.[29]

Third, there is merit in students "unforgetting" the alternatives suppressed in the past as they learn how present practices came to be and how to retrieve historical resources, for the sake of reconstructing certain practices today. By taking "a long look at the private conversations of pastors and their parishioners" in North America over three and half centuries, Holifield argues that the movement from the cure of souls to the care of self, a therapeutic self, took place. In the historical journey toward the twentieth-century's emphasis on pastoral counseling as pastoral care, clergy shifted away from the colonial concern about the cure of souls.

While the twentieth-century clergy lived in a world of selves, the seventeenth- and eighteenth-century clergy resided in a world of souls. As Holifield notes, the cure of souls involved engaging the conscience and was

28. Doug Adams, *Meeting House to Camp Meeting: Toward a History of American Free Church Worship from 1620 to 1835* (Saratoga: Modern Liturgy-Resource Publications and Austin: The Sharing Company, 1981), p. 13.

29. Adams, *Meeting House to Camp Meeting*, p. 10.

seen as "a remedy for sin." Holifield contends that "the aim was always to allay the doubts resulting from sinfulness, or to temper the passions disordered by sinfulness, or to correct the vision clouded by sinfulness . . . to overcome temptations and undermine sinful resolves, to arouse the conscience against sin and to calm anxieties about sin." The self, on the other hand, was understood as the seat of self-centeredness, which needed to be overcome through self-denial. A corporate pastoral care model was preeminent through public preaching, sacraments, public prayer, and pastoral work with families, but private pastoral conversations did also take place.[30]

As the eighteenth century progressed the colonial economy created a new wealthy class and expanded the elite class to include wealthy merchants along with the landed aristocracy. This social change, along with the egalitarian impulses of the time, promoted a shift in culture from a focus on nobility and its forms of deference to a focus on gentility. From 1799 to 1865, within the culture of gentility, "the physician of the souls was to be a gentleman" who supplied "gentlemanly counsel." As the revivals of the early nineteenth century Christianized increasing numbers of women and men, pastoral care played a central role in socialization. For women, "domesticity, piety, and refinement" shaped their pastoral care, with the affections becoming the primary faculty to counsel them. For men, the will became the primary faculty to engage, as "decisiveness of character" became the focus of pastoral care. Advice served the new task of pastoral care giving.[31]

While the twenty-first century clergy live in a world of disintegrating selves, according to some, and multiple selves, according to others, students can probe history to evaluate the endeavors to retrieve the cure of souls in critical and contextual ways as the practice of ministry itself is being reconceived. This metaphor for care may be an especially helpful one today.

Connection at the Center

Teaching that brings history and practice together for the sake of forming ministers will require work across disciplines. But the interdisciplinary

---

30. Holifield, *A History of Pastoral Care in America*, pp. 17-18, 37, 59.
31. Holifield, *A History of Pastoral Care in America*, pp. 70-73, 95, 102, 108, 121-23, 125.

work that we are hoping for does not come from a desire to be interdisciplinary for its own sake, nor from a desire to legitimate our disciplines by linking them to some other discipline that seems more respected or more relevant. It rather grows out of commitments internal to our home fields. Connection is an inside job. Because historians care about what actually happened, we have to offer not only histories of doctrine but also histories of practice. And because homileticians seek to teach a craft we have inherited — not invented — we need to have some sense of how and why it comes to us as it does. Each of our disciplines throws us into the other. And so this work of connecting practice and history cannot be the project only of a few specialists who happen to find it interesting. And it cannot be confined to elective classes that a handful of students might take. The classes we have described here are core introductory courses in our disciplines. History and practice come together not at their edges, but in the deepest parts of their centers. And when we connect the two we get at the heart of what we are trying to do as practical theologians, historians, and teachers of people preparing for ministry.

Many excellent resources to support this kind of teaching already exist. We have named a few in the course of this essay, and more are coming all the time. These books and essays attend to everyday practices. They offer genetic accounts that help students understand how a practice came to be performed in the ways that it is. They give students vocabularies for entering into critical, theological deliberation about good practice. They show students what is at stake in a practice, both for the life of the church and for social and political spheres. And while they help students understand another time and place, the best histories also retain a strong sense of the lostness and strangeness of the past. They remember forgotten and suppressed alternatives to present practice. They trace the rhizomatic development of practices from many centers, in many directions, all at once. They remember the formation of categories of race and ethnicity, even as they remember people, practices, and events that transcended those categories. And — in a few rare cases, like W. E. B. DuBois's history of the sorrow songs — they open onto eschatological horizons.[32]

We already have some books and essays that work well in elective courses. But because history and practice are connected at their centers,

32. See W. E. B. DuBois, "The Sorrow Songs," in *The Souls of Black Folk* (Chicago: A. C. McClurg & Co., 1903; repr. New York: Penguin Classics, 1996), pp. 204-16.

there remains a need for histories of practice designed for use in introductory courses. Books for introductory courses in preaching probably could not attain either the comprehensiveness of recent multivolume works or the detail of carefully limited studies. They could offer short, accessible histories of the topics and practices usually taught in a first course in preaching.[33] And books for introductory courses in church history could not give comprehensive accounts of the developments of even one practice. But they could use core practices of faith to structure their thinner and broader narratives. They might, for instance, ask of each community in each era how they cared for sick and dying people, how they sang their lives, or how they formed people in the faith.[34] Then the histories of these practices would serve to connect the parts of the book to one another and to the present practices that ministers are called to nurture in the lives of others and to take up for themselves.

In addition, because the practices of Christian faith point towards and even embody a grace with which they are not identical, we need more histories of practice told from theological perspectives and more practical theologies that risk claims about the meaning and direction of history. In a time when merely empirical history and idealist theology seem to divide the field between them, theological history can be difficult to imagine. But good examples abound, and their range is wide. Theological history is the genre of the book of Acts and Augustine's *City of God,* of William Seymour's memories of Azusa Street and Reinhold Niebuhr's *The Irony of American History.* The best theological histories place precise descriptive studies in relation to hopes for God's work of redemption. We need more histories of education that remember it as incorporation into the body of Christ, more histories of congregational singing that remember it as participation in the music of the spheres, and more histories of preaching that remember it as the Word of God proclaimed. Such histories, if they are

33. One good example of such a book is Richard Lischer, *The Company of Preachers: An Anthology* (Grand Rapids: Eerdmans, 2002). Lischer's book offers something closer to case studies than to genetic narratives. This allows the book to present a wide range of options for each topic and so to create a rich field of discussion. But the book does not emphasize the historical relationships of these options to one another, or to the reader. They appear instead as an almost synchronous array of ever-present possibilities.

34. A richly researched multi-author book that undertakes something like this for an earlier period is John Van Engen, ed., *Educating People of Faith: Exploring the History of Jewish and Christian Communities* (Grand Rapids: Eerdmans, 2004).

truthful, will remember gaps as much as fulfillment. They will mingle thanksgiving, judgment, lament, repentance, and hope on every page.

Forming women and men for ministry involves helping them to become the sort of people who can receive these mixed and hopeful histories as their own. Receiving these histories as our own requires more than the ability to recite lists of names and dates. It means understanding ourselves as addressed by the past, and so it requires doing all that we can to repair damage from the past and seek life abundant for the future. Knowing the histories as our own commits us to practice. Even so, taking up the practices of life abundant means taking up all the histories that have shaped those practices. We are performing the past, whether we know it or not. Practice tangles us in history, even as history throws us into practice. Forming people for ministry therefore requires holding history and practice together, and holding them open, before a horizon of hope.

Practical Theology on the Quad

The matter of doctoral education in practical theology is a pressing concern. In a 2003 study, the Auburn Center for the Study of Theological Education reported that approximately 31 percent of all seminary and divinity school faculty members teach in the practical fields. In a companion study focused entirely on "practical faculty," Auburn observed that, because a significant percent of faculty in this field have begun to retire, the number of searches for new faculty hires is accelerating rapidly. At the same time, Auburn reported that searching schools are having a great deal of difficulty finding people they deem to be well-qualified for their openings. One significant reason is the dearth of substantive Ph.D. programs in practical theology.*

In this chapter, Thomas G. Long, professor of preaching at Candler School of Theology at Emory University, describes the development of a new Ph.D. program in practical theology at Emory, a largely secular university. Making a place for doctoral education in practical theology in such settings, he argues, is good for practical theology. Moreover, Long claims that practical theology brings to the university perspectives that the university needs if it is to achieve its own larger purposes.

Only about one half of the twenty academic doctoral programs that have educated the most faculty in the practical fields in recent years are university-based. The other half are offered by freestanding theological seminaries. In

---

*See Barbara G. Wheeler et al., "Signs of the Times: Present and Future Theological Faculty," *Auburn Center for the Study of Theological Education Studies* 10 (February 2005), esp. p. 14, and "Hard to Find: Searching for Practical Faculty in the 1990s," *Auburn Center Background Report* 8 (January 2002).

fact, both Thomas Long and I (Craig Dykstra) did our doctoral studies in such a program. Therefore, both of us are keenly aware that Long's case for practical theology on the university quad addresses only part of the picture. This chapter does, however, describe key issues in a way that will help to launch an important conversation in both universities and seminaries about how best to educate and expand the number of people who can be excellent teachers and scholars in practical theology in the decades to come.

10. Practical Theology on the Quad: Doctoral Study in Practical Theology in a University Context

Thomas G. Long

Several years ago, Emory University, the school where I teach, decided to set out on what was for us a bold and somewhat controversial educational venture. We determined that Emory would seek to become a significant provider of newly educated Ph.D.s in the field of practical theology. Also, we decided to do this not by creating a special walled-off doctoral program in practical theology, an isolation ward for students in this field, but instead by placing them in the same educational environment afforded every other doctoral candidate on the campus: the interdisciplinary, interfaith, multicultural, complex, noisy, politically volatile, always argumentative, sometimes conflicted welter of circumstances and conversations that has come to mark educational life at a major research university. In short, we aimed to do practical theology on the university quad. In doing so, Emory joined a few other major universities, including Duke, Vanderbilt, and Boston, who have created innovative educational initiatives in doctoral education in practical theology.

A University and Practical Theology: The Advantages

In some ways, this was a natural and obvious step for Emory. Founded by Methodists and still firmly connected to the United Methodist tradition, Emory has been educating ministers and theologians from its very beginning. There was also a platform on which to build. Emory's Graduate Division of Religion, the arm of the university responsible for Ph.D. work in religion, already had in place a small but vigorous doctoral program in practical theology, producing scholars mostly in religious education and pastoral care. What is more, over the last two decades, Emory has been growing its Ph.D. program in religion generally, steadily climbing into the top tier of graduate universities producing faculty for mainline theological schools.[1]

By expanding its efforts in practical theology, Emory was responding to a clear need in the educational marketplace,[2] no small consideration when many freshly minted Ph.D.s in the humanities bide their time selling Subarus or working at Starbucks while hoping to snag scarce full-time faculty posts. The employment situation is different in practical theology. It has been evident for a long time that, when seminaries and theological schools attempt to fill positions in the area of ministry and practical theology, qualified practical theologians are difficult to come by. In the aptly titled 2002 report "Hard to Find,"[3] the Auburn Center for the Study of Theological Education reported widespread distress among theological schools in filling faculty vacancies in the practical disciplines — preaching, worship, religious education, pastoral care, leadership, and the other so-called arts of ministry. Deans and search committee chairs interviewed by the Auburn researchers consistently reported that faculty searches in the practical fields were "difficult" and presented "more complications" than searches in other fields. One school reported holding a position in homiletics open for twelve years until a suitable candidate could be found!

There are a number of reasons why this is so. In fact, a perfect storm of trouble has been brewing in theological education to create a shortage of practical theologians. The first gale-force wind has been generated by the fact that professors who are currently teaching in the practical fields have been vacating their posts in larger than normal numbers. Some of this attrition is due to the "headhunting effect," namely that practical theologians, because of their skills and their visibility in the church, are often lured away from their academic posts by more lucrative positions in congregations and church agencies. But mainly these losses are a function of age. Currently, the practical theologians on seminary faculties are older on average than faculty in other fields. According to another Auburn study, in

1. See Wheeler et al., "Signs of the Times," esp. p. 14.

2. Some of the material about the scarcity of practical theologians in the job market appeared in a different form in Thomas G. Long, "Teaching Vacancies," *The Christian Century* 21, no. 4 (February 24, 2004): 30-33.

3. See "Hard to Find."

2001, "55% of all faculty members were 52 and older, but 60% of faculty members in the practical fields were in this category."[4]

A second storm surge in practical theology is now roaring on shore because, precisely at the moment when vacancies in the practical fields are increasing and a new generation of teachers is needed, theological schools are often setting higher standards in terms of formal academic credentials for the faculty they employ to teach in the ministry fields. As readers of this volume are well aware, generations ago the practical theological disciplines were often seen as "applied theology," namely, disciplines wherein wisdom generated elsewhere — in biblical studies, theology, ethics, and other places in the theological curriculum — was crafted into methods and procedures that would allow it to shape and govern ministerial and ecclesial practice. Gradually, spurred by the contributions of innovative thinkers in the practical fields, theological educators began to recognize that the label "applied theology" was not sufficient, that the practical disciplines in fact involve critical and original thinking about theologically saturated religious practices. Teaching ministry today, therefore, requires a different kind of expertise, a different level of academic training, and a different set of credentials. Formerly, when theological schools needed professors of church administration, preaching, or worship, many of them were content to search among the ranks of accomplished clergy, seeking people who had a proven track record of doing with excellence the practice they would now teach. Today, however, while performance skills are certainly essential in practical theologians, these are only part of the package. Theological schools want teachers of practical theology who are "cross-trained" in interdisciplinary studies, can conduct original research, forge innovations in their fields, publish substantial books and articles, and participate in the ongoing scholarly conversation among the whole faculty that nourishes the intellectual life of a theological school.

When the Emory faculty were in the planning stages of their new initiative in practical theology, they interviewed a number of prominent theological educators. One of them expressed the view that, while the older generation of practical theologians was often strong in the "how tos" but weak in history, hermeneutics, and theology, a new generation of practical scholars is emerging who combine the pragmatic with careful attention to the tasks of empirical study, historical description, multilayered interpretation, and theo-

---

4. Wheeler et al., "Signs of the Times," p. 9.

logical analysis. In other words, not only is practical theology now deeper, it is also broader. There is an increasing awareness of how the church's ministries of teaching, worship, preaching, education, and leadership connect to the practices of other faiths, to the practices of religious communities throughout history, and to parallel practices in the wider culture.

The fact that theological schools now seek practical theologians who can operate in multidisciplinary environments and engage in creative and critical thinking is not simply a product of faculties looking for bright, interesting, and collaborative colleagues. One of the most dramatic recent changes in theological education involves the recognition that, given our cultural moment, theological students themselves, as they become pastors and church leaders, will need just the sorts of abilities and habits of mind found in the ablest practical theologians. Pastors today are thrown into a complex social environment of colliding cultures, multiple ideologies, and competing demands, and ministry must be creatively negotiated in ways undreamt a generation ago. While Craig Dykstra is surely correct when he observes in this volume that the "pastoral imagination" found in those clergy who grasp and perform ministry well is finally a gift of God's grace, he is also right to say that such imagination requires such qualities as "a truthful and nuanced understanding of how congregations and other institutions actually work" and "a broad awareness and an understanding of the world that the church exists to serve."[5] These are, in part, the benefits of a rigorous and creative theological pedagogy, and if those who teach the practical disciplines cannot engage in social and cultural analysis, do not understand the place of their disciplines historically and in interfaith contexts, and cannot equip their students to do so as well, they will not adequately prepare the next generation of ministers.

So theological schools are now looking for a rare commodity: teachers of the ministry arts who are not only able practitioners but who are also well-trained research scholars able to move nimbly across interdisciplinary and even interfaith lines. The supply of such teachers will have to rise to demand, and graduate schools in religion are simply going to have to step up to the plate and produce more Ph.D.s capable of teaching practical theology. However, and this is the third devastating force in the perfect storm, very few graduate schools are willing or able to do so. On the one hand, the top university programs in religion have mostly not been interested in

5. See Dykstra's chapter in this volume, pp. 42, 52.

practical theology, preferring the "study of" to the "practice of" religion. On the other hand, denominational seminaries, schools where practical theology more readily finds a home and which might be interested in starting new doctoral programs, often lack the finances, the faculty, and the interdisciplinary and interfaith resources needed for excellent advanced programs. Thus the training of practical theologians tends to fall between the educational cracks. Schools that could provide such training usually won't, and schools that desire to provide it often cannot.

Emory University and Practical Theology: The Obstacles

As we have seen, then, because of its heritage, its resources, its commitments, and the urgent need in theological education, Emory's decision to venture more deeply into doctoral education in practical theology makes perfectly good sense. On the other hand, bringing the field of practical theology prominently into the university quad involved walking a delicate, diplomatically sensitive, and somewhat obstacle-strewn path. For a major research university today, one that is both proud and nervous about academic quality, freedom of inquiry, and independence from sectarian ideology, to embrace practical theology as a legitimate field of doctoral level study was no small event.

The issues here are many. To begin with, all of the other areas in the study of religion at the university involve apparent objects of inquiry. Whether it is Judaica, New Testament, West Asian religions, or even the psychology of religion, there is a claimed "there" there, a body of literature, a set of scriptures or rituals, a roughly agreed-upon set of research protocols, an identifiable culture — *something* that scholars can look at, prod, examine, point to, and argue about. While this is not exactly like the medical school geneticist investigating the chromosomal biology of the 22q11 deletion syndrome in newborns, it is close enough to create the aura of a reasonable degree of objectivity in the study of religion. Along comes practical theology, though, looking to some university eyes more like an intramural *activity* than a real field of inquiry, and a confessionally motivated one to boot. To be sure, there are forms of practical theology outside of Christianity, but Christians have essentially operated the franchise. Thus for many outside of the field, practical theology is the exclusive expression of a certain kind of Christian theology or, even more narrowly, of the church and its ministry, not to mention the fact that the word "practical" automatically arouses the suspicion that the field is high on technique and low on theory. In short, practical theology cannot even pretend to put on a lab coat, so what is it doing on the quad?

Ironically, Emory's Christian heritage makes this issue a bit more prickly, not less. While Emory is noteworthy among universities in the widespread intellectual and academic interest in religion on campus (a recent informal Emory survey found that scores of faculty members beyond the theological school and the religion department, dispersed throughout all of the schools of the university, identified their research as connected to religion in some way), the firewall set up between the academic study of religion and the confessional practice of religion remains a firm fixture of university life. Emory's strong and growing religion department is justifiably proud of the broad bandwidth of world religions embraced in its curriculum and the widely respected research of its faculty, a far cry from the simpler "Bible and Christianity" approach found in Emory's churchly origins. In fact, some of the older heads on campus actually believe they can point to the very moment when Emory grew beyond its sleepy, southern roots to become a national university: namely, that day four decades ago when Emory's president decided to stand up for the academic freedom of a young religion professor, Thomas J. J. Altizer, whose defiant bellow that "God is dead" had blown through the Bible Belt and reverberated all the way to the cover of *Time,* precipitating calls for his firing and even death threats. There is always the vague fear in the air that aggressively evangelistic Christians hiding in the bushes outside the religion classrooms could attempt to effect revenge and reclaim their turf. The newly expanded Ph.D. program in practical theology was, therefore, closely inspected to make sure that it was not a Trojan Horse.

Not only must a university-based program of practical theology respond to the suspicion of creeping confessionalism, it must also, quite frankly, navigate the churning waters of campus politics. Academic doctoral programs are prized pieces of real estate in universities because they not only form the educational environment in which universities extend their reach and reputation by producing a new generation of scholars, they also bring to campus a pool of younger scholars who support the work of the faculty by serving as research and teaching assistants and as intellectual protégés. Doctoral programs, despite their steep cost, are, therefore, highly valued by universities and jealously guarded by faculties.

Doctoral programs are also sharply competitive, externally and internally. Emory is typical in that the annual round of Ph.D. admissions in religious studies is a closely watched sporting event among the faculty. We are keenly aware that we are in competition with Harvard, Yale, Chicago, Princeton, and the other top-ranked programs for the same elite group of applicants, and we maintain a mental scorecard of "wins and losses." Less discussed openly, but no less monitored, is the internal scorecard. A Ph.D. student admitted in, say, New Testament means one slot fewer for ethics or theology, and an unwritten set of checks and balances is (sometimes) quietly enforced. Given, then, that doctoral programs lie close to the heart of a university's self-image and mission, that they are key factors in attracting and sustaining a strong senior faculty, and that they place heavy and competition-laced demands on limited resources, the creation of a new program in any field would generate scrutiny and debate. Even those faculty who might welcome practical theological students to the doctoral table want to be sure that they are not sitting in seats otherwise reserved for ethicists or historians.

Practical Theology and "The Idea of a University"

Given the fact that practical theology is best taught from a posture of commitment, not detachment, and given the undeniably competitive environment of contemporary academic life, can practical theology be successfully taught in the quad? Perhaps one helpful response can be found in the thought of John Henry Newman, who a century and a half ago famously advanced "the idea of a university." Newman's lectures by that title were occasioned by a papal proposal to build a Catholic university in Ireland, where, as a beleaguered minority, Catholics could well have been tempted to foster a defensive and sectarian approach to education. Newman countered with a vision of a university that was broad and humane, at one and the same time theological and secular, clear-eyed and honest about human rivalries while steadfastly hopeful about human prospects. A university, Newman said, is "an assemblage of [the] learned," where

> zealots for their own sciences, and rivals of each other, are brought, by familiar intercourse and for the sake of intellectual peace, to adjust together the claims and relations of their respective subjects of investiga-

tion. They learn to respect, to consult, to aid each other. Thus is created a pure and clear atmosphere of thought, which the student also breathes, though in his own case he only pursues a few sciences out of the multitude.

Wherever Newman's view of a university (or anything close to it) prevails, the door is open to practical theology, at least as the field is understood today. Practical theology is a "science" in the way that Newman's statement implies, that is, in the sense that it seeks after and generates knowledge rather than merely applying knowledge acquired elsewhere. Practical theology draws wisdom from the findings of other fields, but it also has a word to speak in the larger conversation that other fields do not have, and its insights are potentially useful to those fields, including those beyond the circle of theology. Moreover, Newman imagined a community of "zealots," scholars not coolly detached from their fields but, to the contrary, passionately convinced that their subjects and epistemologies were ways to Truth. In such a community, the confessional nature of much practical theology, so long as it is accompanied by genuine humility and the openness "to adjust together the claims and relations of their respective subjects of investigation," is not a liability but an asset, not a quality that separates practical theology from other fields but one all fields have in common.

We should be honest, of course, that Newman's dream of a free and open conversation among scholars and disciplines leading to "intellectual peace," when set down in the realities of a university today, sometimes seems as quaint as a lace doily. Although the vision of a community of scholars, free from coercion and unafraid of any ideas, working together on a quest for Truth, still vibrates in the mission statements of universities and in the healthiest places in university life, it must coexist with a more fragmented and market-driven understanding of academic life.

Newman imagined the university as a kind of intellectual peace conference, with all of the parties negotiating earnestly together in a single conversation aiming at a common shalom. What can often impress us most now about a university, however, is not the vitality of the single, overarching conversation, but the electric hum of a thousand conversations. While many people on campuses would still speak reverently of the unified "Search for Truth," frankly it is the quest for multiple, seemingly separate truths that energizes academic life. A concussive discovery in the history department rarely reverberates in the halls of the medical school, nor does an advance in the understanding of the Trinity at the theological school set the business faculty reprogramming their computers.

Universities today sometimes feel less like the Roman Forum, a grand space for common conversation, and more like a shopping mall, a cluster of retail stores, some large and busy (at Emory, the health sciences) and others small boutiques (art history, for example). Each store has internal customers (students) and online customers (industry, government, foundations and other grant makers), and as long as the customer base and bottom line remain strong, each store can conduct business as usual without much thought to the merchant next door. Put this way, the question of the place of practical theology is not simply, "Can you make a contribution to the university-wide quest for Truth?" It is rather, "Is practical theology the kind of store we want in our mall?" Is practical theology like an offbeat art gallery that will increase the mall's trendy reputation and attract intellectually rich customers, or is it more like a nail salon or a tanning studio, the first troubling sign of decline?

There is nevertheless a kind of eschatological hope for Newman's shalom, albeit often in faint and secular form, that shines without ceasing through university life. Signs abound on a university campus, from the constant crossing of paths on the quad to the vague homilies of commencement to the hunger for collaborative work, that we are, at our deepest and best, about some greater whole, some commonly held task. Even when we hide in the shadows of our own library carrels, we nevertheless are still held by the thought that we could together break through to "a pure and clear atmosphere of thought," and that we need "to learn to respect, to consult, to aid each other."

So, can practical theology find a place on the quad? Yes. But a far more interesting and important question is this: *Should* practical theology be taught in a university context? Beyond the obvious advantages of a university's more abundant financial and intellectual resources and the truth that a vision of the university like Newman's earns practical theology a place on the quad, are there compelling reasons, educationally and theologically, why the next generation of practical theologians should be educated in a university environment?

When this question is set down in the context of Emory, or in universities with similar resources and commitments, the answer is yes, precisely because of the character of the new practical theology described in this book. In their own chapter in this volume, Kathleen A. Cahalan and James R. Nieman make this claim about the disciplinary reasoning inherent in the new practical theology:

> The discipline's discourse emerges first through its own direct research in such areas as particular practices, congregational realities, ministerial roles, or educational approaches. It also develops in conversation with adjacent fields in theological education (biblical studies, theology, history) and those beyond it (sociology, psychology, medicine), as well as forms of study outside of academic institutions (for example, in spirituality, leadership, or development). These conversations aid practical theology in seeing how its various contexts can be better described and shaped. They also bring other fields and areas into contact with practical theological reasoning.[6]

In this paragraph, Cahalan and Nieman aptly outline both a sequence for the progress of practical theological research and a disciplinary network needed to support such research. Practical theological inquiry begins, as they present it, by exploring some aspect of the life of a community of faith — its rituals, practices, leadership roles, etc. This is the "there there" of practical theological research: living communities of faith with embodied practices performed in space and in and over time. This exploration is done critically, but not dispassionately. The practical theologian may at times pick up the "scientific" scalpels of the ethnographer or the historian, but the telos of practical theological inquiry — namely the goal of understanding the virtues and deformities of current practice and the reforming of that practice into one of deeper faithfulness — shapes the whole of the inquiry.

At Emory, with its history of theological education as a key activity in the life of the school, there is room on the quad for scholars who take faith communities seriously, who are themselves committed to that faith and those communities, and who bring every intellectual gift to bear on understanding them. As Cahalan and Nieman go on to say, though, such inquiry cannot be done alone. Mutually informing conversations must be started, and the first of these is with "neighbor" disciplines, such as biblical studies and theology. One can neither understand nor help to reform the church's practice of reading Scripture, for example, apart from a pro-

6. See Cahalan and Nieman's chapter in this volume, p. 78.

found understanding of the history, character, and theological significance of Scripture.

To this point, what Cahalan and Nieman describe can be done well within the walls of a freestanding theological school. Looking deeply at the life of the community of faith and talking it over with good friends and neighbors in theology, church history, and biblical studies does not require venturing out onto the quad. However, Cahalan and Nieman push the boundaries out farther when they describe the next two sets of conversation partners: those disciplines beyond theological education (sociology, psychology, medicine) and educational programs operating outside the academy, such as those in spirituality, leadership, and development. It is here that the university as the educational context for practical theology becomes desirable, perhaps even necessary. The university quad is not only a meeting place for all of the disciplines of the school, it is also a public place. Figuratively speaking, good practical theology is not done by going from building to building in the university, engaging in a series of bilateral talks. It is best done out in the sunshine, out on the quad, where everybody passing by, from the university and beyond, can see what is being explored, can ask questions and offer insights and opinions. Theologically, even if it does not yet fully realize it, the whole world has a stake in the outcomes of this research.

There is yet one more claim that Cahalan and Nieman make for practical theology that bears fruit in a university context. When practical theologians engage in conversations with other disciplines, all parties gain. Clearly practical theologians draw wisdom from sociology, linguistics, ethnography, psychology, and other fields of knowledge, but those disciplines are also potential beneficiaries of these conversations. As Cahalan and Nieman put it, these interdisciplinary conversations "also bring other fields and areas into contact with practical theological reasoning." When, for example, practical theologians engage in cross-disciplinary conversations with university colleagues in many fields about child development, underlying conceptions of the nature of childhood, selfhood, and humanity are, of necessity, at play. The practical theologian who brings to the table a view of children as not only biological and psychological beings, but also as gifts from God, changes the equation and adds to the conversation. Or again, when practical theologians engage in dialogue with linguists and rhetoricians, they bring an on-the-ground theological understanding of the telos of language and speech in faith communities, ends that include, but transcend, the normal categories of expression and persuasion and embody such purposes as truth-telling, hospitality, and freedom. Contributions of this kind by practical theology to other fields across the university could become quite significant, because in many ways they challenge the modernist, reductive epistemologies that still govern many fields. Thus practical theology may provide openings to alternative modes of inquiry, practice, and teaching that many in the contemporary university may find compelling.

The Shape of Doctoral Education in Practical Theology

Emory attempted to capture the best of this matrix of inquiry by creating for Ph.D. candidates in religion what is known as a "concentration in religious practices and practical theology." This is not a discrete Ph.D. program, like the programs in Hebrew Bible or Ethics. It is rather something like a "major," a way of focusing a student's program, an educational plan and a meeting place for students in all of the programs who are committed to exploring how their academic disciplines connect to living practices of religious communities. A student in Hebrew Bible, for example, might qualify for this concentration because she is interested in examining how the study of Scripture shapes the life of churches and synagogues. Approximately five students per year who have elected this concentration are admitted to the Ph.D. program every year. A substantial grant from the Lilly Endowment, which undergirds this concentration, allows these admissions to be above and beyond the number of students who would otherwise be admitted to the programs in religion, thus minimizing faculty competition about getting students for the various programs.

Usually most, but not all, of the students admitted each year to the concentration intend eventually to become practical theologians, that is, to teach preaching, Christian education, pastoral care, worship, or another practical theological subdiscipline in a seminary (or religiously affiliated college). All of the students involved in the concentration enroll in a common seminar on "Religious Practices and Practical Theology," in which several methods and perspectives of studying religious practices are examined and employed — for example, ritual theory, ethnography, and performance theory. Practical theology takes its place in the panorama of approaches, and one of the main goals of this seminar is to create a conversation among diverse disciplines, all committed to the critical investigation of living religious practices, in which practical theologians can both discover the contributions that practical theology can make to such a conversation and the benefits derived from other disciplines and methods. One advantage of this seminar is that it immediately introduces students to the kind of multilateral and even interfaith scholarly inquiry characteristic of good practical theology.

The practical theologians in the group also take courses in the history and methods of practical theology per se and seminars in their own subdisciplines (such as homiletics and pastoral care), and are expected to range widely and to find conversation partners in other places in the university. For example, an Emory student studying the practice of marriage in the Christian community might well find resources in the sociology department, the literature department, the law school, the university's Center for the Study of Myth and Ritual in American Life, and other places on campus. Two other aspects of the concentration help to round out the emphasis on doctoral practical theology. First, the director of the concentration arranges frequent extracurricular colloquies and lectures on some aspect of religious practices and practical theology, and, second, the concentration funds two postdoctoral fellowships per year. These are employed primarily to bring to campus recent Ph.D.s who wish either to deepen their capacities in practical theology or even to begin re-tooling their training as historians or biblical scholars into practical theologians. The post-doctoral students participate in the common seminar, teach M.Div. courses in the theological school, and make presentations in the colloquies.

The primary goal of Emory's program is to contribute to the creation of a new generation of practical theologians. Seminars and interdisciplinary conversations are not enough to accomplish this task; students must be formed in the traditions, habits, and skills of a teacher of the practices of the church. Lee S. Shulman, president of the Carnegie Foundation for the Advancement of Teaching, commenting on a study conducted by the foundation concerning the education of clergy,[7] notes that the study group

> found . . . four powerful "signature pedagogies" that run through seminary education: pedagogies of interpretation, pedagogies of formation,

---

7. The study has been published as Charles R. Foster et al., *Educating Clergy: Teaching Practices and Pastoral Imagination* (San Francisco: Jossey-Bass, 2005).

pedagogies of contextualization, and pedagogies of performance. That is, the teachers of clergy must instruct their students in the disciplined analysis of sacred texts; in the formation of their pastoral identities, dispositions, and values; in the understanding of the complex social, political, personal, and congregational conditions in which they are embedded; and in the skills of the preacher, counselor, liturgist, and leader through which they exercise their pastoral, priestly, and rabbinical responsibilities.[8]

The four "signature pedagogies" bear on Emory's program in two ways. First, the new Ph.D. graduates need to be prepared to engage in these pedagogies, but, second, these pedagogies also function in the doctoral education as well in the sense that Ph.D. education in practical theology includes work in reading texts (both sacred texts and the literature of a discipline), formation as a teacher, training in analyzing congregational contexts, and pedagogical methods for teaching performance in some aspect of the practice of ministry.

In terms of forming the habits of mind and practice necessary for the teacher of practical theology, Emory seeks to accomplish this in two ways: through a thorough plan of supervised teaching opportunities and through scheduled extracurricular conversations about practical theology and the task of teaching in theological education. Every Ph.D. student at Emory is responsible for serving not only as a teaching assistant in several practical theological courses at the M.Div. level, under the supervision of a professor, but also for functioning as a full teacher in at least one course, giving lectures, engaging students, and planning the pedagogy. Ph.D. students in practical theology are also gathered with other students working in religious practices for conversation about topics of mutual interest, research projects, the process of finding teaching positions, and general exchanges about life as a scholar in the practices arena.

8. Lee S. Shulman, "From Hermeneutic to Homiletic: The Professional Formation of Clergy," *Change* (March/April 2006): 30. In addition to describing these four "signature pedagogies," Shulman also makes claims about the significance of theological education for higher learning more broadly: "the challenges of [educating clergy] underlie all the other kinds of higher learning as well. Learning for both deep cognitive understanding and the development of character, identity, and moral sensibilities is a goal common to the professions and the liberal arts. We find the education of clergy fascinating and valuable . . . because within its rich complexities we see in microcosm many of the processes that characterize all of higher education" (p. 31).

Emory is not the only university providing this kind of educational opportunity for doctoral students in practical theology.[9] Duke University, for example, offers an innovative Th.D. degree through its divinity school in such areas as evangelism, preaching, and Christian spirituality as well as in interdisciplinary areas such as interpreting Scripture in the church. It is a program that shares much of the same vision of practical theologians out on the university quad engaging in free-ranging conversations with multiple disciplines. Duke describes its approach as follows:

> The program centers upon areas of study often neglected by traditional Ph.D. programs, such as worship, preaching, evangelism, and the arts. At the same time, as an integral component of its mission, the Th.D. program seeks to reconfigure the way in which such practices are brought into creative interdisciplinary conversation with the established academic discourses of biblical studies, historical studies, and theology and ethics. Moreover, the interdisciplinary scope of the program extends to other areas of the university and addresses fresh areas of research such as the intersection of Divinity and Health Care, or Peacemaking and Reconciliation, areas where the Divinity School has been developing significant intellectual and programmatic strength.[10]

While Duke's Th.D. program locates practical theology in new and neglected areas of study, Vanderbilt University's Program in Theology and Practice uses practical theology to reinvigorate long-established disciplines. Fellows in Vanderbilt's program earn a Ph.D. in any one of the existing areas of study within the Graduate Department of Religion. The

---

9. Ph.D. and Th.D. programs in various aspects and sub-disciplines of practical theology are offered by a number of institutions, including Andrews University, Asbury Theological Seminary, Biola University, Boston University, Brite Divinity School, Claremont School of Theology, Columbia Theological Seminary, Concordia Seminary (Mo.), Drew University, Duke Divinity School, Garrett Evangelical Theological Seminary, the Graduate Theological Union, Interdenominational Theological Center, Luther Seminary, Lutheran Theological Seminary at Philadelphia, New Orleans Baptist Seminary, Princeton Theological Seminary, Southeastern Baptist Theological Seminary, Southern Baptist Seminary, Southwestern Baptist Seminary, Toronto School of Theology, Union Theological Seminary and Presbyterian School of Christian Education (Va.), and Vanderbilt University.

10. See the full description of the Duke Th.D. program at their website: http://www .divinity.duke.edu/academics/degrees/thd/. Thanks to Dean L. Gregory Jones of Duke Divinity School for providing further information on this program.

Program in Theology and Practice, as its website explains, seeks to form "a generation of professors who are outstanding teachers of people preparing for ministry and groundbreaking scholars in practical theology." The program stresses teaching for ministry through sustained mentoring, colloquy conversations about the meaning of theological education, seminars that involve ministers of many kinds in the work of doctoral education, and innovative "externships" that let students serve as apprentice teachers in area theological schools. Practical theology — in many senses of the phrase — plays an especially important role in this process of formation. Fellows in every area learn from the distinctive contributions of the academic discipline of practical theology. Fellows in both "classical" and "practical" disciplines learn to think through arts of ministry like preaching, congregational leadership, and pastoral care. Fellows in every discipline learn to attend carefully and critically to the practical theology performed in everyday life. And a capstone presentation pushes Vanderbilt's fellows to stretch their disciplines and work across disciplines in order to do the practical work of public intellectuals.[11]

Boston University, through its School of Theology, initiated a Th.D. program in practical theology nearly ten years ago; the program today is well established and one of the largest doctoral programs in the School of Theology. The Th.D. program has all the rigor of a Ph.D. program, but also has, as the school describes it, the "integrative character and clear connection to the church"[12] that characterize practical theology. Students in this program major in practical theology and choose a concentration area of study among the following fields: (1) congregation and community, (2) ethics, (3) mission, (4) evangelism, (5) mission and evangelism, (6) homiletics, (7) liturgical studies, (8) pastoral theology, or (9) spirituality. They also gain competence in a "complementary discipline" — for example, sociology, psychology, law, or anthropology — upon which they draw in practical theological research. This program is unique in its connection to a range of innovative projects in practical theology, which are coordinated through the Center for Practical Theology at Boston University. The Center for Practical Theology provides fellowships, research sup-

11. Information on the Vanderbilt program can be found on their website: http://www.vanderbilt.edu/gradschool/religion/t&p/index.html. Thanks also to Professor Ted Smith of Vanderbilt for providing further information on this program.

12. Information on the Boston University program can be found on their website: http://www.bu.edu/bulletins/sth/item07.html#anchor30.

port, and teaching assistantships to doctoral students, while also hosting a number of foundation-supported research projects. According to its own stated mission, the Center for Practical Theology

> seeks to provide a bridge between the scholarly resources, questions, and insights of a university-based theological seminary and the wisdom, questions, and traditions of communities of faith. In doing so, the Center provides an infrastructure for sustaining, deepening, and expanding important relationships and connections between Boston University School of Theology and local congregations, denominational offices, and religious centers so that they may be more integrally incorporated into student learning and faculty teaching and research.[13]

These young programs at Boston, Emory, Duke, and Vanderbilt (with other major universities almost sure to follow) are hopeful experiments not only in educating a new generation of teachers in the practical theological fields but also in enabling practical theological discourse to deepen and to mature. The main benefit of such programs, of course, is not in the sheer production of scholars and teachers, but in the life of the church, where pastors who have been guided by those teachers will be able to lead congregations into more faithful Christian living and into mission more significantly engaged with the realities of the society around them.

What should not be lost in all of this, though, is the difference the presence of these programs can make to the larger life of the universities that house them. As Jeffrey Stout has observed, the language of religious commitment is often muted in the public regions of the contemporary university today. Fearing that the language of religious commitment will inevitably alienate, offend, and divide, "we adopt," says Stout, "a thinned-out vocabulary that nearly everyone can use, regardless of their religious differences. This tends not to be a theologically inflected vocabulary, because any such vocabulary will tend to embody assumptions that some of our fellow citizens will have reasons to reject."[14]

It is, of course, impossible to do practical theology with a thinned out,

13. See the website of the Boston University program: http://www.bu.edu/bulletins/sth/item07.html#anchor30. Thanks also to Professor Claire Wolfteich for sharing information about this program.

14. Jeffrey Stout, *Democracy and Tradition* (Princeton: Princeton University Press, 2004), p. 113.

non-theologically inflected vocabulary, and the presence of practical theologians on the university quad, engaged in serious, scholarly, and committed exploration of religious practices, thereby both drawing from and contributing to the many conversations that a university affords, will go a long way toward making it possible for others to imagine that they could function both as good citizens of the university and as those who speak of their deepest religious commitments with clarity, zest, and passion.

Practical Theology
in Ministry

Part 4
and
Learning Ministry over Time

In this section of *For Life Abundant,* our focus shifts from the academy to the congregation. As previous essays have suggested, all the authors of this book are keenly interested in fostering generative relationships between these two settings, an agenda we see as crucial for theological education, Christian ministry, and faithful living in our time. This happens best, we believe, when face-to-face conversation and collaboration across institutional contexts occurs.

The conversations leading to this book have consistently included both pastors and professors. Although the balance of participants tipped toward the academy, we perceived at many points along the way that our work on theological education, ministry, and the Christian life — and indeed the work of practical theology generally — could not thrive without close, personal engagement with those involved in on-the-ground ministry. Each of the authors writing in this section has served as a full-time minister (three of them were serving congregations at the time these essays were written), and together they have pastored congregations in a variety of urban, suburban, and small town settings. These pastors and several others made indispensable contributions to the conversations that shaped this book.

When work on this book began, Christian Scharen was senior pastor of First Lutheran Church of the Reformation (ELCA) in New Britain, Connecticut. In 2004 he accepted a position as associate director of the Center for Faith and Culture at Yale Divinity School, where he teaches congregational studies and works with a project that brings ministers, laity, and academics together to consider "faith as a way of life." Readers will learn more about him in the course of this essay, in which he uses his own pastoral formation as a concrete example of how ministry is learned over time. His emphasis on the importance of ways of knowing that become somatic and intuitive for mature practitioners and his stories of how this kind of knowing began to emerge for him add congregation-based specificity and concreteness to the notion of "know-how" that Bonnie Miller-McLemore takes to be one aim of teaching in practical theology.

In Scharen's depictions of the thinking he did in the midst of specific episodes of ministerial practice, we can see how ministers are themselves practical theologians engaging in many of the moves described in earlier sections of this book. Further, a practical theological question shapes his after-the-fact reflection on these episodes in light of a theory of developmental learning. How, he asks, do people learn to be good pastors? They learn slowly, Scharen argues, and as whole, embodied persons who shape and are shaped by communities. These emphases on time and embodiment challenge theological educators to ponder how the limited but essential years of formal academic preparation can best be used. They also challenge the church to support more extended programs of ministerial development, one of which will be described in the next chapter.

11. Learning Ministry over Time: Embodying Practical Wisdom

Christian Scharen

Practical theology plays a key role in educating and forming ministers far beyond the bounds of the formal theological education offered in colleges, seminaries, and universities. While a brief period of the process of learning ministry is usually spent in theological classrooms, a much larger part takes place in congregations. Such learning begins with God's saving action in the waters of baptism and continues in the midst of a community that has promised to help this new sister or brother in Christ to learn the shape of the Christian life. Thus God and the church give shape to the faith that each future pastor brings to seminary and ministry.[1] We thank them by name in the Acknowledgments.

Attending to learning over time contrasts with much literature on practical theology and theological education — even in this volume — that focuses on teaching rather than learning, and on classrooms rather than congregations and daily life. Other chapters in this book show that practical theology has much to offer through teaching that takes place in college, seminary, or university settings. Here, however, I draw on practical theology to interpret a longer arc of learning. Students come to seminary already formed by a variety of experiences with family, congregation, school, work and the significant relationships in each.[2] Later, the congre-

1. I understand that some who attend seminary have been Christians since childhood while others may have only recently come to faith. In addition, some believe in infant baptism while others affirm believers' baptism. My point does not depend on how long one has been a Christian, or at what age baptism occurs, but that Christian ministry arises from God's saving action and the church's struggle to live faithfully in and for the sake of the world.

2. In a recent major study of teaching in theological education, Charles Foster and his

gations that clergy serve in the years during and following formal theological education act as a forge or furnace of ongoing education and formation for ministry. An especially crucial point in this development is the transition from the relative safety of seminary to the fire of responsible congregational leadership,[3] as the learning that takes place in the midst of intense experiences becomes embodied in the pastor who communicates God's judgment and grace, forgiveness and blessing.

Craig Dykstra has argued that such knowledge of grace and forgiveness, the core knowledge of faith, becomes embodied through practice.[4] For Dykstra, this knowledge is deeply somatic, existential, and personal — knowledge of God's buoyant, trustworthy presence is akin to the knowledge a swimmer has of water. While the initial example here is swimming, Dykstra's larger point is that participation in the practices of faith (prayer, singing, hospitality, forgiveness, and so on) opens us to the work of the Holy Spirit and nurtures in us the sure knowledge of the grace of God in Christ Jesus.[5] Such vibrant knowledge of the grace and love of God is the kind of knowing many seminary teachers and congregational leaders prize in candidates for pastoral ministry exactly because it is the core knowledge for the life of faith. Gaining knowledge of this sort and developing the capacity to articulate it and foster communities in which others can experience it powerfully enough to shape their whole way of life is the core of education and formation for ministry.

Such knowledge, as Dykstra argues, is learned through participation and held in a profoundly embodied way. No instruction or program can simply transmit the wisdom and imagination that good pastors seem to have. Rather, these emerge over time in ministers who entrust themselves

---

fellow researchers regularly note the impact of the divergent life experiences students bring to graduate professional education alongside the question of what the seminary can and cannot be expected to do. See Charles Foster et al., *Educating Clergy: Teaching Practices and Pastoral Imagination* (San Francisco: Jossey-Bass, 2006), pp. 73, 101, 376-77, and passim.

3. See David Wood's chapter in this book.

4. Craig Dykstra, "Reconceiving Practice in Theological Inquiry and Education," in *Virtues and Practices in the Christian Tradition: Christian Ethics after MacIntyre*, ed. Nancey Murphy, Brad J. Kallenberg, and Mark Thiessen Nation (Harrisburg: Trinity, 1997), p. 172. Dykstra writes, "Participation in certain practices provides physical, social, and even intellectual conditions necessary to the knowledge intrinsic to the life of faith."

5. Dykstra elaborates these claims in his chapter on "pastoral and ecclesial imagination" earlier in this volume. See also Craig Dykstra, *Growing in the Life of Faith*, 2nd ed. (Louisville: Westminster/John Knox, 2005), esp. chapter 4.

reflectively and well to participation in the life of faith and to the everyday work of ministry. The notion of embodied learning in this chapter is one way to make sense of how such wisdom and imagination develop. A caveat: by the phrase "embodied learning" I do not mean body *versus* mind, but body-mind, a holistic understanding of one sense-perceiving organism acting in the world.[6] Such knowledge is more like what Aristotle called *phronesis* — practical wisdom — in which one does "quickly" the "right thing, in the right way, and at the right time."[7]

Learning Embodied Practical Wisdom

While I was studying theology in Berkeley, California, I took a philosophy course with Hubert Dreyfus, a philosopher who, with his brother Stuart, had created a theory of how learners develop expertise over time. My wife, Sonja, was simultaneously taking a course from Patricia Benner, whose scholarly research on developmental learning in nursing largely rested upon the work of the Dreyfus brothers.[8] Sonja's father, Paul Batalden, had also discovered Benner and Dreyfus and was using their work in his own thinking about graduate medical education. This generative conversation, with Dreyfus and Benner, initially, and with Sonja and Paul over the years, helped shape the path I took in the process of learning

6. See Bent Flyvbjerg, "Sustaining Non-Rationalized Practices: Body-Mind, Power, and Situational Ethics. An Interview with Hubert and Stuart Dreyfus," *Praxis International* 11, no. 1 (April 1991): 95-96. See also Shawn Gallagher, *How the Body Shapes the Mind* (New York: Oxford University Press, 2005).

7. Aristotle, *The Nicomachean Ethics,* trans. with an introduction by David Ross (New York: Oxford University Press, 1980), p. 150 (Book VI, Chapter 9, §6). Also see Charles Taylor, "To Follow a Rule," in *Philosophical Arguments* (Cambridge, Mass.: Harvard University Press, 1995), p. 177.

8. While both brothers, who teach at the University of California, Berkeley, have written numerous works on this basic theory, the main text is: Hubert L. Dreyfus and Stuart E. Dreyfus, *Mind over Machine: The Power of Human Intuition and Expertise in the Era of the Computer* (New York: The Free Press, 1986). See also Hubert Dreyfus, *On the Internet* (New York: Routledge, 2001). Patricia Benner's work is summarized in a recent article "Using the Dreyfus Model of Skill Acquisition to Describe and Interpret Skill Acquisition and Clinical Judgment in Nursing Practice and Education," *Bulletin of Science, Technology and Society* 24 (June 2004): 188-99. Benner's first major book in this line of research is *From Novice to Expert: Excellence and Power in Clinical Nursing Practice* (Menlo Park: Addison-Wesley Publishing, 1984).

ministry.[9] We each saw the relevance of this description of developmental learning for our respective professions: nursing, medicine, and ministry.

Hubert Dreyfus, a phenomenologist, and Stuart Dreyfus, an applied mathematician, describe a developmental learning pathway from novice to expert. Such development is not a matter of following instinctual neural pathways, as in the case of a baby chicken that immediately scratches the ground for food, but rather a result of disciplined and conscious participation in practices, of "learning by body."[10] In the early stages of learning, they argue, learners need theory — articulated knowledge and rules of thumb — to guide their action. Such learning characterizes the stages Dreyfus and Dreyfus have named "novice," "advanced beginner," and "competent," each normally a part of progress through formal training and into the first years of professional practice.[11] Usually after a number of years of professional practice, however, excellent practitioners develop the capacity to act without rational deliberation — without thinking in the typical sense of conscious reflection. Dreyfus and Dreyfus call these stages "proficient" and "expert." The shift between the thinking characteristic of the first three stages and the final two entails a shift from action based on rational calculation to intuitive action. Through repeated engagement in practice, those who are proficient or expert come to know "of course" — that is, without detaching, reflecting, and planning a rational course of action — just the thing that is needed.[12]

9. Paul has offered me enormous support and encouragement across the years of seminary, graduate school, work in pastoral ministry, and now while I am writing about ministry. His own work is groundbreaking within the field of medicine. See, for example, Paul Batalden, David Leach, Susan Swing, Hubert Dreyfus, and Stuart Dreyfus, "General Competencies and Accreditation in Graduate Medical Education: An Antidote to Overspecification in the Education of Medical Specialists," *Health Affairs* 21 (2002): 103-11.

10. Loïc Wacquant's work to develop a "carnal" sociology, drawing deeply from his mentor Pierre Bourdieu, is among the best sources for thinking about embodied learning. See his *Body and Soul: Notes on Apprenticeship in Boxing* (New York: Oxford University Press, 2004), p. 123.

11. The diversity of life experience and academic preparation students bring to seminary means, among many other things, that the category "novice" fits more or less well depending on the particular person. Some Catholic lay ministers have been working in full-time ministry for decades before entering seminary while other seminarians have only recently had a conversion experience that led them to seminary without much depth in faith formation or experience in congregational life and leadership.

12. Hubert Dreyfus puts it provocatively when he says, "People are at their best when they are not conscious," in "A Conversation with Hubert Dreyfus," interviewed by Russell Schoch, *California Monthly: A Publication of the California Alumni Association* (July 2004).

This phenomenological approach, developed inductively from studies of Air Force pilots, nurses, chess players, and others, has provided me with a theoretical frame for understanding my own process of learning ministry over time. In this chapter, I narrate some of that process as a means of illustrating the Dreyfuses' theory and inviting others to consider their own experience of learning over time. As I begin, a dual confession is in order. First, because the stories I am sharing are about learning, they often show me, to quote a lovely phrase from David Wood, "working at the edges of my competence." At times, as you will see, I fall off that edge. Second, this chapter is confession in the sense that even if I have experienced rocky moments in ministry, my story also points to God's faithfulness and to my gratitude for the community of faith that has guided and taught me along the way. I am well aware that I am far from an expert pastor. I have had only a beginning in ministry, and my story here extends from before my academic and pastoral training through only three years as senior pastor of an urban New England congregation. Clearly, I still have much to learn. In addition, this is only one story, distinct and even unique in many ways. Limited as it is, I hope that rehearsing my story in the midst of a journey in learning ministry may provide a context that will encourage those with different stories to engage in common reflection on the shape and key movements of pastoral formation.

I draw mainly on stories from a few areas of pastoral leadership — worship, preaching, and pastoral care — as a means to focus my reflections.[13] While early on I saw these as relatively distinct tasks or skills (as they are in fact often taught in seminary classrooms), I have come over time to see them as part of a larger, foundational task — that of shaping community.[14] By and large, the Dreyfus and Dreyfus framework will be submerged in footnotes, though I shall also briefly explicate it at the end of the chapter. I hope that this approach will allow the rich narrative of practice — a feature that is essential to the Dreyfuses' approach — to carry much of my argument by showing actual, embodied learning over time.

---

13. I chose these areas of ministry because of my intense focus on those aspects of my work. The obvious point is that one is not equally good at, nor does one develop equally within, the various areas of pastoral practice. Sometimes, because of either interest or capacity, one never develops to the level of mastery in a given area.

14. Jackson Carroll has plowed the ground in this field. See *God's Potters: Pastoral Leadership and the Shaping of Congregations* (Grand Rapids: Eerdmans, 2006) as well as his *As One With Authority: Reflective Leadership in Ministry* (Louisville: Westminster/John Knox, 1991). See also Peter W. Marty's chapter in this volume.

Beginnings

As adult learners, and even as children, we typically do not face learning something new without having first acquired some basic sense of life and some capacities that aid our ability to learn the new thing. Those beginning formal ministerial training come with some level of knowledge of discipleship that, regardless of its depth, provides one foundation for graduate theological education. They also bring other basic knowledge — language, for instance, and some sense of basic trust in relationship to the world — much of it gained through everyday presence within the basic institutions of one's society, such as family, church, school, work, and the strong communities and traditions shaped by and shaping them.[15] All of these kinds of foundational knowledge come through the particular people within those institutions — parents, extended family, friends; pastors and the saints on earth and in heaven; teachers, administrators, fellow students; bosses, coworkers, clients, or customers; and various ideas and ways of life that live through them all in stronger or weaker fashion.[16]

For me, these foundations were laid as I moved through institutions and relationships shaped by a broad and dynamic tradition: Lutheranism.[17] My grandfather, a Lutheran clergyman, invoked God's claim on me in baptism one week after my birth and often told me that I would be a minister when I grew up. Our family practice of daily prayer at the dinner table and hymn-singing around the piano shaped my deep sense of the interconnection between worship and daily life. Yet it was not until my adolescent years that — through my confirmation teacher, Pr. Prinz, and his gentle eyes and attention — I sensed God might care for me. This sense

15. See Emile Durkheim on the moral apprenticeship of the family and school that together inculcate the spirit of discipline within the child: *Moral Education* (New York: The Free Press, 1973), p. 148. See also Robert Bellah et al., *The Good Society* (New York: Alfred A. Knopf, 1991), especially "Introduction: We Live Through Institutions," and Mary Douglas, *How Institutions Think* (Syracuse: Syracuse University Press, 1986), especially Chapter 5, "Institutions Confer Identity."

16. Marcel Mauss's work on the tradition-bound production of the *habitus* through body techniques is essential here. See *Sociology and Psychology: Essays* (New York: Routledge, 1979), pp. 97ff.

17. A beautiful example of this from the Reformed tradition is Nicholas Wolterstorff's essay "The Grace That Shaped My Life," in *Philosophers Who Believe: The Spiritual Journeys of Eleven Leading Thinkers,* ed. Kelly James Clark (Downers Grove, Ill.: InterVarsity, 1993), pp. 273-75.

was deepened through the faithful learning encouraged by campus ministers and professors at a Lutheran college. They gave gentle direction to my searching spirit, teaching me to learn faith not only by doing, serving, and doubting, but also by submitting to the toil of learning the Bible via archaic history and dead languages.[18] After college, through a year of volunteer service in the Lutheran Volunteer Corps, these commitments grew through full-time work as part of a Franciscan ministry with the homeless.

During my LVC year, as it became increasingly evident that I was heading to seminary, the pastor and the organist at my local church began to teach me the lessons of liturgical history and theology. They also gave me my first experiences of preaching (a midweek Lenten meditation) and leading worship (regularly as assisting minister), teaching me posture and vocal projection and modulation along the way. These relationships and institutions were concrete loci of the body of Christ that in turn incorporated me into that body, showing me the way of discipleship and challenging me to join in practicing it. When I began formal seminary education, it was as a next step, not a first step, on the journey of learning ministry.

Novice — Learning the "Rules of the Game"[19]

I was thrilled to be in seminary. The first-year curriculum focused on such basic topics as biblical interpretation, church history, and the theology of Lutheran ministry. In addition, we first-years entered a two-year contextual education program that linked field experience to a weekly "formation group" that provided space for reflection on field experiences. Even at

18. Pierre Bourdieu draws on Durkheim's work on the ascetic practices of negative rites that "produce people who are out of the ordinary, in a word, distinguished," which explains why it is necessary to suffer through "the learning of dead languages" so as to "entrust the body, treated as a kind of memory, with their most precious possessions. . . ." And very little, in the Lutheran view of the Christian faith, is of greater significance than the Word of God found in Scripture. See "Rites of Initiation" in *Language and Symbolic Power* (Stanford: Stanford University Press, 1991), p. 123.

19. In general this stage begins with formal training; that is, it usually begins with the beginning of seminary education. However, for me in fact it had begun earlier, with fits and starts, as I gained clarity about my call to ministry. Key for the novice stage, especially in graduate professional education, is the relation of theory to practice in learning. For the novice stage, theory is a lot of "context-free" information, both theory and rules of thumb, that can be understood at a basic level without experience in the area being learned.

the time, I saw how privileged I was to have the late Timothy Lull, then Dean and Professor of Theology, as my formation group leader and teacher for the course entitled Lutheran Theology and Ministry. We began each class by singing a hymn around the piano in the chapel next door to our classroom — a reflection of Tim's own churchly and pastoral vocation. He emerged for me and many other students as a model of what it meant to be a lively practical theologian in action.

The second-year curriculum included more advanced study in theology and Bible as well as practical theology courses on worship, pastoral care, and homiletics. In addition, I worked at Peace Lutheran in Danville, a suburban congregation served by an intense young pastor named Steve Harms. He thought of suburban America as a more challenging setting than the one in which he had served as a night minister on the streets of downtown San Francisco. The son of a pastor who taught homiletics at an Ohio seminary, Steve was the most powerful preacher I had ever heard. I spent most of that year learning to assist in worship, attending educational and other church events, and talking with Steve about preaching.

My turn to preach finally came during Lent. The text was John 4, the lovely story of Jesus' encounter with the woman at the well. Carefully following a method used in the introductory homiletics course I was taking,[20] I read the biblical text a number of times out loud and then tried to "enter" the text and to grasp the gist in a one-sentence "point" that proclaimed the gospel. I pegged the story as a "liberation" story, an "Exodus" echo in the ministry of the "new Moses." Then I examined other resources and outlined a five-step homiletical plot — an exercise aimed at helping us picture the flow in our minds so that we could avoid having a written manuscript.

On Sunday morning, as I began to preach, I felt a surge of adrenaline because I knew that although I had created the outline, I was not using it. Struggling mightily, I tried both to engage the people and see in my mind's eye the sermon outline I had labored over. Without knowing it, I completely missed one quarter of the sermon — I forgot the section on the Exodus itself!

---

20. The method was from Eugene Lowry's book *The Homiletical Plot* (Louisville: Westminster/John Knox, 1980). Lowry explains five typical movements of a sermonic plot: (1) upsetting the equilibrium; (2) analyzing the discrepancy; (3) disclosing the clue to resolution; (4) experiencing the gospel; (5) anticipating the consequences. This understanding of plotting will enable the preacher to move beyond simple narrative or story telling to actually crafting (mapping) thought in a way that captivates the listener's mind.

After the service, as my stomach churned,[21] Steve kindly said, "Chris, I really thought this was a powerful sermon. It was a little hard to follow at one point — so I wondered if you might have skipped something." My wife Sonja simply said, "Chris, you looked constipated up there." "What?" I remember thinking. "I can't even keep the sermon straight in my head; how am I supposed to remember to smile in the midst of it?"[22] In homiletics class I remembered all the points of the sermon, received good feedback and got a good grade. Still, I couldn't help feeling that my real grade had been mixed. What was the difference between Steve's seemingly effortless preaching, full of spiritual and intellectual connection to the congregation, and my own labored and awkward efforts?

Interlude I

Typically, in the Lutheran pattern, a year-long internship, or vicarage, would have followed these two years of field education directly. Yet I had received encouragement to do "academic" study in theology from college and now seminary professors. In retrospect, I question the distinction between professional and academic coursework, but at the time I was seduced by the invitation to "the harder path" that had been taken by my professors, whom I admired and wanted to emulate. In my first year of seminary, therefore, I had applied to a program that offered an M.A. in religion along with the M.Div. for only one additional year of coursework plus a research thesis. This change, among other things, delayed my full-time parish internship year until I had completed all my coursework and graduated with both degrees.

21. Dreyfus and Dreyfus, in an interview, are asked where emotions reside. In "the whole body," Stuart Dreyfus replies. "In the pit of the stomach." See Flyvbjerg, "Sustaining Non-Rationalized Practices," p. 95.

22. As one accumulates experience with sets of theory and rules of thumb for practice, nascent ability becomes instead overwhelming as one tries to keep everything in mind: biblical and theological interpretation, homiletical theory, sermon flow, dramatic emphasis, and performative grace. David Sudnow beautifully describes a similar circumstance the first night he played jazz piano on stage with a trio: "though at home I'd executed these runs smoothly, under pressure of the situation they were very sloppily produced, and there were many errors." See the end of his chapter titled "Beginnings" in *Ways of the Hand* (Cambridge: MIT Press, 2001), pp. 32-35.

Advanced Beginner — Using Rules in Context[23]

After graduation, I sought out and found an internship at Bethlehem Lutheran, an urban African American Lutheran congregation in downtown Oakland. So as year five of my seminary experience began, I found myself at another beginning point.[24] Rather than a fulfillment along a familiar trajectory, this felt like another world. I was learning simultaneously about a new city, a new neighborhood, and a church quite different from Peace Lutheran in suburban Danville. In my first week, Julius Carroll, the pastor, sat me down and said, "Chris, this internship is going to be largely about listening. That's the best way to succeed as a white boy in the Black Church." I did listen intensely, but even so, I remember my internship not so much as a controlled situation in which I simply listened, but as a series of overwhelmings.[25] Julius tried to foster that by letting waves of congregational life come straight at me.

The first of these waves came within my first month: the death of a 28-year-old woman in a car accident on the night of her graduation from pharmacy school. When Julius heard that Kalani Edwards had died, he told me he wanted me to preach the funeral. My heart stopped. What? Me preach at a tragic funeral like this? I've only been here a month! I've only been to one funeral — my grandmother's — and that was more than a decade ago! He said no: I would lead in pastoral care to the family, and I would preach. He would assist me in the funeral, but I would go alone to the gravesite to lead the committal service.

In some respects, talking with Mr. Edwards, Kalani's father, was the easiest part. I knew how to listen and to be compassionate, and I knew that the Psalms spoke even to the broken heart that cries out, "Why, O Lord?"

23. Typically, the advanced beginning stage would occur later in seminary as students move further along with fieldwork experiences, or in my case, begin a one-year internship in a congregation. This would likely be two to three years after beginning formal graduate theological education.

24. Benner's research found that when people move to new contexts of professional practice, they typically move backwards in skill proficiency. They also move backwards when there has been a period of inactivity — the old use it or lose it factor. However, I believe that it is a mistake to say, as I think Benner does, that simply moving locations or even shifting specialties within a profession *always* means becoming a novice again.

25. Craig Dykstra's comments on overwhelmings are pertinent here; see pp. 53-54 in his chapter in this volume.

Whatever nervousness I had as I drove over, parked, and walked up the steps melted away as I met this bear of a man, shaved head and tattooed arm, quietly weeping as he motioned me into the living room. An hour later, I left with a story of hardship and brokenness despite what could only be called heroic efforts on the part of this father.

Planning the funeral and speaking the gospel of life publicly in the face of death were more difficult. What is a funeral? What are the roles of pastor, funeral director, family, and congregation in such times? My seminary education had not included study of the complex of issues related to a funeral, so I studied whatever Bible, church history, theology, liturgy, and pastoral care I could find in relation to the urgent responsibility of leading this funeral. Then Julius and I outlined the funeral liturgy and walked through its movements in the sanctuary, noting all the points where I might need practice or a written note of reminder.

What I did not know in advance was that I was not in charge of the funeral. That packed funeral was in fact led by the people of God who gathered to send Kalani home to her Lord. The simple line in the order of service that said "Remembrances & Words of Comfort" took longer than the rest of the service. Friends simply kept coming forward to offer words: to Kalani, to Mr. Edwards, and to the gathered friends and family. I followed the rubrics, read the gospel, preached from the pulpit, and tried my best to seem pastoral so that no one would have to ask, "What are you doing here?" or "Where is the pastor?" At the reception afterwards, the most heartening thing to hear was: "That was a real nice message, pastor. It sounds like you knew her real well." In fact, I had never met her, but I learned some profound lessons. First, I learned that what Craig Dykstra calls the "ecclesial imagination" has a vital role in shaping the process of learning ministry. Second, I learned that at a time like this the gospel's promise has to wrap itself in the form of the particular life now lost in order to speak to the grief the loss had caused.

The year had other moments of overwhelming, and a flurry of learning moments large and small. Through it all, I gained experience in fitting the "rules" of worship, preaching, and pastoral care to this context, to these people, though a year was barely enough to begin to know the rules or the context at all well.

Interlude II

Again, as in the transition from my field education experience, I did not follow the typical Lutheran pattern, which would have led next to the pastorate. Having received strong encouragement to pursue doctoral studies, and having been accepted at various schools, I felt yet again that one vocational track (toward pastoral ministry) had to be put off for the sake of another (toward the academy). Doctoral training has a strong gravitational pull toward specialization and erudition. On the one hand, I had to (and chose to) bend to this strong pull, undertaking all the expected coursework and comprehensive exams in theological ethics and sociology of religion. On the other hand, I could be bent only so far away from my longstanding interest in worship, congregations, and the moral life they shape.[26] On the whole, I found that my academic work significantly deepened my understanding of these themes.[27] Close relations with congregations would influence my work at every turn, and my dissertation was based on three full years of fieldwork and study in five different congregations.[28] At the same time, my pastoral identity and churchly commitments were always slightly out of step with that academic setting. I was fortunate to have as a mentor Don Saliers, who is unabashedly connected to the church and active in his denomination and congregation, but some professors worried that my work was too closely associated with the church and were, perhaps, disappointed when I chose to become the pastor of a congregation after I graduated, even though, as one put it, I "didn't have to." Nonetheless, eager to lead an urban congregation and to put to use all the knowledge I had gathered over the years of seminary and doctoral training, I was called to an old Swedish-heritage Lutheran church in the now entirely Puerto Rican downtown of New Britain, Connecticut.

26. A providential conversation with Dorothy Bass during the summer before I began at Emory strongly encouraged my desire to do work grounded in the life of the church. As Thomas Long describes in his chapter, a university-related doctoral program in practical theology offers many distinct advantages, many of which I took advantage of, yet in the absence of a concrete program such as Emory now has, it was difficult to resist the attraction of academic esoterica.

27. The application essay I submitted, written under the guidance of Robert Bellah and Michael Aune, was later published as "To Aid Us to Live: Ideology, Ritual and Christian Subjectivity," *Worship* 70 (September 1996): 406-22.

28. Under the direction of Steve Tipton and Don Saliers, this dissertation was published as *Public Worship and Public Work: Character and Commitment in Local Congregational Life* (Collegeville: The Liturgical Press, 2004).

Competent to Proficient — The Intuitive Leap[29]

Having trusted books so deeply thus far along the way, I naturally read two or three on "how to begin in pastoral ministry." The most significant advice I found was to forget about unpacking my books, to meet people, and to be visible. Little did I know that I would hardly have an option! I was off and running with a funeral on my first day, June 1, 2001. Fortunately for me, the interim associate pastor stayed on for a period of orientation and led the funeral that day. But two weeks later, I presided over the funeral of a one-year-old who had been killed by his psychotic mother. A week later, after I sat by her side as stomach cancer ravaged her body, a stalwart usher from the early service died. And not a week after that, one of the saints of the congregation died of kidney failure. By the end of my first six months, I had presided at 22 funerals, 7 weddings, and 13 baptisms. In addition, my first fall program season was beginning in the midst of the complexity and high emotion evoked by the events of September 11, 2001. Overwhelmings again. My office was not unpacked and neatly organized for a year.

Competence through Agony

Even in the face of the early funerals, and despite the risk of having again and again to speak in the midst of people I did not know well, I did not feel bereft of a sense of what to do.[30] I drew on previous pastoral experiences that had taught me how to be with someone, to listen, and to seek resources

29. Typically, the competent stage occurs during the period when students are making their transition from seminary into full-time leadership in congregational life. Most seminary programs are three years, and Lutherans add a year of full-time internship, so if one develops through this transition from competent to proficient (and that is by no means assured) it most often falls within the first four to six years after finishing formal graduate theological education.

30. Dreyfus, *On the Internet*, pp. 39-41, argues that at the level of competent performance, one has a whole variety of theory and experiences at one's disposal, and the conscious putting together of a plan of action is combined with a real sense of one's responsibility for the outcome. Resistance to the independent decision with all the risk it entails leads to stagnation and regression in skill, but openness to risk and choice leads to the patterning of experiences that allows the leap towards proficiency, a skill level in which one simply "sees" the situation for what it is, a "gut reaction" so to speak, and then decides which of a few options ought to be the response.

of comfort and promise in the Scriptures. Even when shaking in my boots, I nonetheless felt my way forward with a few rules of thumb to guide me.[31] The funeral of the little boy was the hardest. During these early days I began each day reading the Psalms, not as in seminary when I read them out of a romantic attraction to Benedictine life, but out of a sense of absolute necessity, as if somehow my own constant call to speak could only be supported by the ground of God's speaking to me in these ancient hymns of Israel.

Meanwhile, I had grand visions for the mission of the congregation in the city. They had sponsored a "First Fiesta" urban day camp for a decade, and I supposed that they were ready to transform their corporate life more deeply for the sake of neighborhood outreach. On the Sunday of my installation as pastor, I preached a long programmatic sermon in which I critiqued the "Christendom" model of church (none too subtly implying the model fit them), laid out the challenge of mission in a post-Christian society, and proposed a rousing five-point mission strategy.[32] Later that week, Pat Bennett, a longtime church office volunteer and recent widow who was by sheer willpower overcoming the effects of a stroke, took me aside. "Pastor," she said, "you use too many words. Your sermons are too long. Your newsletter articles are too long. I'm sorry to tell you, but it's the truth."

I was crushed, and probably looked it even as I thanked her for her frankness. "What do these people want?" I thought. They called me to help redevelop the church and they don't want to hear my cutting edge redevelopment plans? I had read thirty years of old church reports. I had held meetings with community leaders and studied demographic statistics. I had surveyed the circumstances and thought I was right on target with my proposals. In retrospect, I could see that I didn't know the people, or they

31. Shifting contexts does not cause regression to the novice status as a matter of course. Rather, ability is more narrowly focused on specific aspects of ability in this or that area, which usually are more or less similar to what has been experienced before in a more or less similar context. The less similar, the less transferable are prior experiences and the abilities drawn from them. Here, the shift was not so dramatic to make me feel as if I was starting over.

32. Rereading the sermon today, I think it is exactly right in content. But I now have the perspective to say that it was not a good sermon, not because it wasn't right, but because I didn't yet have the right to say such things to them, and the sermon was not the place to say it. Many people likely went away thinking, "he sure went on today." I might have preached the same content after three years and found more of a hearing, but the sermon would have been constructed much differently and tied to a whole set of conversations with the congregation to see how to take my challenges seriously.

me, so how could I have believed that such a critique would have a salutary effect? I knew a lot, it turns out, about congregational study and very little about the pastoral work of shaping community. The former is required for the latter, but the latter requires more than information. As Peter Marty notes in his winsome chapter for this volume, it requires, for starters, knowing one another's names.[33]

On that warm July day when I was installed as their pastor, I did not know these people well. But that situation rapidly changed in the wake of that horrible and unforgettable Tuesday morning in September. I had already realized that the American flag was an issue for this congregation. While the flag was not displayed in the sanctuary, it was in the fellowship hall — and on each patriotic holiday some members requested that it be placed near the pulpit. I moved the flag to the entryway, thinking I had struck a great compromise. The week after September 11, however, Warren Soneson, who chaired the worship commission, took me aside between the services and said, "Pastor Scharen, we're calling a congregational meeting for next Sunday to vote on returning the flag to its rightful place on the side of the altar. You can be a hero if you just go ahead and do it now." As a child of the post-Vietnam era who had protested U.S.-backed violence in Central America, I failed to understand what was at stake for these veterans of World War II's battle against Hitler, Mussolini, and the Japanese. I said no. My wife, Sonja, strongly urged me to follow my conscience, arguing that if I could not be true to my convictions, how could I be of any use as a spiritual leader? The appeal of this view was tremendous, but I had a feeling of being up against a literal tide of support for the placement of the flag.

Earlier that summer, feeling totally swamped, I had asked the bishop to recommend someone who might serve as a mentor for me. When Pastor Michael Merkel agreed to the plan, he did not know that his first assignment would be working with me in this kind of highly charged situation. Mike agreed with me that I was facing a ministry-defining event, and that how I handled it would shape my subsequent leadership. He thought that I needed to decide if my conscience would let me be pastor, tending to all sides by assuring a good process through education and facilitation, or if I felt called to be prophet, pressing on the question of true worship and idolatry. I chose the former.

After church the next Sunday, I opened the congregational meeting with

33. See Peter Marty, in his chapter in this book, pp. 324-25.

prayer and a set of remarks I had prepared about how one might theologically defend both the exclusion of the flag from the sanctuary and its inclusion. John Darrow, a retired American history teacher from the high school and a lifelong member of the church, argued at length in favor of placing a flag in the sanctuary. His speech, which concluded with a seemingly endless list of other churches in our area that had flags in their worship spaces, was greeted by raucous applause. Then Sonja, shaking from adrenaline and crying openly, gave an impassioned plea for the importance of a sanctuary where we openly worship the God of all nations, and how this truth is confused by the presence of our national flag. Not patriotism but orthodoxy is at stake, she said. When she sat, there was total silence. A few minutes passed and then a World War II veteran and German prison camp survivor stood to declare, "I've never in my life felt a conflict between serving God and country." That was it; the vote was called and the nearly unanimous vote so inspired Warren Soneson that he promptly took the Boy Scouts' flag from the fellowship hall directly up into the sanctuary, placing it just to the side of the pulpit. I consoled myself that although I had not been the prophet on that occasion, it was for the sake of hoped-for prophetic ministry on many occasions down the road. Little did I know that the seeds had already been planted for my eventual departure less than three years later.

Like so many experiences early on at First Lutheran, but most powerfully in this one, I began to feel the weight of the pastoral role. I was now responsible for choosing a course of action and living with the consequences. I thought through what to do with as much input and wisdom as I could gather, and then made a painful choice, not knowing if I had done the right thing.[34] Never having faced such a complex organizational and societal moment before, my attempt to understand the situation and to decide how to respond required me to step back and ask what was at stake. Because the outcome, as Warren put it, either made me a hero or a fool, depending on one's perspective, I felt the emotional weight of the decision. Exactly because of this deliberate choosing amidst responsibility and deep emotional investment, followed by literally years of mulling over the outcome, I began a much more intense tutorial in interpreting whole situa-

---

34. This situation is a classic example for how cognitive scientists, philosophers, and psychologists understand "competent" human thinking. Dreyfus and Dreyfus call it the "Hamlet model of decision-making — the detached, deliberative, and sometimes agonizing selection among alternatives." Dreyfus and Dreyfus, *Mind over Machine*, p. 28.

tions, seeing what was at stake, and engaging with a pastoral response.[35] Such learning can be described in seminary, but it can only be learned once one has made the transition to pastoral leadership. In fact, my three years as a senior pastor were the most intense learning experience of any years of my life, even in comparison to the directly preceding years of doctoral training at Emory University. The practical work of ministry is many things, including intensely academic, if what one means by that is critical reading, research, writing, and teaching. But the learning is much more what Dreyfus calls "know-how," learning that is bodily and intuitive, and no less difficult in its acquisition than theoretical knowledge.[36] This helps underscore why the support of mentors and friendly colleagues is so essential in the first years of ministry.

Proficiency as Intuitive Recognition

My ability to grasp a "sense of the whole" in a given situation came through laying experience upon experience, a bodily sedimentation of many moments of learning with individuals and families.[37] After many moments of such learning, I began to see my regular Sunday preaching in a new way, directly tied to something I only now began to have words for: spiritual education and formation for the congregation as a whole.[38]

---

35. Dreyfus argues (in various places, including *On the Internet*, pp. 36ff.) that emotional involvement in decision-making, and the pain or elation related to varied outcomes, is essential to the development of the capacity for a transition to the stages beyond competent, including expertise and mastery.

36. In the transition to the stages beyond competent, including expertise and mastery, the performer leaves behind calculations that follow rules and maxims to more fluid and intuitive "situational discriminations and accompanied responses" tuned to specific situations and drawing on a whole set of the sort of experiences described in the flag incident.

37. See Pierre Bourdieu, *Pascalian Meditations*, translated by Richard Nice (Stanford: Stanford University Press, 2000), p. 141.

38. Using the term "shaping community" implies something different than does pastoral care (seen typically in terms of individual care in coping with difficulty) or even spiritual direction (seen typically in terms of individual care in reflective conversation about one's relationship to God). It implies both care of the whole (with a focus on those who congregate) and a tending to the work of forming a whole community, not into what I wish them to be, but rather what God desires ("God who has begun a good work in you will perfect it until the day of Jesus Christ" [Phil. 1:5-7]).

While many of the long-time members of First were deeply faithful to this church, only a small core attended anything beyond Sunday morning services. Almost no explicit adult education in the faith had been provided during the history of the congregation, and my early efforts at offering Bible study and adult forums drew only a handful of highly committed and well-educated members.

Late in 2002, a visit from a wise elder in ministry, my former supervisor in LVC, gave me the freedom to become less self-conscious and to ask what God could make of this space we were opening up together as pastor and people. That Christmas Eve, I called in my sermon for a year-long and congregation-wide focus on the Bible. I noted that our confirmation youth were surprised to find the rap artist Coolio's lyrics, "As I walk through the valley of the shadow of death," in the Bible. (Yes, I played part of the song, to the delight of the 25-and-under crowd.) I suggested that we imagine Scripture as the manger in which Christ is laid for us. Tending to the Word revealed in Scripture would help us make the Christmas story matter in our lives daily and open pathways for God to work in our congregation's life as a whole. In response to this challenge, the congregation affirmed a resolution at the January congregational meeting to take up a 2003 "Focus on Bible Study." Things went well at first, but by summer, I felt that the emphasis had stalled with the 20 percent of the congregation that was involved in core leadership. By the end of the year, I wanted to make a connection with the middle 60 percent of the congregation who irregularly came to worship but nothing else.

The death that May of my beloved mentor from seminary, Timothy Lull, sent me back to files from my course with Tim on the Lutheran Confessions. There, I found my answer: a little article on preaching Martin Luther's Small Catechism which was, after all, written by Luther to be "a brief digest and summary of the entire Holy Scriptures." I knew at once this was the way to go; many conversations and experiences taught me that in this congregation confirmation was highly valued and the single experience of education in the faith shared by all. In confirmation, the study of Luther's Small Catechism figured prominently.

With enthusiastic support from the church leadership, I laid plans for a fall series taking us through the main parts: the Ten Commandments, the Creed, and the Lord's Prayer. Each Sunday, after the reading of the lectionary texts, the congregation recited together, in unison, the portion of the Catechism for that day. Then in my sermons I made contemporary connections, for instance between the first commandment's meaning — "we are to fear, love, and trust God above all things" — and our national temptation after September 11 to trust political and especially military power.[39] I ordered copies of the Catechism and sold them after church, selling out each Sunday for weeks.

The Catechism series was very popular. However, it was just the sort of thing I never would have thought of early on in my ministry. It made sense to do, and actually was possible to do, only after I had spent years in the midst of these people, gaining through layers of experiences a congregational "sense of the whole." And because of this sense, I was able to see that I could do what I had thus far failed to do — spark spiritual renewal in the congregational as a whole. Weaving deepening faith commitment to Christ into our common conversation seemed necessary if we were to begin to face the challenges of mission. As I preached on the Catechism, we also began singing in Spanish, elected our first person of Puerto Rican descent as church council president, and identified a proposed sister parish in Dorado, Puerto Rico. Such movement forward in mission was not related directly to studying the Catechism; yet I think it was profoundly related to finding our common ground in a focus on deepening faith commitments. Quoting prophets from the pulpit in my first weeks did not connect; reciting Martin Luther in unison years later did.

It is not that I had become a masterful pastor and preacher. Instead, it was that I had just enough experience to begin to carry on without being so conscious about it all. I had, in other words, begun to see what mastery might entail even if I had not reached it. I just "did" a funeral, or a sermon just "came" to me. I don't mean that in a perfunctory way, as if I did not prepare at all; my point is that I had left behind the experience of obstructive self-awareness. I no longer needed a step-by-step plan or text. Rather the whole made sense to me, so I did not have to think about each piece, about where to stand, or how to hold my hand, or what to say here or there. My body moved, my hand knew where to go, and my voice spoke to the point. My pastoral leadership had become more fluid, a sort of "second

39. My preparations for preaching were no longer consciously focused on technical aspects of sermon construction and delivery. I did those things as a matter of course, and my attention rather focused broadly and intuitively on connections between the text and my working "sense of the whole." Such a shift is implicit in my narrative discussion thus far, but it is worth making it explicit here.

nature."[40] This does not mean that I quit thinking about what I was doing, but rather that the character of my thinking about what I was doing fundamentally changed.[41]

A Theory of Thinking in Action

What does it mean, exactly, to say that the character of my thinking in action fundamentally changed as I learned to do the work of pastoral ministry? According to Stuart and Hubert Dreyfus, humans tend *not* to act skillfully by using "knowing that" in a calculating way: if I do x, and then y, I will get z. Rather, we act in skillful ways by using a less conscious "knowing how" that depends on familiarity and experience. In addition, their stages of developmental learning imply that the "know-how" of expert individuals, whether drivers, plumbers, teachers, or pastors, is not innate, like a bird's ability to build a nest. Human beings have to *learn* to do things like this, usually through trial and error, and often by imitation of those more proficient.

The Dreyfus brothers posit a theory of professional development that includes distinct stages and discernable transition points. The novice stage entails learning context-free elements and rules to be applied to these elements. Thus, my first sermon in field education was shaped by my effort to draw on biblical and theological elements while also following "the rules" for sermon preparation and delivery. The advanced beginner draws on accumulated facility in using a set of rules and also starts to attend to various situational factors. Here a teacher can help a learner to notice relevant situational features and can also offer instructional maxims, as Julius Carroll did. Competence develops out of the advanced be-

---

40. This is exactly what Dreyfus argues is characteristic of the intuitive shift towards proficiency and expertise: fluid performance. In *On the Internet,* he quotes Aristotle as saying "the expert 'straightaway' does 'the appropriate thing, at the appropriate time, in the appropriate way.'"

41. In an article entitled "Peripheral Vision: Expertise in Real World Contexts," *Organizational Studies* 26 (2005): 789, Dreyfus and Dreyfus differentiate between the ways beginners and experts deliberate. One, unsure how to proceed, adopts "calculative rationality" that requires stepping back and rehearsing rules for choosing this or that possible action. The other, with hundreds of experiences at hand, adopts "deliberative rationality," allowing reflection on the goal or perspective that seems evident to them and upon the actions that seem appropriate to achieving that goal.

ginner's experience of being overwhelmed, as I was at Bethlehem and in my early months at First Lutheran. In order to control a multitude of variables, one chooses a plan that helps focus and organize one's performance. In addition — and this is a key difference — one begins to feel ultimate responsibility for the outcome of one's acts and deep emotional investment in the choice of a course of action and its unfolding, about which the responsible leader feels very emotionally involved, as I was at First Lutheran in the days after September 11.

While people often do act in a conscious, problem-solving way when confronted with puzzles or unfamiliar situations, some kinds of intelligent behavior (and exactly that behavior typically called "expert") does not seem to follow this conscious, rule-guided pattern. When one rides a bike, recognizes a face in a crowd, or uses language, one is engaged in a rapid, fluid, involved kind of behavior not associated with the slow, detached reasoning of the problem-solving process. Therefore, moving to the next stages, Dreyfus and Dreyfus describe a qualitatively different sort of thought process.[42]

Proficiency describes a stage at which one acts "without thinking," intuitively, drawing on "know-how" that is the result of many similar experiences that now provide the mental backdrop for an immediate course of action in this current situation. Dreyfus and Dreyfus call this kind of knowing "holistic similarity recognition." The proficient performer will intuitively recognize a situation to which she has to react but then pause to deliberate about the appropriate response. My effort to shape community at First Lutheran became easier and less stressful as I gained enough experience with the congregation to simply see what was needed, rather than to return again and again to a calculative procedure for selecting one of several possible alternatives, each more or less a guess about what would be effective. The difference between the proficient performer and the expert is that the former does not yet have enough experience with the outcomes of a wide variety of possible responses to react automatically. The proficient performer must still decide what to do.

42. Hubert Dreyfus, *On the Internet,* cites recent MRI research showing that amateur and expert chess players use different parts of the brain. Generally, exciting new research is happening on the borders of phenomenology and neuroscience. See "A Phenomenology of Skill Acquisition as the Basis for a Merleau-Pontian Non-representationalist Cognitive Science," unpublished but available on Dreyfus's U.C. Berkeley Philosophy Department website: http://socrates.berkeley.edu/~hdreyfus/pdf/MerleauPontySkillCogSci.pdf. Accessed on January 14, 2008.

Expertise emerges when the conscious decision becomes intuitive also. The performer simply knows what to do, based on mature and practiced understanding. Deliberate practice, usually for at least a decade, makes the learned abilities so much a part of an expert that she needs to be no more aware of what she is doing than of her own body in walking or typing on a computer.[43] Experts do engage in deliberation when something quite important, or something novel, is at stake, but this is not the calculative deliberation of the novice or competent beginner; rather it is a critical reflection on one's intuitions. But for the most part, what distinguishes expertise is fluid performance. What one does, how one reacts, becomes "natural" and indeed in some sense "indescribable."

Mastery, a stage that Hubert Dreyfus sometimes adds to the other five, posits that the highest expertise requires patterns of apprenticeship that allow one to train with various masters sequentially, as is the case in music. Musicians have learned that those who follow one master are not as creative as performers as those who have worked sequentially with several. The reason for this is not because one is good at fingering, another at phrasing, and another at dynamics. Rather, it is because each master has a whole style of his or her own. Each new master destabilizes the apprentice so that she is forced to begin to develop a style of her own.[44] Mastery comes out of serial apprenticeships, but serial apprenticeships do not simply "make" musicians or pastors of very high ability. Time is also a key factor.

Some people might worry about forcing experience into a framework. But for me, the novice to master framework of professional skill development has been very helpful in making sense of my experience, perhaps because it is a phenomenological theory developed out of careful observation of just such experiential learning.

In Conclusion, Some Implications

The stories and theory I have shared lend further support to the apprenticeship model David Wood will advocate in the next chapter, as well as to

43. K. Anders Ericsson, Ralf Th. Krampe, and Clemens Tesch-Romer, "The Role of Deliberate Practice in the Acquisition of Expert Performance," *Psychological Review* 100 (1993): 363-406.

44. Hubert Dreyfus, *On the Internet,* cites Klaus Nielsen, "Musical Apprenticeship: Learning at the Academy of Music as Socially Situated," *Nordisk Pedagogik* 17: 160-69.

other material in this volume. As I conclude this chapter and bring my reflections on my own experiences of learning ministry over time to a close, I want to make note of two points that are not mentioned elsewhere.

When I look back on the apprenticeship I received, the remarkable thing is how varied the important relationships and key moments were. I was profoundly shaped by all my mentors in ministry — by my campus pastors Susan, Martin, and Daniel; by Julius Carroll in Oakland; by Ted Wardlaw and the other pastors of congregations I studied in Atlanta; and by Mike Merkel in Connecticut. In addition, I was blessed by many irregular moments of mentoring, such as Pat Bennett's comment that I used too many words. Tim Lull and Don Saliers were crucial shepherds of my vocation through stages of educational development. Development in pastoral ministry, it seems, is not simply a matter of learning from a handful of the best practitioners, but rather a matter of being open to a more complicated set of encounters that in retrospect seem nothing short of providential. It is important to note that some were intentional relationships and some were not. Perhaps more importantly, however, somewhere along the way I developed a sense of their importance. Even this awareness came in stages, however, for I did not think always about apprenticeship as I do now.[45]

The second point concerns the role evaluation can play in learning ministry. Because the capacity to shape lively Christian communities comes through guided practice over time, the framework of learning described above offers a very nuanced understanding of how even mistakes can become a source of learning. Those who are in guidance roles — teachers, supervising pastors, lay leaders, judicatory officials, and others — can gain from the fine-grained insights a developmental framework of learning provides. As I showed through my own experience at various points, knowing something in theory does not mean one knows what is actually required in practice! When young pastors make mistakes and receive overly critical responses, they may reject necessary reflection on their mistakes and avoid the risks involved in trying again. Such reaction stagnates growth and keeps one from moving to the more sophisticated levels

---

45. One of the most influential moments in my thinking along these lines was while I was in seminary. One of my classmates had an older sibling who was an actor, then starring in a Tennessee Williams play in San Francisco. We went over one night to have dinner with him in his apartment and then to see him in the show. I asked him what actors did for continuing education. He said, "I go to shows and watch really good actors." That really struck me, and I took it as applicable to my professional development as well.

of action marked by intuitive judgment and response. Knowing that mistakes are normal and even necessary for learning at certain stages can help teachers and other guides to do their work well. Moreover, knowing which mistakes are normal and expected at various points along the way can be of great comfort and encouragement as young pastors learn.

Transition into Ministry

David Wood, an American Baptist pastor, has served in a variety of congregational settings over twenty-five years of ordained ministry. He presently serves on the staff of The Fund for Theological Education as the coordinator of the Lilly Endowment–funded Transition into Ministry program. This program provides recent seminary graduates with congregational placements and other forms of engagement designed to foster the learning integral to the experience of the first years of ministry. More than seven hundred new ministers, twenty congregations, and more than fifteen seminaries and other supporting institutions have been directly involved in the program.

Insights gained from the Transition into Ministry program have implications far beyond these participants, however. Studies have shown that what happens in the congregational setting during the early years of a pastor's ministry often has immense influence on his or her lifelong capacity to lead congregations faithfully and well. More deliberate efforts to make this period in a minister's development a thoughtful and fruitful one may prove to contribute in important ways to excellent ministry and to the life-giving communities good ministers can foster.

Coming as it does after a series of other chapters that place practical theology in the academy, this essay represents an expansion of focus that is parallel to the one that new clergy experience as they take up leadership responsibilities in congregations. By encouraging attention to and reflection on this crucial stage within the process of education and formation for ministry, Wood challenges theological educators to regard their present classroom efforts as part of a much longer process of learning that lasts well beyond the seminary years. He also urges theological educators and pastors alike to develop further forms of mutual engagement along an important boundary.

12. Transition into Ministry: Reconceiving the Boundaries between Seminaries and Congregations

David J. Wood

The transition of the medical student from the classroom setting of the medical school to the clinical setting and the actual practice of medicine is not left to chance. There is a carefully structured pedagogical pathway from classroom to clinic and from student to practitioner along which every evolving physician must travel in order to complete his or her training. This pathway of internship and residency is arguably more rigorous, demanding, and transformative than the classroom-centered, book-oriented learning of the first years of graduate medical training. The evolving physician is no less a student in the clinical setting than he or she was in the structured classroom or laboratory of the medical school. However, with the shift of context from classroom to clinic comes a direct engagement with the practice of medicine — with all the uncertainties, contingencies, and intensity of performance that practice entails. This direct engagement also incorporates one into a community that includes fellow learners and mature practitioners. While this participation is peripheral in the sense that the "intern" or "resident" has limited responsibility for the overall enterprise, it does involve immersion into the everyday life-world of being a physician. There is a centripetal trajectory to this participation so that over time, through calibrated engagement with the experience of being a physician, one is drawn into the central practices required of a competent physician.

No such ordered and established pathway exists in the universe of theological education and pastoral preparation. To be sure, the established pathway of formation typically followed by parish pastors[1] re-

1. I will use the term "pastor" to refer primarily to those who exercise ordained pastoral

flects a strong consensus about the need for formal structured learning in the context of a graduate school, under the tutelage of expert theological educators. However, once the focus shifts from the schooling context to the initial years of actual ministerial practice, that consensus dissipates. To be sure, a variety of excellent efforts have sprung up across the ecclesial landscape to apprentice new pastors into the practice of ministry.[2] However, these efforts are too dispersed and scattered to amount to anything as identifiable as a pathway, or even as a set of well-established parallel pathways. A new pastor's experience of the transition from seminary to parish — from classroom to congregation — is, more often than not, abrupt, untutored, and haphazard. As a result, it is a common experience among beginning pastors to feel isolated, unprepared, and devoid of crucial support and guidance. Under such conditions, the learning begun in seminary often fails to grow and bear fruit. As one study conducted by the United Church of Christ concludes, there is increasing evidence that when classroom-based formation is not complemented with congregation-based formation the "very best seminary curriculum is lost or wasted."[3]

In recent years, a growing awareness of the importance of the transition from classroom to congregation has begun to emerge in theological education. Framing these initial years of ministry as the final stage of preparation for ministry establishes a teaching/learning environment beyond the seminary context in which there is explicit freedom to inquire, question, explore, experiment, acknowledge limitations, fail, and succeed. Such freedom paves the way for acquiring the knowledge that is embedded in practice, knowledge that is crucial to growing competence.

A judicatory leader who coordinates a program that attends to pastors

---

leadership in the life of mainline Protestant congregations. This reflects the context for the Transition into Ministry program that provides the background for much of the content of this essay. Having said that, I do assume that the issues and concerns of pastoral formation discussed in this essay also have direct relevance to the formation of priests and lay ecclesial ministers in Roman Catholicism, to the formation of pastoral leadership in congregations in ecclesial traditions beyond mainline Protestantism, and to the formation of pastoral leaders in diverse institutional settings.

2. For an overview of these programs see Michael I. N. Dash, Jimmy Dukes, Gordon T. Smith, "Learning from the First Years: Noteworthy Conclusions from the Parish Experience of Recent Graduates of ATS Schools," *Theological Education* 40, no. 2 (2005): 65-77.

3. See Dash et al., "Learning from the First Years," p. 68.

in their first few years of ministry notes how demanding the initial immersion into the practice of ministry can be.

> New pastors are surprised by many things when entering their first call — by how difficult it is to discern what their pastoral role actually is, by how overwhelmed they feel by the expectations placed upon them, by the pervasiveness of the conflict in their congregations, and by how difficult it can be to garner lay support and leadership. Though they feel well prepared to lead Sunday morning worship, they consistently comment on how ill equipped they feel regarding how to understand and navigate congregational dynamics and decision-making.

What would a well-formed pedagogical pathway from classroom to congregation look like? What are the conditions that provide for a generative transition from classroom-based learning to congregation-based learning? What are the conditions that keep the overwhelmingness of immersion in the practice of ministry in creative tension with one's evolving confidence and competence as a practitioner? These were the pressing questions that inspired the formation of Lilly Endowment's Transition into Ministry (TiM) Grants program. As an embodied response to these enduring questions of pastoral formation, the TiM program is situated squarely on the boundary between seminaries and congregations. Exploring the conception and implementation of this program provides a framework for reconceiving that boundary as a pathway for pastoral formation.

Focusing on the initial years of pastoral practice and the learning curve intrinsic to them, the TiM program began with three fundamental assumptions. The first assumption was that the actual performance of ministry, in local congregations and in relation to mature practitioners, is how and where pastors begin to form pastoral identity. The second assumption was that reflective, appreciative, critical engagement with congregational culture, as well as sustained pastoral involvement with the lives of everyday Christians, are required for the development of pastoral skills. The third assumption was that the habits and practices instilled during the initial years of ministry have a shelf life that impacts one's pastoral practice for years to come.

The first TiM projects were funded in 2000. Since then, the TiM program has grown to twenty congregation-based "residency" projects and more than fifteen institution-based "first-call" projects. In the residency projects, seminary graduates participate in full-time two-year placements in selected local congregations that have agreed to be partners in the TiM program. These programs are designed to give seminary graduates a sustained, reflective, and challenging encounter with the full range of ministerial duties and pastoral life. In each program, there are at least two and as many as four young pastors in residence at any one time. Residents are paid full-time salaries and regarded as full members of a pastoral staff. Many of these programs are now in their second five-year grant cycles. The first-call programs, on the other hand, are hosted by selected seminaries, denominational offices, and other church-related organizations. These ten programs employ a variety of strategies for convening, mentoring, and nurturing young pastors (usually in two- or three-year cycles) who are already ministering in "first-call" situations.

The denominations represented in the TiM program include the Presbyterian Church (USA), the United Methodist Church, the Evangelical Lutheran Church in America, the African Methodist Episcopal Church, the Christian Reformed Church, the Christian Church (Disciples of Christ), the Episcopal Church (USA), the United Church of Christ, the American Baptist Churches (USA), the Progressive National Baptist Convention, and the Cooperative Baptist Fellowship. To date, more than seven hundred young clergy have participated in the TiM program.

Through the TiM program as a whole and the congregation-based programs in particular, we are beginning to learn why the initial years of ministry are so important in the formation of pastoral leaders. An exploration of five constitutive features of these programs will illustrate the content of the pedagogical pathway that is emerging. This exploration may also demonstrate the importance, and indeed the necessity, of further efforts to help new pastors make the transition from preparation for ministry to participation in ministry.

Immersion in a Congregation and in the Pastoral Life

The quotidian life of a congregation is the crucible in which pastoral identity and competence are formed. Here, and nowhere else, is where one learns the shape of the pastoral life that is required of and received by one who leads and serves a congregation. The immersion that comes in the first years of ministry allows for a sustained, intensive encounter with the pastoral life in a way that could only be anticipated, rehearsed, and simulated in the seminary context. While it is true that nearly every seminary includes some form of immersion in practice (either clinical or congregational) during one's seminary experience, this is almost always quite limited in either duration or scope or both.[4]

The sustained immersion characteristic of these programs takes place across the whole range of ministry tasks and responsibilities. Some TiM congregations order this experience through rotations, moving residents from one ministry area to the next every six months or so. A typical range of rotations would include worship planning and leadership, evangelism, adult discipleship, global and regional mission, children's ministry, youth ministry, pastoral care and visitation, and counseling. Other programs allow this to happen in a more ad hoc manner. The point is to establish both a deep and broad encounter with ministerial practice.

One pastoral resident in a Lutheran congregation described what she gained through this kind of tutored immersion in these terms:

> The most obvious benefit of the residency has been the comfort and familiarity I gained with the most basic elements of ministry: planning and leading worship, teaching confirmation, preaching, visiting the sick, preparing candidates for baptism, etc. During seminary the thought of these tasks brought me considerable anxiety, but I feel comfortable in all of them after the hands-on experience and following reflection that I had at Trinity. I had also felt quite anxious about facing conflicts, but the experience of many transitions and personality issues during my two years at Trinity has convinced me of the importance of communicating openly, directly and in a timely fashion.

Central to this dynamic of immersion is the congregation's agreement to grant a resident the status of pastor while simultaneously acknowledging that he or she is a novice. Space is thereby granted for a timely appropriation of the pastoral role — space that is not typically available when a seminary graduate is placed directly into a "first-call" situation as pastor or associate pastor. Unlike most other new pastors, residents receive both pas-

4. This is not to deny the existence of traditions of apprenticeship in American church life — most notably within historic black churches and in Roman Catholic priestly formation. The reference point for the limited attention to immersion in pastoral preparation is the dominant reality within mainline Protestantism.

toral status and freedom from the burden of assuming responsibility for the whole enterprise. Maintaining the dialectic between being a pastor and being a pastor-in-training is critical to the development of a pastoral identity that is also characterized by real growth in competency.

Reflecting back on his TiM experience, a young Lutheran pastor names the importance of this zone of freedom:

> My residency experience spared me from having to take on all the responsibilities of a pastor overnight and without support or mentoring, and instead allowed me to be the first-time pastor I was. I didn't have to pretend to be an expert, but was free to learn and experiment, all the while making valuable contributions to the ministry of the church.

Another participant in an Episcopal program in the Chicago Diocese describes the importance of a calibrated immersion:

> The program allows space for a newly graduated seminarian, newly ordained to the diaconate or priesthood, to learn the crafts of ministry without an undue expectation that they should already know everything. It is a "buffer time" in which the curate does not have to learn everything all at once, but has the time to develop existing skills and acquire new skills.

One final note regarding the significance of immersion: To conceive of this dynamic of immersion only in terms of steadily increasing participation in the performance of ministry is to speak too narrowly of what it is like to experience the major change in status and expectation beginning pastors undergo. Immersion in congregational life brings an intensity of participation and observation that also conveys a wealth of insight into the life-world of being a pastor. Beginning pastors have to ponder such matters as how to order one's time, think on one's feet, handle conflict, and foster good working relationships, as well as the interplay between one's personal, private life and one's professional, public life and the complexity of pastoral relationships more generally. These issues are intrinsic to the pastoral life itself. The opportunity to deal with them for the first time in a setting where one has the freedom to step back and reflect on them makes the insights and judgment pastors need more accessible and supports an important aspect of pastoral development.

DAVID J. WOOD

Integration into a Community of Practitioners

The prevailing consensus that formal theological education is important reflects a related consensus that expert practitioners have an important role to play in the formation of pastors. Within the existing field of formal theological education, professors are those expert practitioners. While it may be true that a similar consensus exists regarding the important role of expert practitioners in the congregational context — namely, seasoned pastors — that consensus has failed to produce a corresponding formal structure of teaching and learning. The TiM program is a serious attempt to give expression to such a structure. Meaningful connections between novice pastors and competent practitioners within the field of practice is a core component of this effort. Central to all these programs is the dynamic of welcome and mentoring by seasoned practitioners. The senior pastor and other members of a pastoral staff work daily with and alongside residents as colleagues, mentors, and supervisors, communicating the skills of ministry and character of ministers in both formal and informal ways. It is the presence of this dynamic of mentorship and collegiality, as well as the movement back and forth between action and reflection it affords, that helps residents to assimilate their experience and integrate it into their emerging pastoral identity.

Beyond weekly staff meetings, most programs maintain weekly seminars and forums for review and feedback on pastoral performance. In the context of these sessions, the performance of the preacher is reviewed (whether senior pastor or resident); pastoral care experiences are discussed; administrative issues are considered; upcoming sermons are previewed; and open-ended give-and-take is encouraged. In many ways, mentors are not seen as master teachers imparting prescriptions for the practice of ministry as much as co-participants in the reflective performance of ministry. The wisdom of the mature practitioner does emerge, to be sure, but it is mediated through shared engagement in the practice of ministry. One pastoral resident in a Baptist congregation described his learning in the following terms:

> Watching [my mentor] in many situations (deacons, staff meetings, worship, Wednesday night Bible study), I feel that I have a good taste of sensing a congregation. If anything, I have learned as a pastor to act as the thermostat and not the thermometer of the congregation.

296

Too often our understanding of the mentor/mentee relationship and the potential learning it provides is too narrow. In their book *Situated Learning: Legitimate Peripheral Participation*, Jean Lave and Etienne Wenger provide a full-orbed description of the range of learning that is available within the context of apprenticeship. In their view apprenticeship provides crucial insight into such things as:

> What everyday life is like; how masters talk, walk, work and generally conduct their lives . . . what other learners are doing; and what learners need to learn to become full practitioners. It includes an increasing understanding of how, when and about what old-timers collaborate, collude, and collide and what they enjoy, dislike, respect and admire.[5]

The significance of the mentor/mentee relationship to the learning of ministry and the cultivation of a well-formed pastoral identity cannot be overstated. In many ways, this relationship becomes the nexus of negotiation of one's pastoral identity and practice. In relation to mature practitioners, novices are able to see what mature practice looks like and thus more gladly to undertake the pathway of formation required for their own maturing. Wherever identity is being negotiated, there is an intensity that is certain to engender conflict along the way. Stories of this intensity and of related occasions of conflict are not uncommon. However, as co-participants in a shared community of practice, it is equally common that these conflicts become a constructive part of learning for both mentor and mentee. Again, Lave and Wenger:

> Conflicts between masters and apprentices (or less individualistically, between generations) take place in the course of everyday participation. Shared participation is the stage on which the old and new, the known and the unknown, the established and the hopeful, act out their differences and discover their commonalities, manifest their fear of one another, and come to terms with their need for one another. Each threatens the fulfillment of the other's destiny, just as it is essential to it. Conflict is experienced and worked out through shared everyday practice in which differing viewpoints and common stakes are in interplay.[6]

5. Jean Lave and Etienne Wenger, *Situated Learning: Legitimate Peripheral Participation* (Cambridge: Cambridge University Press, 1991), p. 95.
6. Lave and Wenger, *Situated Learning*, p. 116.

A senior pastor recalls the first time he met in seminar with his residents. He was anticipating an occasion where he would be called upon by his group of apprentices to share from his reservoir of wisdom distilled from years of pastoral practice. Instead, when he opened the floor for conversation, he was confronted with an array of suggestions for how the practice of ministry in his congregation could be improved upon. His skill as a mentor was expressed in his capacity to utilize their perceptions as a pivot point for reflection on their shared engagement in ministry rather than to become defensive or threatened.

The effective negotiation of continuity and change in the life of a congregation is a crucial dimension of mature pastoral leadership. A good mentor/mentee relationship provides an indispensable context for growing one's capacity for this kind of negotiation on an intensely personal, less public level.

Peer Engagement through Shared Practice

As important as relationships with mature practitioners are to the learning of ministry, being incorporated into a community of *maturing* practitioners is no less important. The TiM program has intentionally cultivated the conditions for a deep and sustained engagement among peers who are engaged with one another in the mutual learning of ministry. The shared risk and anxiety they experience, as well as their mutually discernable growth in skill and identity, establish a deeply formative experience of collegiality. Here are the voices of several young pastors reflecting back on the importance of peers to their vocational formation:

> Being a pastor is a relatively odd thing to do for a living, and if you feel like the only one from your generation taking it on for miles around, it could get quite lonely. I was blessed with terrific peers in this program, who taught me a great deal and provided a wealth of understanding and good humor.

> Perhaps the greatest benefit of the Transition into Ministry program for me was the collegiality and camaraderie and friendships built with fellow participants. The informal network of support was crucial for me in critical moments. I could pick up the phone for instant support, counsel, advice, perspective and good humor.

I have learned the power and grace of friends, particularly those in ministry. Collegiality breeds new ideas and offers new hope and breathes new life into tiring days and closure-free work. Some of my best/most successful moments in the work have been the fruit of collaboration, whether it's a formal meeting, or an informal chat on the phone with a friend.

The importance of peer relationships to the learning of ministry has been a principal finding of the TiM program. It is one that has come to the foreground of our understanding of how ministry is learned through the consensus of feedback from participants themselves. Too often the significance of these relationships has been overlooked because of an emphasis on the mentor/mentee relationship as the principal relational context where learning takes place. Peer relationships have tended to be viewed as supportive of such learning but not essential to it. Lave and Wenger see it otherwise: "It seems typical of apprenticeship that apprentices learn mostly in relation with other apprentices. There is anecdotal evidence . . . that where the circulation of knowledge among peers and near peers is possible, it spreads exceedingly rapidly and effectively."[7] The experience of the TiM program certainly adds to the body of anecdotal evidence.

A Mutually Appreciative Encounter
Between Laity and Pastor

Reading congregational life and negotiating the tricky terrain of pastoral relationality can be two of the most baffling challenges faced by those who come to a congregation without substantial pastoral experience. Yet the capacities to come into a congregation with sensitivity to what is going on there and to relate to laypeople in the situation in a pastorally appropriate way can make or break someone's ministry. Good pastors eventually learn what to look for and how to enter into a range of relationships within a congregation. TiM tries to help new pastors in this learning by establishing structures that bring new pastors into contact with laypeople who understand that part of their role is to help the pastor learn about this aspect of ministry.

---

7. Lave and Wenger, *Situated Learning*, p. 93.

Each TiM program includes advisory groups and support groups that place residents in direct, sustained encounters with laypersons. These ordered relationships, along with informal and pastoral encounters with lay persons, help to train young pastors into appropriate ways of relating to those who identify them as pastors. It is in this close encounter with laity that TiM participants exercise and develop their skills in reading congregational life and negotiating the tricky terrain of pastoral relationality. Here are a few of the ways TiM participants name their experience of congregations.

> It has taught me to observe and name congregational dynamics before and while entering into them — both large-scale (in terms of a congregation's history and culture) and small-scale (committee meetings, interpersonal dynamics, etc.). It has taught me how to say hello well to a congregation (whom to meet, which committees to sit in on, whom in the larger community to meet, which questions to ask of whom). It has taught me how to say good-bye to a congregation. It has shown me where and how to draw boundaries around my relationships when needed and why this is important. It has provided a healthy and beautiful model for loving the people and shown what that looks like — and the power that is loosed for the upbuilding of God's realm — when pastors and congregations love one another.

> The program has helped me grow a pastoral and balanced heart for those who are different from me within the congregation. Engagement with the congregation members is exciting, a joy and a challenge.

The congregation is not simply the object of pastoral practice but is itself a community of practice in which the pastor as newcomer is welcomed and incorporated as a co-participant. A common refrain from these new pastors is how this kind of engagement with the congregation has significantly reformed their view of the congregation in positive and constructive ways. The experience of first-hand, sustained, collaborative encounter with congregations sets up the conditions for a sort of congregational intelligence in these young pastors that provides an essential baseline for a generative encounter with other congregations for years to come.

Ordered Reading and Reflection on Texts
with Fellow Practitioners

The weekly seminar format that is employed across TiM programs provides the setting for the regular and disciplined reading and interpretation of texts as an aspect of pastoral ministry. In many cases the content of the seminar is determined by particular upcoming performances of preaching or teaching. In other cases, the ongoing performance of ministry itself, in all its variations, orients the seminar. So whether the text is a passage of Scripture or a book or an essay, the reading and the ensuing conversation are directly related to the actual practice and performance of ministry. It is the sustained and close proximity of reading to the field of practice that establishes the context for a lively engagement with texts and fellow readers — an engagement that is less driven by papers and other forms of evaluation germane to the classroom and more focused by firsthand, shared participation in a community of practice. In this context, the emphasis is not so much upon mastering the knowledge contained in the text as upon deepening one's understanding of a relevant set of ideas in order to improve one's performance of pastoral work.

Through these seminars, the intellectual life of the pastor and the habits and practices essential to the flourishing of that life come to the foreground. The importance of reading is not simply recommended and promoted — it is practiced and performed. Over time, apprentices learn how reading shapes the practice of ministry, as well as how the practice of ministry shapes reading. The practice of reading and interpreting texts, so central to the seminary context, is thereby integrated into the congregational context of pastoral ministry. In the course of this integration, the novice pastor begins the transition from being, primarily, a student of texts to becoming, over time, a teacher of texts.

In their study of theological education, *Educating Clergy,* Charles Foster and his colleagues identify four pedagogies as essential to the education of clergy: interpretation, formation, contextualization, and performance.[8] The pastoral seminars in TiM programs help to illustrate how all four of these pedagogies can continue to be generative for the ongoing education

8. Charles Foster, Lisa E. Dahill, Lawrence A. Goleman, and Barbara Wang Tolentino, *Educating Clergy: Teaching Practices and Pastoral Imagination* (San Francisco: Jossey-Bass, 2006), p. 33.

and formation of clergy after they have graduated and been placed in congregations. Moreover, they suggest that when a strong apprenticeship is in place, even the pedagogies that are emphasized by seminaries can be extended and enriched, to the benefit of both pastors and congregations. In the process, a bridge can be built between the learning about practice that typically takes place in seminary to the learning from within practice for which the congregation provides the necessary and appropriate context.

Concluding Proposals

These five core features of the congregation-based Transition into Ministry programs shed light on how an experience of apprenticeship can cultivate the rich field of learning new pastors occupy as they make the transition from seminary to congregation. Implicit in this account is that experience in and of itself, garnered by individuals who are isolated from mature and maturing practitioners, is not the wisest teacher. When the complexity of the transition pastors make is not noted and addressed, conversations typically end by making seminaries the target of heavy criticism for their tendency to turn out graduates who are well skilled in the cognitive disciplines (theory) but essentially clueless when it comes to the skills necessary for ministry (practice). Congregations and denominations tend to join forces in demanding that seminaries offer more courses oriented toward the practical skills of ministry and attend more generally to this need across the disciplines of the curriculum.

As long as the seminary context is perceived as the sole, or even as the primary, domain for the learning of ministry, the forms and conditions essential to an education sufficient to the practice of ministry will remain elusive. Instead, both theological educators and church leaders need to empower the practitioners who already reside within congregations, both lay and ordained, to host and foster the kind of learning that becomes possible when a new pastor arrives in their midst. This may happen when all parties recognize the powerful curriculum that is already intrinsic to congregational life itself and devise a range of creative ways to offer it to learners in the early years of ministry.

What can be learned from the TiM program is not that there is some kind of gap between seminaries and congregations that needs to be bridged if clergy are to be well educated. Rather, the TiM program and its exploration of the relevance of apprenticeship to the education and formation of pastors has uncovered the existence of a field where collaboration between the work of seminaries and the life of congregations is crucial. These two domains need to explore more creatively how the boundary between them can become a place of learning to which each can contribute its own distinctive strengths and competencies. Neither exporting faculty to teach in congregations nor inviting pastors into the classroom is sufficient to the needs or adequate to the opportunities inherent in helping new pastors make the transition from seminary into ministry.

As we have seen, however, work at the boundary between these two domains can be an occasion for integration and appropriation that establishes patterns for growth and development that will play out over the course of one's pastoral career. The TiM program is but one example of what it might mean to develop the pedagogical potential that so richly exists along this boundary. The establishment of the conditions of apprenticeship for every seminary graduate who is called to serve in a local congregation would require a new level of collaboration between seminaries, denominations, and congregations. Seasoned pastors and their congregations would need to begin to take greater ownership of their responsibility to be ports of entry for new pastors and would also need to grow in their capacity to serve as pedagogues of ministry, seeing this as an integral part of their service to the church. Seminaries would need to become more intentional about resourcing the teaching and learning of ministry that is resident in the life of congregations, while taking care not to co-opt it.

If characterized by mutual appreciation and sustained conversation, shared work along the boundary between theological education and congregational ministry would not only create a pathway along which new pastors could move from one setting to the other. It would most likely make the pathway itself, and the institutions between which it runs, stronger as well. Theological educators might, for example, be conversation partners for seasoned pastors as they articulate and share the practical knowledge about ministry most possess; in the process, academics and pastors would address significant pedagogical issues of concern to both classroom teachers and on-site mentors. And seasoned pastors could offer theological educators insight and critique as the latter continue to explore the "ways of knowing" that emerge within embodied practice (see the chapter by Bonnie Miller-McLemore in this volume). These concerns are at the heart of practical theology, and several of the essays in this book suggest that practical theologians are prepared to take them up, alongside the seasoned pastors who are their partners and peers in pastoral formation.

Any effort to move forward with reform proposals along the lines suggested in this essay will have to grapple with significant practical questions. The congregation-based TiM projects highlighted in this essay exemplify an apprenticeship model of pastoral formation that comes with a high price tag. Each five-year project received a grant of more than $800,000 to support the residencies of eight or so new pastors. Clearly, if the apprenticeship model is to become feasible across a wide spectrum of congregational settings, the financial bar will need to be lowered significantly.

One possibility is to develop a critical mass of congregations that do not consider this model an adjunct program to be added on to otherwise unchanged staff structures. Rather, the apprenticeship model would restructure the way these congregations are staffed, with one or two full-time positions being consistently dedicated to apprenticeships. To sustain critical attention to the pedagogical and theological depth of such apprenticeship, this plan would also require the development of learning communities where pastoral and lay leaders could collaborate across congregations in resourcing, evaluating, and strengthening their programs. The integration of theological educators into these learning communities would surely strengthen such collaboration. It is not accidental that teaching hospitals are closely tied to medical schools, for both are recognized as domains of teaching and learning essential to the education and formation of physicians. Similarly, if the pathway of pastoral formation is to become as strong as the church needs it to be, a closer collaboration between seminaries and congregations will need to be cultivated around shared pedagogical commitments.

Shaping Communities

Peter W. Marty is Senior Pastor of St. Paul Lutheran Church in Davenport, Iowa, where he has served since 1996. His essay provides a pastor's account of Christian ministry in the congregational setting that emphasizes the overarching goal of ministry rather than its several discrete functions. This emphasis is related to that adopted by the practical theologians writing elsewhere in this book, who insist that the point and purpose of their discipline is, likewise, to serve Christian living in and for the world. Marty's reflections on why shaping a rich communal life in the congregational setting is such an important focus for pastoral leadership, as well as his insights regarding the character of Christian community and the pastoral work that fosters it, thus provide an important example of practical theology from the parish.

As it happens, St. Paul Lutheran Church hosts one of the Transition into Ministry programs described in the previous chapter. This gives Marty an opportunity to mentor young pastors in the pastoral know-how that fosters vital communal identity. The presence of these young pastors in a lively congregation led by a seasoned pastor is also a reminder of the constant need of the church for new pastoral leaders who are able to lead and shape communities in a life-giving way of life in and for the sake of the world. The future of the church depends on this.

13. Shaping Communities: Pastoral Leadership and Congregational Formation

Peter W. Marty

A visit to many late nineteenth- and early twentieth-century churches across America's heartland reveals an interesting detail. Whether in an antiquated country church or a cathedral-like edifice in the central city, a biblical image appears in the artistic features of many of these sanctuaries. The image, often etched in the stained glass high above the altar, or painted on the reredos forming the backdrop to the chancel, is the depiction of Christ's ascension into heaven. From small-town North Dakota to the capital of Nebraska, from the dairy communities of middle Wisconsin to the suburbs of Kansas City, worshipers in many Midwestern churches find themselves Sunday after Sunday looking up at Christ ascending into the clouds.

No one seems to know exactly why this image is so prevalent in churches that were built a century and more ago. Perhaps the ease of painting clouds attracted the interest of amateur artists. Or perhaps the verticality of the image — Christ going up, up, and away — helped northern European immigrants feel a sense of transcendence as they homesteaded such flat land and lived sometimes monotonously hard lives. Or did the image appeal for another reason altogether? Might it have something to do with an empathy evoked by the disciples pictured at the bottom of the painting? In my unscientific study of such sanctuary art over the years, I have rarely discovered an image of Christ ascending into the clouds *without* the disciples gazing up from below. And there is never just one disciple, or two, peering skyward. It is always a group of Jesus' followers, who clearly are wondering what this disappearing Christ will mean for their lives. The more clever the painter and the more meticulous the stained glass artisan, the more intricate the facial expressions on those dis-

ciples standing there with crooked necks. Some of the faces have jaws gap-
ing. Others have furrowed brows, as if to signal some distress. Though
glory and exaltation emanate from the face of the rising Christ, an anxious
look marks the disciples below.

The story that inspires this ascension image tells of the disciples' transition from life in the presence of Jesus Christ to life marked by his sudden
absence. The principal New Testament account of this story is found in
Acts 1, where Jesus, in parting, informs his closest companions that they
will receive power from the Holy Spirit to allow them to rise up from their
confusion and become witnesses throughout the world. What follows next
is telling. The disciples journey back to Jerusalem and find an upper room
in which to gather and pray. The first act of these men and women, who
have the last words of Jesus and the image of his exit seared into their
minds, is to hole up in a room and pray. Jesus has left the keys to the kingdom in their fumbling hands and asked them to be the church. Now they
face the daunting task of figuring out exactly what this means.

Ever since that eventful day, Christian people have been trying to determine how best to be the church — how best to work and function together in a way that honors the spirit and intent of Christ. Followers have
yet to enact a perfectly holy example of what it means to congregate as fellow believers in the rich fellowship that Christ envisioned. But an endless
fascination with the beauty of what those earliest disciples wrestled with,
beginning on the day of the Ascension, continues to inspire our pursuit for
grounding our lives in Christian community.

The consistent witness of Holy Scripture is that God cherishes the idea
of forming a visible body. It is not the spiritual state of individual souls or
personal salvation that preoccupies God throughout the Bible. It isn't even
the achievement of a personal state of holiness. God's intention is to form
a people, an *ekklesia,* a community.

Self and Community: An Enduring Problem

The individual people with whom God has to work in creating *ekklesia,*
whether in our time or any other time, rarely lead entirely secure or easy-
to-manage lives. In fact, the human self is a rather fragile thing. Social scientists and theologians of different stripes have long pointed out the deep
insecurities, the persistent struggles with meaning and significance, and

the universal search for lasting relationships that so steadily define nearly every human life. We can never know exactly what comprised the content of those upper room prayers uttered by the men and women who huddled together on that anxious day when Jesus went up. But it's not unthinkable to imagine them petitioning God for direction. We can understand how natural it would have been for them to pray for a fruitful way to carry out the precious lives God had given them. In the midst of their fragility, how would they acquire the strength to lead lives that truly mattered? What practices or habits might they engage to unlearn sin and gain new hearts of holiness? What would it take to retain a bond of unity long after the shock of Jesus' hasty exit had brought them together? They had no experience to indicate that these questions would all be resolved through the sudden emergence of a new lifestyle. Their simple assignment to constitute a new community of vitality and depth by becoming the Lord's visible body on earth turned out to be not so simple at all.

The unexpected appearance of a guest in their room of prayer, however, changed the dynamics of their assignment. When the Holy Spirit blew through that house, gone were any notions among these Jesus followers that they could hold themselves together in a lasting way with mere grit and determination, or by merely attending to whatever they perceived their own interests to be. Now these disciples would be reckoning with what it means to listen to other voices that sounded nothing like their own. They would be marveling at the ease and delight with which they could associate meaningfully with very different people. This was the great gift of Pentecost.

Luke's account of the beautiful experiences of Christian community that flourished in the earliest days after the Spirit's arrival has continued to inspire Christians across the centuries and today. In Acts 4 we learn that believers began to experience palpable unity with one another ("those who believed were of one heart and soul"). They practiced sharing their possessions ("everything they owned was held in common"). Every individual in the community had the basic necessities of life met ("there was not a needy person among them"). The power of their combined testimony about Jesus' resurrection created an emanation of grace that arose from their togetherness ("great grace was upon them all").

Whatever successes emerged within these earliest examples of Christian community, fragility and insecurity in the human spirit soon had believers questing for the satisfaction of what each one saw as his or her own spiritual needs. The Apostle Paul struggled again and again with faction-ridden communities where living the Christian life was understood primarily as a matter of getting one's personal desires addressed. Instead of honoring God's intent to form a community — a people — these Christians celebrated individual experiences of conversion and transformation above all else. This tendency — which is precisely what the book of Acts is *not* about — became the evolving pattern for much of what would pass as "Christian community" across the years.

Today, we are direct descendants of a pattern of promoting private and personal spirituality that has long overwhelmed the much more difficult work of forming and sustaining Christian community. Some theologians argue that modernity has brought on a rampant individualism never seen before in church history, but it would be more helpful to say that contemporary consumerism and a market ideology have merely exacerbated the longstanding impulse among believers for a privatized faith. Preoccupation with individual salvation is hardly new. The forms for understanding the Christian faith as a life of private piety have merely grown more diverse. In the present culture — where Oprah, James Dobson, and *Chicken Soup for the Soul* daily story e-mails can have more to do with shaping the Christian life than the local congregation does — there is no sign of the private and solitary pursuit of spirituality abating any time soon.

A scene in *Hannah and Her Sisters*, a film written and directed by Woody Allen, offers a good image of the individual and private character of the contemporary journey of faith. Allen plays a guilt-ridden man full of self-doubt who decides to give Jesus a try. To him, this means making a solo visit to the local priest. The viewer sees nothing resembling community or church in the entire scene, only Woody Allen walking away with a stack of books in his arms. Apparently faith in Jesus is an individual project, a private undertaking to be pursued by poring through some books.

As people discover some of the limitations of this approach, they do show signs of hankering for community. These years, many seekers clearly are searching for ways to live less solitary lives. And many Christian believers, too, are aware of their yearning for more complete community and more honest companionship. It is not as if a culture that promotes spiritual individualism finds everyone leading a wonderfully contented life. No, there is today widespread clamoring for more than the self, even if people are not always sure how to fulfill this longing in a meaningful way. The current boom in membership for the all-but-dying 140-year-old Benevolent and Protective Order of Elks is but one example. Droves of young professionals are joining lodges as oases of camaraderie, volunteerism, cheap beer, and private rooms. As one new Elks convert put it, "Where else on a Friday night can you find a room with ten new friends?"[1]

"What life have you if you have not life together?" These words of T. S. Eliot from his 1934 pageant play *The Rock* point to the power of receiving life and nurturing life within the context of relationships with other human beings. "There is no life that is not in community, and no community not lived in praise of God," wrote Eliot.[2] For those who take this playwright's declaration to heart and recognize the connection between life, community, and praise of God, the local congregation becomes a natural place to reverse one's disengagement from others and to rethink one's solitary pursuit of God. It's not the only place, of course, to experience community in the rich biblical understanding of *ekklesia,* wherein God repeatedly resolves to gather a people and form a visible body. But the local congregation can be a powerful place for transcending the individualistic tendencies that creep into so much of life. After all, the church's business has everything to do with relationship, and most especially with putting people in touch with God and with the needs of others.

Life, Community, and Praise in the Christian Congregation

The most critical act a congregation ever undertakes is the praise of God — not the praise of community or the praise of piety, but the praise of God. It is through the regular and disciplined act of communal worship that a congregation manages to transform many disparate individuals into "a people," thus ending the illusion that the best Christian life is one ordered around the satisfaction of personal spiritual preferences. Over time, faithful worship in a congregation becomes its own way of life, a way of communally practicing how to embody the most cherished dimensions of the new life given to us by God in Jesus Christ. It isn't the sudden muttering of religious phrases or the enduring of particular rituals that creates life-giving worship. Rather, it is well-conceived praise that mediates the gospel and redeems people over long stretches of time — redeeming them,

1. Tamara Audi, "Elks, ahead of their time," *USA Today,* March 15, 2006.
2. T. S. Eliot, "Choruses from 'The Rock,'" in *The Complete Poems and Plays: 1909-1950* (New York: Harcourt, Brace & World, Inc., 1962), p. 101.

among other things, from the mistakes of individualistic spirituality. Worshiping together, they are relieved from having to pretend to be God or from worshiping the golden calves created by the bustling spirituality industry. Worshiping together, they grow in their attentiveness to the source, shape, and purpose of the abundant life that is theirs.

Surprisingly, a richly textured communal spirit in the tradition of Acts 4 is absent from many congregations today. This may seem peculiar since the local congregation would appear to be the perfect place in our culture for the intersection of what T. S. Eliot labels "life, community, and the praise of God." But here is where we should clarify some common misconceptions about congregational life. There may be experiences aplenty of social togetherness in the church setting. Friendliness may be an abundant part of all these experiences. But this is not the same as participating generously in, and being deeply entwined with, a spiritually grounded community. Inhabiting the same ecclesiastical space for an hour on Sunday morning is not the same as belonging to a community where your presence truly matters to others and their presence truly matters to you. The difference is often detectable in the very way that a church member expresses her congregational affiliation to a friend: "I *go to* that church on Brady Street," or "I *attend* St. Mary's Catholic Church," which are very different from, "I *belong to a great community of people,* and we call ourselves St. Paul Lutheran Church."

A communal spirit blooms where people are deeply in touch with one another, thriving because of the faithful interaction of their different lives. Outwardly, members of a congregation may have little in common. Inwardly, however, they can be touched by the possibility that they have something to gain and learn from each other. Broad friendship, mutuality of purpose, and an abiding care for one another are all byproducts of a spiritually grounded community that is growing in faith together. The way in which members of a congregation reproduce the love of God through a radical hospitality and an extravagant love for one another will indicate whether they are indeed the body of Christ or simply a religious club.

The Pastoral Work of Shaping Community

Just as the local congregation is not the sole place to experience richly textured Christian community — many institutions from monastic communities to wilderness camps excel in such life — so a pastor is not the only individual capable of encouraging life-giving communal practices that help people love God and one another. But in the large realm of American church life, the pastor is unquestionably a key shaper of congregational habits and practices, a "producer of culture," in Jackson Carroll's description. The pastor serves as the primary agent for interpreting the beliefs and forming the practices that make for a congregation's character. Clergy never function alone in this capacity, of course. The active engagement of laypeople is always a part of the picture, and often vitally so. Most members in a typical congregation possess some intuitive grasp of what it takes to form people together into "a body," having come from family systems that established distinctive habits and practices of their own. Where clergy are completely absent in certain parish configurations, particular individuals usually rise up to give shape to their congregation's own unique way of being, much as a pastor might otherwise do. But for our purposes here the pastor is the lead potter, God's potter "whose work is shaping, glazing and firing those congregational clay jars so that they reveal rather than hide God's power in their life and practices."[3]

In conceptualizing the pastoral role, it is common to refer to a set of core tasks basic to ordained ministry: leading worship, preaching, teaching, providing pastoral care, and overseeing congregational life. There are many variations to this list, and many adjustments according to different pastoral assignments. But two things to note: First, pastoral ministry is greater than any set of tasks. The very existence of a list in a function-based format presents some problems, for mere functionalism does not define the pastorate. Pastoral ministry is a way of life, not a technology or a mechanical execution of actions. Second, rarely if ever do we find the "oversight of congregational life" making its way to the front end of the list. This may be because the church tends to view congregational oversight administratively and sociologically rather than imaginatively and theologically. But if one believes that congregations actually possess a formative power to give life, then *shaping* a rich communal life in the congregational setting is key to the pastoral role — not simply *overseeing* a congregation. The former prizes the congregation as the body of Christ that shares joys and sorrows and seeks to be Christ's ministry of reconciliation to the world. The

---

3. Jackson W. Carroll, *God's Potters: Pastoral Leadership and the Shaping of Congregations* (Grand Rapids: Eerdmans, 2006), p. 2.

latter merely respects realities like the social networks and voluntary character inherent in a congregation, not to mention the need for finding three more helpers to serve the spaghetti dinner this Friday night.

Why elevate attention to the pastoral work of shaping community? For one thing, doing so calls attention to the often unrecognized privilege of being able to live together visibly with other Christians, and the need for someone who is called to nurture this experience of deep communal life. Elsewhere in society such an experience is largely unavailable, and Christians should never take the privilege of community for granted. Dietrich Bonhoeffer in *Life Together* underscores the joy and grace by which "a congregation is permitted to gather visibly around God's word and sacrament in this world." Although he was clearly unaware that a *virtual* world of relationships in our computer age would someday contrast with his articulation of a *visible* fellowship, Bonhoeffer insisted that the *physical* presence of other Christians is a gift of grace and "a source of incomparable joy and strength to the believer."[4]

A pastor can read Bonhoeffer, or the New Testament that inspired him, and know that holiness is born out of communities, not solitary lives. When Peter preaches vigorously at the outset of the book of Acts, he leads thousands of people to repentance and conversion on a single day. But their experience of repentance and conversion deepens and endures only when they become part of the new community that nurtures and embodies the new life they have received. Without a community — namely, the church — to sustain the life and practices of their conversion, they would simply revert back to the old world of tired habits and troubled associations that guided them previously. So Luke consistently emphasizes community, just as Paul in his letters aims for the formation of congregations that will express and embody the new life that comes with being "in Christ."

As we have seen, the New Testament is not about individual experiences of transformation so much as God's resolve to bring a new community into being. This new community is comprised of people willing to foster life in one another. For this reason, molding a communal identity is crucial to meaningful pastoral practice. Helping people in a congregation

---

4. Dietrich Bonhoeffer, *Life Together*, in *Dietrich Bonhoeffer Works*, V, ed. Gerhard Ludwig Mueller, Albrecht Schoenherr, and Geffrey B. Kelly, trans. Daniel W. Bloesch and James H. Burtness (Minneapolis: Fortress, 1996), pp. 28-29.

invest their lives and confidence in one another for the sake of a common dream and a shared mission is indispensable if we are to sustain lives that have been transformed by the gospel. Anything less will lead away from holiness and back to a way of life that disregards the justifying power of God and the requirements of the repentant life.

To speak of God's resolve to bring a "new community" into being is to recognize what some later scholastic and Reformed theologians (including Thomas Aquinas and Martin Luther) understood the church to be — namely, a fellowship of faith. This idea of a "fellowship of faith" meant for them that faith is born out of the matrix of community, not the other way around. It isn't individual acts of faith that mysteriously collect and come together to form a nice community or an interesting fellowship. Instead the emergence of a common faith is the beautiful possibility and new reality that can spring up when all sorts of different believers live in communion. From a pastoral perspective, this is why it is so important to nurture community through particular practices and beliefs that form a congregation and its members in a shared and meaningful way of life. The difference between shaping a richly textured communal spirit and enjoying mere social togetherness — often little more than a result of sharing the same street address — is profound. When the communal fabric of the body of Christ is carefully nurtured, members within it will be surprised by the centrality of faith and the service to the world that rise naturally from their togetherness.

The Catholic theologian John Courtney Murray once described the early church as a "conspiracy." By that he meant that ancient believers "breathed together" (con: *with,* and spire: *breathe*).[5] It wasn't sinister behavior, of course, that held these Christians together. It was their shared sense of reliance on God's gracious Spirit — a Spirit often depicted as wind or breath — that undergirded their *breathing together* as the people of God.

The contemporary church has exactly this same potential and requirement. Effective pastoral leadership in our day will work to have God's people breathing together, modeling a common way of life that is good for the

5. John Courtney Murray, S.J., "America's Four Conspiracies," in *Religion in America,* ed. J. Cogley (New York: Meridian Books, 1958), pp. 12-41. Reprinted in *Catholic Mind* 57 (May-June 1959): 230-41 and in M. Carron, ed., *Readings in the Philosophy of Education* (Detroit: University of Detroit Press, 1960), pp. 84-86.

world. Relying on the guiding power of the Holy Spirit, it will walk people into what Will Willimon and Stanley Hauerwas have referred to as "a community capable of sustaining Christian virtue." Such a community of togetherness, they reason, will "enable us to be better people than we could have been if left to our own devices."[6]

Breathing together can offer all kinds of new life. An illustration from one congregation that engages its members to live in deep commitment to, and appreciation for, one another points to modeling a common way of life that is good for the world. There is in my congregation a woman named Vicky, a thirty-six-year-old mother of three who is dying from a terrible tragedy. A summer job as a swimming pool attendant turned deadly one day when she opened the door to a room full of chlorine vapor. The vapor all but eviscerated her lungs in the ensuing weeks, landing her permanently in a nursing home. Other organ failure has followed in successive years. Depressed by the grim circumstances of her health and their changed family life, Vicky's husband left her and their three elementary-school-aged children. Vicky's sister Donna began adoption proceedings, bringing these nieces into her own family of four young children, plus two other little ones from an incarcerated sister-in-law who also live with Donna and her husband. Nine children living in a three-bedroom apartment, with a stressed-out mother and an overworked dad — it's close to a recipe for death.

Along comes the church. Donna wonders if the school-aged children can start Sunday school. She makes a pleasant call, drops in to meet some church staff, and makes arrangements for the kids to start coming every Sunday. Part of her predicament while tending the home front is her own unavailability to come often, and the frequent absence of her husband, who works two jobs and is away nearly every day of the week. The communal strength of the congregation, forged through a series of intentional practices fostered over a long period of time, leaps into high gear. Families that never envisioned sitting in a church pew with six or seven extra kids suddenly find themselves willing to do so. A sign-up list emerges with individuals committed to helping these sad and lost children know God through the life and love of the congregation. The Monday morning Bible study class pools its resources to plan Thanksgiving and Christmas gifts

6. Stanley Hauerwas and William H. Willimon, *Resident Aliens: Life in the Christian Colony* (Nashville: Abingdon, 1989), p. 81.

and festivities for this family. Not surprisingly, the children have come to love worship and the sense of community visible in this congregation, so much so that they have begun showing up for children's choir rehearsals on Wednesday evenings.

The beauty of a congregation willing to function powerfully as "the body of Christ" to a group of low-income kids is not an act of magic. Nor is it an ad hoc gesture that can be summoned out of thin air. It is a way of life that has grown to become a part of the character of the congregation, a character that runs much deeper than a nice impulse by a few generous individuals eager to help out. The congregational response is part of a larger ethos. The collective behavior of these congregants is closely connected to their whole self-understanding as a group of diverse people drawn together to appreciate the faith and life in one another. If the demands of this one family's situation (wherein a mother and her surrogate flock of children are seeking the best of Christian community) are but a sample of the myriad other human needs likely to confront this congregation on other weeks, there has to be a spirit of common identity that informs the congregation's ministry. Otherwise the congregation will jump spasmodically and unhelpfully at whatever ministry appears urgent. Those members who make the most noise on a specific subject will receive the first attention. The only way to avoid such uneven behavior in congregational life is to draw on a communal strength formed over a sustained period of time that revolves around a shared sense of meaning.

There is something else to note about a congregation that longs to make a difference in the world through its distinctive communal character. If a congregation's shared sense of meaning is to have any lasting value or biblical legitimacy, it must have an impact that extends beyond merely enjoying community for community's sake. Christian communities are capable of being as self-centered as the individualistic pieties and practices exhibited by many devout believers. There is a "service to the world," or a disposition of availability, that is indispensable for any well-formed Christian community that wants to claim Jesus as its Lord. A desire to make life more abundant for someone else, indeed for many others, ought to spring naturally from a congregation that is in touch with the life-giving Spirit of God. Any practical theology worthy of attention will always give high consideration to what the church must do to make life more abundant for those beyond its own fold.

When a band of youth from a congregation gathers at the Salvation

Army meal site to load food onto empty plates in the hands of hungry people, they are doing more than serving up sloppy joes; they are serving up God. In their own spiritually formed way, working with and believing in one another, just as they stand beside and believe in those whom they serve, these youth are offering much more than calories. The results of their efforts exceed what can ever be tallied on the kitchen sign-in clipboard. They have brought life with a human touch to people desperate for any life at all.

When fifty members of a congregation travel to the Gulf Coast to rebuild homes wiped out by Hurricane Katrina twenty months earlier, they are certainly not the first to make such a trip. Whole armies of Rotarians, Habitat for Humanity chapters, college work groups, and scores of generous volunteers arriving on their own have also come and made a difference. But the splendor of the congregation's service to the people of the Gulf Coast exceeds the number of drywall sheets tacked up. It surpasses the number of windows installed. They have come, in all of their diversity, to install more than drywall and windows. They have come to delight in relationships, extend hope to the forgotten elderly, and share the joy they possess that is centered in the gospel. This is more than acting out good intentions, which is the proper work of all volunteers. It is laying those good intentions at the feet of Jesus Christ. It is serving up the medicine of love from the warehouse of their own rich communal strength. Those who participate in such a trip quickly discover that some of the greatest rewards emerge from their capacity to learn from, tolerate, and even delight in each other's idiosyncrasies, such that people whom they serve actually benefit from their common spirit.

Shaping Community — Not the Dream of Community

In light of examples like those just noted, a pastor must have a complex understanding of how a congregation works. This includes a commitment to helping diverse people "breathe together." While many consider uniformity in a congregation to be a virtue, it does not make for a biblical sense of community. Dogged uniformity threatens true community. Clergy who fall in love with a congregation of like-minded parishioners they wish they had, instead of the congregation they actually do have, are seriously missing the mark. Bonhoeffer goes further: "Those who love their dream of a

Christian community more than the Christian community itself become destroyers of that Christian community even though their personal intentions may be ever so honest, earnest, and sacrificial."[7]

Parker Palmer coined the memorable and indispensable definition of community as "that place where the person you least want to live with always lives."[8] A truly Christ-minded community will not emerge so long as individuals are busy surrounding themselves with only those persons with whom they wish to live. Great congregations form where people with a dizzying variety of backgrounds and experiences take an interest in the mystery and the mess of each other's lives. The pastoral challenge is to give shape to this particularly diverse body. It involves leadership that delights more in the beauty of a consciously formed community of Christ than in a community that represents an arbitrary or accidental amalgamation of people seeking God for their individual lives.

One of the Apostle Paul's determinative goals was to take the diversity of the church and, through hard work and grace, form a spirited community. This was how he believed the wisdom of God would get through to the world: "That through the church," he noted, "the wisdom of God in its rich variety might now be made known" (Ephesians 3:10). The pastoral responsibility is to hold rugged individual preferences in check, whether they be the preferences of others or, as importantly, one's own preferences. This guiding responsibility is necessary for a richly textured community to acquire some shape. As the cohesive spirit and common purpose of a diverse community emerges, it is the very rareness of this body that will capture the attention of the world. The manner with which this body or organism begins to move together has more than eye-catching appeal. It also happens to be the church's most effective way for transforming the world.

William H. Whyte, a leader in the study of modern urban street life, spent decades studying the patterns of diverse people on the move. His fascinating analyses of crowd behavior on New York City streets, using time-lapse photography and extensive notes and graphs, are published in his 1988 book *City: Rediscovering the Center.* What Whyte discovered over years of work is that pedestrians walking on busy sidewalks have a natural

7. Bonhoeffer, *Life Together,* p. 36.

8. Parker Palmer, *The Company of Strangers: Christians and the Renewal of America's Public Life* (New York: Crossroad, 1981), p. 124.

way of avoiding collisions with oncoming pedestrians. Without even realizing it, they form a mass or a crowd that is both smooth and efficient.
"They give and they take, at once aggressive and accommodating." The
sidewalk scene comes alive with movement and color — people walking
quickly, walking slowly, skipping up steps, weaving in and out in crossing
patterns, accelerating and retarding to match the moves of others. There is
a beauty, Whyte said of this sight, that is beguiling to watch. "It is indeed a
great dance."[9]

The beauty that Whyte saw in these coordinated crowd movements is
not totally unlike the beauty of a congregation that understands itself as a
community moving forward together. There are obvious differences of
course. Most notably, a congregation is not a mass of people lumped together by default. People make a conscious decision to join a church. Unlike their urban pedestrian counterparts who glob themselves together
quite arbitrarily to cross a street, church members *do* realize quite intentionally that they are creating some form of togetherness. They understand
at least the theory of a congregation being a cohesive community — the
"body of Christ" in New Testament terms — even if they have little sense
of what they must let go of to contribute to the shape of this community.

This is where pastoral leadership figures in. A pastor has the daily
privilege and responsibility of molding an uneven mass of clay and teaching selflessness to people who may be inclined toward a degree of selfishness. No one tells a New York City pedestrian how to pick up the pace or
stutter a step to avoid smashing the heel of the next pedestrian. Every
walker on Fifth Avenue has to decide for himself or herself when and how
to walk based on his or her best guess of what everyone else will do. In a
congregation that is led thoughtfully, members are not left simply to guess
at what everyone else will do. They do not merely decide for their individual selves how to press forward. They are led. They are guided to discover a
sense of their place in the whole because they have been shown how to believe in the significance of the whole. They become captivated by a larger
vision and get wrapped up in the potential of engaging their faith alongside the strength of others' faith. Finding one's place in the fullness of this
kind of spiritual community is a matter of what William Whyte labeled for
another realm, "give and take . . . movement and color . . . walking quickly

9. William H. Whyte, *City: Rediscovering the Center* (New York: Doubleday, 1988), pp.
56-57.

[and] walking slowly." Congregational life is a colorful and complex walk of togetherness, led by a pastoral hand that appreciates the worth inherent in a well-formed community.

As congregations discover their identity in the world and how to engage this complex walk of togetherness, both of which take time and leadership, they have an additional responsibility of their own. It's called molding and shaping their pastors. Pastors, for their part, are not beneath their own patterns of selfishness and rugged individual preference. They are fully capable of leading disordered lives and making poor decisions. So the very humility and generosity of spirit that pastors propose for their parishioners needs to be returned in equal measure by congregations that care about the formation of pastors who will lead effectively. This symbiotic relationship between pastor and people, where both honor the other in a kind of commendable mutuality, should be the desired goal of every pastor interested in forming a life-giving community.

The Pastoral Know-How that Shapes Communities

Christian communities over time have shown a tendency to turn inward and away from a more expansive purpose whenever fear, uncertainty, or aimlessness threatens their identity. The very earliest disciples knew this experience from the very first Easter day, when fear caused them to lock down in a secluded room. The resurrected Christ appeared unexpectedly in their midst that evening, assuring them that a peace and wholeness punctuated their frightened togetherness, whether they knew it or not. Something about his words and presence empowered them to eventually open the door, walk out, and try to be the church. The fuel that would drive the engine for guiding their confidence would be the Lord's very own breath. In what surely must have been a startling move, he breathed on his disciples in that room. That breath would continue to inspire early generations of the church with Spirit-led behavior and leadership. To this day, every community of faith is a gift to the world wherever it embodies the fullness and liveliness that Jesus hoped for on the day he breathed on those first disciples. How this same breath can be exhaled through those who minister in Jesus' name today is our final concern. It is time to ponder some specific moves of pastoral practice that take shaping this kind of community as their goal.

The practical theology articulated in this book takes forming people in a way of life in and for the world as its purpose. All of the best thinking and learning in the world of theology will be pointless if it is not at the service of forming lives that matter. Lives may *change* through a program, an insight, a conversation, a sermon, or any number of other momentary encounters inside or outside of Christian community. But lives are not *transformed* in this rapid or incidental way. Living the Christian life well takes time and practice. It asks the person undertaking this extraordinary life to aim at embodying particular habits and practices that will delight God, feed the joy of others, and grow personal integrity and fulfillment. As we have noted, the ideal setting for giving shape to this extraordinary life is the congregation. But the congregation as a unit or a body can also develop its own communal habits and practices in addition to shaping those who belong to it. Forming Christian communal life takes time and requires constant nurturing. It does not happen automatically, and most often pastoral leadership is what makes the difference. The pastor who commits to shaping this kind of community can provide powerful encouragement by embodying particular personal qualities and pastoral habits that gradually guide a relatively unformed body of people to become a transformed community of vitality and life.

If we remember the words of T. S. Eliot, life and community are linked with praise. Christian community all starts with worship. Leading worship well takes practice. But it also demands something else. It requires the one leading to possess a pastoral eye toward engaging people in a form of life about which they may be very uncertain. The liturgy can baffle. Communal singing can frighten. Ancient words can go unappreciated. Many worshipers stepping into a church will repeatedly ask themselves in the course of the same service why they're there, especially on *this* day! They may be mystified why everyone else around them is "making time" for this "odd exercise" called praise. Leading worship is about engaging these questioning, worried, inquiring, and sometimes sleepy souls in a behavior that asks them to consider everyone else around them. Gestures of welcome and guidance throughout the liturgy (which are not the same as *words* of welcome and guidance) can prompt a worshiper to relax and take in an otherwise anxiety-provoking experience. This kind of leadership also invites each individual to consider what difference he or she might make to the whole. When people in worship think they're doing something exclusively for themselves, they need subtle cues to remember that they're also doing

321

them for God and for others. Dietrich Bonhoeffer took on the subject of singing in this way: "It is the voice of the church that is heard in singing together. It is not I who sing, but the church. However, as a member of the church, I may share in its song."[10]

Engaging people in the dynamism of congregational worship requires a thousand points of connectivity between pastor and people. Thoughtful pastoral leadership is more than going through some motions as the pastor *thinks* they're supposed to be done. It's also going through them as the gathered people *need* them to be done. Reading the consecrating words of the Holy Eucharist is one thing; remembering that there are spiritually hungry people right on the other side of the chalice and bread is another. And they're not just "people." They're friends. They're fellow travelers in the same boat. They're sojourners with the same joys and sorrows as I, the celebrant, am supposed to be able to know about, or candid enough to recognize, in my own life.

Attentiveness and encouragement toward faithful living can take many forms. In my parish ministry, I make a practice of encouraging others to try out capacities they may not even know they possess. When I say, "make a practice," I am referring to almost every conversation in a given day. I invite and sometimes push parishioners to consider forms of service they may never have anticipated or envisioned for themselves — oftentimes, the wilder the imaginative stretch the better. I try to walk people into experiences they probably would have avoided without some serious encouragement. The surprise of this prompting is part of the joy. The delight in the eyes of the other when he or she eventually commits to the prompting is part of the thrill. But two other reasons inspire this ministry of encouragement. First, it automatically connects people with others in the congregation. No matter what the endeavor, encouragement draws the uncertain soul into a quick acknowledgement that she is not quite as solitary as she might have believed or previously experienced. A community surrounds her. Second, the ease and openness, or the seriousness, with which I encourage a parishioner to take something on can allow him to practice in his own mind exactly what it would be like to take on this same behavior within the congregation. After all, he also has the obligation as a full member of the community to be encouraging. Nothing grows a communal spirit like people who are uninhibited to happily encourage one another.

10. Bonhoeffer, *Life Together*, p. 68.

Reflective pastoral leadership that is committed to shaping a strong communal identity also helps people find their theological voice. This is a project that never ends. But neither do the range of experiences for which people need words to converse. It is intimidating to be in a congregation and not know how to think or express oneself in the most basic of theological or biblical ways. In fact, a sense of ineptitude on these fronts only drives a person deeper into his or her private psyche, often offering the impression that he or she was never intended to "fit" into this congregation in the first place. Lacking any kind of confident theological voice also encourages a member to turn inward for spiritual development and renewal.

I make a point of choosing words carefully in public or private conversation that aim to meet the particular parishioner right where he or she may be tuned to think best. I look for straightforward ways to express more complicated theological ideas with an eye toward where the mindsets and linguistic comfort zones of others may be operating. I have noticed that stepping in and out of other people's conversations at artfully timed moments can allow for their own language and insight to flourish. There is no trick to helping people articulate how they might contemplate a given subject in their life or in the world. But if a pastor is to help nurture beliefs, feelings, and practices that foster a communal identity, the people in the community need a vocabulary and grammar with which they can be at home. It is not unusual for all of us to need help imagining some other way of viewing the fullness and goodness of life. Pastors can assist congregants with this imagining. It is a kind of mentoring that can be done humbly and thoughtfully in the context of helping the larger community prosper.

Nothing beats gratitude when it comes to shaping Christian community. It is the blood that should pump through every vein in the body. Our lives and our faith are nothing without thankful expressions to acknowledge the blessing of what the Creator has given us and what we have in each other because of this Creator. I have never met a really grateful person who is unhappy. Never. By implication, a byproduct of giving regular thanks in a community is that happiness becomes part of the shared life. It becomes as ingrained as the gratitude driving it.

Dourness and ingratitude take people nowhere. Yet they often become easy substitutes for the beauty of a generous life when gratitude is not modeled or cultivated. Pastors in the congregational setting ought to be natural purveyors of gratitude. Congregations that are in tune with their high calling to be life-giving bodies in the tradition of the early church in

Acts ought to behave similarly. The spirit pumping forth this gratitude from the midst of a congregation can be nurtured by a pastor's own deep embodiment of this gospel imperative to give thanks. If I, as a pastor, express thanks to a member in my community of faith for anything at all, be it something as valuable as some person's critical involvement in a new program or as small as someone else merely returning a phone call, something other than polite ministerial manners had better be guiding my action. Gratitude must rise from the soul of a pastor. When it does, it will get shared naturally. And when it gets shared naturally, the spirit of generosity that is part and parcel of every rendering of thanks will only grow the abundance of life in the congregation. Those who make a practice of embodying gratitude know how highly contagious it is. It doesn't foster a way of life in a congregation. It *is* its own joyous way of life that is good for the world. Congregations and pastors will grow a more faithful sense of Christian community whenever they encourage gratitude in one another.

It may seem impertinent to mention the importance of learning names of congregational members. But for a pastor bent on the hard work of shaping community, learning and remembering names of big and little people alike is indispensable. The process of knowing names requires determination and practice. But the very exercise of this discipline is part of what it takes to fall in love with people. After all, a person's name is also his or her identity. To speak a person's name is to announce the value of the person. A name opens onto a personality, a history, a world, and the named individual becomes present in an immediate and unforgettable way. The regular use of names, and even the ability to laugh at oneself when forgetting a name, is part of the way friendships are built. When I make a commitment to remember and use someone's name, it reminds me of the value of that person's friendship. It brings two people in touch with one another in a simple yet personal way. In a congregation, this commitment to using first names opens the door for members to employ this way of speaking in their own interactions. Lives get linked. The body of Christ becomes more cohesive as people matter one to another in a personal way.

There are plenty of other qualities and practices in a pastor's life to explore in another place at another time. This mention of a few characteristics of the ministerial life is not meant to be exhaustive. I merely offer them as a sampling of the kind of character and commitments that clergy may need to consider if Christian community along the lines of what is in the book of Acts is ever to flourish. Obviously, every congregation, every setting, and every pastor have their particularities. Thoughtful leadership that is adaptive in nature will always be making adjustments to the gifts and needs of whatever people and traditions are involved. There are histories and challenges unique to every locale. But if fostering abundant life is the aim of every good pastorate, and the practical theology that feeds such ministry is guided by the same desire, then it is fair to highlight common threads to faithful ministry that are vital to any context.

My interest is in wise pastoral leadership that longs to nurture a strong sense of belonging in the congregational setting. This emphasis is not to detract from highlighting dynamic gifts inherent in every congregation, ones that exist independent of any pastoral involvement, and which in their own way may shape and nurture pastors in a critical way. But given the many challenges of our time, where believers do not commonly derive their deepest spirituality from Christian community, it seems imperative that we consider features of the pastoral life that can help raise up the kind of community — or *ekklesia* — that God in Scripture appears to cherish. Clearly, pastors who want their congregations to live the faith in life-giving ways must embody this same life in the depths of their own personhood. And though it may take the duration of a pastor's life to allow every wise practice to become second nature, the very experience of the journey, and the humility required for it, will create an ideal model for a congregation that is hungry for the same rich life.

For Life Abundant

Pastoral leadership is not just a matter of fulfilling specific pastoral functions. It is a matter of performing these functions, and indeed every aspect of daily life and work, in a way that helps a strange menagerie of believers make sense of life as a communal enterprise. It is about fostering a community that is in love with the possibilities of its togetherness in Christ and its responsibility of being available to the needs of others. With an eye on Scripture, a nose for creation, and hands that want to be extended out to the world, a pastor has the privilege of walking fellow believers into the joy of what he or she seeks as well — a chance to experience the abundant life that comes with being a part of this visible body — *ekklesia* — for which God so yearns.

Establishing this togetherness is not a small or quick task. It is a continuous and sometimes strenuous one, performed in the midst of such seemingly small activities as conducting everyday conversations, remembering names, and encouraging new forms of service. But pastors serving in the congregational setting are uniquely positioned to help individuals relinquish their grip on personal preference. They get to help shape a community that breathes around the inspiration of Jesus, intentionally walking people into each other's lives, teaching them how to admire and appreciate fellow members who may often think and live quite differently.

The motivation for this pastoral practice is clear: It is the belief that the love generated by a spiritually coherent community is greater than the sum total of the love emanating from its individual members' lives.

Educating and Forming Disciples for the Reign of God

In this chapter, Gordon Mikoski reflects on more than two decades of learning in and about Israel, the Palestinian Christian community, and the Israeli-Palestinian conflict. The learning began when Mikoski, an American who was then in college, went on a study trip to the Holy Land. It continued as he led other learners on Holy Land pilgrimages during his years as a pastor, and it now shapes how he does his work as a seminary professor of Christian education and practical theology. By ranging somewhat autobiographically across these various settings of education and formation in faith, Mikoski discloses relations among them: a disciple becomes a pastor who fosters discipleship in others, and later this pastor becomes a teacher of other pastors who will go out to teach other disciples.

The ongoing ministry of the church depends on learning like this taking place again and again. More important than this process of generational renewal, however, is a much deeper level of coherence that unites the education of the laity, the work of pastors, and the teaching of theological educators. All of this teaching and learning and ministry cohere because all pursue the same end: a life-giving way of life taken up in response to God's grace in Christ and embodied by communities in and for the world. Mikoski identifies this end as "bear[ing] witness to the transforming power of God in the world" and as an "anticipat[ion] . . . of the Reign of God on earth."

A capable and inspiring pastor plays a central role in Mikoski's account. Archbishop Elias Chacour exemplifies many of the pastoral qualities considered in earlier chapters of this book. In reading this chapter, look for signs of Chacour's pastoral imagination as he sees his troubled homeland through eyes of faith. Note how he embodies practical wisdom through words and gestures

of great integrity. And see him shaping communities, primarily in his own village but now also on a larger world stage.

Practical theology is the explicit focus of attention only on the last few
pages of this chapter. Yet the methods of the discipline (see Kathleen Cahalan
and James Nieman's chapter above) are evident throughout in Mikoski's, and
Chacour's, theological engagement with concrete contexts, current events, and
the needs of the near future. In addition, the chapter as a whole displays both
the ecclesial and the public character of practical theology. While both Mikoski
and Chacour are deeply committed to Christian Scripture, doctrine, and worship, the reconciliation that Chacour pursues, and the education and formation
Mikoski guides, always draw Christians into the public realm — where, Mikoski
argues, practical theology can and must go as well.

14. Educating and Forming Disciples for the Reign of God: Reflections on Youth Pilgrimages to the Holy Land

Gordon S. Mikoski

"I am a Palestinian. I have no bombs." So began one of Father Elias Chacour's summer evening chats with the group of thirty American high school students and their advisors. After hot days of construction work at the Mar Elias high school and technical college, we gathered on the flat roof of *Abuna*'s house to listen intently.[1] He effortlessly wove together captivating stories about his childhood in the hills of northern Galilee, incidents from the ministry of his "compatriot" Jesus Christ, and reports on daily realities of the struggle for peace and justice in the midst of the contemporary Israeli-Palestinian conflict. Those evenings spent under the summer stars on Abuna Chacour's rooftop were the crowning moments of discipleship education and formation on the Israel pilgrimage trips I planned and led in the 1990s. Combined with visits to several biblical sites, physical labor at the schools in Ibillin, and observations of daily aspects of the Israeli-Palestinian conflict as it affects both Palestinians and Jews, Abuna's storytelling profoundly shaped the faith of group participants.[2]

1. The Arabic word *Abuna* means "our father." It is used primarily in reference to Catholic priests. Most English speakers who have had the opportunity to get to know the current Melkite Catholic Archbishop of Akka, Haifa, Nazareth, and all Galilee, Elias Chacour, refer to him simply as "Abuna." The Melkite Church is an ancient Arab Christian community whose patriarch sits in the Vatican under the authority of the Roman Catholic pope.

2. Many responsible books on the background of the Israeli-Palestinian conflict are currently available. I highly recommend the following: Dan Cohn-Sherbok and Dawoud El-Alami, *The Palestinian-Israeli Conflict: A Beginner's Guide,* rev. ed. (Oxford: Oneworld Publications, 2003); Donna Rosenthal, *The Israelis: Ordinary People in an Extraordinary Land* (New York: Free Press, 2003); and Sandy Tolan, *The Lemon Tree: An Arab, a Jew, and the Heart of the Middle East* (London: Bloomsbury, 2006).

The Holy Land youth pilgrimages I led while serving as the Christian education pastor of the Grosse Pointe Memorial Presbyterian Church — in which Abuna Chacour's example and storytelling played a central role — profoundly influenced the emerging Christian faith of the high school and college students from my congregation who participated in them. These trips also shaped the way I think about teaching future pastors and teachers in my current role as professor of Christian education in a theological seminary. They also have influenced the way I engage in and contribute to the academic discipline of practical theology as a Christian educator.

Reflecting on the particular form of the practice of Christian pilgrimage to Israel and the Occupied Territories that I developed for church youth can provide important insights into the various dimensions of education and formation for both discipleship and ministry. It can also provide a way to see something of the rich interplay between the education and formation for discipleship and ministry in congregations, the education of ministers in theological seminaries, and the conceptualization of practical theology in the academy, as all pursue a common telos, the Reign of God. I begin my reflections by describing some of the key features of the trips I led. I will then step back from the task of describing the pilgrimages in order to articulate some of the ways in which these trips have shaped my approach to education and formation for discipleship and ministry in congregational settings, in a theological seminary, and in the field of practical theology.

Youth Pilgrimages to the Holy Land

My First Trip to Israel and the Occupied Territories

As a college student and a recent convert to Christianity, I traveled to Israel and the Occupied Territories for the first time in January of 1983. The purpose of that January term trip sponsored by the religion department of my college was to focus on the historical and geographical backgrounds of the Bible. We visited geographical sites with Bibles in hand and discovered new insights about key events. I probably would have returned happily home with this new knowledge of the backgrounds of the Bible save for two events that occurred. One day, as our group got off the bus in the West

Bank town of Nablus in order to see some sites related to ancient Shechem, a group of Palestinian teenagers rose up seemingly out of nowhere and began to throw rocks at us. They shouted anti-American slogans at us in Arabic as we ran for the bus and drove away. I remember feeling both intense bewilderment and fear as a result of this incident.

A few days later, our group had a couple of unscheduled days in Jerusalem. Two representatives from the Mennonite Central Committee came and offered to give a tour of their work with Palestinian communities in the West Bank. Always one for adventure, I volunteered to go. As we toured agricultural and economic development sites, two realizations began to dawn on me: there were two very different realities in the Holy Land and heretofore our group of Christian college students had been safely enclosed in only one of them. Later, I would come to see that up until my day with the Mennonites in the West Bank, I had been moving about in and reading the Bible from the perspective of an uncritical Christian Zionism. That day of touring with the Mennonites permanently altered the way I interpret the Bible, the way I understand the importance of connecting biblical teachings to contemporary social and political realities, and my perception of what it means to be a disciple of Jesus Christ in the midst of the complexities of today's world.

What I learned from my day with the Mennonites in the West Bank marinated in my heart and mind for several years. Between that college study tour in 1983 and 1990, I finished college, graduated from seminary, got married, and accepted a call to serve as associate pastor for Christian education at the Grosse Pointe Memorial Presbyterian Church in suburban Detroit. In January of 1991, the things I had experienced on my college study tour came to the surface and began to lay the groundwork for a major theme for all of my work in Christian education. In that month, Father Elias Chacour temporarily joined our church staff as Ecumenical Minister.[3]

Chacour began his series of lectures at the church by describing what it means for him to live as a "walking contradiction." He is a Palestinian, but an Israeli citizen. He was baptized in a Maronite church, confirmed by a Ro-

---

3. The Ecumenical Minister program at Grosse Pointe Memorial Church brings pastors from a variety of contexts to serve as a member of the church staff for two to four weeks every January. The Rev. Dr. Ray Kiely developed the concept of this program at Westminster Presbyterian Church in Buffalo, New York, in the 1960s as a way to educate the congregation about the worldwide church. He launched a very similar program in the 1970s at the Grosse Pointe Memorial Church during his tenure there as pastor and head of staff.

man Catholic cardinal, and ordained as a Melkite priest. He celebrates the Orthodox liturgy of St. John Chrysostom, but he is technically a Roman Catholic. He is a victim of Israeli violence, yet he works tirelessly for nonviolence and reconciliation between Jews and Palestinians.[4] Building on this intriguing beginning, he offered his hearers fresh insight into the meaning of Jesus' Sermon on the Mount from the perspective of a contemporary Galilean Christian community that daily faces the complexities and challenges of the contemporary Israeli-Palestinian conflict. The congregation — young and old alike — were enthralled with this man and his message.

The Israel Pilgrimages of Grosse Pointe Memorial Church

Near the end of his time with us, Abuna Chacour invited my wife and me to bring the church's high school youth group to Israel to help with the construction of the high school and technical college in his Palestinian village of Ibillin.[5] We eagerly accepted his invitation and began preparations to take the youth of our church on a series of Christian pilgrimages to the Holy Land.[6]

I intended for the youth participants in these pilgrimages to grow and develop in several important ways. I wanted to enhance and deepen their understanding of Christian history and contemporary witness by visiting places where key biblical events had taken place and by standing in solidarity with Palestinian Christians who have struggled for decades with injustice, unrelenting conflict, and economic discrimination. I intended for participants to develop an action-reflection habit of mind as a key feature of Christian discipleship. Further, I wanted the young people on these trips

4. Elias Chacour, *We Belong to the Land: The Story of a Palestinian Israeli Who Lives for Peace and Reconciliation* (Notre Dame: University of Notre Dame Press, 2001), p. 7. For the origin and meaning of the term "Melkite" see p. 9 of Chacour's book.

5. My wife, Nancy, also served as an associate pastor in Christian education at the Grosse Pointe Memorial Church. We carried out our work in educational ministry in that congregation in a differentiated partnership. We jointly developed and led the youth pilgrimages to Israel.

6. The Israel trips were actually cooperative ecumenical ventures. We invited the local Episcopal and Lutheran churches to join us for these youth pilgrimages. At various points, the trips also had contingents from Westminster Presbyterian Church in Sacramento, California, under the leadership of the Rev. Dr. Donald Griggs.

to develop a hopeful vision of a shared and reconciled future for Israelis and Palestinians. Finally, I wanted them to gain some critical distance on their own privileged situation back home and to participate reflectively in American conversations about the Israeli-Palestinian conflict.

Each trip sought to realize these aims through a carefully constructed itinerary and daily rhythm. The itinerary began with touring important biblical and religious sites in and around Jerusalem. In Jerusalem, we would take the pilgrims on visits to ancient sites like the Church of the Holy Sepulchre, the Western Wall of the Temple, the Dome of the Rock, the Garden of Gethsemane, and the Mount of Olives. We also incorporated experiences that disclosed the pain of people who today live in that land, including a visit to Yad Vashem (the Israeli Holocaust Memorial) and meetings with Palestinian human rights workers and church leaders. One day was spent in Bethlehem at sites like the Church of the Nativity and the Shepherds' Field (Beit Sahour). The group also traveled to Jericho, the Dead Sea, and Masada on one very long day.

Each day the group met for breakfast and morning prayers before venturing out on a day of touring. At each site we visited, relevant biblical passages would be read. Often, the group would pray and sing hymns or spiritual songs that had some connection to the site. Throughout the day, the group would observe and comment on visible aspects of the Israeli-Palestinian conflict — particularly signs of the military occupation of the West Bank by Israel. After dinner, the group would gather for an extended period of worship that included opportunities to discuss and reflect on discoveries, perplexities, and questions that arose during the course of the day's itinerary.

The second half of the trip took place in Galilee. In this portion of the experience, the group used the campus of the Mar Elias High School and Technical College as its home base. Each morning at 6:00, the pilgrims would gather for breakfast followed by a period of physical labor at the Mar Elias schools. From early morning until early afternoon, group members painted classrooms, built retaining walls, moved masonry materials, landscaped, and cleaned buildings. In the heat of midday, work ceased, and we took excursions to Nazareth or the Sea of Galilee. After dinner back in Ibillin, the group would gather for worship and conversations with Abuna Chacour about Jesus' life, teaching, passion, and ongoing ministry in the world. For most pilgrims, the most important element of the entire Holy Land experience was the time spent listening to and interacting with Abuna Chacour. With dexterity, humor, and profundity, he wove all the strands of the pilgrimage experience into a remarkable tapestry of Christian faith and discipleship during our nightly sessions with him.

The education and formation that took place on the pilgrimages did not end with the group's arrival at Detroit Metro Airport. Much of the discipleship education and integration of what had been experienced began only at the point of reentry into the pilgrims' daily lives back home. The intensity and length of these Holy Land pilgrimages provided enough dehabituation from familiar routines to enable participants to see with new eyes realities that they usually took for granted. The experience of being away from home in radically different cultural contexts for two weeks helped trip participants to appreciate some "ordinary" things like hot water on demand, grocery stores stocked with familiar foods, civil rights for all, and the absence of soldiers and military equipment. That part of maturation in Christian discipleship which has to do with the process of disembedding from and gaining critical perspective on the givenness of one's family, community, and culture was greatly aided by the experience of these pilgrimages. These trips to the Middle East provided powerful stimulus for developing what educational theorist Maxine Greene described as the insight that "things could be otherwise."[7] Upon returning home, the familiar became strange for a time. The process of making sense out of the pilgrimage experience while dealing with the dynamics of reentry into that which had previously been taken for granted often proved extraordinarily important for the development of a faith that embodies Christ's abundant life in and for the world.

The Unique Influence of Elias Chacour's Discipleship, Ministry, and Practical Theology

It may at first seem surprising that most of these young pilgrims told us that the most formative part of the trip was their time with Abuna Chacour. Given that the participants in the Israel pilgrimages were in the Middle East — some traveling outside of the United States for the very first time — and given the rich historical, geographical, and social context of Israel and the Occupied Territories, one might have thought that other as-

---

7. "My focal interest is in human freedom, in the capacity to surpass the given and look at things as if they could be otherwise." Maxine Greene, *The Dialectic of Freedom* (New York: Teachers College Press, 1988), p. 3.

pects of the experience would exert the most shaping influence. In order to see why participants consistently said that their sense of Christian disciple-ship had grown the most through exposure to Abuna Chacour, one needs to know a bit more about his life story and ministry.

Elias Chacour was seven years old when disruptive and disorienting political realities burst upon his quiet life in the Christian agricultural vil-lage of Biram nestled high in the verdant hills of upper Galilee. From 1948 until today, Chacour has been a refugee in his own land. The ancestral homeland of Galilean Palestine upon which his family cultivated figs and other produce for centuries has nearly all been confiscated by the state of Israel. The trauma of losing his home and the harmonious way of life that his family had known for generations has profoundly marked the subse-quent unfolding of his life and vocation. He refers to this as his deepest wound.[8]

As a citizen of the state of Israel, Chacour has been spared some of the cruelest aspects of life in the Occupied Territories and in the Palestinian refugee camps. Nevertheless, he and the other Palestinians who live as citi-zens of the state of Israel have suffered greatly as second-class citizens. He carries with him the wounds of homelessness as well as those arising from repeatedly having experienced and been witness to the traumatization of his fellow Palestinians. As a Palestinian Christian, he has struggled against intense pressures exerted on him and on his community by both Israeli Jews and Palestinian Muslims.[9]

Facing the twin dangers of debilitating grief — which all too often metastasizes into hatred — and the prospect of a life of permanent exile abroad in the West, Chacour has instead sought to build a future in which Palestinians and Jews can live together in peace with justice. Chacour's own sense of discipleship has given him resources with which to resist forces of injustice, violence, and death and to work toward a democratic, pluralistic, and reconciled future for Jews and Palestinians. His profound and direct relationship with Jesus Christ, his "compatriot" from Galilee, has given him strength to stay and to build when so many others in his sit-

8. Elias Chacour, *Blood Brothers* (Grand Rapids: Chosen Books, 2003), p. 108.

9. For a fuller discussion of the issue of Palestinian Christian emigration, see Mitri Raheb, *I Am a Palestinian Christian,* trans. Ruth C. L. Gritsch (Minneapolis: Fortress, 1995), pp. 15-25. For a comprehensive treatment of Arab Christians in the Middle East, see Kenneth Cragg, *The Arab Christian: A History in the Middle East* (Louisville: Westminster/John Knox, 1991).

uation have emigrated, become chronically depressed, or even chosen the path of violence.

Chacour's parents and the Christian community into which he was born imparted to him a deeply Christian way of life. From his mother, he learned the power of biblical narratives and their potential for connecting with the challenges of contemporary circumstances. From his father, he learned the Christian practice of forgiveness and the way of love in the face of violence and injustice. From both parents, he learned the importance of a life suffused with prayer and the call to love one's enemies. From his church, he learned to connect liturgy to the issues and challenges of daily life. Early in his life as a displaced and vulnerable person, Chacour discovered on his own the value of mystical contemplation. In his early adolescence, he would seek solace from the bitter social and political realities he faced daily by wandering the Galilean hills and praying to his Galilean "compatriot," Jesus Christ. The practices of prayer and contemplation have anchored his remarkable work as parish priest, ecumenical partner, interfaith catalyst, public witness, and, lately, archbishop.

As fleet-footed parish priest, determined school builder, and creative public witness, Abuna Chacour moves easily from theological reflection on situations to strategic action aimed at changing them in the direction of a more desirable future. Responding to the challenging problems within the church, between religious communities, and in the wider public context of the Palestinian-Israeli conflict, Chacour has developed and implemented a range of strategies for effective social transformation: reconciliation, prayerful activism, boundary crossing, coalition building, creative transgression, comic reframing, and nonviolent resistance as the power of love.

The ultimate ground of Chacour's practical theological vision is his interpretation of the coming, life, teachings, death, and resurrection of Jesus Christ, the Man from Galilee. In Chacour's view, the teachings of the Sermon on the Mount about love for enemies, forgiveness, and peacemaking have their ultimate grounding in the reconciling events of Good Friday and Easter. Taking cues from the Man from Galilee, Chacour has endeavored to serve as an agent of divine reconciliation in the church, among different religious communities, and between Israelis and Palestinians.

In searching for effective strategies of response to the pressing human needs confronting him, Chacour always begins with prayer, seeking guidance from the Risen Christ and empowerment by the Holy Spirit before venturing off into some plan of action. The themes of the gathered church in prayer as expressed in the Melkite version of the Byzantine liturgy of St. John Chrysostom often provide the themes and vision that give rise to Chacour's plans for social or political action.[10] Each time his community gathers for worship, they sing such things as "Blessed are those who hunger and thirst for righteousness, for they shall be filled" and "Blessed are the peacemakers, for they shall be called the children of God." In this way, the liturgy has helped Chacour to see that prayer inexorably leads to concrete social action. Rightly understood, prayer cannot lead to withdrawal into pietistic abstraction; instead, it puts those who pray in direct personal touch with the "Man from Galilee" who healed, taught, transformed, forgave, reconciled enemies, and loved the world. Prayer is, therefore, the first and, in some ways, the most effective element of faithful strategic action in and for the world. Regular engagement in the liturgy forms a community that exists not for its own sake, but for the sake of God and all creation.

Abuna Chacour possesses an uncanny ability to connect personally with adversaries and enemies. He speaks in a way that communicates both truth and love. One could interpret his ministry as an extended exercise in making friends with people with whom he shouldn't even be talking. Such openness to others means that one must accept the truth that sometimes "my enemy is also right and I am also wrong." Chacour's courage to cross boundaries that separate individuals and communities from one another finds a complement in his spirit of dialectical vulnerability.

Chacour possesses unusual gifts for coalition building. He is able to enlist people to work toward the realization of a common project through the personal relationships he establishes with a variety of people and groups. In the beginning of his ministry, he was able to bring about reconciliation in the village of Ibillin largely through his efforts — with the assistance of three nuns from Nazareth — to build relationships through a pattern of regular visits to the homes of all the inhabitants of the village. When he was called upon to lead a march for peace in Jerusalem while a graduate student working on Talmud at Hebrew University, he enlisted the support of Jewish

10. Most tellingly, the Melkite version of Chrysostom's liturgy directs the clergy and the gathered congregation to sing the Beatitudes from the Sermon on the Mount every Sunday during the procession of the Gospels through the congregation immediately prior to the reading and interpretation of Scripture. For the full text of the Melkite version of the Divine Liturgy of St. John Chrysostom, see http://www.melkite.org/Dliturgy.htm. Accessed February 19, 2007.

faculty and students, Arab Christians, and Muslims. When he set his sights on building a Christian-based and religiously plural school, he persuaded local skilled workers to make in-kind contributions of labor to the project. He also invited a number of Jews to join the faculty. In order to secure a building permit from the state of Israel after the building already existed and after several years of struggle, he creatively found a way to enlist the direct personal support of then–Secretary of State James Baker III.

Chacour's strategy involves not only resolving conflict, but sometimes deliberately generating conflict. When faced with corruption, manifest injustice, or bureaucratic absurdities, Chacour has often intentionally broken rules and transgressed legally or socially constructed barriers. He baptizes grapevines and builds school buildings without permits. He insists on joint funeral services for priests of rival churches and invites Muslims to pray in his church when a mosque has been destroyed. He refuses to allow himself to be boxed in by the norms and expectations of others. He tells bishops that they will win his respect only when they follow Jesus' example in their ministries. Much of Chacour's life and work has been characterized by creative transgression of socially constructed rules that constrain and disfigure human dignity.

Chacour often uses humor to reframe situations that would otherwise perpetuate and reinforce the existing order of things. By turning assumptions upside down and by juxtaposing the unexpected with the taken for granted, Chacour frequently offers both radical critique of an unjust situation and an invitation into a better future. His quick wit, combined with a well-developed sense of the gap between the "is" and the "ought," often creates disarming strategies for change. Whether throwing open his jacket to Western audiences to show that one can be Palestinian and not necessarily a terrorist, renaming "monstrous" mountains as beacons of light, or disclosing the incivilities of a government that treats a portion of its citizens as second-class citizens, Chacour refuses to give in to despair. His faith in the present and future actions of the Triune God in particular situations gives him an unshakable hope for a better future. The behaviors of this self-described "crazy priest" ultimately make sense only in a comic mode: the certain knowledge that in the end all shall be well. On the way to that comic end, a healthy dose of the unexpected, the ironic, and the ridiculous may well be necessary to get things moving in a more hopeful direction in such a complicated, prolonged, and toxic situation as the Israeli-Palestinian conflict.

Means matter. They matter as much as the ends to which they are employed. Chacour demonstrates in the variety of contexts in which his practical theological work has unfolded that nonviolent love provides the only way to break out of the cycle of violence. Drawing from and echoing Mohandas Gandhi and Martin Luther King Jr., Chacour strategically interrupts the mimetic pattern of violence by the active and resistant power of love. As a Melkite Christian, he affirms that the Triune God made known in the person and work of Jesus Christ is the source of this counterintuitive force for healing and reconciliation.

Each of these themes — reconciliation, prayerful activism, boundary crossing, coalition building, creative transgression, comic reframing, and nonviolent resistance as the power of love — comes into play when Abuna Chacour talks with young people on the roof of his home during warm summer evenings. Weaving together powerful insights from the life and teachings of Jesus, his own experience as a displaced Palestinian Christian, and contemporary experiences of peacemaking in the highly conflicted context in which he lives and works, Chacour's narratives have a positively transforming and lasting effect on young American disciples on pilgrimage.

Discipleship Education and Formation in Congregations

The Israel pilgrimages that contributed greatly to the formation of late adolescent Christian disciples at the Grosse Pointe Memorial Church throughout the 1990s have had several important long-term effects on the youth participants. They have also had lasting impact on me. For example, my understanding of the task of discipleship education and formation in congregational settings in relation to Jesus Christ, whom I now have come to know as the Man from Galilee, has been significantly impacted by this particular practice of pilgrimage. The way in which I engage the field of practical theology as a Christian educator working in a theological school also bears the marks of having been influenced by these pilgrimages. In this section and the next I will sketch some of the effects that the experiences of taking youth to the Holy Land and having them interact with Abuna Chacour have had on my subsequent work as pastor, theological educator, and practical theologian.

Christian disciples are educated and formed to a significant degree by engaging in religious practices. Many practices, such as prayer, Bible reading, service to others, and the like, are quotidian in character. That is, Christian individuals and communities engage in them regularly, often daily. These practices make up part of the ordinary pattern of their lives. Over time, engagement in such practices can powerfully shape the development of Christian faith and discipleship.

Quotidian religious practices, however, do not exhaust the entire range of religious practices that have potential to form and educate Christian disciples. Some formative religious practices — like pilgrimage — take people out of their ordinary, daily routines and place them at the margins of comfort, safety, and understanding for carefully delineated periods of time. Such liminal practices — especially when combined with a well-developed pattern of quotidian religious practices — can have a profound effect on emerging disciples.

For many centuries, Christianity, Islam, and other religious traditions have encouraged the liminal practice of pilgrimage as a way of forming and reinforcing religious commitment among their adherents.[11] In Christianity, many accounts exist of pilgrimages to the Holy Land. Egeria, a fourth-century pilgrim from Spain, provided rich and detailed accounts of her encounters with the geography and the key liturgical activities of the Christian church in and around Palestine. Celebrating the Easter Vigil in the Church of the Holy Sepulchre in Jerusalem helped Egeria to enter much more deeply into the baptismal mystery of participation in the death and resurrection of Jesus Christ than had been the case previously at home in Spain.[12] One of the earliest and perhaps the most famous account of a journey to the Holy Land by a Christian, Egeria's diary has provided compelling witness to the powerful, forming effects of the practice of pilgrimage for nearly fifteen centuries.[13]

11. I borrow the term "liminal" from Victor and Edith Turner, *Image and Pilgrimage in Christian Culture: Anthropological Perspectives* (New York: Columbia University Press, 1978), pp. 34-35 and 249-50.

12. The Church of the Holy Sepulchre (derived from the word for "tomb" in Latin) is thought by many archaeologists and scholars to have been built over the actual sites of Golgotha and Christ's tomb. See, for example, James H. Charlesworth, ed., *Jesus and Archaeology* (Grand Rapids: Eerdmans, 2006), pp. 35-37.

13. George E. Gingras in the introduction to the Ancient Christian Writers edition of Egeria's diaries wrote, "The facts Egeria presents in recounting her journeys are always subordinate and incidental to her central purpose, which was to vivify and confirm her faith in the truths of Scripture through personal contact with those places marked by the action of

The practice of pilgrimage has continued in the three main Christian traditions down to the present day. In the Eastern Orthodox and Roman Catholic traditions, pilgrimage has always enjoyed an important place in the constellation of practices associated with discipleship formation. Even Protestants, whose forebears in the sixteenth century strongly criticized and generally devalued the practice of pilgrimage as a reaction to medieval Catholic excesses, have often found ways through the centuries to engage in the practice of pilgrimage. Untold numbers of Protestant pilgrims have journeyed to places like Wittenberg, Geneva, Le Chambon, and Taizé — not to mention the Holy Land — in order to deepen their faith and to equip them more effectively to live out their faith in daily life.

One could make the argument that most youth mission trips sponsored by mainline Protestant churches in America today bear a significant pilgrimage dimension. Most mission trips are not only about putting discipleship into action by serving other people; they are also about forming disciples by taking them temporarily out of the familiar, the comfortable, and the routine so that they can have a more profound experience of Jesus Christ. By most accounts, tremendous growth in faith can and does take place through mission trip experiences.[14] I think that the formative potential of such trips could be significantly enhanced by bringing to the fore the pilgrimage dimension of such experiences. The formative potential of pilgrimages is so great that it raises the possibility that approaches to discipleship education and formation in local congregations may need to be reformulated so as to feature explicitly a combination of quotidian and liminal practices.

Pilgrimages to Israel and the Occupied Territories represent a special case of pilgrimage for youth. They include all the benefits of other kinds of pilgrimage while bringing the Bible alive for young people in ways that years of participation in church school and youth group often cannot. For example, reading a passage of Scripture while actually seeing and exploring the place where it occurred almost always stimulates a deeper appreciation for and understanding of that passage. Even the most polished multimedia

---

God on man, and to meet and pray in the company of those who she considered best exemplified the Christian life, the monks of Sinai, Palestine, Mesopotamia, and Isauria." *Egeria: Diary of a Pilgrimage,* trans. George E. Gingras, Ancient Christian Writers, vol. 38 (New York: Newman Press, 1970), p. 19.

14. See Don C. Richter, *Mission Trips That Matter: Embodied Faith for the Sake of the World* (Nashville: Upper Room Books, 2008).

Bible studies cannot compare with the experiences of reflecting on biblical stories like the account of Jesus' entry into Jerusalem on Palm Sunday while retracing his steps from the top of the Mount of Olives to the Temple Mount. The story of Jesus and the Samaritan woman becomes three-dimensional when told to a group that is gathered around the site of Jacob's well in Nablus. Likewise, maintaining group interest in a passage from 2 Kings 20 or 2 Chronicles 32 tends not to be a problem when the passage is read moments before the group plunges into a quarter-mile underground slog through knee-deep water running through Hezekiah's actual tunnel. For many participants on these trips, the Bible comes alive for the first time. For the rest of their lives as they read, hear, and study the Bible, participants will vividly recall having been to many of its important places.

Encountering something of the complexity and pathos on both sides of the contemporary Israeli-Palestinian conflict plays just as important a part in shaping disciples as does the geographical contextualization of biblical narratives. Though many American groups travel to this region and receive a nearly antiseptic biblical-backgrounds experience (like my college study tour in 1983), the Israel youth pilgrimages I led sought to expose trip participants to both the backgrounds of the Bible and the rudiments of the contemporary Israeli-Palestinian conflict. I believe combining exposure to this complicated conflict with on-site biblical education helps young people learn that Christian discipleship is not and cannot be a matter of spiritual practices and feelings disconnected from the context in which Christian communities are actually situated. Bringing students into limited exposure to the vortex of the Israeli-Palestinian conflict as part of a church-sponsored trip teaches young disciples that following Christ necessarily and inescapably has social and political dimensions. Furthermore, hearing from Palestinian Christians about the ways in which the resources of their Christian faith help them to address creatively and courageously the daily challenges posed by contemporary political struggles often leaves mainline American Protestant young people with a powerful impression of the transformative character of Christian discipleship.

Exposure to the dynamics of the Israeli-Palestinian conflict as part of a Christian pilgrimage helps foster engaged discipleship in the American context when pilgrims return home. Inasmuch as the Israeli-Palestinian conflict feeds Arab and worldwide Muslim resentment against the United States, informed perspectives on this very difficult issue is of vital importance for American young people who are on the verge of taking up civic responsibility and engagement.[15] American Christian ignorance about or silence in relation to this complicated set of issues serves only to perpetuate destruction and a downward spiral into violent chaos. Informed American Christian disciples, on the other hand, can make significant contributions toward the resolution of this conflict through their informed participation in the American political process.

Physical labor in the Christian-based, religiously pluralistic schools founded by Archbishop Chacour also provided a formative experience for these American pilgrims. Trip participants spent a week doing physically demanding tasks to help build the schools in Ibillin that are informed by Jesus' teachings in the Sermon on the Mount and that seek to foster a peacefully coexistent, pluralistic, and democratic future for Jews, Muslims, Druze, and Christians in the Holy Land. Through classroom construction, painting, landscaping, and light carpentry, pilgrimage participants learned that following Jesus Christ means performing humble acts for others in service to a transformative vision of the Reign of God in the world. Discipleship associated with such tasks literally means getting one's hands dirty for the Lord. To help make these connections, Abuna Chacour would help the group to see how their manual labor played an important part in building a better future for Israelis and Palestinians each evening as he spent several hours with them. These evening sessions with Abuna Chacour combined with daily worship and reflection helped to cement an action-reflection pattern of discipleship for young pilgrims.

Teaching Those Responsible for Discipleship Education and Formation

As my teaching vocation has shifted from a congregational setting to a church-related theological seminary, I work now to equip the next genera-

---

15. It is important to point out here that the Israel pilgrimages sought to expose participants to the perspectives and grievances of both sides of the Israeli-Palestinian conflict. In keeping with the stance of the Presbyterian Church (U.S.A.), we emphasized the following points: the right of the state of Israel to exist with safe and secure borders, the central importance of ending Israel's occupation of the Occupied Territories (i.e., the West Bank, the Golan Heights, and the Gaza Strip), the denunciation of all violence (whether by Palestinian suicide bombers or by Israeli military incursions and home demolitions in the Occupied Territories), and the hope for a future for Israelis and Palestinians characterized by peace with justice.

tion of church leaders for effective leadership in discipleship education and formation in congregations. Several aspects of the Holy Land pilgrimages I led in the 1990s inform the way I teach future pastors and teachers.

First, I want my students to develop an approach to discipleship education and formation that simultaneously mines the depths of Christian identity and participates in the ongoing activity of God in and for the world. That is to say, I want them to foster the development of disciples who live not primarily for themselves, their families, or even for the church, but for God, the transformation of society, and the good of all creation. I want them to aim at forming disciples who will participate in the *Missio Dei* in and for the world.[16] In my Master of Divinity level classes, I try to inspire a vision for educational ministry that will emphasize the central importance of personal knowledge of Jesus Christ as he is known through Scripture and through faithful engagement with the pressing issues and challenges of the contemporary world situation. I want my students to avoid the twin errors of stressing Christian identity to the point of withdrawing into homogenous countercultural enclaves (conservative distortion) and of minimizing attention to Christian identity in order to cooperate with communities and individuals in the public square who do not share Christian views and values (liberal distortion). This vision of discipleship resonates well with Johannes Baptist Metz's conviction that "following Christ . . . is at one and the same time mystical and political."[17]

16. Jürgen Moltmann writes of this concept, "In the movements of the Trinitarian history of God's dealings with the world the church finds and discovers itself, in all the relationships which comprehend its life. It finds itself on the path traced by this history of God's dealings with the world, and it discovers itself as one element in the movements of the divine sending, gathering together and experience. It is not that the church has a mission of salvation to fulfill to the world; it is the mission of the Son and the Spirit through the Father that includes the church, creating a church as it goes on its way. . . . The church participates in Christ's messianic mission and in the creative mission of the Spirit." *The Church in the Power of the Spirit: A Contribution to Messianic Ecclesiology* (New York: Harper & Row, 1975), pp. 64-65.

17. Johannes B. Metz, *Followers of Christ: The Religious Life and the Church*, trans. Thomas Linton (New York: Paulist, 1978), p. 41. Metz also rejects distortions on the side of disconnected identity assertion and minimalist pluralistic cooperation. He writes, "When the double mystical and political composition of following Christ is ignored, what is eventually accepted is an understanding of following Christ that ends up by exemplifying only half of what is involved. On the one hand you have following Christ as something purely subjective, and on the other following Christ as an exclusively regulatory idea, as a purely humanistic political concept. What happens is either the reduction of following Christ to a purely social and political dimension of behavior or its reduction to private religious spirituality" (p. 44).

The Holy Land pilgrimages and repeated exposure to Abuna Chacour's example have helped me to see that educational ministry should aim to hold together Christian identity formation — funded by participation in distinctively Christian practices and deep appropriation of Scripture and ecclesial traditions — and radical openness to non-Christian others through the practices of democratic conversation, creative collaboration, compassionate activism, and advocacy for human rights.[18]

Second, I have learned from the pilgrimage experiences that teaching the teachers of disciples must be characterized by rich and complex interplay between interpretation and action. Preparation for the pilgrimages always involved providing participants with interpretive frameworks for understanding the religious and political dimensions of the journey. Each day's activities during a pilgrimage was capped by processing experiences in relation to the interpretive frameworks provided during the preparation phase. Upon their return home, pilgrims continued to deepen, revise, and rework their understanding of discipleship in light of their intense experiences on the pilgrimage.

A key part of teaching for discipleship in the church involves initiating learning experiences that encourage the appropriation of an action-reflection rhythm akin to what pilgrims experienced on the Holy Land pilgrimages. Pastors and teachers need to provide ecclesial learners with interpretive frameworks for understanding Scripture, Christian traditions, and the various challenges posed by contemporary life. Such interpretive frameworks should, then, equip and lead learners into reflective engagement in following Christ through engagement in Christian practices in the concrete and highly contextual circumstance of daily life.[19] Experiences of reflective action, in turn, lead to both deepening and revising the various

18. For a longer discussion of my conception of the aims of Christian education, see my forthcoming book tentatively entitled *Baptism and Christian Identity* (Grand Rapids: Eerdmans).

19. J. B. Metz captures a key aspect of this theory-practice dynamic when he writes, "Christ must always be thought of in such a way that he is never merely thought of. Christology does not simply lecture about following Christ but feeds itself, for its own truth's sake on the practice of following Christ. Essentially it expresses a practical knowledge. In this sense every Christology is subject to the primacy of practice. This one could term Christological dialectic or the dialectic of following Christ. . . . It is a dialectic of theory and practice, a dialectic of subject and object. It is by following him that we know whom we are dealing with and who saves us." Metz, *Followers of Christ*, pp. 39-40.

interpretive frameworks provided. Teaching future congregational leaders about Christian education in a theological school, then, needs to teach about the importance and centrality of an action-reflection dynamic in discipleship education. Seminary-level teaching in this area must do more than merely teach it, however; even more, it must employ methods of teaching that provide experiences of the interplay of theory and practice. The methods of teaching should convey and reinforce the subject matter at this point.[20] Teaching about discipleship education and formation through lectures and textual analysis has important but limited value. Because the manner of teaching also teaches, preparing future pastors and teachers for leadership in educational ministry needs also to include a rich experiential dimension. In an environment with unlimited resources, it would be ideal actually to take ministerial students on a trip to the Holy Land with an eye toward teaching how to teach in light of that experience. Because that is not possible in most theological schools, one must get creative in developing the experiential dimension of action-reflection learning. This can mean developing experiential learning opportunities in the classroom. It can also mean encouraging students to engage in religious practices outside of the classroom or assigning site visits to congregations. Whatever the particular learning activities, it is important to keep in mind the importance of providing both rich learning experiences and mechanisms for reflecting on and learning from those experiences in a theory-practice loop.

Third, my practice of teaching Christian education in a theological school has been informed by these trips in relation to the content of what I teach in Christian education courses. The Holy Land pilgrimages for youth helped me to see that spiritual practices and worship should, whenever possible, be connected with the social and political challenges posed by contemporary life. The juxtaposition of religious practices and public engagement offers a vision of the Christian life that avoids sectarian withdrawal and the collapsing of attentiveness to divine transcendence into an immanence of mere social concern. Partly as a result of the structure of these pilgrimages and repeated encounters with Abuna Chacour's practical theological vision along similar lines, I teach my Master of Divinity students that

20. Katherine Turpin, professor of Christian education at Iliff School of Theology, calls this "the need to teach how to teach by teaching." This is the focal point of her article in *The International Journal of Practical Theology* 12, no. 1 (Spring 2008).

Christian education is the necessary linkage between liturgy and life. Effective Christian education provides opportunities for learners in the local church to connect the dots between what occurs in relation to font, table, and pulpit and what happens in their daily lives as they interact with the problems and possibilities of social contexts. To that end, Christian education leaders need proficiency in understanding the dynamics of both Christian worship and contemporary social or political problems, as well as the habits of mind necessary to relate the two in discerning and creative ways.

Issues like the multilayered aspects of the biblical-political complex can be explored in greater depth with theological students than with children or youth in the local church. For example, it is imperative that today's theological students come to see with clarity and precision the dangers of both tacit and overt forms of Christian Zionism. Because uncritical Christian Zionism is so prevalent among American Protestants — especially among more literal-minded evangelicals — I see it as my duty as a theological educator to promote critical perspectives on a range of important issues such as biblical teachings on questions related to land, the status of the Jews, anti-Semitism, the relationships among the three main Abrahamic religious traditions, and the character of Christian witness and mission.

The Holy Land pilgrimages for youth also served as a catalyst for my thinking about practical Trinitarianism. In the opening of her book, *God for Us: The Trinity and Christian Life,* Catherine Mowry LaCugna wrote that "The doctrine of the Trinity is ultimately a practical doctrine with radical consequences for Christian life."[21] Her assertion — and many others like it by a large company of contemporary Trinitarian theologians — has opened

---

21. Catherine Mowry LaCugna, *God for Us: The Trinity and Christian Life* (San Francisco: HarperSanFrancisco, 1991), p. 1. There has been an explosion of books on the theme of the Trinity as a practical doctrine in the past couple of decades. No book has been more influential along these lines than Jürgen Moltmann's *The Trinity and the Kingdom: The Doctrine of God* (San Francisco: Harper & Row, 1981). For other important treatments of this theme see the following: Leonardo Boff, *Trinity and Society,* trans. Paul Burns (Maryknoll, N.Y.: Orbis, 1997); David S. Cunningham, *These Three Are One: The Practice of Trinitarian Theology* (Oxford: Blackwell, 1998); Colin E. Gunton, *The One, the Three, and the Many: God, Creation, and the Culture of Modernity* (Cambridge: Cambridge University Press, 1993); Elizabeth A. Johnson, *She Who Is: The Mystery of God in Feminist Theological Discourse* (New York: Crossroad, 1992); Joy Ann McDougall, *Pilgrimage of Love: Moltmann on the Trinity and Christian Life* (New York: Oxford University Press, 2005); and Miroslav Volf, *Exclusion and Embrace: A Theological Exploration of Identity, Otherness, and Reconciliation* (Nashville: Abingdon, 1996). This list represents only a sampling from the ever-growing body of literature on this subject.

up a whole range of issues and questions in relation to the development of a distinctively Trinitarian approach to the aims, methods, and curriculum of teaching for discipleship.[22] Part of my thinking about this matter in relation to the theory and practice of Christian education has been influenced by my encounters with the ministry and teachings of Abuna Chacour while leading youth pilgrimage. In all his work, Chacour affirms that the Triune God works in the world, not just in and through particular Christian churches. On the basis of his understanding of the way in which the Spirit works with the Son to bring justice, peace, reconciliation, and harmony among all peoples and groups to the glory of the Father, Chacour has developed impressive bridge-building and community-organizing activities among Christian traditions and between Christian and non-Christian religious communities. In turn, I seek to give those who will assume responsibility for the education of disciples in local churches tools for discerning and participating in the ongoing work of the Triune God's transforming activity in church and world.

Fourth, these trips have contributed to my understanding of the role of those responsible for the Christian education and formation of others. Pastors and teachers in local congregations are greatly aided in their educational ministry by seeing themselves as, among other appropriate metaphors, pilgrimage leaders. As those who have some shaping responsibility for the journey of pilgrims through this life, they must attend to the different phases of the pilgrimage experience. They must take great care in preparation for learning experiences — whether in distant lands or at home — by providing interpretive frameworks. They need to assume in their work the basic posture of inviting people to travel with them on challenging journeys of discovery and engagement. They need to do all that they can to provide engaging learning experiences. As they do so, they should also provide enough in the way of interpretive frameworks that learning will be enhanced, but not so much as to interfere with participants' own meaning-making processes. Finally, they need to provide opportunities for pilgrims to deepen, revise, and rework their understanding of the transformative experiences they have encountered along the journey of discipleship.

---

22. For a fuller treatment of the relation between practical Trinitarianism and Christian education see my forthcoming book. For another approach, see Robert W. Pazmiño's *God Our Teacher: Theological Basics in Christian Education* (Grand Rapids: Baker Academic, 2001).

Reflections in Relation to the Discipline of Practical Theology

Several important themes for the field of practical theology come into focus as I step back from a consideration of the inner workings of the Holy Land pilgrimages for youth and the things that can be learned from them for the education of disciples in congregations and for the task of preparing leaders for the church in a theological school. Reflecting on this particular form of the liminal practice of pilgrimage provides some clarification about the aims, methods, and subject matter of the field of practical theology.

The central aim of practical theology ought to be the transformation of society in the direction of the Reign of the Triune God. Even though human effort alone will not bring about the full realization of God's Reign on earth, Christian churches do have an important proleptic or anticipatory role to play here and now with regard to the divinely determined future for the world. Funded by eschatological hope and grounded in liturgical practices like baptism and Eucharist which "remember the future," Christian communities bear witness in word and deed to the transforming power of God in the world toward a coming future marked by the knowledge and praise of God and the experience of justice, peace, and reconciliation among all peoples.[23]

The unique character of the Israel pilgrimages also has clarified for me some controversial matters of method in practical theology. My experiences in leading trips to the Holy Land for youth have helped me to come to an essentially Chalcedonian approach to practical theology. By this I mean that practical theology needs to take its theological cues about method from the Christological work of the Council of Chalcedon in 451. That ecumenical council affirmed both the divine and human natures of Christ existing in one Person without mixing and without confusion. Further, the two natures of Christ do not exist in reciprocal or symmetrical parity; the divine nature has a certain kind of primacy without trumping or obliterating the human nature.[24] These Chalcedo-

23. For a similar, if less explicitly Trinitarian, formulation of the aim of practical theology, see Johannes van der Ven's discussion of the "basileia symbol" in his *Practical Theology: An Empirical Approach* (Leuven: Peeters Press, 1998), pp. 69-76. I see the Reign of God model I am advocating as consonant with the telos of "abundant life for all creation" that guides this volume as a whole; see p. 1.

24. For more developed treatments of a Chalcedonian approach to practical theology, see the work of my Princeton Seminary colleague Deborah van Deusen Hunsinger in her

nian themes inform my approach to method in practical theology in a very important way.

Theological normativity and the contextuality of human experience must be held closely together and in such a way that the thickness of human situatedness is given its proper due and that matters theological and ecclesial are always given primacy. A Chalcedonian approach to practical theological method seeks to avoid excessive stress on human experience at the expense of or loss of nerve about theological normativity born of revelation. It equally eschews too much emphasis on revelation at the expense of rich hermeneutical engagement with actual lived human situations and experiences. There must be instead a dialectical interaction between revelation and context. However, this dialectic can never be seen as strictly symmetrical. Inasmuch as practical theology is an academic discipline primarily in and for the church, it must take its bearings from biblical narratives, norms, visions, and principles. It aims to foster lives of authentic discipleship that creatively engage the pressing social issues of the day, but emphatically and unapologetically in the direction of the Reign of God. Likewise, the meaning of complex social situations can only be fully discerned and disclosed in relation to the biblical witness. My understanding of method in practical theology could perhaps be characterized best as a liberal Barthianism (richly funded by Chalcedonian Christology) that is constantly engaged in dialogue and engagement with social contexts.

This all can seem rather abstract and technical until one sees it played out in reading the Bible with pilgrims at holy sites situated in the midst of the Israeli-Palestinian conflict. One goes on pilgrimage to Israel and the West Bank in part to gain a deeper understanding of Scripture so that, in turn, one can be a better disciple of Christ for the sake of God and the world. Reading Scripture in a decontextualized, antiseptic, and apolitical manner only functions to support the social, political, and economic status quo. Reading Scripture in that way runs the very serious risk of missing the entire point of revelation as the definitive witness to the transforming

---

Theology and Pastoral Counseling: A New Interdisciplinary Approach (Grand Rapids: Eerdmans, 1995), pp. 61-104. Also, my predecessor at Princeton Seminary, James E. Loder, combined the insights of Chalcedon and the Danish philosopher Søren Kierkegaard to produce a distinctive Barthian formulation of method in practical theology. See Loder's *The Knight's Move: The Relational Logic of the Spirit in Theology and Science* (Colorado Springs: Helmers & Howard, 1992), pp. 81-122, and his *The Logic of the Spirit: Human Development in Theological Perspective* (San Francisco: Jossey-Bass, 1998), pp. 26-45.

work of the Spirit in history through the Son toward the glorification of the Father. More pointedly, such decontextualized approaches to reading Scripture tend to support tacit, if not explicit, forms of Christian Zionism that hinder rather than help the process of peace with justice in the Israeli-Palestinian conflict. In contrast, my experience of leading Holy Land pilgrimages helped me to see that properly interpreting Scripture means that one must keep one's eyes on the page while keeping one's ears close to the ground.

My Chalcedonian considerations of method in practical theology — especially when taken in the light of experience with Christian pilgrimage in the midst of the Israeli-Palestinian conflict — lead to another key insight with regard to methods in practical theology. It is increasingly clear to me that the ministerial, ecclesial, and public paradigms for the field of practical theology should not be seen as competing alternatives. Rather, they should be viewed as component parts of a larger, differentiated whole that is held together by a hopeful vision of the Reign of God. In other words, taxonomies of approaches to practical theology that put ministerial, ecclesial, and public paradigms into competing silos may do more harm than good.[25] Inasmuch as it is theological in character — and, therefore, also ecclesial — practical theology seeks to foster followers of Jesus Christ who participate in the life of the church for the sake of the transformation of the world in the direction of the Reign of the Triune God. In order for such disciples to emerge in the church, ministerial leaders with highly specialized training and skills — including in the area of educational ministry — are needed to promote, guide, and galvanize their development. In other words, all three paradigms — the ministerial, the ecclesial, and the public — of practical theology need to function together in a larger differentiated whole in order most effectively to advance the cause of the Reign of God in the world.

Finally, my reflections on Israel pilgrimages for youth lead me to an increasingly deep conviction about the subject matter or substantive focus for the field of practical theology. In the panoply of human problems that call for engagement by practical theologians, the Israeli-Palestinian conflict stands out. Because of its pathos, complexity, and influence in the lives

---

25. For a discussion of these three paradigms in the field of practical theology, see van der Ven, *Practical Theology,* pp. 34-41. See also James W. Fowler, *Faith Development and Pastoral Care* (Philadelphia: Fortress, 1987), pp. 17-25.

of millions of Jews, Muslims, and Christians — both in the Middle East and in the West — this conflict needs to be taken up by practical theologians as a matter of urgent and pressing concern. Addressing this problem with all the tools of the discipline of practical theology can have enormously constructive benefits for Israelis, Palestinians, and Americans — as well as for Christians, Muslims, and Jews in all three societies and beyond.

PART 5

For Life Abundant

15. In Anticipation

Bringing a book project to completion is an experience that brings mixed feelings. A review of what has been accomplished brings satisfaction, of course. At the same time, authors usually know that there is much more that needs to be explored and written. Both feelings are ours as we offer this book to readers.

Our sense that much remains to be done is a source not of regret but of anticipation, for it points to the dynamic and ongoing character of practical theology itself. Practical theology that takes as its telos a life-giving way of life in and for the world is necessarily open-ended, for that way of life emerges in specific times and places that are constantly in flux. Moreover, this kind of theology is undertaken not only for the sake of, but also in the midst of, the potentially unlimited range of actual situations and communities within which abundant life can emerge. The authors of this book know only a few of these situations and communities well, for we come from a limited set of locations. We hope that our efforts here will encourage other people of faith to undertake practical theology in the midst of their own situated lives as citizens, ministers, educators, and members of families and communities of many kinds. At a historical moment when faithful living in and for a world torn by violence and injustice could hardly be more urgent, the call to engage in theology of this kind comes to Christians in many walks of life.

Practical theologians have long insisted that theological reflection finds its most generative starting points in concrete, nearby situations: the effort of a teenager to live faithfully in a certain town, the design of a course for a specific group of students, the preparations of a pastor for the

funeral of a child, the work of a Palestinian-Israeli priest to shape community in the midst of social conflict. The authors of this book have long
stressed the significance of concrete situations like these, but in the course
of talking and writing together, we realized the generativity of practice
with new clarity. In the conversations that led to this book, intellectual
breakthroughs often came when we were working on such situations at
close range and with some degree of personal involvement, looking carefully at a specific syllabus, say, or at an episode in which one of us had
learned something important about offering care or shaping a community.
Later, we also did the necessary work of stepping back to consider what we
were learning in a more systematic and abstract way. Yet the importance of
trying to understand and address that which is particular, embodied,
timed, and placed constantly reasserted itself.

The life-giving way of life that is God's promise and provision itself
emerges precisely in the midst of such concrete and specific locations,
where it unsettles, comforts, disrupts, and reconfigures persons and communities through the gift of new creation. Practical theology's capacity to
engage theologically with lives that are actually lived and communities
that really exist thus yields forms of scholarship, teaching, reflection, and
action that are remarkably well suited to their subject matter. The shape of
practical theology *fits* the shape of the way of life it tries to describe, critique, sustain, and embody. We note especially five salient features that
characterize both a life-giving way of life in the world and practical theology as we are coming to understand it:

Undertaken within and over time

A way of life that embodies Christ's abundant life in and for the world
takes shape over time and in time. It draws on Scripture, traditions, and
practices while also adapting constantly to new situations. It involves faithful response not just of the right kind, but at the right time. Attending to
this temporal dimension has opened us to a range of new understandings.
One of the major theses of this book is that education and formation for
ministry also take place across periods of time much longer than the three
or four years of graduate theological education. Similarly, the passage of
time shapes projects in practical theology; the book we now offer is not at
all the book we envisioned at the authors' first meeting. Both historically
and in the recent past and present, Christian living, ministry, and theology
mature in time and through action over time — including failed action,

when we learn from it. Moreover, participants in Christian living, ministry, and theology are aware of the instability of given arrangements and open to change. Indeed, they readily seek change for the sake of life abundant.

Embodied and placed

Christian living takes place somewhere in particular and emerges through the actual daily conduct of particular human beings who together are the body of Christ in and for that place. Moreover, these same human beings are embodied persons who both require and provide for others the care and respect that are such crucial aspects of a way of life abundant. The locatedness of Christian life and ministry, like its temporality, sustains certain kinds of continuity but also means that Christian practices must adapt to a wide range of cultural, social, and natural contexts. Practical theology likewise does its work with an eye to the particularity of each location, for example by suiting a course to a specific seminary or by incorporating a reading of the culture of a given congregation into its proposals for action there. Indeed, its capacity to guide practice and to craft proposals for action arises in large part from close attention to situatedness and specificity. In addition, of course, practical theologians are themselves embodied and placed; acknowledging this is one reason why the editors have introduced each author before his or her chapter. Finally, practical theology's attention to that which is local, nearby, situated, particular, and concrete reflects an incarnational turn that both honors God's presence in all these locations and reminds teachers, students, ministers, and other Christians of our own immersion in the life of a specific part of God's vast creation.

Shared and collaborative

The Christian life cannot be lived in isolation, for God's promise of abundant life is received and realized in and through relationships with others. Practical theologians in the academy, the church, and public life seek to comprehend, serve, and transform communities of many kinds for the sake of abundant life. Moreover, they necessarily do so in collaboration with others, integrating insights that come from various disciplines and spheres of life. There is no other way to gather insights, methods, and resources that are adequate to portray the complex realities on which this field focuses. Practical theology cannot thrive apart from collaboration — especially, perhaps, the kind of collaboration that crosses boundaries between the academy, the church, and other settings. In the conversations that led to this book, the presence of pastors and of educators from a range of disciplines alongside those trained in the discipline of practical theology added depth, challenge, and enjoyment. We were also quite aware that our work was influenced by many others who have been important teachers, ministers, colleagues, authors, and fellow disciples to each of us. In coming years, practical theology needs to collaborate far more closely than we have done here with many others, including ethicists and biblical scholars in the academy and people of faith who are eager to engage practical theological questions in their places of work, family life, leisure, and civic engagement.

Affirming the intelligence of practice

Texts and propositions alone cannot carry or communicate the knowledge of God's grace in Christ that is at the heart of Christian existence. This life-giving knowledge, which dwells in the bodies of believers and in the body they comprise, is gained through forms of active and receptive participation that engage a wide range of human capacities. Likewise, the specific practices by which we respond to God's grace — practices such as prayer, forgiveness, and hospitality — bear knowledge of God, ourselves, and the world that cannot be reduced to words, even though words are often indispensable in helping us to learn and participate faithfully in them. Such practices embody certain kinds of wisdom and foster certain kinds of intelligence when engaged in serious and critical ways. The practice of Christian ministry also requires and imbues forms of knowledge, wisdom, and intelligence that include but reach far beyond cognition alone. Practical theology serves the church and the world by honoring and articulating such knowledge, wisdom, and intelligence as they emerge in actual persons and communities, and by considering how they might most faithfully be deepened and shared for the sake of abundant life. In doing so, practical theology seeks to clarify the intelligence of practice without reducing it, and to query its reasons even while acknowledging that it is impossible fully to comprehend either the concrete uniqueness or the Spirit-led possibility inherent in any given instance of practice. Like faithful ministry and discipleship, practical theology pursues the telos of a life-giving way of life in awareness that the means employed in doing so — the practices of faith, including the arts of ministry — are not merely tools. Rather they are both the goal and the path of the Christian life.

Nourished by Scripture and reliant on the grace of God

As Christian people respond together to God's promise and presence in particular times and places, they are provided with wisdom and life that are not of their own making. Through Scripture, the Holy Spirit addresses each new situation, judging falsehood and renewing courage, gratitude, and hope. Here the church receives an inexhaustible and indispensable (and sometimes puzzling) source of wisdom. Drinking deeply from this source over time nourishes and shapes the imagination of the church and its ministers, transforming how we see ourselves and others and challenging the distortions that human communities, including our own, so readily embrace. We see that what is usually called "the environment" is a creation of God of which we are part, and we hear our greed named as sin and those who are poor called "brothers and sisters" by Jesus. Moreover, we see that Christian life and ministry belong first and last not to us but to God. This awareness brings both humility about the reach of our own practices and a renewed sense of the importance of doing them faithfully and well. A Scripture-shaped attentiveness to God and the qualities to which such attentiveness gives rise — including humility about the incomplete and often ungodly character of our teaching and research as well as earnest commitment to make both as true and excellent as possible — are likewise marks of good practical theology.

In all of these ways, practical theology provides approaches that fit the shape of its subject matter and furnish points of view that are suited to the reality under consideration. These features not only summarize the subject matter of practical theology and the fittingness of its approach, however. They also give practical shape to our commitment to attend in all our work to the presence of the Triune God in and for the life of the world. The practical, communal, temporal, and situated features of this field reflect our desire to serve One whose very being is relational, and whose creative presence infuses all that is, and who meets humankind as a person born in a body like our own at a specific time and place, and whose Spirit breathes new life in countless actual situations today. In the presence of this Triune God, all our endeavors are set on an eschatological horizon of judgment and hope on which both the dreadful inadequacy of our efforts and God's gracious capacity to work in, through, and in spite of them are revealed.

A volume-ending piece such as this one is necessarily general, even when its purpose is to commend attention to specific, local, and concrete practices that comprise a way of life in and for the world. Yet these few pages are meant less as summary than as summons. Far from being a conclusion, they instead record some thoughts gathered in the midst of a journey that the authors of this book are taking in the company of many other disciples, ministers, and theological educators. We offer these pages, and this book as a whole, in anticipation of the conversations and writing — and ministry and living — that lie ahead.

Acknowledgments

This book grew out of the work of the Seminar on Practical Theology and Christian Ministry, which included Arturo Bañuelas, Dorothy C. Bass, Elizabeth M. Bounds, Kathleen A. Cahalan, David D. Daniels III, Craig Dykstra, Robert Dykstra, L. Gregory Jones, Serene Jones, Verity Jones, Thomas G. Long, Peter W. Marty, Gordon S. Mikoski, Bonnie Miller-McLemore, James R. Nieman, Stephanie Paulsell, Ana María Piñeda, Christian Scharen, John D. Witvliet, and David J. Wood. The contributions of pastors who shared their insights about learning ministry also deepened this work immensely: Arturo Bañuelos, Paul Block, Tony Celino, Martin Copenhaver, Lillian Daniel, David Dragseth, Robert Fritch, Moises Gutierrez, David Keill, Brian Maas, Martin Malzahn, Linda McCrae, Bruce Modahl, Shawnthea Monroe Muller, Michael Mooty, Cherie Parker, Vincent Petersen, Dudley Rose, Maria Lulu Santana, Wendy Scherbart, Gary Simpson, Richard Sotelo, John Stowe, Sandy Velasco Scott, Maria Guadalupe Vital Cruz, Andrea Walker, Bill White, Mike Wilker, and Albert (Sandy) Williams.

The Seminar on Practical Theology and Christian Ministry was supported by the Valparaiso Project on the Education and Formation of People in Faith, a project funded by Lilly Endowment Inc. and based at Valparaiso University. For a full account of the project, its guiding concepts, and the activities it has supported, see www.practicingourfaith.org. The coeditors of *For Life Abundant* have understood prior Valparaiso Project books, and the work of the project as a whole, as endeavors in practical theology. Work on the present book has allowed us to develop this understanding more fully and also to learn from and with an excellent group of colleagues in practical theology. We wish especially to thank the other authors of the 1997 book that laid the groundwork for subsequent efforts, *Practicing Our Faith:* M. Shawn Copeland, Thomas Hoyt Jr., L. Gregory Jones, John Koenig, Sharon Daloz Parks, Stephanie Paulsell, Amy Plantinga Pauw, Ana María Piñeda, Larry Rasmussen, Frank Rogers Jr., and Don E. Saliers. We also thank our colleagues in a seminar on the theology of Christian practices that led to the book *Practicing Theology: Beliefs and Practices in Christian Life:* Nancy E. Bedford, Gilbert I. Bond, Sarah Coakley, Reinhard Hütter, L. Gregory Jones, Serene Jones, Amy Plantinga Pauw, Christine D. Pohl, Kathryn Tanner, Miroslav Volf, and Tammy R. Williams. We are immensely grateful to all of these colleagues, as well as to the many others with whom we have been in conversation over the years about a way of life shaped by Christian practices. We also thank Doretta Kurzinski for her faithful work of hospitality, coordination, and manuscript preparation. In all our work, we are grateful for the support of our spouses, Betsy Dykstra and Mark Schwehn.

CRAIG DYKSTRA
DOROTHY C. BASS

Contributors

Dorothy C. Bass is director of the Valparaiso Project on the Education and Formation of People in Faith and a member of the Evangelical Lutheran Church in America.

Kathleen A. Cahalan, a Roman Catholic, is associate professor of theology at Saint John's University School of Theology and Seminary.

David D. Daniels III is professor of church history at McCormick Theological Seminary and a minister in the Church of God in Christ.

Craig Dykstra is senior vice president for religion at Lilly Endowment Inc. and a minister in the Presbyterian Church (U.S.A.). He was formerly Thomas W. Synnott Professor of Christian Education at Princeton Theological Seminary.

Serene Jones is Titus Street Professor of Theology and chair of Women's, Gender, and Sexuality Studies at Yale University. She is a minister in the Christian Church (Disciples of Christ) and the United Church of Christ.

Thomas G. Long is Bandy Professor of Preaching, Candler School of Theology, Emory University. He is a minister in the Presbyterian Church (U.S.A.).

Peter W. Marty is pastor of St. Paul Lutheran Church (ELCA) in Davenport, Iowa.

Gordon S. Mikoski, a minister in the Presbyterian Church (U.S.A.), is assistant professor of Christian education at Princeton Theological Seminary.

Bonnie J. Miller-McLemore is E. Rhodes and Leona B. Carpenter Professor of Pastoral Theology at Vanderbilt University Divinity School and a minister in the Christian Church (Disciples of Christ).

James R. Nieman is professor of practical theology at Hartford Seminary and a pastor in the Evangelical Lutheran Church in America.

Christian Scharen is director of the Faith as a Way of Life Program at the Yale Center for Faith and Culture and teaches practical theology and congregational studies at Yale Divinity School. He is a pastor in the Evangelical Lutheran Church in America.

Ted A. Smith is director of the Program in Theology and Practice and assistant professor of ethics and preaching at Vanderbilt University. He is a minister in the Presbyterian Church (U.S.A.).

John D. Witvliet is director of the Calvin Institute of Christian Worship and associate professor of worship, theology, and music at Calvin College and Calvin Theological Seminary. He is a minister in the Christian Reformed Church.

David J. Wood, an American Baptist minister, is director of the Transition into Ministry Coordination Program of the Fund for Theological Education.

Index

Candler School of Theology (Emory University), 241

Cane Ridge Revival, 224

Carnegie Foundation for the Advancement of Teaching, 166n.8, 255

Carroll, Jackson, 269n.14, 312

Carroll, Julius, 274-75, 284, 287

Cassirer, Ernst, 135

Center for Practical Theology (Boston University), 258-59

Certeau, Michel de, 4n.7, 219

Chacour, Elias, 327-30, 331-39, 343, 345-46, 348

Chalcedon, Council of, 349

Christ. *See* Jesus Christ

Christian community. *See* community

Christian practices. *See* practices

Chrysostom, John, 332, 337

church: early, 307-9, 320; examples of, 43-45, 56-57, 62; questions for the, 11

City: Rediscovering the Center (Whyte), 318

City of God (Augustine), 239

Clifford, James, 231-32

Collins, John, 71n.8

Come Shouting to Zion: African American Protestantism in the American South and British Caribbean to 1828 (Frey and Wood), 230

community, 21-23, 31, 58n.19, 67-68, 71-73, 315-20, 322; as described in the book of Acts, 308-9, 311, 313, 323-24; God's intention to form, 307, 309, 313-14, 325; and individualism, 309-11, 313; pastoral work of shaping, 58-59, 269, 279, 281n.38, 312-14, 317-26

compassion fatigue, 204, 209

confirmation, 282

Couture, Pamela, 175-76, 179-81, 186

Cross, the, 203

Dahill, Lisa E., 170n.1. *See also Educating Clergy*

Daniels, David, 16, 213, 215

Darrow, John, 280

death, 39-40, 154, 156, 201, 233-34, 274-75. *See also* funerals

Deleuze, Gilles, 231

dementia, ministry to persons with, 105, 107, 110, 112

developmental learning: advanced beginner, 268, 274-75, 284-85; competency, 268, 277, 280n.34, 283nn.35-36, 284-85; expertise, 268, 283nn.35-36, 286nn.40-41, 285-86; mastery, 283nn.35-36, 283, 286; novice, 268, 271-73, 284; proficiency, 268, 279nn.29-30, 281, 284n.40, 285; stages of, 267-68, 284-87

discipleship, 71-76; education and formation, 339-41, 343-46, 348; and practical theology, 66-70, 74, 77-78, 80-81, 84

diversity. *See* race and ethnicity

doctrine, teaching of, 106-8, 199-202

Dreyfus, Hubert, 181, 267-69, 273n.21, 280n.34, 284-86; *On the Internet*, 277n.30, 281, 285n.42, 286

Dreyfus, Stuart E., 181, 267-69, 273n.21, 280n.34, 284-86

DuBois, W. E. B., 238

Duke, James, 128n.17

Duke University, 243, 257

Durkheim, Emile, 270n.15, 271n.18

Dykstra, Craig, 12n.17, 14, 28, 30-31, 46, 105n.23, 171n.3, 172n.4, 200n.2, 229, 246, 266, 274n.25, 275

ecclesial imagination, 43-44, 57-61, 275. *See also* pastoral imagination

ecclesial memory, 228

Educating Clergy (Foster et al.), 92, 98n.16, 103n.20, 112n.29, 170n.1, 255n.7, 265n.2, 301

education, theological. *See* theological education

Educational Imagination, The (Eisner), 135